The Twentieth Century

Other Books by Howard Zinn

La Guardia in Congress   1959

The Southern Mystique   1964

SNCC: The New Abolitionists   1964

New Deal Thought (editor)   1965

Vietnam: The Logic of Withdrawal   1967

Disobedience and Democracy   1968

The Politics of History   1970

The Pentagon Papers: Critical Essays   1972
(editor, with Noam Chomsky)

Postwar America   1973

Justice in Everyday Life (editor)   1974

A People's History of the United States   1980

The Twentieth Century
A People's History

HOWARD ZINN

From the author's *A People's History of the United States,*
with a new chapter on the Carter and Reagan presidencies

PERENNIAL LIBRARY

Harper & Row, Publishers, New York
Grand Rapids, Philadelphia, St. Louis, San Francisco
London, Singapore, Sydney, Tokyo, Toronto

ACKNOWLEDGMENTS

To Akwesasne Notes, Mohawk Nation, for the passage from Ila Abernathy's poem.

To Dodd, Mead & Company, for the passage from "We Wear the Mask" from *The Complete Poems of Paul Laurence Dunbar*.

To Harper & Row, for "Incident" from *On These I Stand* by Countee Cullen. Copyright 1925 by Harper & Row, Publishers, Inc.; renewed 1953 by Ida M. Cullen. Reprinted by permission of the publisher.

To *The New Trail*, 1953 School Yearbook of the Phoenix Indian School, Phoenix, Arizona, for the poem "It Is Not!"

To Random House, Inc., for the passage from "I, Too," copyright 1926 by Alfred A. Knopf, Inc., and renewed 1954 by Langston Hughes; and for the "Dream Deferred" passage from "Lenox Avenue Mural," copyright 1951 by Langston Hughes. Reprinted from *Selected Poems of Langston Hughes*, by permission of the publisher.

To Esta Seaton, for her poem "Her Life," which first appeared in *The Ethnic American Woman* by Edith Blicksilver, Kendall/Hunt Publishing Company, 1978. By permission of *Minnesota Review*.

To Warner Bros., for the excerpt from "Brother Can You Spare a Dime?" Lyric by Jay Gorney, Music by E.Y. Harburg. © 1932 Warner Bros. Inc. Copyright Renewed. All Rights Reserved. Used By Permission.

This work is an abridgement of *A People's History of the United States*.

First HARPER COLOPHON edition published 1984.

Library of Congress Cataloging in Publication Data

Zinn, Howard, 1922-
   The twentieth century, a people's history.

(Harper colophon books)
Bibliography: p.
Includes index.
   1. United States—History—20th century. I. Title.
E741.Z55 1984   973.9   83-48397
ISBN 0-06-091103-4 (pbk.)

---

91 92 MPC 20 19 18 17 16 15 14 13 12 11 10 9 8

For Willow and his generation

Contents

Preface

My book *A People's History of the United States* started with Christopher Columbus and ended in the mid-1970s. This volume, drawn from the latter half of that book, is intended for the reader who wants to concentrate on this century. It is also an opportunity for me to carry the story further, into the 1980s, with a new chapter, "The Challenge of 1984."

But I must explain my point of view. It is obvious in the very first pages of the larger *People's History,* when I tell about Columbus and emphasize not his navigational skill and fortitude in making his way to the Western Hemisphere, but his cruel treatment of the Indians he found here, torturing them, exterminating them in his greed for gold, his desperation to bring riches to his patrons back in Spain. In other words, my focus is not on the achievements of the heroes of traditional history, but on all those people who were the victims of those achievements, who suffered silently or fought back magnificently.

The rest of what I have to say about my view of history is reprinted from the first chapter of *A People's History of the United States.*

To emphasize the heroism of Columbus and his successors as navigators and discoverers, and to deemphasize their genocide, is not a technical necessity but an ideological choice. It serves—unwittingly—to justify what was done.

My point is not that we must, in telling history, accuse, judge, condemn Columbus *in absentia.* It is too late for that; it would be a useless scholarly exercise in morality. But the easy acceptance of atrocities as a deplorable but necessary price to pay for progress (Hiroshima and Vietnam to save Western civilization; Kronstadt and Hungary to save socialism; nuclear proliferation to save us all)—that is still with us. One reason these atrocities are still with us is that we have learned to bury them in a mass of other facts, as radioactive wastes are buried in containers in the earth. We have learned to give them exactly the same proportion of attention that teachers and writers often give them in the most respectable of classrooms and textbooks. This learned sense of moral proportion, coming from the apparent objectivity of the scholar, is accepted more easily than when it comes from politicians at press conferences. It is therefore more deadly.

The treatment of heroes (Columbus) and their victims (the Arawaks)—the quiet acceptance of conquest and murder in the name of progress—is only one aspect of a certain approach to history, in which the past is told from the point of view of governments, conquerors, diplomats, leaders. It is as if they, like Columbus, deserve universal acceptance, as if they—the Founding Fathers, Jackson, Lincoln, Wilson, Roosevelt, Kennedy, the leading members of Congress, the famous Justices of the Supreme Court—represent the nation as a whole. The pretense is that there really is such a thing as "the United States," subject to occasional conflicts and quarrels, but fundamentally a community of people with common interests. It is as if there really is a "national interest," represented in the Constitution, in territorial expansion, in the laws passed by Congress, the decisions of the courts, the development of capitalism, the culture of education and the mass media.

"History is the memory of states," wrote Henry Kissinger in his first book, *A World Restored,* in which he proceeded to tell the history of nineteenth-century Europe from the viewpoint of the leaders of Austria and England, ignoring the millions who suffered from those statesmen's policies. From his standpoint, the "peace" that Europe had before the French Revolution was "restored" by the diplomacy of a few national leaders. But for factory workers in England, farmers in France, colored people in Asia and Africa, women and children everywhere except in the upper classes, it was a world of conquest, violence, hunger, exploitation —a world not restored but disintegrated.

My viewpoint, in telling the history of the United States, is different: that we must not accept the memory of states as our own. Nations are not communities and never have been. The history of any country, presented as the history of a family, conceals fierce conflicts of interest (sometimes exploding, most often repressed) between conquerors and conquered, masters and slaves, capitalists and workers, dominators and dominated in race and sex. And in such a world of conflict, a world of victims and executioners, it is the job of thinking people, as Albert Camus suggested, not to be on the side of the executioners.

Thus, in that inevitable taking of sides which comes from selection and emphasis in history, I prefer to try to tell the story of the discovery of America from the viewpoint of the Arawaks, of the Constitution from the standpoint of the slaves, of Andrew Jackson as seen by the Cherokees, of the Civil War as seen by the New York Irish, of the Mexican War as seen by the deserting soldiers of Scott's army, of the rise of industrialism as seen by the young women in the Lowell textile mills, of the Spanish-American War as seen by the Cubans, the conquest of the Philippines as seen by black soldiers on Luzon, the Gilded Age as seen by southern farmers, the First World War as seen by socialists, the Second World War as seen by pacifists, the New Deal as seen by blacks in Harlem, the postwar American empire as seen by peons in Latin America. And so on, to the limited extent that any one person, however he or she strains, can "see" history from the standpoint of others.

My point is not to grieve for the victims and denounce the executioners. Those tears, that anger, cast into the past, deplete our moral energy for the present. And the lines are not always clear. In the long run, the oppressor is also a victim. In the short run (and so far, human history has consisted only of short runs), the victims, themselves desperate and tainted with the culture that oppresses them, turn on other victims.

Still, understanding the complexities, this book will be skeptical of governments and their attempts, through politics and culture, to ensnare ordinary people in a giant web of nationhood pretending to a common interest. I will try not to overlook the cruelties that victims inflict on one another as they are jammed together in the boxcars of the system. I don't want to romanticize them. But I do remember (in rough paraphrase) a statement I once read: "The cry of the poor is not always just, but if you don't listen to it, you will never know what justice is."

I don't want to invent victories for people's movements. But to think that history-writing must aim simply to recapitulate the failures that dominate the past is to make historians collaborators in an endless cycle of defeat. If history is to be creative, to anticipate a possible future without denying the past, it should, I believe, emphasize new possibilities by disclosing those hidden episodes of the past when, even if in brief flashes, people showed their ability to resist, to join together, occasionally to win. I am supposing, or perhaps only hoping, that our future may be found in the past's fugitive moments of compassion rather than in its solid centuries of warfare.

That, being as blunt as I can, is my approach to the history of the United States. The reader may as well know that before going on.

Boston, 1980, 1984

The Twentieth Century

1.

The Empire and the People

Theodore Roosevelt wrote to a friend in the year 1897: "In strict confidence . . . I should welcome almost any war, for I think this country needs one."

The year of the massacre at Wounded Knee, 1890, it was officially declared by the Bureau of the Census that the internal frontier was closed. The profit system, with its natural tendency for expansion, had already begun to look overseas. The severe depression that began in 1893 strengthened an idea developing within the political and financial elite of the country: that overseas markets for American goods might relieve the problem of underconsumption at home and prevent the economic crises that in the 1890s brought class war.

And would not a foreign adventure deflect some of the rebellious energy that went into strikes and protest movements toward an external enemy? Would it not unite people with government, with the armed forces, instead of against them? This was probably not a conscious plan among most of the elite—but a natural development from the twin drives of capitalism and nationalism.

Expansion overseas was not a new idea. Even before the war against Mexico carried the United States to the Pacific, the Monroe Doctrine looked southward into and beyond the Caribbean. Issued in 1823 when the countries of Latin America were winning independence from Spanish control, it made plain to European nations that the United States considered Latin America its sphere of influence. Not long after, some Americans began thinking into the Pacific: of Hawaii, Japan, and the great markets of China.

There was more than thinking; the American armed forces had made forays overseas. A State Department list, "Instances of the Use of United States Armed Forces Abroad 1798–1945" (presented by Secretary of State Dean Rusk to a Senate committee in 1962 to cite precedents for the use of armed force against Cuba), shows 103 interventions in the affairs of other countries between 1798 and 1895. A sampling from the list, with the exact description given by the State Department:

1852–53—Argentina. Marines were landed and maintained in Buenos Aires to protect American interests during a revolution.

1853—Nicaragua—to protect American lives and interests during political disturbances.

1853–54—Japan—The "Opening of Japan" and the Perry Expedition. [The State Department does not give more details, but this involved the use of warships to force Japan to open its ports to the United States.]

1853–54—Ryukyu and Bonin Islands—Commodore Perry on three visits before going to Japan and while waiting for a reply from Japan made a naval demonstration, landing marines twice, and secured a coaling concession from the ruler of Naha on Okinawa. He also demonstrated in the Bonin Islands. All to secure facilities for commerce.

1854—Nicaragua—San Juan del Norte [Greytown was destroyed to avenge an insult to the American Minister to Nicaragua.]

1855—Uruguay—U.S. and European naval forces landed to protect American interests during an attempted revolution in Montevideo.

1859—China—For the protection of American interests in Shanghai.

1860—Angola, Portuguese West Africa—To protect American lives and property at Kissembo when the natives became troublesome.

1893—Hawaii—Ostensibly to protect American lives and property; actually to promote a provisional government under Sanford B. Dole. This action was disavowed by the United States.

1894—Nicaragua—To protect American interests at Bluefields following a revolution.

Thus, by the 1890s, there had been much experience in overseas probes and interventions. The ideology of expansion was widespread in the upper circles of military men, politicians, businessmen—and even among some of the leaders of farmers' movements who thought foreign markets would help them.

Captain A. T. Mahan of the U.S. navy, a popular propagandist for expansion, greatly influenced Theodore Roosevelt and other American leaders. The countries with the biggest navies would inherit the earth, he said. "Americans must now begin to look outward." Senator Henry Cabot Lodge of Massachusetts wrote in a magazine article:

In the interests of our commerce . . . we should build the Nicaragua canal, and for the protection of that canal and for the sake of our commercial supremacy in the Pacific we should control the Hawaiian islands and maintain our influence in Samoa. . . . and when the Nicaraguan canal is built, the island of Cuba . . . will become a necessity. . . . The great nations are rapidly absorbing for their future expansion and their present defense all the waste places of the earth. It is a movement which makes for civilization and the advancement of the race. As one of the great nations of the world the United States must not fall out of the line of march.

A Washington *Post* editorial on the eve of the Spanish-American war:

A new consciousness seems to have come upon us—the consciousness of strength—and with it a new appetite, the yearning to show our strength. . . . Ambition, interest, land hunger, pride, the mere joy of fighting, whatever it may be, we are animated by a new sensation. We are face to face with a strange destiny. The taste of Empire is in the mouth of the people even as the taste of blood in the jungle. . . .

Was that taste in the mouth of the people through some instinctive lust for aggression or some urgent self-interest? Or was it a taste (if indeed it existed) created, encouraged, advertised, and exaggerated by the millionaire press, the military, the government, the eager-to-please scholars of the time? Political scientist John Burgess of Columbia University said the Teutonic and Anglo-Saxon races were "particularly endowed with the capacity for establishing national states . . . they are entrusted . . . with the mission of conducting the political civilization of the modern world."

Several years before his election to the presidency, William McKinley said: "We want a foreign market for our surplus products." Senator Albert Beveridge of Indiana in early 1897 declared: "American factories are making more than the American people can use; American soil is producing more than they can consume. Fate has written our policy for us; the trade of the world must and shall be ours." The Department of State explained in 1898:

It seems to be conceded that every year we shall be confronted with an increasing surplus of manufactured goods for sale in foreign markets if American operatives and artisans are to be kept employed the year around. The enlargement of foreign consumption of the products of our mills and workshops has, therefore, become a serious problem of statesmanship as well as of commerce.

These expansionist military men and politicians were in touch with one another. One of Theodore Roosevelt's biographers tells us: "By 1890, Lodge, Roosevelt, and Mahan had begun exchanging views," and that they tried to get Mahan off sea duty "so that he could continue full-time his propaganda for expansion." Roosevelt once sent Henry Cabot Lodge a copy of a poem by Rudyard Kipling, saying it was "poor poetry, but good sense from the expansionist standpoint."

When the United States did not annex Hawaii in 1893 after some Americans (the combined missionary and pineapple interests of the Dole family) set up their own government, Roosevelt called this hesitancy "a crime against white civilization." And he told the Naval War College: "All the great masterful races have been fighting races. . . . No triumph of peace is quite so great as the supreme triumph of war."

Roosevelt was contemptuous of races and nations he considered inferior. When a mob in New Orleans lynched a number of Italian immigrants, Roosevelt thought the United States should offer the Italian government some remuneration, but privately he wrote his sister that he thought the lynching was "rather a good thing" and told her he had said as much at a dinner with "various dago diplomats . . . all wrought up by the lynching."

William James, the philosopher, who became one of the leading anti-imperialists of his time, wrote about Roosevelt that he "gushes over war as the ideal condition of human society, for the manly strenuousness which it involves, and treats peace as a condition of blubberlike and swollen ignobility, fit only for huckstering weaklings, dwelling in gray twilight and heedless of the higher life. . . ."

Roosevelt's talk of expansionism was not just a matter of manliness and heroism; he was conscious of "our trade relations with China." Lodge was aware of the textile interests in Massachusetts that looked to Asian markets. Historian Marilyn Young has written of the work of the American China Development Company to expand American influence in China for commercial reasons, and of State Department instructions to the American emissary in China to "employ all proper methods for the extension of American interests in China." She says *(The Rhetoric of Empire)* that the talk about markets in China was far greater than the actual amount of dollars involved at the time, but this talk was important in shaping American policy toward Hawaii, the Philippines, and all of Asia.

While it was true that in 1898, 90 percent of American products were sold at home, the 10 percent sold abroad amounted to a billion dollars. Walter Lafeber writes *(The New Empire)*: "By 1893, American trade exceeded that of every country in the world except England. Farm products, of course, especially in the key tobacco, cotton, and wheat areas, had long depended heavily on international markets for their prosperity." And in the twenty years up to 1895, new investments by American capitalists overseas reached a billion dollars. In 1885, the steel industry's publication *Age of Steel* wrote that the internal markets were insufficient and the overproduction of industrial products "should be relieved and prevented in the future by increased foreign trade."

Oil became a big export in the 1880s and 1890s: by 1891, the Rockefeller family's Standard Oil Company accounted for 90 percent of American exports of kerosene and controlled 70 percent of the world market. Oil was now second to cotton as the leading product sent overseas.

There were demands for expansion by large commercial farmers, including some of the Populist leaders, as William Appleman Williams has shown in *The Roots of the Modern American Empire*. Populist Congressman Jerry Simpson of Kansas told Congress in 1892 that with a huge agricultural surplus, farmers "must of necessity seek a foreign market." True, he was not calling for aggression or conquest—but once foreign markets were seen as important to prosperity, expansionist policies, even war, might have wide appeal.

Such an appeal would be especially strong if the expansion looked like an act of generosity—helping a rebellious group overthrow foreign rule—as in Cuba. By 1898, Cuban rebels had been fighting their Spanish conquerors for three years in an attempt to win independence. By that time, it was possible to create a national mood for intervention.

It seems that the business interests of the nation did not at first want military intervention in Cuba. American merchants did not need colonies or wars of conquest if they could just have free access to markets. This idea of an "open door" became the dominant theme of American foreign policy in the twentieth century. It was a more sophisticated approach to imperialism than the traditional empire-building of Europe. William Appleman Williams, in *The Tragedy of American Diplomacy*, says:

> This national argument is usually interpreted as a battle between imperialists led by Roosevelt and Lodge and anti-imperialists led by William Jennings Bryan and Carl Schurz. It is far more accurate and illuminating, however, to view it as a three-cornered fight. The third group was a coalition of businessmen, intellectuals, and politicians who opposed traditional colonialism and advocated instead a policy of an open door through which America's preponderant economic strength would enter and dominate all underdeveloped areas of the world.

However, this preference on the part of some business groups and politicians for what Williams calls the idea of "informal empire," without war, was always subject to change. If peaceful imperialism turned out to be impossible, military action might be needed.

For instance, in late 1897 and early 1898, with China weakened by a recent war with Japan, German military forces occupied the Chinese port of Tsingtao at the mouth of Kiaochow Bay and demanded a naval station there, with rights to railways and coal mines on the nearby peninsula of Shantung. Within the next few months, other European powers moved in on China, and the partition of China by the major imperialist powers was under way, with the United States left behind.

At this point, the New York *Journal of Commerce*, which had advocated peaceful development of free trade, now urged old-fashioned military colonialism. Julius Pratt, a historian of U.S. expansionism, describes the turnabout:

> This paper, which has been heretofore characterized as pacifist, anti-imperialist, and devoted to the development of commerce in a free-trade world, saw the foundation of its faith crumbling as a result of the threatened partition of China. Declaring that free access to the markets of China, with its 400,-000,000 people, would largely solve the problem of the disposal of our surplus manufactures, the *Journal* came out not only for a stern insistence upon complete equality of rights in China but unreservedly also for an isthmian canal, the acquisition of Hawaii, and a material increase in the navy—three measures which it had hitherto strenuously opposed. Nothing could be more significant than the manner in which this paper was converted in a few weeks. . . .

There was a similar turnabout in U.S. business attitudes on Cuba in 1898. Businessmen had been interested, from the start of the Cuban revolt against Spain, in the effect on commercial possibilities there. There already was a substantial economic interest in the island, which President Grover Cleveland summarized in 1896:

> It is reasonably estimated that at least from $30,000,000 to $50,000,000 of American capital are invested in the plantations and in railroad, mining, and other business enterprises on the island. The volume of trade between the United States and Cuba, which in 1889 amounted to about $64,000,000, rose in 1893 to about $103,000,000.

Popular support of the Cuban revolution was based on the thought that they, like the Americans of 1776, were fighting a war for their own liberation. The United States government, however, the conservative product of another revolutionary war, had power and profit in mind as it observed the events in Cuba. Neither Cleveland, President during the first years of the Cuban revolt, nor McKinley, who followed, recognized the insurgents officially as belligerents; such legal recognition would have enabled the United States to give aid to the rebels without sending an army. But there may have been fear that the rebels would win on their own and keep the United States out.

There seems also to have been another kind of fear. The Cleveland administration said a Cuban victory might lead to "the establishment of a white and a black republic," since Cuba had a mixture of the two races. And the black republic might be dominant. This idea was expressed in 1896 in an article in *The Saturday Review* by a young and eloquent imperialist, whose mother was American and whose father was English—Winston Churchill. He wrote that while Spanish rule was bad and the rebels had the support of the people, it would be better for Spain to keep control:

A grave danger represents itself. Two-fifths of the insurgents in the field are negroes. These men would, in the event of success, demand a predominant share in the government of the country . . . the result being, after years of fighting, another black republic.

The reference to "another" black republic meant Haiti, whose revolution against France in 1803 had led to the first nation run by blacks in the New World. The Spanish minister to the United States wrote to the U.S. Secretary of State:

In this revolution, the negro element has the most important part. Not only the principal leaders are colored men, but at least eight-tenths of their supporters. . . . and the result of the war, if the Island can be declared independent, will be a secession of the black element and a black Republic.

As Philip Foner says in his two-volume study *The Spanish-Cuban-American War*, "The McKinley Administration had plans for dealing with the Cuban situation, but these did not include independence for the island." He points to the administration's instructions to its minister to Spain, Stewart Woodford, asking him to try to settle the war because it "injuriously affects the normal function of business, and tends to delay the condition of prosperity," but not mentioning freedom and justice for the Cubans. Foner explains the rush of the McKinley administration into war (its ultimatum gave Spain little time to negotiate) by the fact that "if the United States waited too long, the Cuban revolutionary forces would emerge victorious, replacing the collapsing Spanish regime."

In February 1898, the U.S. battleship *Maine*, in Havana harbor as a symbol of American interest in the Cuban events, was destroyed by a mysterious explosion and sank, with the loss of 268 men. There was no evidence ever produced on the cause of the explosion, but excitement grew swiftly in the United States, and McKinley began to move in the direction of war. Walter Lafeber says:

The President did not want war; he had been sincere and tireless in his efforts to maintain the peace. By mid-March, however, he was beginning to discover that, although he did not want war, he did want what only a war could provide; the disappearance of the terrible uncertainty in American political and economic life, and a solid basis from which to resume the building of the new American commercial empire.

At a certain point in that spring, both McKinley and the business community began to see that their object, to get Spain out of Cuba, could not be accomplished without war, and that their accompanying object, the securing of American military and economic influence in Cuba, could not be left to the Cuban rebels, but could be ensured only by U.S. intervention. The New York *Commercial Advertiser*, at first against war, by March 10 asked intervention in Cuba for "humanity and love of freedom, and above all, the desire that the commerce and industry of every part of the world shall have full freedom of development in the whole world's interest."

Before this, Congress had passed the Teller Amendment, pledging the United States not to annex Cuba. It was initiated and supported by those people who were interested in Cuban independence and opposed to American imperialism, and also by business people who saw the "open door" as sufficient and military intervention unnecessary. But by the spring of 1898, the business community had developed a hunger for action. The *Journal of Commerce* said: "The Teller amendment . . . must be interpreted in a sense somewhat different from that which its author intended it to bear."

There were special interests who would benefit directly from war. In Pittsburgh, center of the iron industry, the Chamber of Commerce advocated force, and the *Chattanooga Tradesman* said that the possibility of war "has decidedly stimulated the iron trade." It also noted that "actual war would very decidedly enlarge the business of transportation." In Washington, it was reported that a "belligerent spirit" had infected the Navy Department, encouraged "by the contractors for projectiles, ordnance, ammunition and other supplies, who have thronged the department since the destruction of the Maine."

Russell Sage, the banker, said that if war came, "There is no question as to where the rich men stand." A survey of businessmen said that John Jacob Astor, William Rockefeller, and Thomas Fortune Ryan were "feeling militant." And J. P. Morgan believed further talk with Spain would accomplish nothing.

On March 21, 1898, Henry Cabot Lodge wrote McKinley a long letter, saying he had talked with "bankers, brokers, businessmen, editors, clergymen and others" in Boston, Lynn, and Nahant, and "everybody," including "the most conservative classes," wanted the Cuban question "solved." Lodge reported: "They said for business one shock and then an end was better than a succession of spasms such as we must have if this war in Cuba went on." On March 25, a telegram arrived at the White House from an adviser to McKinley, saying: "Big corporations here now believe we will have war. Believe all would welcome it as relief to suspense."

Two days after getting this telegram, McKinley presented an ultimatum to Spain, demanding an armistice. He said nothing about independence for Cuba. A spokesman for the Cuban rebels, part of a group of Cubans in New York, interpreted this to mean the U.S. simply wanted to replace Spain. He responded:

In the face of the present proposal of intervention without previous recognition of independence, it is necessary for us to go a step farther and say that we must and will regard such intervention as nothing less than a declaration of war by the United States against the Cuban revolutionists. . . .

Indeed, when McKinley asked Congress for war on April 11, he did not recognize the rebels as belligerents or ask for Cuban independence. Nine days later, Congress, by joint resolution, gave McKinley the power to intervene. When American forces moved into Cuba, the rebels welcomed them, hoping the Teller Amendment would guarantee Cuban independence.

Many histories of the Spanish-American war have said that "public opinion" in the United States led McKinley to declare war on Spain and send forces to Cuba. True, certain influential newspapers had been pushing hard, even hysterically. And many Americans, seeing the aim of intervention as Cuban independence—and with the Teller Amendment as guarantee of this intention—supported the idea. But would McKinley have gone to war because of the press and some portion of the public (we had no public opinion surveys at that time) without the urging of the business community? Several years after the Cuban

war, the chief of the Bureau of Foreign Commerce of the Department
of Commerce wrote about that period:

> Underlying the popular sentiment, which might have evaporated in time,
> which forced the United States to take up arms against Spanish rule in Cuba,
> were our economic relations with the West Indies and the South American
> republics. . . . The Spanish-American War was but an incident of a general
> movement of expansion which had its roots in the changed environment of
> an industrial capacity far beyond our domestic powers of consumption. It
> was seen to be necessary for us not only to find foreign purchasers for our
> goods, but to provide the means of making access to foreign markets easy,
> economical and safe.

American labor unions had sympathy for the Cuban rebels as soon
as the insurrection against Spain began in 1895. But they opposed American expansionism. Both the Knights of Labor and the American Federation of Labor spoke against the idea of annexing Hawaii, which McKinley proposed in 1897. Despite the feeling for the Cuban rebels, a
resolution calling for U.S. intervention was defeated at the 1897 convention of the AFL. Samuel Gompers of the AFL wrote to a friend: "The
sympathy of our movement with Cuba is genuine, earnest, and sincere,
but this does not for a moment imply that we are committed to certain
adventurers who are apparently suffering from Hysteria. . . ."

When the explosion of the *Maine* in February led to excited calls
for war in the press, the monthly journal of the International Association
of Machinists agreed it was a terrible disaster, but it noted that the
deaths of workers in industrial accidents drew no such national clamor.
It pointed to the Lattimer Massacre of September 10, 1897, during a
coal strike in Pennsylvania. Miners marching on a highway to the Lattimer mine—Austrians, Hungarians, Italians, Germans—who had originally been imported as strikebreakers but then organized themselves,
refused to disperse, whereupon the sheriff and his deputies opened fire,
killing nineteen of them, most shot in the back, with no outcry in the
press. The labor journal said that the

> . . . carnival of carnage that takes place every day, month and year in the
> realm of industry, the thousands of useful lives that are annually sacrificed
> to the Moloch of greed, the blood tribute paid by labor to capitalism, brings
> forth no shout for vengeance and reparation. . . . Death comes in thousands
> of instances in mill and mine, claims his victims, and no popular uproar is
> heard.

The official organ of the Connecticut AFL, *The Craftsman,* also warned about the hysteria worked up by the sinking of the *Maine:*

A gigantic . . . and cunningly-devised scheme is being worked ostensibly to place the United States in the front rank as a naval and military power. The real reason is that the capitalists will have the whole thing and, when any workingmen dare to ask for the living wage . . . they will be shot down like dogs in the streets.

Some unions, like the United Mine Workers, called for U.S. intervention after the sinking of the *Maine.* But most were against war. The treasurer of the American Longshoremen's Union, Bolton Hall, wrote "A Peace Appeal to Labor," which was widely circulated:

If there is a war, you will furnish the corpses and the taxes, and others will get the glory. Speculators will make money out of it—that is, out of you. Men will get high prices for inferior supplies, leaky boats, for shoddy clothes and pasteboard shoes, and you will have to pay the bill, and the only satisfaction you will get is the privilege of hating your Spanish fellow-workmen, who are really your brothers and who have had as little to do with the wrongs of Cuba as you have.

Socialists opposed the war. One exception was the Jewish *Daily Forward. The People,* newspaper of the Socialist Labor party, called the issue of Cuban freedom "a pretext" and said the government wanted war to "distract the attention of the workers from their real interests." The *Appeal to Reason,* another Socialist newspaper, said the movement for war was "a favorite method of rulers for keeping the people from redressing domestic wrongs." In the San Francisco *Voice of Labor* a Socialist wrote: "It is a terrible thing to think that the poor workers of this country should be sent to kill and wound the poor workers of Spain merely because a few leaders may incite them to do so."

But after war was declared, Foner says, "the majority of the trade unions succumbed to the war fever." Samuel Gompers called the war "glorious and righteous" and claimed that 250,000 trade unionists had volunteered for military service. The United Mine Workers pointed to higher coal prices as a result of the war and said: "The coal and iron trades have not been so healthy for some years past as at present."

The war brought more employment and higher wages, but also higher prices. Foner says: "Not only was there a startling increase in the cost of living, but, in the absence of an income tax, the poor found themselves paying almost entirely for the staggering costs of the war through increased levies on sugar, molasses, tobacco, and other taxes.

. . ." Gompers, publicly for the war, privately pointed out that the war had led to a 20 percent reduction of the purchasing power of workers' wages.

On May Day, 1898, the Socialist Labor party organized an antiwar parade in New York City, but the authorities would not allow it to take place, while a May Day parade called by the Jewish *Daily Forward,* urging Jewish workers to support the war, was permitted. The Chicago *Labor World* said: "This has been a poor man's war—paid for by the poor man. The rich have profited by it, as they always do. . . ."

The Western Labor Union was founded at Salt Lake City on May 10, 1898, because the AFL had not organized unskilled workers. It wanted to bring together all workers "irrespective of occupation, nationality, creed or color" and "sound the death knell of every corporation and trust that has robbed the American laborer of the fruits of his toil. . . ." The union's publication, noting the annexation of Hawaii during the war, said this proved that "the war which started as one of relief for the starving Cubans has suddenly changed to one of conquest."

The prediction made by longshoreman Bolton Hall, of wartime corruption and profiteering, turned out to be remarkably accurate. Richard Morris's *Encyclopedia of American History* gives startling figures:

Of the more than 274,000 officers and men who served in the army during the Spanish-American War and the period of demobilization, 5,462 died in the various theaters of operation and in camps in the U.S. Only 379 of the deaths were battle casualties, the remainder being attributed to disease and other causes.

The same figures are given by Walter Millis in his book *The Martial Spirit.* In the *Encyclopedia* they are given tersely, and without mention of the "embalmed beef" (an army general's term) sold to the army by the meatpackers—meat preserved with boric acid, nitrate of potash, and artificial coloring matter.

In May of 1898, Armour and Company, the big meatpacking company of Chicago, sold the army 500,000 pounds of beef which had been sent to Liverpool a year earlier and had been returned. Two months later, an army inspector tested the Armour meat, which had been stamped and approved by an inspector of the Bureau of Animal Industry, and found 751 cases containing rotten meat. In the first sixty cases he opened, he found fourteen tins already burst, "the effervescent putrid contents of which were distributed all over the cases." (The description comes from the *Report of the Commission to Investigate the Conduct of the War Department in the War with Spain,* made to the Senate in 1900.) Thousands of soldiers got food poisoning. There are no figures on how many of the five thousand noncombat deaths were caused by that.

The Spanish forces were defeated in three months, in what John Hay, the American Secretary of State, later called a "splendid little war." The American military pretended that the Cuban rebel army did not exist. When the Spanish surrendered, no Cuban was allowed to confer on the surrender, or to sign it. General William Shafter said no armed rebels could enter the capital city of Santiago, and told the Cuban rebel leader, General Calixto García, that not Cubans, but the old Spanish civil authorities, would remain in charge of the municipal offices in Santiago.

American historians have generally ignored the role of the Cuban rebels in the war; Philip Foner, in his history, was the first to print García's letter of protest to General Shafter:

I have not been honored with a single word from yourself informing me about the negotiations for peace or the terms of the capitulation by the Spaniards.

. . . when the question arises of appointing authorities in Santiago de Cuba . . . I cannot see but with the deepest regret that such authorities are not elected by the Cuban people, but are the same ones selected by the Queen of Spain. . . .

A rumor too absurd to be believed, General, describes the reason of your measures and of the orders forbidding my army to enter Santiago for fear of massacres and revenge against the Spaniards. Allow me, sir, to protest against even the shadow of such an idea. We are not savages ignoring the rules of civilized warfare. We are a poor, ragged army, as ragged and poor as was the army of your forefathers in their noble war for independence. . . .

Along with the American army in Cuba came American capital. Foner writes:

Even before the Spanish flag was down in Cuba, U.S. business interests set out to make their influence felt. Merchants, real estate agents, stock speculators, reckless adventurers, and promoters of all kinds of get-rich schemes flocked to Cuba by the thousands. Seven syndicates battled each other for control of the franchises for the Havana Street Railway, which were finally won by Percival Farquhar, representing the Wall Street interests of New York. Thus, simultaneously with the military occupation began . . . commercial occupation.

The *Lumbermen's Review,* spokesman for the lumber industry, said in the midst of the war: "The moment Spain drops the reigns of government in Cuba . . . the moment will arrive for American lumber interests to move into the island for the products of Cuban forests. Cuba still possesses 10,000,000 acres of virgin forest abounding in valuable timber . . . nearly every foot of which would be saleable in the United States and bring high prices."

Americans began taking over railroad, mine, and sugar properties when the war ended. In a few years, $30 million of American capital was invested. United Fruit moved into the Cuban sugar industry. It bought 1,900,000 acres of land for about twenty cents an acre. The American Tobacco Company arrived. By the end of the occupation, in 1901, Foner estimates that at least 80 percent of the export of Cuba's minerals were in American hands, mostly Bethlehem Steel.

During the military occupation a series of strikes took place. In September 1899, a gathering of thousands of workers in Havana launched a general strike for the eight-hour day, saying, ". . . we have determined to promote the struggle between the worker and the capitalist. For the workers of Cuba will no longer tolerate remaining in total subjection." The American General William Ludlow ordered the mayor of Havana to arrest eleven strike leaders, and U.S. troops occupied railroad stations and docks. Police moved through the city breaking up meetings. But the economic activity of the city had come to a halt. Tobacco workers struck. Printers struck. Bakers went on strike. Hundreds of strikers were arrested, and some of the imprisoned leaders were intimidated into calling for an end to the strike.

The United States did not annex Cuba. But a Cuban Constitutional Convention was told that the United States army would not leave Cuba until the Platt Amendment, passed by Congress in February 1901, was incorporated into the new Cuban Constitution. This Amendment gave the United States "the right to intervene for the preservation of Cuban independence, the maintenance of a government adequate for the protection of life, property, and individual liberty. . . ." It also provided for the United States to get coaling or naval stations at certain specified points.

The Teller Amendment and the talk of Cuban freedom before and during the war had led many Americans—and Cubans—to expect genuine independence. The Platt Amendment was now seen, not only by the radical and labor press, but by newspapers and groups all over the United States, as a betrayal. A mass meeting of the American Anti-

Imperialist League at Faneuil Hall in Boston denounced it, ex-governor George Boutwell saying: "In disregard of our pledge of freedom and sovereignty to Cuba we are imposing on that island conditions of colonial vassalage."

In Havana, a torchlight procession of fifteen thousand Cubans marched on the Constitutional Convention, urging them to reject the Amendment. But General Leonard Wood, head of the occupation forces, assured McKinley: "The people of Cuba lend themselves readily to all sorts of demonstrations and parades, and little significance should be attached to them."

A committee was delegated by the Constitutional Convention to reply to the United States' insistence that the Platt Amendment be included in the Constitution. The committee report, *Penencia a la Convención,* was written by a black delegate from Santiago. It said:

> For the United States to reserve to itself the power to determine when this independence was threatened, and when, therefore, it should intervene to preserve it, is equivalent to handing over the keys to our house so that they can enter it at any time, whenever the desire seizes them, day or night, whether with good or evil design.

And:

> The only Cuban governments that would live would be those which count on the support and benevolence of the United States, and the clearest result of this situation would be that we would only have feeble and miserable governments . . . condemned to live more attentive to obtaining the blessings of the United States than to serving and defending the interests of Cuba. . . .

The report termed the request for coaling or naval stations "a mutilation of the fatherland." It concluded:

> A people occupied militarily is being told that before consulting their own government, before being free in their own territory, they should grant the military occupants who came as friends and allies, rights and powers which would annul the sovereignty of these very people. That is the situation created for us by the method which the United States has just adopted. It could not be more obnoxious and inadmissible.

With this report, the Convention overwhelmingly rejected the Platt Amendment.

Within the next three months, however, the pressure from the United States, the military occupation, the refusal to allow the Cubans to set up their own government until they acquiesced, had its effect;

the Convention, after several refusals, adopted the Platt Amendment. General Leonard Wood wrote in 1901 to Theodore Roosevelt: "There is, of course, little or no independence left Cuba under the Platt Amendment."

Cuba was thus brought into the American sphere, but not as an outright colony. However, the Spanish-American war did lead to a number of direct annexations by the United States. Puerto Rico, a neighbor of Cuba in the Caribbean, belonging to Spain, was taken over by U.S. military forces. The Hawaiian Islands, one-third of the way across the Pacific, which had already been penetrated by American missionaries and pineapple plantation owners, and had been described by American officials as "a ripe pear ready to be plucked," was annexed by joint resolution of Congress in July of 1898. Around the same time, Wake Island, 2,300 miles west of Hawaii, on the route to Japan, was occupied. And Guam, the Spanish possession in the Pacific, almost all the way to the Philippines, was taken. In December of 1898, the peace treaty was signed with Spain, officially turning over to the United States Guam, Puerto Rico, and the Philippines, for a payment of $20 million.

There was heated argument in the United States about whether or not to take the Philippines. As one story has it, President McKinley told a group of ministers visiting the White House how he came to his decision:

Before you go I would like to say just a word about the Philippine business. . . . The truth is I didn't want the Philippines, and when they came to us as a gift from the gods, I did not know what to do with them. . . . I sought counsel from all sides—Democrats as well as Republicans—but got little help.

I thought first we would only take Manila; then Luzon, then other islands, perhaps, also.

I walked the floor of the White House night after night until midnight; and I am not ashamed to tell you, gentlemen, that I went down on my knees and prayed Almighty God for light and guidance more than one night. And one night late it came to me this way—I don't know how it was, but it came:

1) That we could not give them back to Spain—that would be cowardly and dishonorable.

2) That we could not turn them over to France or Germany, our commercial rivals in the Orient—that would be bad business and discreditable.

3) That we could not leave them to themselves—they were unfit for self-government—and they would soon have anarchy and misrule over there worse than Spain's was; and

4) That there was nothing left for us to do but to take them all and to

educate the Filipinos, and uplift and civilize and Christianize them, and by God's grace do the very best we could by them, as our fellow men for whom Christ also died. And then I went to bed and went to sleep and slept soundly.

The Filipinos did not get the same message from God. In February 1899, they rose in revolt against American rule, as they had rebelled several times against the Spanish. Emilio Aguinaldo, a Filipino leader, who had earlier been brought back from China by U.S. warships to lead soldiers against Spain, now became leader of the *insurrectos* fighting the United States. He proposed Filipino independence within a U.S. protectorate, but this was rejected.

It took the United States three years to crush the rebellion, using seventy thousand troops—four times as many as were landed in Cuba— and thousands of battle casualties, many times more than in Cuba. It was a harsh war. For the Filipinos the death rate was enormous from battle casualties and from disease.

The taste of empire was on the lips of politicians and business interests throughout the country now. Racism, paternalism, and talk of money mingled with talk of destiny and civilization. In the Senate, Albert Beveridge spoke, January 9, 1900, for the dominant economic and political interests of the country:

Mr. President, the times call for candor. The Philippines are ours forever. . . . And just beyond the Philippines are China's illimitable markets. We will not retreat from either. . . . We will not renounce our part in the mission of our race, trustee, under God, of the civilization of the world. . . .

The Pacific is our ocean. . . . Where shall we turn for consumers of our surplus? Geography answers the question. China is our natural customer. . . . The Philippines give us a base at the door of all the East. . . .

No land in America surpasses in fertility the plains and valleys of Luzon. Rice and coffee, sugar and cocoanuts, hemp and tobacco. . . . The wood of the Philippines can supply the furniture of the world for a century to come. At Cebu the best informed man on the island told me that 40 miles of Cebu's mountain chain are practically mountains of coal. . . .

I have a nugget of pure gold picked up in its present form on the banks of a Philippine creek. . . .

My own belief is that there are not 100 men among them who comprehend what Anglo-Saxon self-government even means, and there are over 5,000,000 people to be governed.

It has been charged that our conduct of the war has been cruel. Senators, it has been the reverse. . . . Senators must remember that we are not dealing with Americans or Europeans. We are dealing with Orientals.

The fighting with the rebels began, McKinley said, when the insurgents attacked American forces. But later, American soldiers testified that the United States had fired the first shot. After the war, an army officer speaking in Boston's Faneuil Hall said his colonel had given him orders to provoke a conflict with the insurgents.

In February 1899, a banquet took place in Boston to celebrate the Senate's ratification of the peace treaty with Spain. President McKinley himself had been invited by the wealthy textile manufacturer W. B. Plunkett to speak. It was the biggest banquet in the nation's history: two thousand diners, four hundred waiters. McKinley said that "no imperial designs lurk in the American mind," and at the same banquet, to the same diners, his Postmaster General, Charles Emory Smith, said that "what we want is a market for our surplus."

William James, the Harvard philosopher, wrote a letter to the Boston *Transcript* about "the cold pot grease of McKinley's cant at the recent Boston banquet" and said the Philippine operation "reeked of the infernal adroitness of the great department store, which has reached perfect expertness in the art of killing silently, and with no public squalling or commotion, the neighboring small concerns."

James was part of a movement of prominent American businessmen, politicians, and intellectuals who formed the Anti-Imperialist League in 1898 and carried on a long campaign to educate the American public about the horrors of the Philippine war and the evils of imperialism. It was an odd group (Andrew Carnegie belonged), including antilabor aristocrats and scholars, united in a common moral outrage at what was being done to the Filipinos in the name of freedom. Whatever their differences on other matters, they would all agree with William James's angry statement: "God damn the U.S. for its vile conduct in the Philippine Isles."

The Anti-Imperialist League published the letters of soldiers doing duty in the Philippines. A captain from Kansas wrote: "Caloocan was supposed to contain 17,000 inhabitants. The Twentieth Kansas swept through it, and now Caloocan contains not one living native." A private from the same outfit said he had "with my own hand set fire to over fifty houses of Filipinos after the victory at Caloocan. Women and children were wounded by our fire."

A volunteer from the state of Washington wrote: "Our fighting blood was up, and we all wanted to kill 'niggers.' . . . This shooting human beings beats rabbit hunting all to pieces."

It was a time of intense racism in the United States. In the years between 1889 and 1903, on the average, every week, two Negroes were lynched by mobs—hanged, burned, mutilated. The Filipinos were brown-skinned, physically identifiable, strange-speaking and strange-looking to Americans. To the usual indiscriminate brutality of war was thus added the factor of racial hostility.

In November 1901, the Manila correspondent of the Philadelphia *Ledger* reported:

The present war is no bloodless, opera bouffe engagement; our men have been relentless, have killed to exterminate men, women, children, prisoners and captives, active insurgents and suspected people from lads of ten up, the idea prevailing that the Filipino as such was little better than a dog. . . . Our soldiers have pumped salt water into men to make them talk, and have taken prisoners people who held up their hands and peacefully surrendered, and an hour later, without an atom of evidence to show that they were even *insurrectos*, stood them on a bridge and shot them down one by one, to drop into the water below and float down, as examples to those who found their bullet-loaded corpses.

Early in 1901 an American general returning to the United States from southern Luzon, said:

One-sixth of the natives of Luzon have either been killed or have died of the dengue fever in the last few years. The loss of life by killing alone has been very great, but I think not one man has been slain except where his death has served the legitimate purposes of war. It has been necessary to adopt what in other countries would probably be thought harsh measures.

Secretary of War Elihu Root responded to the charges of brutality: "The war in the Philippines has been conducted by the American army with scrupulous regard for the rules of civilized warfare. . . . with self-restraint and with humanity never surpassed."

In Manila, a Marine named Littletown Waller, a major, was accused of shooting eleven defenseless Filipinos, without trial, on the island of Samar. Other marine officers described his testimony:

The major said that General Smith instructed him to kill and burn, and said that the more he killed and burned the better pleased he would be; that it was no time to take prisoners, and that he was to make Samar a howling wilderness. Major Waller asked General Smith to define the age limit for killing, and he replied "Everything over ten."

In the province of Batangas, the secretary of the province estimated that of the population of 300,000, one-third had been killed by combat, famine, or disease.

Mark Twain commented on the Philippine war:

We have pacified some thousands of the islanders and buried them; destroyed their fields; burned their villages, and turned their widows and orphans out-of-doors; furnished heartbreak by exile to some dozens of disagreeable patriots; subjugated the remaining ten millions by Benevolent Assimilation, which is the pious new name of the musket; we have acquired property in the three hundred concubines and other slaves of our business partner, the Sultan of Sulu, and hoisted our protecting flag over that swag.

And so, by these Providences of God—and the phrase is the government's, not mine—we are a World Power.

American firepower was overwhelmingly superior to anything the Filipino rebels could put together. In the very first battle, Admiral Dewey steamed up the Pasig River and fired 500-pound shells into the Filipino trenches. Dead Filipinos were piled so high that the Americans used their bodies for breastworks. A British witness said: "This is not war; it is simply massacre and murderous butchery." He was wrong; it was war.

For the rebels to hold out against such odds for years meant that they had the support of the population. General Arthur MacArthur, commander of the Filipino war, said: ". . . I believed that Aguinaldo's troops represented only a faction. I did not like to believe that the whole population of Luzon—the native population, that is—was opposed to us." But he said he was "reluctantly compelled" to believe this because the guerrilla tactics of the Filipino army "depended upon almost complete unity of action of the entire native population."

Despite the growing evidence of brutality and the work of the Anti-Imperialist League, some of the trade unions in the United States supported the action in the Philippines. The Typographical Union said it liked the idea of annexing more territory because English-language schools in those areas would help the printing trade. The publication of the glassmakers saw value in new territories that would buy glass. The railroad brotherhoods saw shipment of U.S. goods to the new territories meaning more work for railroad workers. Some unions repeated what big business was saying, that territorial expansion, by creating a market for surplus goods, would prevent another depression.

On the other hand, when the *Leather Workers' Journal* wrote that an increase in wages at home would solve the problem of surplus by creating more purchasing power inside the country, the *Carpenters' Journal* asked: "How much better off are the workingmen of England through all its colonial possessions?" The *National Labor Tribune,* publication of the Iron, Steel, and Tin Workers, agreed that the Philippines were rich with resources, but added:

The same can be said of this country, but if anybody were to ask you if you owned a coal mine, a sugar plantation, or railroad you would have to say no . . . all those things are in the hands of the trusts controlled by a few. . . .

When the treaty for annexation of the Philippines was up for debate in Congress in early 1899, the Central Labor Unions of Boston and New York opposed it. There was a mass meeting in New York against annexation. The Anti-Imperialist League circulated more than a million pieces of literature against taking the Philippines. (Foner says that while the League was organized and dominated by intellectuals and business people, a large part of its half-million members were working-class people, including women and blacks.) Locals of the League held meetings all over the country. The campaign against the Treaty was a powerful one, and when the Senate did ratify it, it was by one vote.

The mixed reactions of labor to the war—lured by economic advantage, yet repelled by capitalist expansion and violence—ensured that labor could not unite either to stop the war or to conduct class war against the system at home. The reactions of black soldiers to the war were also mixed: there was the simple need to get ahead in a society where opportunities for success were denied the black man, and the military life gave such possibilities. There was race pride, the need to show that blacks were as courageous, as patriotic, as anyone else. And yet, there was with all this the consciousness of a brutal war, fought against colored people, a counterpart of the violence committed against black people in the United States.

Willard Gatewood, in his book *Smoked Yankees and the Struggle for Empire,* reproduces and analyzes 114 letters to Negro newspapers written by black soldiers in the period 1898–1902. The letters show all those conflicting emotions. Black soldiers encamped in Tampa, Florida, ran into bitter race hatred by white inhabitants there. And then, after they fought with distinction in Cuba, Negroes were not rewarded with officers' commissions; white officers commanded black regiments.

Negro soldiers in Lakeland, Florida, pistol-whipped a drugstore owner when he refused to serve one of them, and then, in a confrontation with a white crowd, killed a civilian. In Tampa, a race riot began when drunken white soldiers used a Negro child as a target to show their marksmanship; Negro soldiers retaliated, and then the streets "ran red with negro blood," according to press dispatches. Twenty-seven Negro soldiers and three whites were severely wounded. The chaplain of a black regiment in Tampa wrote to the Cleveland *Gazette:*

Is America any better than Spain? Has she not subjects in her very midst who are murdered daily without a trial of judge or jury? Has she not subjects in her own borders whose children are half-fed and half-clothed, because their father's skin is black. . . . Yet the Negro is loyal to his country's flag.

The same chaplain, George Prioleau, talks of black veterans of the Cuban war "unkindly and sneeringly received" in Kansas City, Missouri. He says that "these black boys, heroes of our country, were not allowed to stand at the counters of restaurants and eat a sandwich and drink a cup of coffee, while the white soldiers were welcomed and invited to sit down at the tables and eat free of cost."

But it was the Filipino situation that aroused many blacks in the United States to militant opposition to the war. The senior bishop of the African Methodist Episcopal Church, Henry M. Turner, called the campaign in the Philippines "an unholy war of conquest" and referred to the Filipinos as "sable patriots."

There were four black regiments on duty in the Philippines. Many of the black soldiers established rapport with the brown-skinned natives on the islands, and were angered by the term "nigger" used by white troops to describe the Filipinos. An "unusually large number" of black troops deserted during the Philippines campaign, Gatewood says. The Filipino rebels often addressed themselves to "The Colored American Soldier" in posters, reminding them of lynchings back home, asking them not to serve the white imperialist against other colored people.

Some deserters joined the Filipino rebels. The most famous of these was David Fagan of the 24th Infantry. According to Gatewood: "He accepted a commission in the insurgent army and for two years wreaked havoc upon the American forces."

From the Philippines, William Simms wrote:

I was struck by a question a little Filipino boy asked me, which ran about this way: "Why does the American Negro come . . . to fight us where we are much a friend to him and have not done anything to him. He is all the same as me and me all the same as you. Why don't you fight those people in America who burn Negroes, that make a beast of you . . ."?

Another soldier's letter of 1899:

Our racial sympathies would naturally be with the Filipinos. They are fighting manfully for what they conceive to be their best interests. But we cannot for the sake of sentiment turn our back upon our own country.

Patrick Mason, a sergeant in the 24th Infantry, wrote to the Cleveland *Gazette*, which had taken a strong stand against annexation of the Philippines:

Dear Sir: I have not had any fighting to do since I have been here and don't care to do any. I feel sorry for these people and all that have come under the control of the United States. I don't believe they will be justly dealt by. The first thing in the morning is the "Nigger" and the last thing at night is the "Nigger." . . . You are right in your opinions. I must not say much as I am a soldier. . . .

A black infantryman named William Fulbright wrote from Manila in June 1901 to the editor of a paper in Indianapolis: "This struggle on the islands has been naught but a gigantic scheme of robbery and oppression."

Back home, while the war against the Filipinos was going on, a group of Massachusetts Negroes addressed a message to President McKinley:

We the colored people of Massachusetts in mass meeting assembled . . . have resolved to address ourselves to you in an open letter, notwithstanding your extraordinary, your incomprehensible silence on the subject of our wrongs. . . .

. . . you have seen our sufferings, witnessed from your high place our awful wrongs and miseries, and yet you have at no time and on no occasion opened your lips on our behalf. . . .

With one accord, with an anxiety that wrenched our hearts with cruel hopes and fears, the Colored people of the United States turned to you when Wilmington, North Carolina was held for two dreadful days and nights in the clutch of a bloody revolution; when Negroes, guilty of no crime except the color of their skin and a desire to exercise the rights of their American citizenship, were butchered like dogs in the streets of that ill-fated town . . . for want of federal aid, which you would not and did not furnish. . . .

It was the same thing with that terrible ebullition of mob spirit at Phoenix, South Carolina, when black men were hunted and murdered, and white men [these were white radicals in Phoenix] shot and driven out of that place by a set of white savages. . . . We looked in vain for some word or some act from you. . . .

And when you made your Southern tour a little later, and we saw how cunningly you catered to Southern race prejudice. . . . How you preached patience, industry, moderation to your long-suffering black fellow citizens, and patriotism, jingoism and imperialism to your white ones. . . .

The "patience, industry, and moderation" preached to blacks, the "patriotism" preached to whites, did not fully sink in. In the first years of the twentieth century, despite all the demonstrated power of the state, large numbers of blacks, whites, men, women became impatient, immoderate, unpatriotic.

2.
The Socialist Challenge

War and jingoism might postpone, but could not fully suppress, the class anger that came from the realities of ordinary life. As the twentieth century opened, that anger reemerged. Emma Goldman, the anarchist and feminist, whose political consciousness was shaped by factory work, the Haymarket executions, the Homestead strike, the long prison term of her lover and comrade, Alexander Berkman, the depression of the 1890s, the strike struggles of New York, her own imprisonment on Blackwell's Island, spoke at a meeting some years after the Spanish-American war:

> How our hearts burned with indignation against the atrocious Spaniards!
> . . . But when the smoke was over, the dead buried, and the cost of the war came back to the people in an increase in the price of commodities and rent—that is, when we sobered up from our patriotic spree—it suddenly dawned on us that the cause of the Spanish-American war was the price of sugar.
> . . . that the lives, blood, and money of the American people were used to protect the interests of the American capitalists.

Mark Twain was neither an anarchist nor a radical. By 1900, at sixty-five, he was a world-acclaimed writer of funny-serious-American-to-the-bone stories. He watched the United States and other Western countries go about the world and wrote in the New York *Herald* as the century began: "I bring you the stately matron named Christendom, returning bedraggled, besmirched, and dishonored from pirate raids in Kiao-Chou, Manchuria, South Africa, and the Philippines, with her soul full of meanness, her pocket full of boodle, and her mouth full of pious hypocrisies."

There were writers of the early twentieth century who spoke for socialism or criticized the capitalist system harshly—not obscure pamphleteers, but among the most famous of American literary figures, whose books were read by millions: Upton Sinclair, Jack London, Theodore Dreiser, Frank Norris.

Upton Sinclair's novel *The Jungle*, published in 1906, brought the conditions in the meatpacking plants of Chicago to the shocked attention of the whole country, and stimulated demand for laws regulating the meat industry. But also, through the story of an immigrant laborer, Jurgis Rudkus, it spoke of socialism, of how beautiful life might be if people cooperatively owned and worked and shared the riches of the earth. *The Jungle* was first published in the Socialist newspaper *Appeal to Reason;* it was then read by millions as a book, and was translated into seventeen languages.

One of the influences on Upton Sinclair's thinking was a book, *People of the Abyss,* by Jack London. London was a member of the Socialist party. He had come out of the slums of San Francisco, the child of an unwed mother. He had been a newsboy, a cannery worker, a sailor, a fisherman, had worked in a jute mill and a laundry, hoboed the railroads to the East Coast, been clubbed by a policeman on the streets of New York and arrested for vagrancy in Niagara Falls, watched men beaten and tortured in jail, pirated oysters in San Francisco Bay, read Flaubert, Tolstoy, Melville, and the *Communist Manifesto,* preached socialism in the Alaskan gold camps in the winter of 1896, sailed 2,000 miles back through the Bering Sea, and became a world-famous writer of adventure books. In 1906, he wrote his novel *The Iron Heel,* with its warning of a fascist America, its ideal of a socialist brotherhood of man. In the course of it, through his characters, he indicts the system.

In the face of the facts that modern man lives more wretchedly than the cave-man, and that his producing power is a thousand times greater than that of the cave-man, no other conclusion is possible than that the capitalist class has mismanaged . . . criminally and selfishly mismanaged.

And with this attack, the vision:

Let us not destroy those wonderful machines that produce efficiently and cheaply. Let us control them. Let us profit by their efficiency and cheapness. Let us run them for ourselves. That, gentlemen, is socialism. . . .

It was a time when even a self-exiled literary figure living in Europe and not prone to political statements—the novelist Henry James—could tour the United States in 1904 and see the country as a "huge Rappacini garden, rank with each variety of the poison-plant of the money passion."

"Muckrakers," who raked up the mud and the muck, contributed to the atmosphere of dissent by simply telling what they saw. Some of the new mass-circulation magazines, ironically enough in the interest of profit, printed their articles: Ida Tarbell's exposure of the Standard Oil Company; Lincoln Steffens's stories of corruption in the major American cities.

By 1900, neither the patriotism of the war nor the absorption of energy in elections could disguise the troubles of the system. The process of business concentration had gone forward; the control by bankers had become more clear. As technology developed and corporations became larger, they needed more capital, and it was the bankers who had this capital. By 1904, more than a thousand railroad lines had been consolidated into six great combinations, each allied with either Morgan or Rockefeller interests. As Cochran and Miller say:

The imperial leader of the new oligarchy was the House of Morgan. In its operations it was ably assisted by the First National Bank of New York (directed by George F. Baker) and the National City Bank of New York (presided over by James Stillman, agent of the Rockefeller interests). Among them, these three men and their financial associates occupied 341 directorships in 112 great corporations. The total resources of these corporations in 1912 was $22,245,000,000, more than the assessed value of all property in the twenty-two states and territories west of the Mississippi River. . . .

Morgan had always wanted regularity, stability, predictability. An associate of his said in 1901:

With a man like Mr. Morgan at the head of a great industry, as against the old plan of many diverse interests in it, production would become more regular, labor would be more steadily employed at better wages, and panics caused by over-production would become a thing of the past.

But even Morgan and his associates were not in complete control of such a system. In 1907, there was a panic, financial collapse, and crisis. True, the very big businesses were not hurt, but profits after 1907 were not as high as capitalists wanted, industry was not expanding as fast as it might, and industrialists began to look for ways to cut costs.

One way was Taylorism. Frederick W. Taylor had been a steel company foreman who closely analyzed every job in the mill, and worked out a system of finely detailed division of labor, increased mechanization, and piecework wage systems, to increase production and profits. In 1911, he published a book on "scientific management" that became powerfully influential in the business world. Now management could control every detail of the worker's energy and time in the factory. As Harry Braverman said (Labor and Monopoly Capital), the purpose of Taylorism was to make workers interchangeable, able to do the simple tasks that the new division of labor required—like standard parts divested of individuality and humanity, bought and sold as commodities.

It was a system well fitted for the new auto industry. In 1909, Ford sold 10,607 autos; in 1913, 168,000; in 1914, 248,000 (45 percent of all autos produced). The profit: $30 million.

With immigrants a larger proportion of the labor force (in the Carnegie plants of Allegheny County in 1907, of the 14,359 common laborers, 11,694 were Eastern Europeans), Taylorism, with its simplified unskilled jobs, became more feasible.

In New York City, the new immigrants went to work in the sweatshops. The poet Edwin Markham wrote in *Cosmopolitan* magazine, January 1907:

In unaired rooms, mothers and fathers sew by day and by night. Those in the home sweatshop must work cheaper than those in the factory sweatshops. . . . And the children are called in from play to drive and drudge beside their elders. . . .

All the year in New York and in other cities you may watch children radiating to and from such pitiful homes. Nearly any hour on the East Side of New York City you can see them—pallid boy or spindling girl—their faces dulled, their backs bent under a heavy load of garments piled on head and shoulders, the muscles of the whole frame in a long strain. . . .

Is it not a cruel civilization that allows little hearts and little shoulders to strain under these grown-up responsibilities, while in the same city, a pet cur is jeweled and pampered and aired on a fine lady's velvet lap on the beautiful boulevards?

The city became a battlefield. On August 10, 1905, the New York *Tribune* reported that a strike at Federman's bakery on the Lower East Side led to violence when Federman used scab labor to continue producing:

Strikers or their sympathizers wrecked the bake shop of Philip Federman at No. 183 Orchard Street early last night amid scenes of the most tumultuous excitement. Policemen smashed heads right and left with their nightsticks after two of their number had been roughly dealt with by the mob. . . .

There were five hundred garment factories in New York. A woman later recalled the conditions of work:

. . . dangerously broken stairways . . . windows few and so dirty. . . . The wooden floors that were swept once a year. . . . Hardly any other light but the gas jets burning by day and by night . . . the filthy, malodorous lavatory in the dark hall. No fresh drinking water. . . . mice and roaches. . . .

During the winter months . . . how we suffered from the cold. In the summer we suffered from the heat. . . .

In these disease-breeding holes we, the youngsters together with the men and women toiled from seventy and eighty hours a week! Saturdays and Sundays included! . . . A sign would go up on Saturday afternoon: "If you don't come in on Sunday, you need not come in on Monday." . . . Children's dreams of a day off shattered. We wept, for after all, we were only children. . . .

At the Triangle Shirtwaist Company, in the winter of 1909, women organized and decided to strike. Soon they were walking the picket line in the cold, knowing they could not win while the other factories were operating. A mass meeting was called of workers in the other shops, and Clara Lemlich, in her teens, an eloquent speaker, still bearing the signs of her recent beating on the picket line, stood up: "I offer a resolution that a general strike be declared now!" The meeting went wild; they voted to strike.

Pauline Newman, one of the strikers, recalled years later the beginning of the general strike:

Thousands upon thousands left the factories from every side, all of them walking down toward Union Square. It was November, the cold winter was just around the corner, we had no fur coats to keep warm, and yet there was the spirit that led us on and on until we got to some hall. . . .

I can see the young people, mostly women, walking down and not caring what might happen . . . the hunger, cold, loneliness. . . . They just didn't care on that particular day; that was their day.

The union had hoped three thousand would join the strike. Twenty thousand walked out. Every day a thousand new members joined the union, the International Ladies Garment Workers Union, which before this had few women. Colored women were active in the strike, which went on through the winter, against police, against scabs, against arrests and prison. In more than three hundred shops, workers won their demands. Women now became officials in the union. Pauline Newman again:

We tried to educate ourselves. I would invite the girls to my rooms, and we took turns reading poetry in English to improve our understanding of the language. One of our favorites was Thomas Hood's "Song of the Shirt," and another . . . Percy Bysshe Shelley's "Mask of Anarchy." . . .

> "Rise like lions after slumber
> In unvanquishable number!

Shake your chains to earth, like dew
Which in sleep had fallen on you—
Ye are many, they are few!"

The conditions in the factories did not change much. On the afternoon of March 25, 1911, a fire at the Triangle Shirtwaist Company
that began in a rag bin swept through the eighth, ninth, and tenth
floors, too high for fire ladders to reach. The fire chief of New York
had said that his ladders could reach only to the seventh floor. But
half of New York's 500,000 workers spent all day, perhaps twelve hours,
above the seventh floor. The laws said factory doors had to open outward. But at the Triangle Company the doors opened in. The law
said the doors could not be locked during working hours, but at the
Triangle Company doors were usually locked so the company could
keep track of the employees. And so, trapped, the young women were
burned to death at their worktables, or jammed against the locked
exit door, or leaped to their deaths down the elevator shafts. The New
York *World* reported:

. . . screaming men and women and boys and girls crowded out on the many
window ledges and threw themselves into the streets far below. They jumped
with their clothing ablaze. The hair of some of the girls streamed up aflame
as they leaped. Thud after thud sounded on the pavements. It is a ghastly
fact that on both the Greene Street and Washington Place sides of the building
there grew mounds of the dead and dying. . . .

From opposite windows spectators saw again and again pitiable compan-
ionships formed in the instant of death—girls who placed their arms around
each other as they leaped.

When it was over, 146 Triangle workers, mostly women, were
burned or crushed to death. There was a memorial parade down Broadway, and 100,000 marched.

There were more fires. And accidents. And sickness. In the year
1904, 27,000 workers were killed on the job, in manufacturing, transport, and agriculture. In one year, 50,000 accidents took place in New
York factories alone. Hat and cap makers were getting respiratory diseases, quarrymen were inhaling deadly chemicals, lithographic printers
were getting arsenic poisoning. A New York State Factory Investigation
Commission reported in 1912:

Sadie is an intelligent, neat, clean girl, who has worked from the time
she got her working papers in embroidery factories. . . . In her work she
was accustomed to use a white powder (chalk or talcum was usual) which

was brushed over the perforated designs and thus transferred to the cloth. The design was easily brushed off when made of chalk or of talcum. . . . Her last employer therefore commenced using white lead powder, mixed with rosin, which cheapened the work as the powder could not be rubbed off and necessitate restamping.

None of the girls knew of the change in powder, nor of the danger in its use. . . .

Sadie had been a very strong, healthy girl, good appetite and color; she began to be unable to eat. . . . Her hands and feet swelled, she lost the use of one hand, her teeth and gums were blue. When she finally had to stop work, after being treated for months for stomach trouble, her physician advised her to go to a hospital. There the examination revealed the fact that she had lead poisoning. . . .

According to a report of the Commission on Industrial Relations, in 1914, 35,000 workers were killed in industrial accidents and 700,000 injured. That year the income of forty-four families making $1 million or more equaled the total income of 100,000 families earning $500 a year. The record shows an exchange between Commissioner Harris Weinstock of the Commission on Industrial Relations and President John Osgood, head of a Colorado coal company controlled by the Rockefellers:

WEINSTOCK: If a worker loses his life, are his dependents compensated in any way?

OSGOOD: Not necessarily. In some cases they are and in some cases not.

WEINSTOCK: If he is crippled for life is there any compensation?

OSGOOD: No sir, there is none. . . .

WEINSTOCK: Then the whole burden is thrown directly upon their shoulders.

OSGOOD: Yes, sir.

WEINSTOCK: The industry bears none of it?

OSGOOD: No, the industry bears none of it.

Unionization was growing. Shortly after the turn of the century there were 2 million members of labor unions (one in fourteen workers), 80 percent of them in the American Federation of Labor. The AFL was an exclusive union—almost all male, almost all white, almost all skilled workers. Although the number of women workers kept growing—it doubled from 4 million in 1890 to 8 million in 1910, and women were one-fifth of the labor force—only one in a hundred belonged to a union.

Black workers in 1910 made one-third of the earnings of white workers. Although Samuel Gompers, head of the AFL, would make speeches about its belief in equal opportunity, the Negro was excluded from most AFL unions. Gompers kept saying he did not want to interfere with the "internal affairs" of the South: "I regard the race problem as one with which you people of the Southland will have to deal; without the interference, too, of meddlers from the outside."

In the reality of struggle, rank-and-file workers overcame these separations from time to time. Foner quotes Mary McDowell's account of the formation of a women's union in the Chicago stockyards:

> It was a dramatic occasion on that evening, when an Irish girl at the door called out—"A Colored sister asks admission. What shall I do with her?" And the answer came from the Irish young woman in the chair—"Admit her, of course, and let all of you give her a hearty welcome!"

In New Orleans in 1907 a general strike on the levees, involving ten thousand workers (longshoremen, teamsters, freight handlers), black and white, lasted twenty days. The head of the Negro longshoremen, E. S. Swan, said:

> The whites and Negroes were never before so strongly cemented in a common bond and in my 39 years of experience of the levee, I never saw such solidarity. In all the previous strikes the Negro was used against the white man but that condition is now past and both races are standing together for their common interests. . . .

These were exceptions. In general, the Negro was kept out of the trade union movement. W. E. B. Du Bois wrote in 1913: "The net result of all this has been to convince the American Negro that his greatest enemy is not the employer who robs him, but his fellow white workingman."

Racism was practical for the AFL. The exclusion of women and foreigners was also practical. These were mostly unskilled workers, and the AFL, confined mostly to skilled workers, was based on the philosophy of "business unionism" (in fact, the chief official of each AFL union was called the "business agent"), trying to match the monopoly of production by the employer with a monopoly of workers by the union. In this way it won better conditions for some workers, and left most workers out.

AFL officials drew large salaries, hobnobbed with employers, even moved in high society. A press dispatch from Atlantic City, New Jersey, the fashionable seaside resort, in the summer of 1910:

> Engaged in a game of bathing suit baseball with President Sam Gompers, Secretary Frank Morrison and other leaders of the A.F. of L. on the beach

this morning, John Mitchell, former head of the mine workers' union, lost a $1000 diamond ring presented to him by his admirers after the settlement of the big Pennsylvania coal strike. Capt. George Berke, a veteran life guard, found the ring, whereupon Mitchell peeled a hundred dollar bill from a roll he carried in his pocket and handed it to the captain as a reward for his find.

The well-paid leaders of the AFL were protected from criticism by tightly controlled meetings and by "goon" squads—hired toughs originally used against strikebreakers but after a while used to intimidate and beat up opponents inside the union.

In this situation—terrible conditions of labor, exclusivity in union organization—working people wanting radical change, seeing the root of misery in the capitalist system, moved toward a new kind of labor union. One morning in June 1905, there met in a hall in Chicago a convention of two hundred socialists, anarchists, and radical trade unionists from all over the United States. They were forming the I.W.W.— the Industrial Workers of the World. Big Bill Haywood, a leader of the Western Federation of Miners, recalled in his autobiography that he picked up a piece of board that lay on the platform and used it for a gavel to open the convention:

Fellow workers. . . . This is the Continental Congress of the working-class. We are here to confederate the workers of this country into a working-class movement that shall have for its purpose the emancipation of the working-class from the slave bondage of capitalism. . . . The aims and objects of this organization shall be to put the working-class in possession of the economic power, the means of life, in control of the machinery of production and distribution, without regard to the capitalist masters.

On the speakers' platform with Haywood were Eugene Debs, leader of the Socialist party, and Mother Mary Jones, a seventy-five-year-old white-haired woman who was an organizer for the United Mine Workers of America. The convention drew up a constitution, whose preamble said:

The working class and the employing class have nothing in common. There can be no peace so long as hunger and want are found among millions of working people and the few, who make up the employing class, have all the good things of life.

Between these two classes a struggle must go on until all the toilers come together on the political as well as on the industrial field, and take and hold that which they produce by their labor, through an economic organization of the working class without affiliation with any political party. . . .

One of the IWW pamphlets explained why it broke with the AFL idea of craft unions:

The directory of unions of Chicago shows in 1903 a total of 56 different unions in the packing houses, divided up still more in 14 different national trades unions of the American Federation of Labor.

What a horrible example of an army divided against itself in the face of a strong combination of employers. . . .

The IWW (or "Wobblies," as they came to be called, for reasons not really clear) aimed at organizing all workers in any industry into "One Big Union," undivided by sex, race, or skills. They argued against making contracts with the employer, because this had so often prevented workers from striking on their own, or in sympathy with other strikers, and thus turned union people into strikebreakers. Negotiations by leaders for contracts replaced continuous struggle by the rank and file, the Wobblies believed.

They spoke of "direct action":

Direct action means industrial action directly by, for, and of the workers themselves, without the treacherous aid of labor misleaders or scheming politicians. A strike that is initiated, controlled, and settled by the workers directly affected is direct action. . . . Direct action is industrial democracy.

One IWW pamphlet said: "Shall I tell you what direct action means? The worker on the job shall tell the boss when and where he shall work, how long and for what wages and under what conditions."

The IWW people were militant, courageous. Despite a reputation given them by the press, they did not believe in initiating violence, but did fight back when attacked. In McKees Rocks, Pennsylvania, they led a strike of six thousand workers in 1909 against an affiliate of the U.S. Steel Company, defied the state troopers, and battled with them. They promised to take a trooper's life for every worker killed (in one gun battle four strikers and three troopers were killed), and managed to keep picketing the factories until the strike was won.

The IWW saw beyond strikes:

Strikes are mere incidents in the class war; they are tests of strength, periodical drills in the course of which the workers train themselves for concerted action. This training is most necessary to prepare the masses for the final "catastrophe," the general strike which will complete the expropriation of the employers.

The idea of anarcho-syndicalism was developing strongly in Spain and Italy and France at this time—that the workers would take power, not by seizing the state machinery in an armed rebellion, but by bringing the economic system to a halt in a general strike, then taking it over to use for the good of all. IWW organizer Joseph Ettor said:

If the workers of the world want to win, all they have to do is recognize their own solidarity. They have nothing to do but fold their arms and the world will stop. The workers are more powerful with their hands in their pockets than all the property of the capitalists. . . .

It was an immensely powerful idea. In the ten exciting years after its birth, the IWW became a threat to the capitalist class, exactly when capitalist growth was enormous and profits huge. The IWW never had more than five to ten thousand enrolled members at any one time; people came and went, and perhaps a hundred thousand were members at one time or another. But their energy, their persistence, their inspiration to others, their ability to mobilize thousands at one place, one time, made them an influence on the country far beyond their numbers. They traveled everywhere (many were unemployed or migrant workers); they organized, wrote, spoke, sang, spread their message and their spirit.

They were attacked with all the weapons the system could put together: the newspapers, the courts, the police, the army, mob violence. Local authorities passed laws to stop them from speaking; the IWW defied these laws. In Missoula, Montana, a lumber and mining area, hundreds of Wobblies arrived by boxcar after some had been prevented from speaking. They were arrested one after another until they clogged the jails and the courts, and finally forced the town to repeal its anti-speech ordinance.

In Spokane, Washington, in 1909, an ordinance was passed to stop street meetings, and an IWW organizer who insisted on speaking was arrested. Thousands of Wobblies marched into the center of town to speak. One by one they spoke and were arrested, until six hundred were in jail. Jail conditions were brutal, and several men died in their cells, but the IWW won the right to speak.

In Fresno, California, in 1911, there was another free speech fight. The San Francisco *Call* commented:

It is one of those strange situations which crop up suddenly and are hard to understand. Some thousands of men, whose business it is to work with their hands, tramping and stealing rides, suffering hardships and facing dangers—to get into jail. . . .

In jail they sang, they shouted, they made speeches through the bars to groups that gathered outside the prison. As Joyce Kornbluh reports in her remarkable collection of IWW documents, *Rebel Voices:*

They took turns lecturing about the class struggle and leading the singing of Wobbly songs. When they refused to stop, the jailor sent for fire department trucks and ordered the fire hoses turned full force on the prisoners. The men used their mattresses as shields, and quiet was only restored when the icy water reached knee-high in the cells.

When city officials heard that thousands more were planning to come into town, they lifted the ban on street speaking and released the prisoners in small groups.

That same year in Aberdeen, Washington, once again laws against free speech, arrests, prison, and, unexpectedly, victory. One of the men arrested, "Stumpy" Payne, a carpenter, farm hand, editor of an IWW newspaper, wrote about the experience:

Here they were, eighteen men in the vigor of life, most of whom came long distances through snow and hostile towns by beating their way, penniless and hungry, into a place where a jail sentence was the gentlest treatment that could be expected, and where many had already been driven into the swamps and beaten nearly to death. . . . Yet here they were, laughing with boyish glee at tragic things that to them were jokes. . . .

But what was the motive behind the actions of these men? . . . Why were they here? Is the call of Brotherhood in the human race greater than any fear or discomfort, despite the efforts of the masters of life for six thousand years to root out that call of Brotherhood from our minds?

In San Diego, Jack White, a Wobbly arrested in a free-speech fight in 1912, sentenced to six months in the county jail on a bread and water diet, was asked if he had anything to say to the court. A stenographer recorded what he said:

The prosecuting attorney, in his plea to the jury, accused me of saying on a public platform at a public meeting, "To hell with the courts, we know what justice is." He told a great truth when he lied, for if he had searched the innermost recesses of my mind he could have found that thought, never expressed by me before, but which I express now, "To hell with your courts, I know what justice is," for I have sat in your court room day after day and have seen members of my class pass before this, the so-called bar of justice. I have seen you, Judge Sloane, and others of your kind, send them to prison because they dared to infringe upon the sacred rights of property.

You have become blind and deaf to the rights of man to pursue life and happiness, and you have crushed those rights so that the sacred right of property shall be preserved. Then you tell me to respect the law. I do not. I did violate the law, as I will violate every one of your laws and still come before you and say "To hell with the courts." . . .

The prosecutor lied, but I will accept his lie as a truth and say again so that you, Judge Sloane, may not be mistaken as to my attitude, "To hell with your courts, I know what justice is."

There were also beatings, tarrings and featherings, defeats. One IWW member, John Stone, tells of being released from the jail at San Diego at midnight with another IWW man and forced into an automobile:

We were taken out of the city, about twenty miles, where the machine stopped. . . . a man in the rear struck me with a blackjack several times on the head and shoulders; the other man then struck me on the mouth with his fist. The men in the rear then sprang around and kicked me in the stomach. I then started to run away; and heard a bullet go past me. I stopped. . . . In the morning I examined Joe Marko's condition and found that the back of his head had been split open.

In 1916, in Everett, Washington, a boatload of Wobblies was fired on by two hundred armed vigilantes gathered by the sheriff, and five Wobblies were shot to death, thirty-one wounded. Two of the vigilantes were killed, nineteen wounded. The following year—the year the United States entered World War I—vigilantes in Montana seized IWW organizer Frank Little, tortured him, and hanged him, leaving his body dangling from a railroad trestle.

Joe Hill, an IWW organizer, wrote dozens of songs—biting, funny, class-conscious, inspiring—that appeared in IWW publications and in its *Little Red Song Book*. He became a legend in his time and after. His song "The Preacher and the Slave" had a favorite IWW target, the church:

> Long-haired preachers come out every night,
> Try to tell you what's wrong and what's right;
> But when asked how 'bout something to eat
> They will answer with voices so sweet:
>
> You will eat, bye and bye,
> In that glorious land above the sky;
> Work and pray, live on hay,
> You'll get pie in the sky when you die.

His song "Rebel Girl" was inspired by the strike of women at the textile mills in Lawrence, Massachusetts, and especially by the IWW leader of that strike, Elizabeth Gurley Flynn:

> There are women of many descriptions
> In this queer world, as everyone knows,
> Some are living in beautiful mansions,
> And are wearing the finest of clothes.
> There are blue-blooded queens and princesses,
> Who have charms made of diamonds and pearl,
> But the only and Thoroughbred Lady
> Is the Rebel Girl.

In November 1915, Joe Hill was accused of killing a grocer in Salt Lake City, Utah, in a robbery. There was no direct evidence presented to the court that he had committed the murder, but there were enough pieces of evidence to persuade a jury to find him guilty. The case became known throughout the world, and ten thousand letters went to the governor in protest, but with machine guns guarding the entrance to the prison, Joe Hill was executed by a firing squad. He had written Bill Haywood just before this: "Don't waste any time in mourning. Organize."

The IWW became involved in a set of dramatic events in Lawrence, Massachusetts, in the year 1912, where the American Woolen Company owned four mills. The work force were immigrant families—Portuguese, French-Canadian, English, Irish, Russian, Italian, Syrian, Lithuanian, German, Polish, Belgian—who lived in crowded, flammable wooden tenements. The average wage was $8.76 a week. A woman physician in Lawrence, Dr. Elizabeth Shapleigh, wrote:

A considerable number of the boys and girls die within the first two or three years after beginning work . . . thirty-six out of every 100 of all the men and women who work in the mill die before or by the time they are twenty-five years of age.

It was in January, midwinter, when pay envelopes distributed to weavers at one of the mills—Polish women—showed that their wages, already too low to feed their families, had been reduced. They stopped their looms and walked out of the mill. The next day, five thousand workers at another mill quit work, marched to still another mill, rushed the gates, shut off the power to the looms, and called on the other workers to leave. Soon ten thousand workers were on strike.

A telegram went to Joseph Ettor, a twenty-six-year-old Italian, an IWW leader in New York, to come to Lawrence to help conduct the strike. He came. A committee of fifty was set up, representing every nationality among the workers, to make the important decisions. Less than a thousand millworkers belonged to the IWW, but the AFL had ignored the unskilled workers, and so they turned to the IWW leadership in the strike.

The IWW organized mass meetings and parades. The strikers had to supply food and fuel for 50,000 people (the entire population of Lawrence was 86,000); soup kitchens were set up, and money began arriving from all over the country—from trade unions, IWW locals, socialist groups, individuals.

The mayor called out the local militia; the governor ordered out the state police. A parade of strikers was attacked by police a few weeks after the strike began. This led to rioting all that day. In the evening, a striker, Anna LoPizzo, was shot and killed. Witnesses said a policeman did it, but the authorities arrested Joseph Ettor and another IWW organizer who had come to Lawrence, a poet named Arturo Giovanitti. Neither was at the scene of the shooting, but the charge was that "Joseph Ettor and Arturo Giovanitti did incite, procure, and counsel or command the said person whose name is not known to commit the said murder. . . ."

With Ettor, head of the strike committee, in jail, Big Bill Haywood was called in to replace him; other IWW organizers, including Elizabeth Gurley Flynn, came into Lawrence. Now there were twenty-two companies of militia and two troops of cavalry in the city. Martial law was declared, and citizens were forbidden to talk on the street. Thirty-six strikers were arrested, many sentenced to a year in prison. On Tuesday, January 30, a young Syrian striker, John Ramy, was bayoneted to death. But the strikers were still out, and the mills were not working. Ettor said: "Bayonets cannot weave cloth."

In February, the strikers began mass picketing, seven thousand to ten thousand pickets in an endless chain, marching through the mill districts, with white armbands: "Don't be a scab." But their food was running out and the children were hungry. It was proposed by the New York *Call*, a Socialist newspaper, that the children of strikers be sent to sympathetic families in other cities to take care of them, while the strike lasted. This had been done by strikers in Europe, never in the United States—but in three days, the *Call* got four hundred letters offering to take children. The IWW and the Socialist party began to organize the children's exodus, taking applications from families who wanted them, arranging medical exams for the youngsters.

On February 10, over a hundred children, aged four to fourteen, left Lawrence for New York City. They were greeted at Grand Central Station by five thousand Italian Socialists singing the "Marseillaise" and the "Internationale." The following week, another hundred children came to New York, and thirty-five to Barre, Vermont. It was becoming clear: if the children were taken care of, the strikers could stay out, for their spirit was high. The city officials in Lawrence, citing a statute on child neglect, said no more children would be permitted to leave Lawrence.

Despite the city edict, a group of forty children assembled on February 24 to go to Philadelphia. The railroad station was filled with police, and the scene that followed was described to Congressmen by a member of the Women's Committee of Philadelphia:

When the time approached to depart, the children arranged in a long line, two by two, in orderly procession, with their parents near at hand, were about to make their way to the train when the police closed in on us with their clubs, beating right and left, with no thought of children, who were in the most desperate danger of being trampled to death. The mothers and children were thus hurled in a mass and bodily dragged to a military truck, and even then clubbed, irrespective of the cries of the panic-stricken women and children. . . .

A week after that, women returning from a meeting were surrounded by police and clubbed; one pregnant woman was carried unconscious to a hospital and gave birth to a dead child.

Still, the strikers held out. "They are always marching and singing," reporter Mary Heaton Vorse wrote. "The tired, gray crowds ebbing and flowing perpetually into the mills had waked and opened their mouths to sing."

The American Woolen Company decided to give in. It offered raises of 5 to 11 percent (the strikers insisted that the largest increases go to the lowest-paid), time and a quarter for overtime, and no discrimination against those who had struck. On March 14, 1912, ten thousand strikers gathered on the Lawrence Common and, with Bill Haywood presiding, voted to end the strike.

Ettor and Giovanitti went on trial. Support for them had been mounting all over the country. There were parades in New York and Boston; on September 30, fifteen thousand Lawrence workers struck for twenty-four hours to show their support for the two men. After

that, two thousand of the most active strikers were fired, but the IWW
threatened to call another strike, and they were put back. A jury found
Ettor and Giovanitti not guilty, and that afternoon, ten thousand people
assembled in Lawrence to celebrate.

The IWW took its slogan "One Big Union" seriously. Women,
foreigners, black workers, the lowliest and most unskilled of workers,
were included when a factory or mine was organized. When the Brotherhood of Timber Workers organized in Louisiana and invited Bill Haywood to speak to them in 1912 (shortly after the Lawrence victory),
he expressed surprise that no Negroes were at the meeting. He was
told it was against the law to have interracial meetings in Louisiana.
Haywood told the convention:

> You work in the same mills together. Sometimes a black man and a
> white man chop down the same tree together. You are meeting in convention
> now to discuss the conditions under which you labor. . . . Why not be sensible
> about this and call the Negroes into the Convention? If it is against the law,
> this is one time when the law should be broken.

Negroes were invited into the convention, which then voted to affiliate
with the IWW.

In 1900 there were 500,000 women office workers—in 1870 there
had been 19,000. Women were switchboard operators, store workers,
nurses. Half a million were teachers. The teachers formed a Teachers
League that fought against the automatic firing of women who became
pregnant. The following "Rules for Female Teachers" were posted by
the school board of one town in Massachusetts:

1. Do not get married.
2. Do not leave town at any time without permission of the school board.
3. Do not keep company with men.
4. Be home between the hours of 8 P.M. and 6 A.M.
5. Do not loiter downtown in ice cream stores.
6. Do not smoke.
7. Do not get into a carriage with any man except your father or brother.
8. Do not dress in bright colors.
9. Do not dye your hair.
10. Do not wear any dress more than two inches above the ankle.

The conditions of women working in a Milwaukee brewery were
described by Mother Mary Jones, who worked there briefly in 1910
(she was close to eighty at this time):

Condemned to slave daily in the wash-room in wet shoes and wet clothes, surrounded with foul-mouthed, brutal foremen . . . the poor girls work in the vile smell of sour beer, lifting cases of empty and full bottles weighing from 100 to 150 pounds. . . . Rheumatism is one of the chronic ailments and is closely followed by consumption. . . . The foreman even regulates the time the girls may stay in the toilet room. . . . Many of the girls have no home nor parents and are forced to feed and clothe and shelter themselves . . . on $3.00 a week. . . .

In the laundries, women organized. In 1909, the *Handbook* of the Women's Trade Union Industrial League wrote about women in steam laundries:

How would you like to iron a shirt a minute? Think of standing at a mangle just above the washroom with the hot steam pouring up through the floor for 10, 12, 14 and sometimes 17 hours a day! Sometimes the floors are made of cement and then it seems as though one were standing on hot coals, and the workers are dripping with perspiration. . . . They are . . . breathing air laden with particles of soda, ammonia, and other chemicals! The Laundry Workers Union . . . in one city reduced this long day to 9 hours, and has increased the wages 50 percent. . . .

Labor struggles could make things better, but the country's resources remained in the hands of powerful corporations whose motive was profit, whose power commanded the government of the United States. There was an idea in the air, becoming clearer and stronger, an idea not just in the theories of Karl Marx but in the dreams of writers and artists through the ages: that people might cooperatively use the treasures of the earth to make life better for everyone, not just a few.

Around the turn of the century, strike struggles were multiplying— in the 1890s there had been about a thousand strikes a year; by 1904 there were four thousand strikes a year. Law and military force again and again took the side of the rich. It was a time when hundreds of thousands of Americans began to think of socialism.

Debs wrote in 1904, three years after the formation of the Socialist party:

The "pure and simple" trades union of the past does not answer the requirements of today. . . .

The attempt of each trade to maintain its own independence separately and apart from others results in increasing jurisdictional entanglements, fruitful of dissension, strife and ultimate disruption. . . .

The members of a trades union should be taught . . . that the labor movement means more, infinitely more, than a paltry increase in wages and the strike necessary to secure it; that while it engages to do all that possibly can be done to better the working conditions of its members, its higher object is to overthrow the capitalist system of private ownership of the tools of labor, abolish wage-slavery and achieve the freedom of the whole working class and, in fact, of all mankind. . . .

What Debs accomplished was not in theory, or analysis, but in expressing eloquently, passionately, what people were feeling. The writer Heywood Broun once quoted a fellow Socialist speaking of Debs: "That old man with the burning eyes actually believes that there can be such a thing as the brotherhood of man. And that's not the funniest part of it. As long as he's around I believe it myself."

Eugene Debs had become a Socialist while in jail in the Pullman strike. Now he was the spokesman of a party that made him its presidential candidate five times. The party at one time had 100,000 members, and 1,200 office holders in 340 municipalities. Its main newspaper, *Appeal to Reason,* for which Debs wrote, had half a million subscribers, and there were many other Socialist newspapers around the country, so that, all together, perhaps a million people read the Socialist press.

Socialism moved out of the small circles of city immigrants—Jewish and German socialists speaking their own languages—and became American. The strongest Socialist state organization was in Oklahoma, which in 1914 had twelve thousand dues-paying members (more than New York State), and elected over a hundred Socialists to local office, including six to the Oklahoma state legislature. There were fifty-five weekly Socialist newspapers in Oklahoma, Texas, Louisiana, Arkansas, and summer encampments that drew thousands of people.

James Green describes these Southwest radicals, in his book *Grass-Roots Socialism,* as "indebted homesteaders, migratory tenant farmers, coal miners and railroad workers, 'redbone' lumberjacks from the piney woods, preachers and schoolteachers from the sunbaked prairies . . . village artisans and atheists . . . the unknown people who created the strongest regional Socialist movement in United States history." Green continues:

The Socialist movement . . . was painstakingly organized by scores of former Populists, militant miners, and blacklisted railroad workers, who were assisted by a remarkable cadre of professional agitators and educators and inspired by occasional visits from national figures like Eugene V. Debs and Mother Jones. . . . This core of organizers grew to include indigenous dissenters. . . . a much larger group of amateur agitators who canvassed the region selling newspapers, forming reading groups, organizing locals, and making soapbox speeches.

There was almost a religious fervor to the movement, as in the eloquence of Debs. In 1906, after the imprisonment in Idaho of Bill Haywood and two other officers of the Western Federation of Miners on an apparently faked murder charge, Debs wrote a flaming article in the *Appeal to Reason:*

Murder has been plotted and is about to be executed in the name and under the forms of law. . . .

It is a foul plot; a damnable conspiracy; a hellish outrage. . . .

If they attempt to murder Moyer, Haywood and their brothers, a million revolutionists, at least, will meet them with guns. . . .

Capitalist courts never have done, and never will do, anything for the working class. . . .

A special revolutionary convention of the proletariat . . . would be in order, and, if extreme measures are required, a general strike could be ordered and industry paralyzed as a preliminary to a general uprising.

If the plutocrats begin the program, we will end it.

Theodore Roosevelt, after reading this, sent a copy to his Attorney General, W. H. Moody, with a note: "Is it possible to proceed against Debs and the proprietor of this paper criminally?"

As the Socialists became more successful at the polls (Debs got 900,000 votes in 1912, double what he had in 1908), and more concerned with increasing that appeal, they became more critical of IWW tactics of "sabotage" and "violence," and in 1913 removed Bill Haywood from the Socialist Party Executive Committee, claiming he advocated violence (although some of Debs's writings were far more inflammatory).

Women were active in the socialist movement, more as rank-and-file workers than as leaders—and, sometimes, as sharp critics of socialist policy. Helen Keller, for instance, the gifted blind-mute-deaf woman with her extraordinary social vision, commented on the expulsion of Bill Haywood in a letter to the New York *Call:*

It is with the deepest regret that I have read the attacks upon Comrade Haywood . . . such an ignoble strife between two factions which should be one, and that, too, at a most critical period in the struggle of the proletariat. . . .

What? Are we to put difference of party tactics before the desperate needs of the workers? . . . While countless women and children are breaking their hearts and ruining their bodies in long days of toil, we are fighting one another. Shame upon us!

Only 3 percent of the Socialist party's members were women in 1904. At the national convention that year, there were only eight women delegates. But in a few years, local socialist women's organizations, and a national magazine, *Socialist Woman,* began bringing more women into the party, so that by 1913, 15 percent of the membership was women. The editor of *Socialist Woman,* Josephine Conger-Kaneko, insisted on the importance of separate groups for women:

In the separate organization the most unsophisticated little woman may soon learn to preside over a meeting, to make motions, and to defend her stand with a little "speech". After a year or two of this sort of practice she is ready to work with the men. And there is a mighty difference between working *with* the men, and simply sitting in obedient reverence under the shadow of their aggressive power.

Socialist women were active in the feminist movement of the early 1900s. According to Kate Richards O'Hare, the Socialist leader from Oklahoma, New York women socialists were superbly organized. During the 1915 campaign in New York for a referendum on women's suffrage, in one day at the climax of the campaign, they distributed 60,000 English leaflets, 50,000 Yiddish leaflets, sold 2,500 one-cent books and 1,500 five-cent books, put up 40,000 stickers, and held 100 meetings.

But were there problems of women that went beyond politics and economics, that would not be solved automatically by a socialist system? Once the economic base of sexual oppression was corrected, would equality follow? Battling for the vote, or for anything less than revolutionary change—was that pointless? The argument became sharper as the women's movement of the early twentieth century grew, as women spoke out more, organized, protested, paraded—for the vote, and for recognition as equals in every sphere, including sexual relations and marriage.

Charlotte Perkins Gilman, whose writing emphasized the crucial question of economic equality between the sexes, wrote a poem called "The Socialist and the Suffragist," ending with:

> "A lifted world lifts women up,"
> The Socialist explained.
> "You cannot lift the world at all
> While half of it is kept so small,"
> the Suffragist maintained.

The world awoke, and tartly spoke:
"Your work is all the same;
Work together or work apart,
Work, each of you, with all your heart—
Just get into the game!"

When Susan Anthony, at eighty, went to hear Eugene Debs speak (twenty-five years before, he had gone to hear her speak, and they had not met since then), they clasped hands warmly, then had a brief exchange. She said, laughing: "Give us suffrage, and we'll give you socialism." Debs replied: "Give us socialism and we'll give you suffrage."

There were women who insisted on uniting the two aims of socialism and feminism, like Crystal Eastman, who imagined new ways of men and women living together and retaining their independence, different from traditional marriage. She was a socialist, but wrote once that a woman "knows that the whole of woman's slavery is not summed up in the profit system, nor her complete emancipation assured by the downfall of capitalism."

In the first fifteen years of the twentieth century, there were more women in the labor force, more with experience in labor struggles. Some middle-class women, conscious of women's oppression and wanting to do something, were going to college and becoming aware of themselves as not just housewives. The historian William Chafe writes (*Women and Equality*):

Female college students were infused with a self-conscious sense of mission and a passionate commitment to improve the world. They became doctors, college professors, settlement house workers, business women, lawyers, and architects. Spirited by an intense sense of purpose as well as camaraderie, they set a remarkable record of accomplishment in the face of overwhelming odds. Jane Addams, Grace and Edith Abbott, Alice Hamilton, Julia Lathrop, Florence Kelley—all came out of this pioneering generation and set the agenda of social reform for the first two decades of the 20th century.

They were defying the culture of mass magazines, which were spreading the message of woman as companion, wife, homemaker. Some of these feminists married; some did not. All struggled with the problem of relations with men, like Margaret Sanger, pioneer of birth control education, who suffered a nervous breakdown inside an apparently happy but confining marriage; she had to leave husband and children to make a career for herself and feel whole again. Sanger had written in *Woman and the New Race:* "No woman can call herself free who does not own and control her own body. No woman can call herself free until she can choose conscientiously whether she will or will not be a mother."

It was a complicated problem. Kate Richards O'Hare, for example, believed in the home, but thought socialism would make that better. When she ran for Congress in 1910 in Kansas City she said: "I long for domestic life, home and children with every fiber of my being. . . . Socialism is needed to restore the home."

On the other hand, Elizabeth Gurley Flynn wrote in her autobiography, *Rebel Girl:*

A domestic life and possibly a large family had no attraction for me. . . . I wanted to speak and write, to travel, to meet people, to see places, to organize for the I.W.W. I saw no reason why I, as a woman, should give up my work for this. . . .

While many women in this time were radicals, socialists, anarchists, an even larger number were involved in the campaign for suffrage, and the mass support for feminism came from them. Veterans of trade union struggles joined the suffrage movement, like Rose Schneiderman of the Garment Workers. At a Cooper Union meeting in New York, she replied to a politician who said that women, given the vote, would lose their femininity:

Women in the laundries . . . stand for thirteen or fourteen hours in the terrible steam and heat with their hands in hot starch. Surely these women won't lose any more of their beauty and charm by putting a ballot in a ballot box once a year than they are likely to lose standing in foundries or laundries all year round.

Every spring in New York, the parades for women's suffrage kept growing. In 1912, a news report:

All along Fifth Avenue from Washington Square, where the parade formed, to 57th Street, where it disbanded, were gathered thousands of men and women of New York. They blocked every cross street on the line of march. Many were inclined to laugh and jeer, but none did. The sight of the impressive column of women striding five abreast up the middle of the street stifled all thought of ridicule. . . . women doctors, women lawyers . . . women architects, women artists, actresses and sculptors; women waitresses, domestics; a huge division of industrial workers . . . all marched with an intensity and purpose that astonished the crowds that lined the streets.

From Washington, in the spring of 1913, came a *New York Times* report:

In a woman's suffrage demonstration to-day the capital saw the greatest parade of women in its history. . . . In the parade over 5000 women passed down Pennsylvania Avenue. . . . It was an astonishing demonstration. It was estimated . . . that 500,000 persons watched the women march for their cause.

Some women radicals were skeptical. Emma Goldman, the anarchist and feminist, spoke her mind forcefully, as always, on the subject of women's suffrage:

Our modern fetish is universal suffrage. . . . The women of Australia and New Zealand can vote, and help make the laws. Are the labor conditions better there . . . ?

The history of the political activities of man proves that they have given him absolutely nothing that he could not have achieved in a more direct, less costly, and more lasting manner. As a matter of fact, every inch of ground he has gained has been through a constant fight, a ceaseless struggle for self-assertion, and not through suffrage. There is no reason whatever to assume that woman, in her climb to emancipation, has been, or will be, helped by the ballot. . . .

Her development, her freedom, her independence, must come from and through herself. First, by asserting herself as a personality. Second, by refusing the right to anyone over her body; by refusing to bear children, unless she wants them; by refusing to be a servant to God, the State, society, the husband, the family, etc. by making her life simpler, but deeper and richer. . . . Only that, and not the ballot, will set woman free. . . .

And Helen Keller, writing in 1911 to a suffragist in England:

Our democracy is but a name. We vote? What does that mean? It means that we choose between two bodies of real, though not avowed, autocrats, We choose between Tweedledum and Tweedledee. . . .

You ask for votes for women. What good can votes do when ten-elevenths of the land of Great Britain belongs to 200,000 and only one-eleventh to the rest of the 40,000,000? Have your men with their millions of votes freed themselves from this injustice?

Emma Goldman was not postponing the changing of woman's condition to some future socialist era—she wanted action more direct, more immediate, than the vote. Helen Keller, while not an anarchist, also believed in continuous struggle outside the ballot box. Blind, deaf, she fought with her spirit, her pen. When she became active and openly socialist, the Brooklyn *Eagle,* which had previously treated her as a heroine, wrote that "her mistakes spring out of the manifest limitations of her development." Her response was not accepted by the *Eagle,* but printed in the New York *Call.* She wrote that when once she met the editor of the Brooklyn *Eagle* he complimented her lavishly. "But now that I have come out for socialism he reminds me and the public that I am blind and deaf and especially liable to error. . . ." She added:

> Oh, ridiculous Brooklyn *Eagle!* What an ungallant bird it is! Socially blind and deaf, it defends an intolerable system, a system that is the cause of much of the physical blindness and deafness which we are trying to prevent. . . . The *Eagle* and I are at war. I hate the system which it represents. . . . When it fights back, let it fight fair. . . . It is not fair fighting or good argument to remind me and others that I cannot see or hear. I can read. I can read all the socialist books I have time for in English, German and French. If the editor of the Brooklyn *Eagle* should read some of them, he might be a wiser man, and make a better newspaper. If I ever contribute to the Socialist movement the book that I sometimes dream of, I know what I shall name it: Industrial Blindness and Social Deafness.

Mother Jones did not seem especially interested in the feminist movement. She was busy organizing textile workers and miners, and organizing their wives and children. One of her many feats was the organization of a children's march to Washington to demand the end of child labor (as the twentieth century opened, 284,000 children between the ages of ten and fifteen worked in mines, mills, factories). She described this:

> In the spring of 1903, I went to Kensington, Pennsylvania, where seventy-five thousand textile workers were on strike. Of this number at least ten thousand were little children. The workers were striking for more pay and shorter hours. Every day little children came into Union Headquarters, some with their hands off, some with the thumb missing, some with their fingers off at the knuckle. They were stooped little things, round shouldered and skinny. . . .
>
> I asked some of the parents if they would let me have their little boys and girls for a week or ten days, promising to bring them back safe and sound. . . . A man named Sweeny was marshall. . . . A few men and women went with me. . . . The children carried knapsacks on their backs in which was a knife and fork, a tin cup and plate. . . . One little fellow had a drum and another had a fife. . . . We carried banners that said: . . . "We want time to play. . . .

The children marched through New Jersey and New York and down to Oyster Bay to try to see President Theodore Roosevelt, but he refused to see them. "But our march had done its work. We had drawn the attention of the nation to the crime of child labor."

That same year, children working sixty hours a week in textile mills in Philadelphia went on strike, carrying signs: "WE WANT TO GO TO SCHOOL!" "55 HOURS OR NOTHING!"

One gets a sense of the energy and fire of some of those turn-of-the-century radicals by looking at the police record of Elizabeth Gurley Flynn:

> 1906–16, Organizer, lecturer for I.W.W.
> 1918–24, Organizer, Workers Defense Union
> Arrested in New York, 1906, free-speech case, dismissed; active in Spokane, Washington, free-speech fight, 1909; arrested, Missoula, Montana, 1909, in free-speech fight of I.W.W., Spokane, Washington, free-speech fight of I.W.W., hundreds arrested; in Philadelphia arrested three times, 1911, at strike meetings of Baldwin Locomotive Works; active in Lawrence textile strike, 1912; hotel-workers strike, 1912, New York; Paterson textile strike, 1913; defense work for Ettor-Giovanitti case, 1912; Mesaba Range strike, Minnesota, 1916; Everett IWW case, Spokane, Washington, 1916; Joe Hill defense, 1914. Arrested Duluth, Minnesota, 1917, charged with vagrancy under law passed to stop I.W.W. and pacifist speakers, case dismissed. Indicted in Chicago IWW case, 1917. . . .

Black women faced double oppression. A Negro nurse wrote to a newspaper in 1912:

> We poor colored women wage-earners in the South are fighting a terrible battle. . . . On the one hand, we are assailed by black men, who should be our natural protectors; and, whether in the cook kitchen, at the washtub, over the sewing machine, behind the baby carriage, or at the ironing board, we are but little more than pack horses, beasts of burden, slaves! . . .

In this early part of the twentieth century, labeled by generations of white scholars as "the Progressive period," lynchings were reported every week; it was the low point for Negroes, North and South, "the nadir," as Rayford Logan, a black historian, put it. In 1910 there were 10 million Negroes in the United States, and 9 million of them were in the South.

The government of the United States (between 1901 and 1921, the Presidents were Theodore Roosevelt, William Howard Taft, Woodrow Wilson)—whether Republican or Democrat—watched Negroes being lynched, observed murderous riots against blacks in Statesboro, Georgia, Brownsville, Texas, and Atlanta, Georgia, and did nothing.

There were Negroes in the Socialist party, but the Socialist party did not go much out of its way to act on the race question. As Ray Ginger writes of Debs: "When race prejudice was thrust at Debs, he always publicly repudiated it. He always insisted on absolute equality. But he failed to accept the view that special measures were sometimes needed to achieve this equality."

Blacks began to organize: a National Afro-American Council formed in 1903 to protest against lynching, peonage, discrimination, disfranchisement; the National Association of Colored Women, formed around the same time, condemned segregation and lynchings. In Georgia in 1906 there was an Equal Rights Convention, which pointed to 260 Georgia Negroes lynched since 1885. It asked the right to vote, the right to enter the militia, to be on juries. It agreed blacks should work hard. "And at the same time we must agitate, complain, protest and keep protesting against the invasion of our manhood rights. . . ."

W. E. B. Du Bois, teaching in Atlanta, Georgia, in 1905, sent out a letter to Negro leaders throughout the country, calling them to a conference just across the Canadian border from Buffalo, near Niagara Falls. It was the start of the "Niagara Movement."

Du Bois, born in Massachusetts, the first black to receive a Ph.D. degree from Harvard University (1895), had just written and published his poetic, powerful book *The Souls of Black Folk.* Du Bois was a Socialist sympathizer, although only briefly a party member.

One of his associates in calling the Niagara meeting was William Monroe Trotter, a young black man in Boston, of militant views, who edited a weekly newspaper, the *Guardian.* In it he attacked the moderate ideas of Booker T. Washington. When, in the summer of 1903, Washington spoke to an audience of two thousand at a Boston church, Trotter and his supporters prepared nine provocative questions, which caused a commotion and led to fistfights. Trotter and a friend were arrested. This may have added to the spirit of indignation which led Du Bois to spearhead the Niagara meeting. The tone of the Niagara group was strong:

We refuse to allow the impression to remain that the Negro-American assents to inferiority, is submissive under oppression and apologetic before insults. Through helplessness we may submit, but the voice of protest of ten million Americans must never cease to assail the ears of their fellows so long as America is unjust.

A race riot in Springfield, Illinois, prompted the formation of the National Association for the Advancement of Colored People in 1910. Whites dominated the leadership of the new organization; Du Bois was the only black officer. He was also the first editor of the NAACP periodical *The Crisis.* The NAACP concentrated on legal action and education, but Du Bois represented in it that spirit which was embodied in the Niagara movement's declaration: "Persistent manly agitation is the way to liberty."

What was clear in this period to blacks, to feminists, to labor organizers and socialists, was that they could not count on the national government. True, this was the "Progressive Period," the start of the Age of Reform; but it was a reluctant reform, aimed at quieting the popular risings, not making fundamental changes.

What gave it the name "Progressive" was that new laws were passed. Under Theodore Roosevelt, there was the Meat Inspection Act, the Hepburn Act to regulate railroads and pipelines, a Pure Food and Drug Act. Under Taft, the Mann-Elkins Act put telephone and telegraph systems under the regulation of the Interstate Commerce Commission. In Woodrow Wilson's presidency, the Federal Trade Commission was introduced to control the growth of monopolies, and the Federal Reserve Act to regulate the country's money and banking system. Under Taft were proposed the Sixteenth Amendment to the Constitution, allowing a graduated income tax, and the Seventeenth Amendment, providing for the election of Senators directly by popular vote instead of by the state legislatures, as the original Constitution provided. Also at this time, a number of states passed laws regulating wages and hours, providing for safety inspection of factories and compensation for injured workmen.

It was a time of public investigations aimed at soothing protest. In 1913 the Pujo Committee of Congress studied the concentration of power in the banking industry, and the Commission on Industrial Relations of the Senate held hearings on labor-management conflict.

Undoubtedly, ordinary people benefited to some extent from these changes. The system was rich, productive, complex; it could give enough of a share of its riches to enough of the working class to create a protective shield between the bottom and the top of the society. A study of immigrants in New York between 1905 and 1915 finds that 32 percent of Italians and Jews rose out of the manual class to higher levels (although not to *much* higher levels). But it was also true that many Italian immigrants did not find the opportunities inviting enough for them to stay. In one four-year period, seventy-three Italians left New York for every one hundred that arrived. Still, enough Italians became construction workers, enough Jews became businessmen and professionals, to create a middle-class cushion for class conflict.

Fundamental conditions did not change, however, for the vast majority of tenant farmers, factory workers, slum dwellers, miners, farm laborers, working men and women, black and white. Robert Wiebe sees in the Progressive movement an attempt by the system to adjust to changing conditions in order to achieve more stability. "Through rules with impersonal sanctions, it sought continuity and predictability in a world of endless change. It assigned far greater power to government . . . . and it encouraged the centralization of authority." Harold Faulkner concluded that this new emphasis on strong government was for the benefit of "the most powerful economic groups."

Gabriel Kolko calls it the emergence of "political capitalism," where the businessmen took firmer control of the political system because the private economy was not efficient enough to forestall protest from below. The businessmen, Kolko says, were not opposed to the new reforms; they initiated them, pushed them, to stabilize the capitalist system in a time of uncertainty and trouble.

For instance, Theodore Roosevelt made a reputation for himself as a "trust-buster" (although his successor, Taft, a "conservative," while Roosevelt was a "Progressive," launched more antitrust suits that did Roosevelt). In fact, as Wiebe points out, two of J. P. Morgan's men—Elbert Gary, chairman of U.S. Steel, and George Perkins, who would later become a campaigner for Roosevelt—"arranged a general understanding with Roosevelt by which . . . they would cooperate in any investigation by the Bureau of Corporations in return for a guarantee of their companies' legality." They would do this through private negotiations with the President. "A gentleman's agreement between reasonable people" Wiebe says, with a bit of sarcasm.

The panic of 1907, as well as the growing strength of the Socialists, Wobblies, and trade unions, speeded the process of reform. According to Wiebe: "Around 1908 a qualitative shift in outlook occurred among large numbers of these men of authority. . . ." The emphasis was now on "enticements and compromises." It continued with Wilson, and "a great many reform-minded citizens indulged the illusion of a progressive fulfillment."

What radical critics now say of those reforms was said at the time (1901) by the *Bankers' Magazine:* "As the business of the country has learned the secret of combination, it is gradually subverting the power of the politician and rendering him subservient to its purposes. . . ."

There was much to stabilize, much to protect. By 1904, 318 trusts, with capital of more than seven billion dollars, controlled 40% of the U.S. manufacturing.

In 1909, a manifesto of the new Progressivism appeared—a book called *The Promise of American Life* by Herbert Croly, editor of the *New Republic* and an admirer of Theodore Roosevelt. He saw the need for discipline and regulation if the American system were to continue. Government should do more, he said, and he hoped to see the "sincere and enthusiastic imitation of heroes and saints"—by whom he may have meant Theodore Roosevelt.

Richard Hofstadter, in his biting chapter on the man the public saw as the great lover of nature and physical fitness, the war hero, the Boy Scout in the White House, says: "The advisers to whom Roosevelt listened were almost exclusively representatives of industrial and finance capital—men like Hanna, Robert Bacon, and George W. Perkins of the House of Morgan, Elihu Root, Senator Nelson W. Aldrich . . . and James Stillman of the Rockefeller interests." Responding to his worried brother-in-law writing from Wall Street, Roosevelt replied: "I intend to be most conservative, but in the interests of the corporations themselves and above all in the interests of the country."

Roosevelt supported the regulatory Hepburn Act because he feared something worse. He wrote to Henry Cabot Lodge that the railroad lobbyists who opposed the bill were wrong: "I think they are very short-sighted not to understand that to beat it means to increase the movement for government ownership of the railroads." His action against the trusts was to induce them to accept government regulation, in order to prevent destruction. He prosecuted the Morgan railroad monopoly in the Northern Securities Case, considering it an antitrust victory, but it hardly changed anything, and, although the Sherman Act provided for criminal penalties, there was no prosecution of the men who had planned the monopoly—Morgan, Harriman, Hill.

As for Woodrow Wilson, Hofstadter points out he was a conservative from the start. As a historian and political scientist, Wilson wrote *(The State):* "In politics nothing radically novel may safely be attempted." He urged "slow and gradual" change. His attitude toward labor, Hofstadter says, was "generally hostile," and he spoke of the "crude and ignorant minds" of the Populists.

James Weinstein *(The Corporate Ideal in the Liberal State)* has studied the reforms of the Progressive period, especially the process by which business and government, sometimes with the aid of labor leaders, worked out the legislative changes they thought necessary.

Weinstein sees "a conscious and successful effort to guide and control the economic and social policies of federal, state, and municipal governments by various business groupings in their own long-range interest. . . ." While the "original impetus" for reform came from protesters and radicals, "in the current century, particularly on the federal level, few reforms were enacted without the tacit approval, if not the guidance, of the large corporate interests." These interests assembled liberal reformers and intellectuals to aid them in such matters.

Weinstein's definition of liberalism—as a means of stabilizing the system in the interests of big business—is different from that of the liberals themselves. Arthur Schlesinger writes: "Liberalism in America has been ordinarily the movement on the part of the other sections of society to restrain the power of the business community." If Schlesinger is describing the hope or intent of these other sections, he may be right. If he is describing the actual effect of these liberal reforms, that restraint has not happened.

The controls were constucted skillfully. In 1900, a man named Ralph Easley, a Republican and conservative, a schoolteacher and journalist, organized the National Civic Federation. Its aim was to get better relations between capital and labor. Its officers were mostly big businessmen, and important national politicians, but its first vice-president, for a long time, was Samuel Gompers of the AFL. Not all big businesses liked what the National Civic Federation was doing. Easley called these critics anarchists, opposed to the rational organization of the system. "In fact," Easley wrote, "our enemies are the Socialists among the labor people and the anarchists among the capitalists."

The NCF wanted a more sophisticated approach to trade unions, seeing them as an inevitable reality, therefore wanting to come to agreements with them rather than fight with them: better to deal with a conservative union than face a militant one. After the Lawrence textile strike of 1912, John Golden, head of the conservative AFL Textile Union Workers, wrote Easley that the strike had given manufacturers "a very rapid education" and "some of them are falling all over themselves now to do business with our organization."

The National Civic Federation did not represent all opinions in the business world; the National Association of Manufacturers didn't want to recognize organized labor in any way. Many businessmen did not want even the puny reforms proposed by the Civic Federation— but the Federation's approach represented the sophistication and authority of the modern state, determined to do what was best for the capitalist class as a whole, even if this irritated some capitalists. The new approach was concerned with the long-range stability of the system, even at the cost, sometimes, of short-term profits.

Thus, the Federation drew up a model workmen's compensation bill in 1910, and the following year twelve states passed laws for compensation or accident insurance. When the Supreme Court said that year that New York's workmen's compensation law was unconstitutional because it deprived corporations of property without due process of law, Theodore Roosevelt was angry. Such decisions, he said, added "immensely to the strength of the Socialist Party." By 1920, forty-two states had workmen's compensation laws. As Weinstein says: "It represented a growing maturity and sophistication on the part of many large corporation leaders who had come to understand, as Theodore Roosevelt often told them, that social reform was truly conservative."

As for the Federal Trade Commission, established by Congress in 1914 presumably to regulate trusts, a leader of the Civic Federation reported after several years of experience with it that it "has apparently been carrying on its work with the purpose of securing the confidence of well-intentioned business men, members of the great corporations as well as others."

In this period, cities also put through reforms, many of them giving power to city councils instead of mayors, or hiring city managers. The idea was more efficiency, more stability. "The end result of the movements was to place city government firmly in the hands of the business class," Weinstein says. What reformers saw as more democracy in city government, urban historian Samuel Hays sees as the centralization of power in fewer hands, giving business and professional men more direct control over city government.

The Progressive movement, whether led by honest reformers like Senator Robert La Follette of Wisconsin or disguised conservatives like Roosevelt (who was the Progressive party candidate for President in 1912), seemed to understand it was fending off socialism. The Milwaukee *Journal,* a Progressive organ, said the conservatives "fight socialism blindly . . . while the Progressives fight it intelligently and seek to remedy the abuses and conditions upon which it thrives."

Frank Munsey, a director of U.S. Steel, writing to Roosevelt, seeing him as the best candidate for 1912, confided in him that the United States must move toward a more "parental guardianship of the people" who needed "the sustaining and guiding hand of the State." It was "the work of the state to think for the people and plan for the people," the steel executive said.

It seems quite clear that much of this intense activity for Progressive reform was intended to head off socialism. Easley talked of "the menace of Socialism as evidenced by its growth in the colleges, churches, newspapers." In 1910, Victor Berger became the first member of the Socialist party elected to Congress; in 1911, seventy-three Socialist mayors were elected, and twelve hundred lesser officials in 340 cities and towns. The press spoke of "The Rising Tide of Socialism."

A privately circulated memorandum suggested to one of the departments of the National Civic Federation: "In view of the rapid spread in the United States of socialistic doctrines," what was needed was "a carefully planned and wisely directed effort to instruct public opinion as to the real meaning of socialism." The memorandum suggested that the campaign "must be very skillfully and tactfully carried out," that it "should not violently attack socialism and anarchism as such" but should be "patient and persuasive" and defend three ideas: "individual liberty; private property; and inviolability of contract."

It is hard to say how many Socialists saw clearly how useful reform was to capitalism, but in 1912, a left-wing Socialist from Connecticut, Robert LaMonte, wrote: "Old age pensions and insurance against sickness, accident and unemployment are cheaper, are better business than jails, poor houses, asylums, hospitals." He suggested that progressives would work for reforms, but Socialists must make only "impossible demands," which would reveal the limitations of the reformers.

Did the Progressive reforms succeed in doing what they intended— stabilize the capitalist system by repairing its worst defects, blunt the edge of the Socialist movement, restore some measure of class peace in a time of increasingly bitter clashes between capital and labor? To some extent, perhaps. But the Socialist party continued to grow. The IWW continued to agitate. And shortly after Woodrow Wilson took office there began in Colorado one of the most bitter and violent struggles between workers and corporate capital in the history of the country.

This was the Colorado coal strike that began in September 1913 and culminated in the "Ludlow Massacre" of April 1914. Eleven thousand miners in southern Colorado, mostly foreign-born—Greeks, Italians, Serbs—worked for the Colorado Fuel & Iron Corporation, which was owned by the Rockefeller family. Aroused by the murder of one of their organizers, they went on strike against low pay, dangerous conditions, and feudal domination of their lives in towns completely controlled by the mining companies. Mother Jones, at this time an organizer for the United Mine Workers, came into the area, fired up the miners with her oratory, and helped them in those critical first months of the strike, until she was arrested, kept in a dungeonlike cell, and then forcibly expelled from the state.

When the strike began, the miners were immediately evicted from their shacks in the mining towns. Aided by the United Mine Workers Union, they set up tents in the nearby hills and carried on the strike, the picketing, from these tent colonies. The gunmen hired by the Rockefeller interests—the Baldwin-Felts Detective Agency—using Gatling guns and rifles, raided the tent colonies. The death list of miners grew, but they hung on, drove back an armored train in a gun battle, fought to keep out strikebreakers. With the miners resisting, refusing to give in, the mines not able to operate, the Colorado governor (referred to by a Rockefeller mine manager as "our little cowboy governor") called out the National Guard, with the Rockefellers supplying the Guard's wages.

The miners at first thought the Guard was sent to protect them, and greeted its arrivals with flags and cheers. They soon found out the Guard was there to destroy the strike. The Guard brought strikebreakers in under cover of night, not telling them there was a strike. Guardsmen beat miners, arrested them by the hundreds, rode down with their horses parades of women in the streets of Trinidad, the central town in the area. And still the miners refused to give in. When they lasted through the cold winter of 1913–1914, it became clear that extraordinary measures would be needed to break the strike.

In April 1914, two National Guard companies were stationed in the hills overlooking the largest tent colony of strikers, the one at Ludlow, housing a thousand men, women, children. On the morning of April 20, a machine gun attack began on the tents. The miners fired back. Their leader, a Greek named Lou Tikas, was lured up into the hills to discuss a truce, then shot to death by a company of National Guardsmen. The women and children dug pits beneath the tents to escape the gunfire. At dusk, the Guard moved down from the hills with torches, set fire to the tents, and the families fled into the hills; thirteen people were killed by gunfire.

The following day, a telephone linesman going through the ruins of the Ludlow tent colony lifted an iron cot covering a pit in one of the tents and found the charred, twisted bodies of eleven children and two women. This became known as the Ludlow Massacre.

The news spread quickly over the country. In Denver, the United Mine Workers issued a "Call to Arms"—"Gather together for defensive purposes all arms and ammunition legally available." Three hundred armed strikers marched from other tent colonies into the Ludlow area, cut telephone and telegraph wires, and prepared for battle. Railroad workers refused to take soldiers from Trinidad to Ludlow. At Colorado Springs, three hundred union miners walked off their jobs and headed for the Trinidad district, carrying revolvers, rifles, shotguns.

In Trinidad itself, miners attended a funeral service for the twenty-six dead at Ludlow, then walked from the funeral to a nearby building, where arms were stacked for them. They picked up rifles and moved into the hills, destroying mines, killing mine guards, exploding mine shafts. The press reported that "the hills in every direction seem suddenly to be alive with men."

In Denver, eighty-two soldiers in a company on a troop train headed for Trinidad refused to go. The press reported: "The men declared they would not engage in the shooting of women and children. They hissed the 350 men who did start and shouted imprecations at them."

Five thousand people demonstrated in the rain on the lawn in front of the state capital at Denver asking that the National Guard officers at Ludlow be tried for murder, denouncing the governor as an accessory. The Denver Cigar Makers Union voted to send five hundred armed men to Ludlow and Trinidad. Women in the United Garment Workers Union in Denver announced four hundred of their members had volunteered as nurses to help the strikers.

All over the country there were meetings, demonstrations. Pickets marched in front of the Rockefeller office at 26 Broadway, New York City. A minister protested in front of the church where Rockefeller sometimes gave sermons, and was clubbed by the police.

The *New York Times* carried an editorial on the events in Colorado, which were now attracting international attention. The *Times* emphasis was not on the atrocity that had occurred, but on the mistake in tactics that had been made. Its editorial on the Ludlow Massacre began: "Somebody blundered. . . ." Two days later, with the miners armed and in the hills of the mine district, the *Times* wrote: "With the deadliest weapons of civilization in the hands of savage-minded men, there can be no telling to what lengths the war in Colorado will go unless it is quelled by force. . . . The President should turn his attention from Mexico long enough to take stern measures in Colorado."

The governor of Colorado asked for federal troops to restore order, and Woodrow Wilson complied. This accomplished, the strike petered out. Congressional committees came in and took thousands of pages of testimony. The union had not won recognition. Sixty-six men, women, and children had been killed. Not one militiaman or mine guard had been indicted for crime.

Still, Colorado had been a scene of ferocious class conflict, whose emotional repercussions had rolled through the entire country. The threat of class rebellion was clearly still there in the industrial conditions of the United States, in the undeterred spirit of rebellion among working people—whatever legislation had been passed, whatever liberal reforms were on the books, whatever investigations were undertaken and words of regret and conciliation uttered.

The *Times* had referred to Mexico. On the morning that the bodies were discovered in the tent pit at Ludlow, American warships were attacking Vera Cruz, a city on the coast of Mexico—bombarding it, occupying it, leaving a hundred Mexicans dead—because Mexico had arrested American sailors and refused to apologize to the United States with a twenty-one-gun salute. Could patriotic fervor and the military spirit cover up class struggle? Unemployment, hard times, were growing in 1914. Could guns divert attention and create some national consensus against an external enemy? It surely was a coincidence—the bombardment of Vera Cruz, the attack on the Ludlow colony. Or perhaps it was, as someone once described human history, "the natural selection of accidents." Perhaps the affair in Mexico was an instinctual response of the system for its own survival, to create a unity of fighting purpose among a people torn by internal conflict.

The bombardment of Vera Cruz was a small incident. But in four months the First World War would begin in Europe.

3.
War Is the Health of the State

"War is the health of the state," the radical writer Randolph Bourne said, in the midst of the First World War. Indeed, as the nations of Europe went to war in 1914, the governments flourished, patriotism bloomed, class struggle was stilled, and young men died in frightful numbers on the battlefields—often for a hundred yards of land, a line of trenches.

In the United States, not yet in the war, there was worry about the health of the state. Socialism was growing. The IWW seemed to be everywhere. Class conflict was intense. In the summer of 1916, during a Preparedness Day parade in San Francisco, a bomb exploded, killing nine people; two local radicals, Tom Mooney and Warren Billings, were arrested and would spend twenty years in prison. Shortly after that Senator James Wadsworth of New York suggested compulsory military training for all males to avert the danger that "these people of ours shall be divided into classes." Rather: "We must let our young men know that they owe some responsibility to this country."

The supreme fulfillment of that responsibility was taking place in Europe. Ten million were to die on the battlefield; 20 million were to die of hunger and disease related to the war. And no one since that day has been able to show that the war brought any gain for humanity that would be worth one human life. The rhetoric of the socialists, that it was an "imperialist war," now seems moderate and hardly arguable. The advanced capitalist countries of Europe were fighting over boundaries, colonies, spheres of influence; they were competing for Alsace-Lorraine, the Balkans, Africa, the Middle East.

The war came shortly after the opening of the twentieth century, in the midst of exultation (perhaps only among the elite in the Western world) about progress and modernization. One day after the English declared war, Henry James wrote to a friend: "The plunge of civilization into this abyss of blood and darkness . . . is a thing that so gives away the whole long age during which we have supposed the world to be . . . gradually bettering." In the first Battle of the Marne,

the British and French succeeded in blocking the German advance
on Paris. Each side had 500,000 casualties.

The killing started very fast, and on a large scale. In August 1914,
a volunteer for the British army had to be 5 feet 8 inches to enlist.
By October, the requirement was lowered to 5 feet 5 inches. That month
there were thirty thousand casualties, and then one could be 5 feet 3.
In the first three months of war, almost the entire original British army
was wiped out.

For three years the battle lines remained virtually stationary in
France. Each side would push forward, then back, then forward again—
for a few yards, a few miles, while the corpses piled up. In 1916 the
Germans tried to break through at Verdun; the British and French
counterattacked along the Seine, moved forward a few miles, and lost
600,000 men. One day, the 9th Battalion of the King's Own Yorkshire
Light Infantry launched an attack with eight hundred men. Twenty-
four hours later, there were eighty-four left.

Back home, the British were not told of the slaughter. One English
writer recalled: "The most bloody defeat in the history of Britain . . .
might occur . . . and our Press come out bland and copious and graphic
with nothing to show that we had not had quite a good day—a victory
really. . . ." The same thing was happening on the German side; as
Erich Maria Remarque wrote in his great novel, on days when men
by the thousands were being blown apart by machine guns and shells,
the official dispatches announced "All Quiet on the Western Front."

In July 1916, British General Douglas Haig ordered eleven divisions
of English soldiers to climb out of their trenches and move toward
the German lines. The six German divisions opened up with their machine guns. Of the 110,000 who attacked, 20,000 were killed, 40,000
more wounded—all those bodies strewn on no man's land, the ghostly
territory between the contending trenches. On January 1, 1917, Haig
was promoted to field marshal. What happened that summer is described
tersely in William Langer's *An Encyclopedia of World History:*

Despite the opposition of Lloyd George and the skepticism of some of
his subordinates, Haig proceeded hopefully to the main offensive. The third
battle of Ypres was a series of 8 heavy attacks, carried through in driving
rain and fought over ground water-logged and muddy. No break-through was
effected, and the total gain was about 5 miles of territory, which made the
Ypres salient more inconvenient than ever and cost the British about 400,000
men.

The people of France and Britain were not told the extent of the casualties. When, in the last year of the war, the Germans attacked ferociously on the Somme, and left 300,000 British soldiers dead or wounded, London newspapers printed the following, we learn from Paul Fussell's *The Great War and Modern Memory:*

WHAT CAN I DO?

How the Civilian May Help in this Crisis.
Be cheerful. . . .
Write encouragingly to friends at the front. . . .
Don't repeat foolish gossip.
Don't listen to idle rumors.
Don't think you know better than Haig.

Into this pit of death and deception came the United States, in the spring of 1917. Mutinies were beginning to occur in the French army. Soon, out of 112 divisions, 68 would have mutinies; 629 men would be tried and condemned, 50 shot by firing squads. American troops were badly needed.

President Woodrow Wilson had promised that the United States would stay neutral in the war: "There is such a thing as a nation being too proud to fight." But in April of 1917, the Germans had announced they would have their submarines sink any ship bringing supplies to their enemies; and they had sunk a number of merchant vessels. Wilson now said he must stand by the right of Americans to travel on merchant ships in the war zone. "I cannot consent to any abridgement of the rights of American citizens in any respect. . . ."

As Richard Hofstadter points out *(The American Political Tradition):* "This was rationalization of the flimsiest sort. . . ." The British had also been intruding on the rights of American citizens on the high seas, but Wilson was not suggesting we go to war with them. Hofstadter says Wilson "was forced to find legal reasons for policies that were based not upon law but upon the balance of power and economic necessities."

It was unrealistic to expect that the Germans should treat the United States as neutral in the war when the U.S. had been shipping great amounts of war materials to Germany's enemies. In early 1915, the British liner *Lusitania* was torpedoed and sunk by a German submarine. She sank in eighteen minutes, and 1,198 people died, including 124 Americans. The United States claimed the *Lusitania* carried an innocent cargo, and therefore the torpedoing was a monstrous German atrocity. Actually, the *Lusitania* was heavily armed: it carried 1,248 cases of 3-inch shells, 4,927 boxes of cartridges (1,000 rounds in each box), and 2,000 more cases of small-arms ammunition. Her manifests were falsified to hide this fact, and the British and American governments lied about the cargo.

Hofstadter wrote of "economic necessities" behind Wilson's war policy. In 1914 a serious recession had begun in the United States. J. P. Morgan later testified: "The war opened during a period of hard times. . . . Business throughout the country was depressed, farm prices were deflated, unemployment was serious, the heavy industries were working far below capacity and bank clearings were off." But by 1915, war orders for the Allies (mostly England) had stimulated the economy, and by April 1917 more than $2 billion worth of goods had been sold to the Allies. As Hofstadter says: "America became bound up with the Allies in a fateful union of war and prosperity."

Prosperity depended much on foreign markets, it was believed by the leaders of the country. In 1897, the private foreign investments of the United States amounted to $700 million dollars. By 1914 they were $3½ billion. Wilson's Secretary of State, William Jennings Bryan, while a believer in neutrality in the war, also believed that the United States needed overseas markets; in May of 1914 he praised the President as one who had "opened the doors of all the weaker countries to an invasion of American capital and American enterprise."

Back in 1907, Woodrow Wilson had said in a lecture at Columbia University: "Concessions obtained by financiers must be safeguarded by ministers of state, even if the sovereignty of unwilling nations be outraged in the process. . . . the doors of the nations which are closed must be battered down." In his 1912 campaign he said: "Our domestic markets no longer suffice, we need foreign markets." In a memo to Bryan he described his aim as "an open door to the world," and in 1914 he said he supported "the righteous conquest of foreign markets."

With World War I, England became more and more a market for American goods and for loans at interest. J. P. Morgan and Company acted as agents for the Allies, and when, in 1915, Wilson lifted the ban on private bank loans to the Allies, Morgan could now begin lending money in such great amounts as to both make great profit and tie American finance closely to the interest of a British victory in the war against Germany.

The industrialists and the political leaders talked of prosperity as if it were classless, as if everyone gained from Morgan's loans. True, the war meant more production, more employment, but did the workers in the steel plants gain as much as U.S. Steel, which made $348 million in profit in 1916 alone? When the United States entered the war, it was the rich who took even more direct charge of the economy. Financier Bernard Baruch headed the War Industries Board, the most powerful of the wartime government agencies. Bankers, railroad men, and industrialists dominated these agencies.

A remarkably perceptive article on the nature of the First World War appeared in May 1915 in the *Atlantic Monthly*. Written by W. E. B. Du Bois, it was titled "The African Roots of War." It was a war for empire, of which the struggle between Germany and the Allies over Africa was both symbol and reality: ". . . in a very real sense Africa is a prime cause of this terrible overturning of civilization which we have lived to see." Africa, Du Bois said, is "the Land of the Twentieth Century," because of the gold and diamonds of South Africa, the cocoa of Angola and Nigeria, the rubber and ivory of the Congo, the palm oil of the West Coast.

Du Bois saw more than that. He was writing several years before Lenin's *Imperialism,* which noted the new possibility of giving the working class of the imperial country a share of the loot. He pointed to the paradox of greater "democracy" in America alongside "increased aristocracy and hatred toward darker races." He explained the paradox by the fact that "the white workingman has been asked to share the spoil of exploiting 'chinks and niggers.' " Yes, the average citizen of England, France, Germany, the United States, had a higher standard of living than before. But: "Whence comes this new wealth? . . . It comes primarily from the darker nations of the world—Asia and Africa, South and Central America, the West Indies, and the islands of the South Seas."

Du Bois saw the ingenuity of capitalism in uniting exploiter and exploited—creating a safety valve for explosive class conflict. "It is no longer simply the merchant prince, or the aristocratic monopoly, or even the employing class, that is exploiting the world: it is the nation, a new democratic nation composed of united capital and labor."

The United States fitted that idea of Du Bois. American capitalism needed international rivalry—and periodic war—to create an artificial community of interest between rich and poor, supplanting the genuine community of interest among the poor that showed itself in sporadic movements. How conscious of this were individual entrepreneurs and statesmen? That is hard to know. But their actions, even if half-conscious, instinctive drives to survive, matched such a scheme. And in 1917 this demanded a national consensus for war.

The government quickly succeeded in creating such a consensus, according to the traditional histories. Woodrow Wilson's biographer Arthur Link wrote: "In the final analysis American policy was determined by the President and public opinion." In fact, there is no way of measuring public opinion at that time, and there is no persuasive evidence that the public wanted war. The government had to work hard to create its consensus. That there was no spontaneous urge to fight is suggested by the strong measures taken: a draft of young men, an elaborate propaganda campaign throughout the country, and harsh punishment for those who refused to get in line.

Despite the rousing words of Wilson about a war "to end all wars" and "to make the world safe for democracy," Americans did not rush to enlist. A million men were needed, but in the first six weeks after the declaration of war only 73,000 volunteered. Congress voted overwhelmingly for a draft.

George Creel, a veteran newspaperman, became the government's official propagandist for the war; he set up a Committee on Public Information to persuade Americans the war was right. It sponsored 75,000 speakers, who gave 750,000 four-minute speeches in five thousand American cities and towns. It was a massive effort to excite a reluctant public. At the beginning of 1917, a member of the National Civic Federation had complained that "neither workingmen nor farmers" were taking "any part or interest in the efforts of the security or defense leagues or other movements for national preparedness."

The day after Congress declared war, the Socialist party met in emergency convention in St. Louis and called the declaration "a crime against the people of the United States." In the summer of 1917, Socialist antiwar meetings in Minnesota drew large crowds—five thousand, ten thousand, twenty thousand farmers—protesting the war, the draft, profiteering. A local newspaper in Wisconsin, the Plymouth *Review,* said that probably no party ever gained more rapidly in strength than the Socialist party just at the present time." It reported that "thousands assemble to hear Socialist speakers in places where ordinarily a few hundred are considered large assemblages." The Akron *Beacon-Journal,* a conservative newspaper in Ohio, said there was "scarcely a political observer . . . but what will admit that were an election to come now a mighty tide of socialism would inundate the Middle West." It said the country had "never embarked upon a more unpopular war."

In the municipal elections of 1917, against the tide of propaganda and patriotism, the Socialists made remarkable gains. Their candidate for mayor of New York, Morris Hillquit, got 22 percent of the vote, five times the normal Socialist vote there. Ten Socialists were elected to the New York State legislature. In Chicago, the party vote went from 3.6 percent in 1915 to 34.7 percent in 1917. In Buffalo, it went from 2.6 percent to 30.2 percent.

George Creel and the government were behind the formation of an American Alliance for Labor and Democracy, whose president was Samuel Gompers and whose aim was to "unify sentiment in the nation" for the war. There were branches in 164 cities; many labor leaders went along. According to James Weinstein, however, the Alliance did not work: "Rank-and-file working class support for the war remained lukewarm. . . ." And although some prominent Socialists—Jack London, Upton Sinclair, Clarence Darrow—became prowar after the U.S. entered, most Socialists continued their opposition.

Congress passed, and Wilson signed, in June of 1917, the Espionage Act. From its title one would suppose it was an act against spying. However, it had a clause that provided penalties up to twenty years in prison for "Whoever, when the United States is at war, shall wilfully cause or attempt to cause insubordination, disloyalty, mutiny, or refusal of duty in the military or naval forces of the United States, or shall wilfully obstruct the recruiting or enlistment service of the U.S. . . ." Unless one had a theory about the nature of governments, it was not clear how the Espionage Act would be used. It even had a clause that said "nothing in this section shall be construed to limit or restrict . . . any discussion, comment, or criticism of the acts or policies of the Government. . . ." But its double-talk concealed a singleness of purpose. The Espionage Act was used to imprison Americans who spoke or wrote against the war.

Two months after the law passed, a Socialist named Charles Schenck was arrested in Philadelphia for printing and distributing fifteen thousand leaflets that denounced the draft law and the war. The leaflet recited the Thirteenth Amendment provision against "involuntary servitude" and said the Conscription Act violated this. Conscription, it said, was "a monstrous deed against humanity in the interests of the financiers of Wall Street." And: "Do not submit to intimidation."

Schenck was indicted, tried, found guilty, and sentenced to six months in jail for violating the Espionage Act. (It turned out to be one of the shortest sentences given in such cases.) Schenck appealed, arguing that the Act, by prosecuting speech and writing, violated the First Amendment: "Congress shall make no law . . . abridging the freedom of speech, or of the press. . . ."

The Supreme Court's decision was unanimous and was written by its most famous liberal, Oliver Wendell Holmes. He summarized the contents of the leaflet and said it was undoubtedly intended to "obstruct" the carrying out of the draft law. Was Schenck protected by the First Amendment? Holmes said:

The most stringent protection of free speech would not protect a man in falsely shouting fire in a theatre and causing a panic. . . . The question in every case is whether the words used are used in such circumstances and are of such a nature as to create a clear and present danger that they will bring about the substantive evils that Congress has a right to prevent.

Holmes's analogy was clever and attractive. Few people would think free speech should be conferred on someone shouting fire in a theater and causing a panic. But did that example fit criticism of the war? Zechariah Chafee, a Harvard law school professor, wrote later (Free Speech in the United States) that a more apt analogy for Schenck was someone getting up between the acts at a theater and declaring that there were not enough fire exits. To play further with the example: was not Schenck's act more like someone shouting, not falsely, but truly, to people about to buy tickets and enter a theater, that there was a fire raging inside?

Perhaps free speech could not be tolerated by any reasonable person if it constituted a "clear and present danger" to life and liberty; after all, free speech must compete with other vital rights. But was not the war itself a "clear and present danger," indeed, more clear and more present and more dangerous to life than any argument against it? Did citizens not have a right to object to war, a right to be a danger to dangerous policies?

(The Espionage Act, thus approved by the Supreme Court, has remained on the books all these years since World War I, and although it is supposed to apply only in wartime, it has been constantly in force since 1950, because the United States has legally been in a "state of emergency" since the Korean war. In 1963, the Kennedy administration pushed a bill [unsuccessfully] to apply the Espionage Act to statements uttered by Americans abroad; it was concerned, in the words of a cable from Secretary of State Rusk to Ambassador Lodge in Vietnam, about journalists in Vietnam writing "critical articles . . . on Diem and his government" that were "likely to impede the war effort.")

The case of Eugene Debs soon came before the Supreme Court. In June of 1918, Debs visited three Socialists who were in prison for opposing the draft, and then spoke, across the street from the jail, to an audience he kept enthralled for two hours. He was one of the country's great orators, and was interrupted again and again by laughter and applause. "Why, the other day, by a vote of five-to-four—a kind of craps game, come seven, come eleven—they declared the child labor law unconstitutional." He spoke of his comrades in jail. He dealt with the charges that Socialists were pro-German. "I hate, I loathe, I despise Junkers and Junkerdom. I have no earthly use for the Junkers of Germany, and not one particle more use for the Junkers in the United States." (Thunderous applause and cheers.)

They tell us that we live in a great free republic, that our institutions are democratic; that we are a free and self-governing people. That is too much, even for a joke. . . .

Wars throughout history have been waged for conquest and plunder. . . . And that is war in a nutshell. The master class has always declared the wars; the subject class has always fought the battles. . . .

Debs was arrested for violating the Espionage Act. There were draft-age youths in his audience, and his words would "obstruct the recruiting or enlistment service."

His words were intended to do much more than that:

Yes, in good time we are going to sweep into power in this nation and throughout the world. We are going to destroy all enslaving and degrading capitalist institutions and re-create them as free and humanizing institutions. The world is daily changing before our eyes. The sun of capitalism is setting; the sun of Socialism is rising. . . . In due time the hour will strike and this great cause triumphant . . . will proclaim the emancipation of the working class and the brotherhood of all mankind. (Thunderous and prolonged applause.)

Debs refused at his trial to take the stand in his defense, or to call a witness on his behalf. He denied nothing about what he said. But before the jury began its deliberations, he spoke to them:

I have been accused of obstructing the war. I admit it. Gentlemen, I abhor war. I would oppose war if I stood alone. . . . I have sympathy with the suffering, struggling people everywhere. It does not make any difference under what flag they were born, or where they live. . . .

The jury found him guilty of violating the Espionage Act. Debs addressed the judge before sentencing:

Your honor, years ago I recognized my kinship with all living beings, and I made up my mind that I was not one bit better than the meanest on earth. I said then, and I say now, that while there is a lower class, I am in it; while there is a criminal element, I am of it; while there is a soul in prison, I am not free.

The judge denounced those "who would strike the sword from the hand of this nation while she is engaged in defending herself against a foreign and brutal power." He sentenced Debs to ten years in prison.

Debs's appeal was not heard by the Supreme Court until 1919. The war was over. Oliver Wendell Holmes, for a unanimous court, affirmed Debs's guilt. Holmes discussed Debs's speech: "He then expressed opposition to Prussian militarism in a way that naturally might have been thought to be intended to include the mode of proceeding in the United States." Holmes said Debs made "the usual contrasts between capitalists and laboring men . . . with the implication running through it all that the working men are not concerned in the war." Thus, Holmes said, the "natural and intended effect" of Debs's speech would be to obstruct recruiting.

Debs was locked up in the West Virginia state penitentiary, and then in the Atlanta federal penitentiary, where he spent thirty-two months until, at the age of sixty-six, he was released by President Harding in 1921.

About nine hundred people went to prison under the Espionage Act. This substantial opposition was put out of sight, while the visible national mood was represented by military bands, flag waving, the mass buying of war bonds, the majority's acquiescence to the draft and the war. This acquiescence was achieved by shrewd public relations and by intimidation—an effort organized with all the power of the federal government and the money of big business behind it. The magnitude of that campaign to discourage opposition says something about the spontaneous feelings of the population toward the war.

The newspapers helped create an atmosphere of fear for possible opponents of the war. In April of 1917, the *New York Times* quoted Elihu Root (former Secretary of War, a corporation lawyer) as saying: "We must have no criticism now." A few months later it quoted him again that "there are men walking about the streets of this city tonight who ought to be taken out at sunrise tomorrow and shot for treason."

At the same time, Theodore Roosevelt was talking to the Harvard Club about Socialists, IWWs, and others who wanted peace as "a whole raft of sexless creatures."

In the summer of 1917, the American Defense Society was formed. The New York *Herald* reported: "More than one hundred men enrolled yesterday in the American Vigilante Patrol at the offices of the American Defense Society. . . . The Patrol was formed to put an end to seditious street oratory."

The Department of Justice sponsored an American Protective League, which by June of 1917 had units in six hundred cities and towns, a membership of nearly 100,000. The press reported that their members were "the leading men in their communities . . . bankers . . . railroad men . . . hotel men." One study of the League describes their methods:

The mails are supposed to be sacred. . . . But let us call the American Protective League sometimes almost clairvoyant as to letters done by suspects. . . . It is supposed that breaking and entering a man's home or office place without warrant is burglary. Granted. But the League has done that thousands of times and has never been detected!

The League claimed to have found 3 million cases of disloyalty. Even if these figures are exaggerated, the very size and scope of the League gives a clue to the amount of "disloyalty."

The states organized vigilante groups. The Minnesota Commission of Public Safety, set up by state law, closed saloons and moving picture theaters, took count of land owned by aliens, boosted Liberty bonds, tested people for loyalty. The Minneapolis *Journal* carried an appeal by the Commission "for all patriots to join in the suppression of anti-draft and seditious acts and sentiment."

The national press cooperated with the government. The *New York Times* in the summer of 1917 carried an editorial: "It is the duty of every good citizen to communicate to proper authorities any evidence of sedition that comes to his notice." And the *Literary Digest* asked its readers "to clip and send to us any editorial utterances they encounter which seem to them seditious or treasonable." Creel's Committee on Public Information advertised that people should "report the man who spreads pessimistic stories. Report him to the Department of Justice." In 1918, the Attorney General said: "It is safe to say that never in its history has this country been so thoroughly policed."

Why these huge efforts? On August 1, 1917, the New York *Herald* reported that in New York City ninety of the first hundred draftees claimed exemption. In Minnesota, headlines in the Minneapolis *Journal* of August 6 and 7 read: "DRAFT OPPOSITION FAST SPREADING IN STATE," and "CONSCRIPTS GIVE FALSE ADDRESSES." In Florida, two Negro farm hands went into the woods with a shotgun and mutilated themselves to avoid the draft: one blew off four fingers of his hand; the other shot off his arm below the elbow. Senator Thomas Hardwick of Georgia said "there was undoubtedly general and widespread opposition on the part of many thousands . . . to the enactment of the draft law. Numerous and largely attended mass meetings held in every part of the State protested against it. . . ." Ultimately, over 330,000 men were classified as draft evaders.

In Oklahoma, the Socialist party and the IWW had been active among tenant farmers and sharecroppers who formed a "Working Class Union." At a mass meeting of the Union, plans were made to destroy a railroad bridge and cut telegraph wires in order to block military enlistments. A march on Washington was planned for draft objectors throughout the country. (This was called the Green Corn Rebellion because they planned to eat green corn on their march.) Before the Union could carry out its plans, its members were rounded up and arrested, and soon 450 individuals accused of rebellion were in the state penitentiary. Leaders were given three to ten years in jail, others sixty days to two years.

On July 1, 1917, radicals organized a parade in Boston against the war, with banners:

Is this a Popular War, Why Conscription?
Who Stole Panama? Who Crushed Haiti?
We Demand Peace.

The New York *Call* said eight thousand people marched, including "4000 members of the Central Labor Union, 2000 members of the Lettish Socialist Organizations, 1500 Lithuanians, Jewish members of cloak trades, and other branches of the party." The parade was attacked by soldiers and sailors, on orders from their officers.

The Post Office Department began taking away the mailing privileges of newspapers and magazines that printed antiwar articles. *The Masses,* a socialist magazine of politics, literature, and art, was banned from the mails. It had carried an editorial by Max Eastman in the summer of 1917, saying, among other things: "For what specific purposes are you shipping our bodies, and the bodies of our sons, to Europe?

For my part, I do not recognize the right of a government to draft me to a war whose purposes I do not believe in."

In Los Angeles, a film was shown that dealt with the American Revolution and depicted British atrocities against the colonists. It was called *The Spirit of '76*. The man who made the film was prosecuted under the Espionage Act because, the judge said, the film tended "to question the good faith of our ally, Great Britain." He was sentenced to ten years in prison. The case was officially listed as *U.S.* v. *Spirit of '76*.

In a small town in South Dakota, a farmer and socialist named Fred Fairchild, during an argument about the war, said, according to his accusers: "If I were of conscription age and had no dependents and were drafted, I would refuse to serve. They could shoot me, but they could not make me fight." He was tried under the Espionage Act, sentenced to a year and a day at Leavenworth penitentiary. And so it went, multiplied two thousand times (the number of prosecutions under the Espionage Act).

About 65,000 men declared themselves conscientious objectors and asked for noncombatant service. At the army bases where they worked, they were often treated with sadistic brutality. Three men who were jailed at Fort Riley, Kansas, for refusing to perform any military duties, combatant or noncombatant, were taken one by one into the corridor and:

. . . a hemp rope slung over the railing of the upper tier was put about their necks, hoisting them off their feet until they were at the point of collapse. Meanwhile the officers punched them on their ankles and shins. They were then lowered and the rope was tied to their arms, and again they were hoisted off their feet. This time a garden hose was played on their faces with a nozzle about six inches from them, until they collapsed completely. . . .

Schools and universities discouraged opposition to the war. At Columbia University, J. McKeen Cattell, a psychologist, a long-time critic of the Board of Trustees' control of the university, and an opponent of the war, was fired. A week later, in protest, the famous historian Charles Beard resigned from the Columbia faculty, charging the trustees with being "reactionary and visionless in politics, narrow and medieval in religion. . . ."

In Congress, a few voices spoke out against the war. The first woman in the House of Representatives, Jeannette Rankin, did not respond when her name was called in the roll call on the declaration of war. One of the veteran politicians of the House, a supporter of the war, went to her and whispered, "Little woman, you cannot afford not to vote. You represent the womanhood of the country. . . ." On the next roll call she stood up: "I want to stand by my country, but I cannot vote for war. I vote No." A popular song of the time was: "I Didn't Raise My Boy to Be a Soldier." It was overwhelmed, however, by songs like "Over There," "It's a Grand Old Flag," and "Johnny Get Your Gun."

Socialist Kate Richards O'Hare, speaking in North Dakota in July of 1917, said, it was reported, that "the women of the United States were nothing more nor less than brood sows, to raise children to get into the army and be made into fertilizer." She was arrested, tried, found guilty, and sentenced to five years in the Missouri state penitentiary. In prison she continued to fight. When she and fellow prisoners protested the lack of air, because the window above the cell block was kept shut, she was pulled out in the corridor by guards for punishment. In her hand she was carrying a book of poems, and as she was dragged out she flung the book up at the window and broke it, the fresh air streaming in, her fellow prisoners cheering.

Emma Goldman and her fellow anarchist, Alexander Berkman (he had already been locked up fourteen years in Pennsylvania; she had served a year on Blackwell's Island) were sentenced to prison for opposing the draft. She spoke to the jury:

Verily, poor as we are in democracy how can we give of it to the world? . . . a democracy conceived in the military servitude of the masses, in their economic enslavement, and nurtured in their tears and blood, is not democracy at all. It is despotism—the cumulative result of a chain of abuses which, according to that dangerous document, the Declaration of Independence, the people have the right to overthrow. . . .

The war gave the government its opportunity to destroy the IWW. The IWW newspaper, the *Industrial Worker,* just before the declaration of war, wrote: "Capitalists of America, we will fight against you, not for you! Conscription! There is not a power in the world that can make the working class fight if they refuse." Philip Foner, in his history of the IWW, says that the Wobblies were not as active against the war as the Socialists, perhaps because they were fatalistic, saw the war as inevitable, and thought that only victory in class struggle, only revolutionary change, could end war.

In early September 1917, Department of Justice agents made simultaneous raids on forty-eight IWW meeting halls across the country, seizing correspondence and literature that would become courtroom evidence. Later that month, 165 IWW leaders were arrested for conspiring to hinder the draft, encourage desertion, and intimidate others in connection with labor disputes. One hundred and one went on trial in April 1918; it lasted five months, the longest criminal trial in American history up to that time. John Reed, the Socialist writer just back from reporting on the Bolshevik Revolution in Russia *(Ten Days That Shook the World),* covered the IWW trial for *The Masses* magazine and described the defendants:

I doubt if ever in history there has been a sight just like them. One hundred and one lumberjacks, harvest hands, miners, editors . . . who believe the wealth of the world belongs to him who creates it . . . the outdoor men, hard-rock blasters, tree-fellers, wheat-binders, longshoremen, the boys who do the strongwork of the world. . . .

The IWW people used the trial to tell about their activities, their ideas. Sixty-one of them took the stand, including Big Bill Haywood, who testified for three days. One IWW man told the court:

You ask me why the I.W.W. is not patriotic to the United States. If you were a bum without a blanket; if you had left your wife and kids when you went west for a job, and had never located them since; if your job had never kept you long enough in a place to qualify you to vote; if you slept in a lousy, sour bunkhouse, and ate food just as rotten as they could give you and get by with it; if deputy sheriffs shot your cooking cans full of holes and spilled your grub on the ground; if your wages were lowered on you when the bosses thought they had you down; if there was one law for Ford, Suhr, and Mooney, and another for Harry Thaw; if every person who represented law and order and the nation beat you up, railroaded you to jail, and the good Christian people cheered and told them to go to it, how in hell do you expect a man to be patriotic? This war is a business man's war and we don't see why we should go out and get shot in order to save the lovely state of affairs that we now enjoy.

The jury found them all guilty. The judge sentenced Haywood and fourteen others to twenty years in prison; thirty-three were given ten years, the rest shorter sentences. They were fined a total of $2,500,000. The IWW was shattered. Haywood jumped bail and fled to revolutionary Russia, where he remained until his death ten years later.

The war ended in November 1918. Fifty thousand American soldiers had died, and it did not take long, even in the case of patriots, for bitterness and disillusionment to spread through the country. This was reflected in the literature of the postwar decade. John Dos Passos, in his novel *1919*, wrote of the death of John Doe:

> In the tarpaper morgue at Chalons-sur-Marne in the reek of chloride of lime and the dead, they picked out the pine box that held all that was left of . . . John Doe. . . .
> . . . the scraps of dried viscera and skin bundled in khaki
> they took to Chalons-sur-Marne
> and laid it out neat in a pine coffin
> and took it home to God's Country on a battleship
> and buried it in a sarcophagus in the Memorial Amphitheatre in the Arlington National Cemetery
> and draped the Old Glory over it
> and the bugler played taps
> and Mr. Harding prayed to God and the diplomats and the generals and the admirals and the brass hats and the politicians and the handsomely dressed ladies out of the society column of the Washington Post stood up solemn
> and thought how beautiful sad Old Glory God's Country it was to have the bugler play taps and the three volleys made their ears ring.
> Where his chest ought to have been they pinned the Congressional Medal. . . .

Ernest Hemingway would write *A Farewell to Arms*. Years later a college student named Irwin Shaw would write a play, *Bury the Dead*. And a Hollywood screenwriter named Dalton Trumbo would write a powerful and chilling antiwar novel about a torso and brain left alive on the battlefield of World War I, *Johnny Got His Gun*. Ford Madox Ford wrote *No More Parades*.

With all the wartime jailings, the intimidation, the drive for national unity, when the war was over, the Establishment still feared socialism. There seemed to be a need again for the twin tactics of control in the face of revolutionary challenge: reform and repression.

The first was suggested by George L. Record, one of Wilson's friends, who wrote to him in early 1919 that something would have to be done for economic democracy, "to meet this menace of socialism." He said: "You should become the real leader of the radical forces in America, and present to the country a constructive program of fundamental reform, which shall be an alternative to the program presented by the socialists, and the Bolsheviki. . . ."

That summer of 1919, Wilson's adviser Joseph Tumulty reminded him that the conflict between the Republicans and Democrats was unimportant compared with that which threatened them both:

What happened in Washington last night in the attempt upon the Attorney General's life is but a symptom of the terrible unrest that is stalking about the country. . . . As a Democrat I would be disappointed to see the Republican Party regain power. That is not what depresses one so much as to see growing steadily from day to day, under our very eyes, a movement that, if it is not checked, is bound to express itself in attack upon everything we hold dear. In this era of industrial and social unrest both parties are in disrepute with the average man. . . .

"What happened in Washington last night" was the explosion of a bomb in front of the home of Wilson's Attorney General A. Mitchell Palmer. Six months after that bomb exploded, Palmer carried out the first of his mass raids on aliens—immigrants who were not citizens. A law passed by Congress near the end of the war provided for the deportation of aliens who opposed organized government or advocated the destruction of property. Palmer's men, on December 21, 1919, picked up 249 aliens of Russian birth (including Emma Goldman and Alexander Berkman), put them on a transport, and deported them to what had become Soviet Russia. The Constitution gave no right to Congress to deport aliens, but the Supreme Court had said, back in 1892, in affirming the right of Congress to exclude Chinese, that as a matter of self-preservation, this was a natural right of the government.

In January 1920, four thousand persons were rounded up all over the country, held in seclusion for long periods of time, brought into secret hearings, and ordered deported. In Boston, Department of Justice agents, aided by local police, arrested six hundred people by raiding meeting halls or by invading their homes in the early morning. A troubled federal judge described the process:

Pains were taken to give spectacular publicity to the raid, and to make it appear that there was great and imminent public danger. . . . The arrested aliens, in most instances perfectly quiet and harmless working people, many of them not long ago Russian peasants, were handcuffed in pairs, and then, for the purposes of transfer on trains and through the streets of Boston, chained together. . . .

In the spring of 1920, a typesetter and anarchist named Andrea Salsedo was arrested in New York by FBI agents and held for eight weeks in the FBI offices on the fourteenth floor of the Park Row Building, not allowed to contact family or friends or lawyers. Then his crushed body was found on the pavement below the building and the FBI said he had committed suicide by jumping from the fourteenth floor window.

Two friends of Salsedo, anarchists and workingmen in the Boston area, having just learned of his death, began carrying guns. They were arrested on a streetcar in Brockton, Massachusetts, and charged with a holdup and murder that had taken place two weeks before at a shoe factory. These were Nicola Sacco and Bartolomeo Vanzetti. They went on trial, were found guilty, and spent seven years in jail while appeals went on, and while all over the country and the world, people became involved in their case. The trial record and the surrounding circumstances suggested that Sacco and Vanzetti were sentenced to death because they were anarchists and foreigners. In August 1927, as police broke up marches and picket lines with arrests and beatings, and troops surrounded the prison, they were electrocuted.

Sacco's last message to his son Dante, in his painfully learned English was a message to millions of others in the years to come:

> So, Son, instead of crying, be strong, so as to be able to comfort your mother . . . take her for a long walk in the quiet country, gathering wild flowers here and there. . . . But remember always, Dante, in the play of happiness, don't you use all for yourself only. . . . help the persecuted and the victim because they are your better friends. . . . In this struggle of life you will find more and love and you will be loved.

There had been reforms. The patriotic fervor of war had been invoked. The courts and jails had been used to reinforce the idea that certain ideas, certain kinds of resistance, could not be tolerated. And still, even from the cells of the condemned, the message was going out: the class war was still on in that supposedly classless society, the United States. Through the twenties and the thirties, it was still on.

4.
Self-help in Hard Times

The war was hardly over, it was February 1919, the IWW leadership was in jail, but the IWW idea of the general strike became reality for five days in Seattle, Washington, when a walkout of 100,000 working people brought the city to a halt.

It began with 35,000 shipyard workers striking for a wage increase. They appealed for support to the Seattle Central Labor Council, which recommended a city-wide strike, and in two weeks 110 locals—mostly American Federation of Labor, only a few IWW—voted to strike. The rank and file of each striking local elected three members to a General Strike Committee, and on February 6, 1919, at 10:00 A.M., the strike began.

Unity was not easy to achieve. The IWW locals were in tension with the AFL locals. Japanese locals were admitted to the General Strike Committee but were not given a vote. Still, sixty thousand union members were out, and forty thousand other workers joined in sympathy.

Seattle workers had a radical tradition. During the war, the president of the Seattle AFL, a socialist, was imprisoned for opposing the draft, was tortured, and there were great labor rallies in the streets to protest.

The city now stopped functioning, except for activities organized by the strikers to provide essential needs. Firemen agreed to stay on the job. Laundry workers handled only hospital laundry. Vehicles authorized to move carried signs "Exempted by the General Strike Committee." Thirty-five neighborhood milk stations were set up. Every day thirty thousand meals were prepared in large kitchens, then transported to halls all over the city and served cafeteria style, with strikers paying twenty-five cents a meal, the general public thirty-five cents. People were allowed to eat as much as they wanted of the beef stew, spaghetti, bread, and coffee.

A Labor War Veteran's Guard was organized to keep the peace. On the blackboard at one of its headquarters was written: "The purpose of this organization is to preserve law and order without the use of force. No volunteer will have any police power or be allowed to carry weapons of any sort, but to use persuasion only." During the strike, crime in the city decreased. The commander of the U.S. army detachment sent into the area told the strikers' committee that in forty years of military experience he hadn't seen so quiet and orderly a city. A poem printed in the Seattle *Union Record* (a daily newspaper put out by labor people) by someone named Anise:

> What scares them most is
> That NOTHING HAPPENS!
> They are ready
> For DISTURBANCES.
> They have machine guns
> And soldiers,
> But this SMILING SILENCE
>   Is uncanny.
> The business men
> Don't understand
> That sort of weapon . . .
> It is your SMILE
> That is UPSETTING
> Their reliance
>   On Artillery, brother!
> It is the garbage wagons
> That go along the street
> Marked "EXEMPT
> by STRIKE COMMITTEE."
> It is the milk stations
> That are getting better daily,
> And the three hundred
> WAR Veterans of Labor
> Handling the crowds
> WITHOUT GUNS,
> For these things speak
> Of a NEW POWER
> And a NEW WORLD
> That they do not feel
> At HOME in.

The mayor swore in 2,400 special deputies, many of them students at the University of Washington. Almost a thousand sailors and marines were brought into the city by the U.S. government. The general strike ended after five days, according to the General Strike Committee because of pressure from the international officers of the various unions, as well as the difficulties of living in a shut-down city.

The strike had been peaceful. But when it was over, there were raids and arrests: on the Socialist party headquarters, on a printing plant. Thirty-nine members of the IWW were jailed as "ring-leaders of anarchy."

In Centralia, Washington, where the IWW had been organizing lumber workers, the lumber interests made plans to get rid of the IWW. On November 11, 1919, Armistice Day, the Legion paraded through town with rubber hoses and gas pipes, and the IWW prepared for an attack. When the Legion passed the IWW hall, shots were fired—it is unclear who fired first. They stormed the hall, there was more firing, and three Legion men were killed.

Inside the headquarters was an IWW member, a lumberjack named Frank Everett, who had been in France as a soldier while the IWW national leaders were on trail for obstructing the war effort. Everett was in army uniform and carrying a rifle. He emptied it into the crowd, dropped it, and ran for the woods, followed by a mob. He started to wade across the river, found the current too strong, turned, shot the leading man dead, threw his gun into the river, and fought the mob with his fists. They dragged him back to town behind an automobile, suspended him from a telegraph pole, took him down, locked him in jail. That night, his jailhouse door was broken down, he was dragged out, put on the floor of a car, his genitals were cut off, and then he was taken to a bridge, hanged, and his body riddled with bullets.

No one was ever arrested for Everett's murder, but eleven Wobblies were put on trial for killing an American Legion leader during the parade, and six of them spent fifteen years in prison.

Why such a reaction to the general strike, to the organizing of the Wobblies? A statement by the mayor of Seattle suggests that the Establishment feared not just the strike itself but what it symbolized. He said:

The so-called sympathetic Seattle strike was an attempted revolution. That there was no violence does not alter the fact. . . . The intent, openly and covertly announced, was for the overthrow of the industrial system; here first, then everywhere. . . . True, there were no flashing guns, no bombs, no killings. Revolution, I repeat, doesn't need violence. The general strike, as practiced in Seattle, is of itself the weapon of revolution, all the more dangerous because quiet. To succeed, it must suspend everything; stop the entire life stream of

a community. . . . That is to say, it puts the government out of operation.
And that is all there is to revolt—no matter how achieved.

Furthermore, the Seattle general strike took place in the midst of a
wave of postwar rebellions all over the world. A writer in *The Nation*
commented that year:

> The most extraordinary phenomenon of the present time . . . is the unpre-
> cedented revolt of the rank and file. . . .
> In Russia it has dethroned the Czar. . . . In Korea and India and Egypt
> and Ireland it keeps up an unyielding resistance to political tyranny. In England
> it brought about the railway strike, against the judgement of the men's own
> executives. In Seattle and San Francisco it has resulted in the stevedores'
> recent refusal to handle arms or supplies destined for the overthrow of the
> Soviet Government. In one district of Illinois it manifested itself in a resolution
> of striking miners, unanimously requesting their state executive "to go to Hell".
> In Pittsburgh, according to Mr. Gompers, it compelled the reluctant American
> Federation officers to call the steel strike, lest the control pass into the hands
> of the I.W.W.'s and other "radicals". In New York, it brought about the
> longshoremen's strike and kept the men out in defiance of union officials,
> and caused the upheaval in the printing trade, which the international officers,
> even though the employers worked hand in glove with them, were completely
> unable to control.
> The common man . . . losing faith in the old leadership, has experienced
> a new access of self-confidence, or at least a new recklessness, a readiness to
> take chances on his own account . . . authority cannot any longer be imposed
> from above; it comes automatically from below.

In the steel mills of western Pennsylvania later in 1919, where
men worked twelve hours a day, six days a week, doing exhausting
work under intense heat, 100,000 steel workers were signed up in twenty
different AFL craft unions. A National Committee attempting to tie
them together in their organizing drive found in the summer of 1919
"the men are letting it be known that if we do not do something for
them they will take the matter into their own hands."

The National Council was getting telegrams like the one from
the Johnstown Steel Workers Council: "Unless the National Committee
authorizes a national strike vote to be taken this week we will be compelled to go on strike here alone." William Z. Foster (later a Communist
leader, at this time secretary-treasurer to the National Committee in
charge of organizing) received a telegram from organizers in the Youngstown district: "We cannot be expected to meet the enraged workers,
who will consider us traitors if strike is postponed."

There was pressure from President Woodrow Wilson and Samuel Gompers, AFL president, to postpone the strike. But the steelworkers were too insistent, and in September 1919, not only the 100,000 union men but 250,000 others went out on strike.

The sheriff of Allegheny County swore in as deputies five thousand employees of U.S. Steel who had not gone on strike, and announced that outdoor meetings would be forbidden. A report of the Interchurch World Movement made at the time said:

In Monessen . . . the policy of the State Police was simply to club men off the streets and drive them into their homes. . . . In Braddock . . . when a striker was clubbed in the street he would be taken to jail, kept there over night. . . . Many of those arrested in Newcastle . . . were ordered not to be released until the strike was over.

The Department of Justice moved in, carrying out raids on workers who were aliens, holding them for deportation. At Gary, Indiana, federal troops were sent in.

Other factors operated against the strikers. Most were recent immigrants, of many nationalities, many languages. Sherman Service, Inc., hired by the steel corporations to break the strike, instructed its men in South Chicago: "We want you to stir up as much bad feeling as you possibly can between the Serbians and the Italians. Spread data among the Serbians that the Italians are going back to work. . . . Urge them to go back to work or the Italians will get their jobs." More than thirty thousand black workers were brought into the area as strikebreakers—they had been excluded from AFL unions and so felt no loyalty to unionism.

As the strike dragged on, the mood of defeat spread, and workers began to drift back to work. After ten weeks, the number of strikers was down to 110,000, and then the National Committee called the strike off.

In the year following the war, 120,000 textile workers struck in New England and New Jersey, and 30,000 silk workers struck in Paterson, New Jersey. In Boston the police went out on strike, and in New York City cigarmakers, shirtmakers, carpenters, bakers, teamsters, and barbers were out on strike. In Chicago, the press reported, "More strikes and lockouts accompany the mid-summer heat than ever known before at any one time." Five thousand workers at International Harvester and five thousand city workers were in the streets.

When the twenties began, however, the situation seemed under control. The IWW was destroyed, the Socialist party falling apart. The strikes were beaten down by force, and the economy was doing just well enough for just enough people to prevent mass rebellion.

Congress, in the twenties, put an end to the dangerous, turbulent flood of immigrants (14 million between 1900 and 1920) by passing laws setting immigration quotas: the quotas favored Anglo-Saxons, kept out black and yellow people, limited severely the coming of Latins, Slavs, Jews. No African country could send more than 100 people; 100 was the limit for China, for Bulgaria, for Palestine; 34,007 could come from England or Northern Ireland, but only 3,845 from Italy; 51,227 from Germany, but only 124 from Lithuania; 28,567 from the Irish Free State, but only 2,248 from Russia.

The Ku Klux Klan was revived in the 1920s, and it spread into the 'North. By 1924 it had 4½ million members. The NAACP seemed helpless in the face of mob violence and race hatred everywhere. The impossibility of the black person's ever being considered equal in white America was the theme of the nationalist movement led in the 1920s by Marcus Garvey. He preached black pride, racial separation, and a return to Africa, which to him held the only hope for black unity and survival. But Garvey's movement, inspiring as it was to some blacks, could not make much headway against the powerful white supremacy currents of the postwar decade.

There was some truth to the standard picture of the twenties as a time of prosperity and fun—the Jazz Age, the Roaring Twenties. Unemployment was down, from 4,270,000 in 1921 to a little over 2 million in 1927. The general level of wages for workers rose. Some farmers made a lot of money. The 40 percent of all families who made over $2,000 a year could buy new gadgets: autos, radios, refrigerators. Millions of people were not doing badly—and they could shut out of the picture the others—the tenant farmers, black and white, the immigrant families in the big cities either without work or not making enough to get the basic necessities.

But prosperity was concentrated at the top. While from 1922 to 1929 real wages in manufacturing went up per capita 1.4 percent a year, the holders of common stocks gained 16.4 percent a year. Six million families (42 percent of the total) made less than $1,000 a year. One-tenth of 1 percent of the families at the top received as much income as 42 percent of the families at the bottom, according to a report of the Brookings Institution. Every year in the 1920s, about 25,000 workers were killed on the job and 100,000 permanently disabled.

Two million people in New York City lived in tenements condemned as firetraps.

The country was full of little industrial towns like Muncie, Indiana, where, according to Robert and Helen Lynd *(Middletown)*, the class system was revealed by the time people got up in the morning: for two-thirds of the city's families, "the father gets up in the dark in winter, eats hastily in the kitchen in the gray dawn, and is at work from an hour to two and a quarter hours before his children have to be at school."

There were enough well-off people to push the others into the background. And with the rich controlling the means of dispensing information, who would tell? Historian Merle Curti observed about the twenties:

It was, in fact, only the upper ten percent of the population that enjoyed a marked increase in real income. But the protests which such facts normally have evoked could not make themselves widely or effectively felt. This was in part the result of the grand strategy of the major political parties. In part it was the result of the fact that almost all the chief avenues to mass opinion were now controlled by large-scale publishing industries.

Some writers tried to break through: Theodore Dreiser, Sinclair Lewis, Lewis Mumford. F. Scott Fitzgerald, in an article, "Echoes of the Jazz Age," said: "It was borrowed time anyway—the whole upper tenth of a nation living with the insouciance of a grand duc and the casualness of chorus girls." He saw ominous signs amid that prosperity: drunkenness, unhappiness, violence:

A classmate killed his wife and himself on Long Island, another tumbled "accidentally" from a skyscraper in Philadelphia, another purposely from a skyscraper in New York. One was killed in a speak-easy in Chicago; another was beaten to death in a speak-easy in New York and crawled home to the Princeton Club to die; still another had his skull crushed by a maniac's axe in an insane asylum where he was confined.

Sinclair Lewis captured the false sense of prosperity, the shallow pleasure of the new gadgets for the middle classes, in his novel *Babbitt:*

It was the best of nationally advertised and quantitatively produced alarm-clocks, with all modern attachments, including cathedral chime, intermittent alarm, and a phosphorescent dial. Babbitt was proud of being awakened by such a rich device. Socially it was almost as creditable as buying expensive cord tires.

He sulkily admitted now that there was no more escape, but he lay and detested the grind of the real-estate business, and disliked his family, and disliked himself for disliking them.

Women had finally, after long agitation, won the right to vote in 1920 with the passage of the Nineteenth Amendment, but voting was still a middle-class and upper-class activity. Eleanor Flexner, recounting the history of the movement, says the effect of female suffrage was that "women have shown the same tendency to divide along orthodox party lines as male voters."

Few political figures spoke out for the poor of the twenties. One was Fiorello La Guardia, a Congressman from a district of poor immigrants in East Harlem (who ran, oddly, on both Socialist and Republican tickets). In the mid-twenties he was made aware by people in his district of the high price of meat. When La Guardia asked Secretary of Agriculture William Jardine to investigate the high price of meat, the Secretary sent him a pamphlet on how to use meat economically. La Guardia wrote back:

I asked for help and you send me a bulletin. The people of New York City cannot feed their children on Department bulletins. . . . Your bulletins . . . are of no use to the tenement dwellers of this great city. The housewives of New York have been trained by hard experience on the economical use of meat. What we want is the help of your department on the meat profiteers who are keeping the hard-working people of this city from obtaining proper nourishment.

During the presidencies of Harding and Coolidge in the twenties, the Secretary of the Treasury was Andrew Mellon, one of the richest men in America. In 1923, Congress was presented with the "Mellon Plan," calling for what looked like a general reduction of income taxes, except that the top income brackets would have their tax rates lowered from 50 percent to 25 percent, while the lowest-income group would have theirs lowered from 4 percent to 3 percent. A few Congressmen from working-class districts spoke against the bill, like William P. Connery of Massachusetts:

I am not going to have my people who work in the shoe factories of Lynn and in the mills in Lawrence and the leather industry of Peabody, in these days of so-called Republican prosperity when they are working but three days in the week think that I am in accord with the provisions of this bill. . . . When I see a provision in this Mellon tax bill which is going to save Mr. Mellon himself $800,000 on his income tax and his brother $600,000 on his, I cannot give it my support.

The Mellon Plan passed. In 1928, La Guardia toured the poorer districts of New York and said: "I confess I was not prepared for what I actually saw. It seemed almost incredible that such conditions of poverty could really exist."

Buried in the general news of prosperity in the twenties were, from time to time, stories of bitter labor struggles. In 1922, coal miners and railroad men went on strike, and Senator Burton Wheeler of Montana, a Progressive elected with labor votes, visited the strike area and reported:

All day long I have listened to heartrending stories of women evicted from their homes by the coal companies. I heard pitiful pleas of little children crying for bread. I stood aghast as I heard most amazing stories from men brutally beaten by private policemen. It has been a shocking and nerve-racking experience.

A textile strike in Rhode Island in 1922 among Italian and Portuguese workers failed, but class feelings were awakened and some of the strikers joined radical movements. Luigi Nardella recalled:

. . . my oldest brother, Guido, he started the strike. Guido pulled the handles on the looms in the Royal Mills, going from one section to the next shouting, "Strike! Strike!" . . . When the strike started we didn't have any union organizers. . . . We got together a group of girls and went from mill to mill, and that morning we got five mills out. We'd motion to the girls in the mills, "Come out! Come out!" Then we'd go on to the next. . . .

Somebody from the Young Workers' League came out to bring a check, and invited me to a meeting, and I went. Then I joined, and in a few years I was in the Risorgimento Club in Providence. We were anti-Fascists. I spoke on street corners, bring a stand, jump up and talk to good crowds. And we led the support for Sacco and Vanzetti. . . .

After the war, with the Socialist party weakened, a Communist party was organized, and Communists were involved in the organization of the Trade Union Education League, which tried to build a militant spirit inside the AFL. When a Communist named Ben Gold, of the furriers' section of the TUEL, challenged the AFL union leadership at a meeting, he was knifed and beaten. But in 1926, he and other Communists organized a strike of furriers who formed mass picket lines, battled the police to hold their lines, were arrested and beaten, but kept striking, until they won a forty-hour week and a wage increase.

Communists again played a leading part in the great textile strike that spread through the Carolinas and Tennessee in the spring of 1929.

The mill owners had moved to the South to escape unions, to find more subservient workers among the poor whites. But these workers rebelled against the long hours, the low pay. They particularly resented the "stretch-out"—an intensification of work. For instance, a weaver who had operated twenty-four looms and got $18.91 a week would be raised to $23, but he would be "stretched out" to a hundred looms and had to work at a punishing pace.

The first of the textile strikes was in Tennessee, where five hundred women in one mill walked out in protest against wages of $9 to $10 a week. Then at Gastonia, North Carolina, workers joined a new union, the National Textile Workers Union, led by Communists, which admitted both blacks and whites to membership. When some of them were fired, half of the two thousand workers went out on strike. An atmosphere of anti-Communism and racism built up and violence began. Textile strikes began to spread across South Carolina.

One by one the various strikes were settled, with some gains, but not at Gastonia. There, with the textile workers living in a tent colony, and refusing to renounce the Communists in their leadership, the strike went on. But strikebreakers were brought in and the mills kept operating. Desperation grew; there were violent clashes with the police. One dark night, the chief of police was killed in a gun battle and sixteen strikers and sympathizers were indicted for murder, including Fred Beal, a Communist party organizer. Ultimately seven were tried and given sentences of from five to twenty years. They were released on bail, and left the state; the Communists escaped to Soviet Russia. Through all the defeats, the beatings, the murders, however, it was the beginning of textile mill unionism in the South.

The stock market crash of 1929, which marked the beginning of the Great Depression of the United States, came directly from wild speculation which collapsed and brought the whole economy down with it. But, as John Galbraith says in his study of that event (The Great Crash), behind that speculation was the fact that "the economy was fundamentally unsound." He points to very unhealthy corporate and banking structures, an unsound foreign trade, much economic misinformation, and the "bad distribution of income" (the highest 5 percent of the population received about one-third of all personal income).

A socialist critic would go further and say that the capitalist system was by its nature unsound: a system driven by the one overriding motive of corporate profit and therefore unstable, unpredictable, and blind to human needs. The result of all that: permanent depression for many of its people, and periodic crises for almost everybody. Capitalism, despite its attempts at self-reform, its organization for better control, was still in 1929 a sick and undependable system.

After the crash, the economy was stunned, barely moving. Over five thousand banks closed and huge numbers of businesses, unable to get money, closed too. Those that continued laid off employees and cut the wages of those who remained, again and again. Industrial production fell by 50 percent, and by 1933 perhaps 15 million (no one knew exactly)—one-fourth or one-third of the labor force—were out of work. The Ford Motor Company, which in the spring of 1929 had employed 128,000 workers, was down to 37,000 by August of 1931. By the end of 1930, almost half the 280,000 textile mill workers in New England were out of work. Former President Calvin Coolidge, commented with his customary wisdom: "When more and more people are thrown out of work, unemployment results." He spoke again in early 1931, "This country is not in good condition."

Clearly, those responsible for organizing the economy did not know what had happened, were baffled by it, refused to recognize it, and found reasons other than the failure of the system. Herbert Hoover had said, not long before the crash: "We in America today are nearer to the final triumph over poverty than ever before in the history of any land." Henry Ford, in March 1931, said the crisis was here because "the average man won't really do a day's work unless he is caught and cannot get out of it. There is plenty of work to do if people would do it." A few weeks later he laid off 75,000 workers.

There were millions of tons of food around, but it was not profitable to transport it, to sell it. Warehouses were full of clothing, but people could not afford it. There were lots of houses, but they stayed empty because people couldn't pay the rent, had been evicted, and now lived in shacks in quickly formed "Hoovervilles" built on garbage dumps.

Brief glimpses of reality in the newspapers could have been multiplied by the millions: A *New York Times* story in early 1932:

After vainly trying to get a stay of dispossession until January 15 from his apartment at 46 Hancock Street in Brooklyn, yesterday, Peter J. Cornell, 48 years old, a former roofing contractor out of work and penniless, fell dead in the arms of his wife.

A doctor gave the cause of his death as heart disease, and the police said it had at least partly been caused by the bitter disappointment of a long day's fruitless attempt to prevent himself and his family being put out on the street. . . .

Cornell owed $5 in rent in arrears and $39 for January which his landlord required in advance. Failure to produce the money resulted in a dispossess order being served on the family yesterday and to take effect at the end of the week.

After vainly seeking assistance elsewhere, he was told during the day by the Home Relief Bureau that it would have no funds with which to help him until January 15.

A dispatch from Wisconsin to *The Nation,* in late 1932:

Throughout the middle west the tension between the farmers and authorities has been growing . . . as a result of tax and foreclosure sales. In many cases evictions have been prevented only by mass action on the part of the farmers. However, until the Cichon homestead near Elkhorn, Wisconsin, was besieged on December 6 by a host of deputy sheriffs armed with machine-guns, rifles, shotguns, and tear-gas bombs, there had been no actual violence. Max Cichon's property was auctioned off at a foreclosure sale last August, but he refused to allow either the buyer or the authorities to approach his home. He held off unwelcome visitors with a shotgun. The sheriff called upon Cichon to submit peacefully. When he refused to do so, the sheriff ordered deputies to lay down a barrage of machine-gun and rifle fire . . . Cichon is now in jail in Elkhorn, and his wife and two children, who were with him in the house, are being cared for in the county hospital. Cichon is not a trouble-maker. He enjoys the confidence of his neighbors, who only recently elected him justice of the peace of the town of Sugar Creek. That a man of his standing and disposition should go to such lengths in defying the authorities is a clear warning that we may expect further trouble in the agricultural districts unless the farmers are soon helped.

A tenement dweller on 113th Street in East Harlem wrote to Congressman Fiorello La Guardia in Washington:

You know my condition is bad. I used to get pension from the government and they stopped. It is now nearly seven months I am out of work. I hope you will try to do something for me. . . . I have four children who are in need of clothes and food. . . . My daughter who is eight is very ill and not recovering. My rent is due two months and I am afraid of being put out.

In Oklahoma, the farmers found their farms sold under the auctioneer's hammer, their farms turning to dust, the tractors coming in and taking over. John Steinbeck, in his novel of the depression, *The Grapes of Wrath,* describes what happened:

And the dispossessed, the migrants, flowed into California, two hundred and fifty thousand, and three hundred thousand. Behind them new tractors were going on the land and the tenants were being forced off. And new waves were on the way, new waves of the dispossessed and the homeless, hard, intent, and dangerous. . . .

And a homeless hungry man, driving the road with his wife beside him and his thin children in the back seat, could look at the fallow fields which might produce food but not profit, and that man could know how a fallow field is a sin and the unused land a crime against the thin children. . . .

And in the south he saw the golden oranges hanging on the trees, the little golden oranges on the dark green trees; and guards with shotguns patrolling the lines so a man might not pick an orange for a thin child, oranges to be dumped if the price was low. . . .

These people were becoming "dangerous," as Steinbeck said. The spirit of rebellion was growing. Mauritz Hallgren, in a 1933 book, *Seeds of Revolt,* compiled newspaper reports of things happening around the country:

England, Arkansas, January 3, 1931. The long drought that ruined hundreds of Arkansas farms last summer had a dramatic sequel late today when some 500 farmers, most of them white men and many of them armed, marched on the business section of this town. . . . Shouting that they must have food for themselves and their families, the invaders announced their intention to take it from the stores unless it were provided from some other source without cost.

Detroit, July 9, 1931: An incipient riot by 500 unemployed men turned out of the city lodging house for lack of funds was quelled by police reserves in Cadillac Square tonight. . . .

Indiana Harbor, Indiana, August 5, 1931: Fifteen hundred jobless men stormed the plant of the Fruit Growers Express Company here, demanding that they be given jobs to keep from starving. The company's answer was to call the city police, who routed the jobless with menacing clubs.

Boston, November 10, 1931. Twenty persons were treated for injuries, three were hurt so seriously that they may die, and dozens of others were nursing wounds from flying bottles, lead pipe, and stones after clashes between striking longshoremen and Negro strikebreakers along the Charlestown–East Boston waterfront.

Detroit, November 28, 1931. A mounted patrolman was hit on the head with a stone and unhorsed and one demonstrator was arrested during a disturbance in Grand Circus Park this morning when 2000 men and women met there in defiance of police orders.

Chicago, April 1, 1932. Five hundred school children, most with haggard faces and in tattered clothes, paraded through Chicago's downtown section to the Board of Education offices to demand that the school system provide them with food.

Boston, June 3, 1932. Twenty-five hungry children raided a buffet lunch set up for Spanish War veterans during a Boston parade. Two automobile-loads of police were called to drive them away.

New York, January 21, 1933. Several hundred jobless surrounded a restaurant just off Union square today demanding they be fed without charge. . . .

Seattle, February 16, 1933. A two-day siege of the County-City Building, occupied by an army of about 5,000 unemployed, was ended early tonight, deputy sheriffs and police evicting the demonstrators after nearly two hours of efforts.

Yip Harburg, the songwriter, told Studs Terkel about the year 1932: "I was walking along the street at that time, and you'd see the bread lines. The biggest one in New York City was owned by William Randolph Hearst. He had a big truck with several people on it, and big cauldrons of hot soup, bread. Fellows with burlap on their feet were lined up all around Columbus Circle, and went for blocks and blocks around the park, waiting." Harburg had to write a song for the show *Americana*. He wrote "Brother, Can You Spare a Dime."

> Once in khaki suits,
> Gee, we looked swell,
> Full of that Yankee Doodle-de-dum.
> Half a million boots went sloggin' through Hell,
> I was the kid with the drum.
> Say, don't you remember, they called me Al—
> It was Al all the time.
> Say, don't you remember I'm your pal—
> Brother, can you spare a dime.

It was not just a song of despair. As Yip Harburg told Terkel:

In the song the man is really saying: I made an investment in this country. Where the hell are my dividends? . . . It's more than just a bit of pathos. It doesn't reduce him to a beggar. It makes him a dignified human, asking questions—and a bit outraged, too, as he should be.

The anger of the veteran of the First World War, now without work, his family hungry, led to the march of the Bonus Army to Washington in the spring and summer of 1932. War veterans, holding government bonus certificates which were due years in the future, demanded that Congress pay off on them now, when the money was desperately needed. And so they began to move to Washington from all over the country, with wives and children or alone. They came in broken-down old autos, stealing rides on freight trains, or hitchhiking. They were miners from West Virginia, sheet metal workers from Columbus, Georgia, and unemployed Polish veterans from Chicago. One family—husband, wife, three-year-old boy—spent three months on freight trains coming from California. Chief Running Wolf, a jobless Mescalero Indian from New Mexico, showed up in full Indian dress, with bow and arrow.

More than twenty thousand came. Most camped across the Potomac River from the Capitol on Anacostia Flats where, as John Dos Passos wrote, "the men are sleeping in little lean-tos built out of old newspapers, cardboard boxes, packing crates, bits of tin or tarpaper roofing, every kind of cockeyed makeshift shelter from the rain scraped together out of the city dump." The bill to pay off on the bonus passed the House, but was defeated in the Senate, and some veterans, discouraged, left. Most stayed—some encamped in government buildings near the Capitol, the rest on Anacostia Flats, and President Hoover ordered the army to evict them.

Four troops of cavalry, four companies of infantry, a machine gun squadron, and six tanks assembled near the White House. General Douglas MacArthur was in charge of the operation, Major Dwight Eisenhower his aide. George S. Patton was one of the officers. MacArthur led his troops down Pennsylvania Avenue, used tear gas to clear veterans out of the old buildings, and set the buildings on fire. Then the army moved across the bridge to Anacostia. Thousands of veterans, wives, children, began to run as the tear gas spread. The soldiers set fire to some of the huts, and soon the whole encampment was ablaze. When it was all over, two veterans had been shot to death, an eleven-week-old baby had died, an eight-year-old boy was partially blinded by gas, two police had fractured skulls, and a thousand veterans were injured by gas.

The hard, hard times, the inaction of the government in helping, the action of the government in dispersing war veterans—all had their effect on the election of November 1932. Democratic party candidate Franklin D. Roosevelt defeated Herbert Hoover overwhelmingly, took office in the spring of 1933, and began a program of reform legislation which became famous as the "New Deal." When a small veterans' march on Washington took place early in his administration, he greeted them and provided coffee; they met with one of his aides and went home. It was a sign of Roosevelt's approach.

The Roosevelt reforms went far beyond previous legislation. They had to meet two pressing needs: to reorganize capitalism in such a way to overcome the crisis and stabilize the system; also, to head off the alarming growth of spontaneous rebellion in the early years of the Roosevelt administration—organization of tenants and the unemployed, movements of self-help, general strikes in several cities.

That first objective—to stabilize the system for its own protection—was most obvious in the major law of Roosevelt's first months in office, the National Recovery Act (NRA). It was designed to take control of the economy through a series of codes agreed on by management, labor, and the government, fixing prices and wages, limiting competition. From the first, the NRA was dominated by big businesses and served their interests. As Bernard Bellush says *(The Failure of the N.R.A.)*, its Title I "turned much of the nation's power over to highly organized, well-financed trade associations and industrial combines. The unorganized public, otherwise known as the consumer, along with the members of the fledgling trade-union movement, had virtually nothing to say about the initial organization of the National Recovery Administration, or the formulation of basic policy."

Where organized labor was strong, Roosevelt moved to make some concessions to working people. But: "Where organized labor was weak, Roosevelt was unprepared to withstand the pressures of industrial spokesmen to control the . . . NRA codes." Barton Bernstein *(Towards a New Past)* confirms this: "Despite the annoyance of some big businessmen with Section 7a, the NRA reaffirmed and consolidated their power. . . ." Bellush sums up his view of the NRA:

The White House permitted the National Association of Manufacturers, the Chamber of Commerce, and allied business and trade associations to assume overriding authority. . . . Indeed, private administration became public administration, and private government became public government, insuring the marriage of capitalism with statism.

When the Supreme Court in 1935 declared the NRA unconstitutional, it claimed it gave too much power to the President, but, according to Bellush, ". . . FDR surrendered an inordinate share of the power of government, through the NRA, to industrial spokesmen throughout the country."

Also passed in the first months of the new administration, the AAA (Agricultural Adjustment Administration) was an attempt to organize agriculture. It favored the larger farmers as the NRA favored big business. The TVA (Tennessee Valley Authority) was an unusual entrance of government into business—a government-owned network of dams and hydroelectric plants to control floods and produce electric power in the Tennessee Valley. It gave jobs to the unemployed, helped the consumer with lower electric rates, and in some respect deserved the accusation that it was "socialistic." But the New Deal's organization of the economy was aimed mainly at stabilizing the economy, and secondly at giving enough help to the lower classes to keep them from turning a rebellion into a real revolution.

That rebellion was real when Roosevelt took office. Desperate people were not waiting for the government to help them; they were helping themselves, acting directly. Aunt Molly Jackson, a woman who later became active in labor struggles in Appalachia, recalled how she walked into the local store, asked for a 24-pound sack of flour, gave it to her little boy to take it outside, then filled a sack of sugar and said to the storekeeper, "Well, I'll see you in ninety days. I have to feed some children . . . I'll pay you, don't worry." And when he objected, she pulled out her pistol (which, as a midwife traveling alone through the hills, she had a permit to carry) and said: "Martin, if you try to take this grub away from me, God knows that if they electrocute me for it tomorrow, I'll shoot you six times in a minute." Then, as she recalls, "I walked out, I got home, and these seven children was so hungry that they was a-grabbin the raw dough off-a their mother's hands and crammin it into their mouths and swallowing it whole."

All over the country, people organized spontaneously to stop evictions. In New York, in Chicago, in other cities—when word spread that someone was being evicted, a crowd would gather; the police would remove the furniture from the house, put it out in the street, and the crowd would bring the furniture back. The Communist party was active in organizing Workers Alliance groups in the cities. Mrs. Willye Jeffries, a black woman, told Studs Terkel about evictions:

A lot of 'em was put out. They'd call and have the bailiffs come and sit them out, and as soon as they'd leave, we would put 'em back where they came out. All we had to do was call Brother Hilton. . . . Look, such and such a place, there's a family sittin' out there. Everybody passed through the neighborhood, was a member of the Workers Alliance, had one person they would call. When that one person came, he'd have about fifty people with him. . . . Take that stuff right on back up there. The men would connect those lights and go to the hardware and get gas pipe, and connect that stove back. Put the furniture back just like you had it, so it don't look like you been out the door.

Unemployed Councils were formed all over the country. They were described by Charles R. Walker, writing in *The Forum* in 1932:

I find it is no secret that Communists organize Unemployed Councils in most cities and usually lead them, but the councils are organized democratically and the majority rules. In one I visited at Lincoln Park, Michigan, there were three hundred members of which eleven were Communists. . . . The Council had a right wing, a left wing, and a center. The chairman of the Council . . . was also the local commander of the American Legion. In Chicago there are 45 branches of the Unemployed Council, with a total membership of 22,000.

The Council's weapon is democratic force of numbers, and their function is to prevent evictions of the destitute, or if evicted to bring pressure to bear on the Relief Commission to find a new home; if an unemployed worker has his gas or his water turned off because he can't pay for it, to see the proper authorities; to see that the unemployed who are shoeless and clothesless get both; to eliminate through publicity and pressure discriminations between Negroes and white persons, or against the foreign born, in matters of relief . . . to march people down to relief headquarters and demand they be fed and clothed. Finally to provide legal defense for all unemployed arrested for joining parades, hunger marches, or attending union meetings.

People organized to help themselves, since business and government were not helping them in 1931 and 1932. In Seattle, the fishermen's union caught fish and exchanged them with people who picked fruit and vegetables, and those who cut wood exchanged that. There were twenty-two locals, each with a commissary where food and firewood were exchanged for other goods and services: barbers, seamstresses, and doctors gave of their skills in return for other things. By the end of 1932, there were 330 self-help organizations in thirty-seven states, with over 300,000 members. By early 1933, they seem to have collapsed; they were attempting too big a job in an economy that was more and more a shambles.

Perhaps the most remarkable example of self-help took place in the coal district of Pennsylvania, where teams of unemployed miners dug small mines on company property, mined coal, trucked it to cities, and sold it below the commercial rate. By 1934, 5 million tons of this "bootleg" coal were produced by twenty thousand men using four thousand vehicles. When attempts were made to prosecute, local juries would not convict, local jailors would not imprison.

These were simple actions, taken out of practical need, but they had revolutionary possibilities. Paul Mattick, a Marxist writer, commented:

All that is really necessary for the workers to do in order to end their miseries is to perform such simple things as to take from where there is, without regard to established property principles or social philosophies, and to start to produce for themselves. Done on a broad social scale, it will lead to lasting results; on a local, isolated plane it will be . . . defeated. . . . The bootleg miners have shown in a rather clear and impressive way, that the so-much bewailed absence of a socialist ideology on the part of the workers really does not prevent workers from acting quite anticapitalistically, quite in accordance with their own needs. Breaking through the confines of private property in order to live up to their own necessities, the miners' action is, at the same time a manifestation of the most important part of class consciousness—namely, that the problems of the workers can be solved only by themselves.

Were the New Dealers—Roosevelt and his advisers, the businessmen who supported him—also class-conscious? Did they understand that measures must be quickly taken, in 1933 and 1934, to give jobs, food baskets, relief, to wipe out the idea "that the problems of the workers can be solved only by themselves"? Perhaps, like the workers' class consciousness, it was a set of actions arising not from held theory, but from instinctive practical necessity.

Perhaps it was such a consciousness that led to the Wagner-Connery Bill, introduced in Congress in early 1934, to regulate labor disputes. The bill provided elections for union representation, a board to settle problems and handle grievances. Was this not exactly the kind of legislation to do away with the idea that "the problems of the workers can be solved only by themselves"? Big business thought it was too helpful to labor and opposed it. Roosevelt was cool to it. But in the year 1934 a series of labor outbursts suggested the need for legislative action.

A million and a half workers in different industries went on strike in 1934. That spring and summer, longshoremen on the West Coast, in a rank-and-file insurrection against their own union leadership as well as against the shippers, held a convention, demanded the abolition of the shape-up (a kind of early-morning slave market where work gangs were chosen for the day), and went out on strike.

Two thousand miles of Pacific coastline were quickly tied up. The teamsters cooperated, refusing to truck cargo to the piers, and maritime workers joined the strike. When the police moved in to open the piers, the strikers resisted en masse, and two were killed by police gunfire. A mass funeral procession for the strikers brought together tens of thousands of supporters. And then a general strike was called in San Francisco, with 130,000 workers out, the city immobilized.

Five hundred special police were sworn in and 4,500 National Guardsmen assembled, with infantry, machine gun, tank and artillery units. The Los Angeles *Times* wrote:

The situation in San Francisco is not correctly described by the phrase "general strike." What is actually in progress there is an insurrection, a Communist-inspired and led revolt against organized government. There is but one thing to be done—put down the revolt with any force necessary.

The pressure became too strong. There were the troops. There was the AFL pushing to end the strike. The longshoremen accepted a compromise settlement. But they had shown the potential of a general strike.

That same summer of 1934, a strike of teamsters in Minneapolis was supported by other working people, and soon nothing was moving in the city except milk, ice, and coal trucks given exemptions by the strikers. Farmers drove their products into town and sold them directly to the people in the city. The police attacked and two strikers were killed. Fifty thousand people attended a mass funeral. There was an enormous protest meeting and a march on City Hall. After a month, the employers gave in to the teamsters' demands.

In the fall of that same year, 1934, came the largest strike of all—325,000 textile workers in the South. They left the mills and set up flying squadrons in trucks and autos to move through the strike areas, picketing, battling guards, entering the mills, unbelting machinery. Here too, as in the other cases, the strike impetus came from the rank and file, against a reluctant union leadership at the top. The *New York Times* said: "The grave danger of the situation is that it will get completely out of the hands of the leaders."

Again, the machinery of the state was set in motion. Deputies and armed strikebreakers in South Carolina fired on pickets, killing seven, wounding twenty others. But the strike was spreading to New England. In Lowell, Massachusetts, 2,500 textile workers rioted; in Saylesville, Rhode Island, a crowd of five thousand people defied state troopers who were armed with machine guns, and shut down the textile mill. In Woonsocket, Rhode Island, two thousand people, aroused because someone had been shot and killed by the National Guard, stormed through the town and closed the mill.

By September 18, 421,000 textile workers were on strike throughout the country. There were mass arrests, organizers were beaten, and the death toll rose to thirteen. Roosevelt now stepped in and set up a board of mediation, and the union called off the strike.

In the rural South, too, organizing took place, often stimulated by Communists, but nourished by the grievances of poor whites and blacks who were tenant farmers or farm laborers, always in economic difficulties but hit even harder by the Depression. The Southern Tenant Farmers Union started in Arkansas, with black and white sharecroppers, and spread to other areas. Roosevelt's AAA was not helping the poorest of farmers; in fact by encouraging farmers to plant less, it forced tenants and sharecroppers to leave the land. By 1935, of 6,800,000 farmers, 2,800,000 were tenants. The average income of a sharecropper was $312 a year. Farm laborers, moving from farm to farm, area to area, no land of their own, in 1933 were earning about $300 a year.

Black farmers were the worst off, and some were attracted to the strangers who began appearing in their area during the Depression, suggesting they organize. Nate Shaw recalls, in Theodore Rosengarten's remarkable interview (All God's Dangers):

And durin of the pressure years, a union begin to operate in this country, called it the Sharecroppers Union—that was a nice name, I thought . . . and I knowed what was goin on was a turnabout on the southern man, white and colored; it was somethin unusual. And I heard about it bein a organization for the poor class of people—that's just what I wanted to get into, too. I wanted to know the secrets of it enough that I could become in the knowledge of it. . . .

Mac Sloane, white man, said "You stay out of it. These niggers runnin around here carryin on some kind of meetin—you better stay out of it."

I said to myself, "You a fool if you think you can keep me from joinin". I went right on and joined it, just as quick as the next meetin come. . . . And he done just the thing to push me into it—gived me orders not to join.

The teachers of this organization begin to drive through this country— they couldn't let what they was doin be known. One of em was a colored fella; I disremember his name but he did a whole lot of time, holdin meetins with us—that was part of this job. . . .

Had the meetins at our houses or anywhere we could keep a look and a watch-out that nobody was comin in on us. Small meetins, sometimes there'd be a dozen . . . niggers was scared, niggers was scared, that's tellin the truth.

Nate Shaw told of what happened when a black farmer who hadn't paid his debts was about to be dispossessed:

The deputy said, "I'm goin to take all old Virgil Jones got this mornin." . . .

I begged him not to do it, begged him. "You'll dispossess him of bein able to feed his family."

Nate Shaw then told the deputy he was not going to allow it. The deputy came back with more men, and one of them shot and wounded Shaw, who then got his gun and fired back. He was arrested in late 1932, and served twelve years in an Alabama prison. His story is a tiny piece of the great unrecorded drama of the southern poor in those years of the Sharecroppers Union. Years after his release from prison, Nate Shaw spoke his mind on color and class:

O, it's plain as your hand. The poor white man and the poor black man is sittin in the same saddle today—big dudes done branched em off that way. The control of a man, the controllin power, is in the hands of the rich man. . . . That class is standin together and the poor white man is out there on the colored list—I've caught that: ways and actions a heap of times speaks louder than words. . . .

Hosea Hudson, a black man from rural Georgia, at the age of ten a plowhand, later an iron worker in Birmingham, was aroused by the case of the Scottsboro Boys in 1931 (nine black youths accused of raping two white girls and convicted on flimsy evidence by all-white juries). That year he joined the Communist party. In 1932 and 1933, he organized unemployed blacks in Birmingham. He recalls:

Deep in the winter of 1932 we Party members organized a unemployed mass meeting to be held on the old courthouse steps, on 3rd Avenue, North Birmingham. . . . It was about 7000 or more people turned out . . . Negroes and whites. . . .

In 1932 and '33 we began to organize these unemployed block committees in the various communities of Birmingham. . . . If someone get out of food. . . . We wouldn't go around and just say, "That's too bad". We make it our business to go see this person. . . . And if the person was willing . . . we'd work with them. . . .

Block committees would meet every week, had a regular meeting. We talked about the welfare question, what was happening, we read the *Daily Worker* and the *Southern Worker* to see what was going on about unemployed relief, what people doing in Cleveland . . . struggles in Chicago . . . or we talk about the latest developments in the Scottsboro case. We kept up, we was on top, so people always wanted to come cause we had something different to tell them every time.

In 1934 and 1935 hundreds of thousands of workers, left out of the tightly controlled, exclusive unions of the American Federation of Labor, began organizing in the new mass production industries—auto, rubber, packinghouse. The AFL could not ignore them; it set up a Committee for Industrial Organization to organize these workers outside of craft lines, by industry, all workers in a plant belonging to one union. This Committee, headed by John Lewis, then broke away and became the CIO—the Congress of Industrial Organizations.

But it was rank-and-file strikes and insurgencies that pushed the union leadership, AFL and CIO, into action. Jeremy Brecher tells the story in his book *Strike!* A new kind of tactic began among rubber workers in Akron, Ohio, in the early thirties—the sit-down strike. The workers stayed in the plant instead of walking out, and this had clear advantages: they were directly blocking the use of strikebreakers; they did not have to act through union officials but were in direct control of the situation themselves; they did not have to walk outside in the cold and rain, but had shelter; they were not isolated, as in their work, or on the picket line; they were thousands under one roof, free to talk to one another, to form a community of struggle. Louis Adamic, a labor writer, describes one of the early sit-downs:

Sitting by their machines, cauldrons, boilers and work benches, they talked. Some realized for the first time how important they were in the process of rubber production. Twelve men had practically stopped the works! . . . Superintendents, foremen, and straw bosses were dashing about. . . . In less than an hour the dispute was settled, full victory for the men.

In early 1936, at the Firestone rubber plant in Akron, makers of truck tires, their wages already too low to pay for food and rent, were faced with a wage cut. When several union men were fired, others began to stop work, to sit down on the job. In one day the whole of plant #1 was sitting down. In two days, plant #2 was sitting down, and management gave in. In the next ten days there was a sit-down at Goodyear. A court issued an injunction against mass picketing. It was ignored, and 150 deputies were sworn in. But they soon faced ten thousand workers from all over Akron. In a month the strike was won.

The idea spread through 1936. In December of that year began the longest sit-down strike of all, at Fisher Body plant #1 in Flint,

Michigan. It started when two brothers were fired, and it lasted until February 1937. For forty days there was a community of two thousand strikers. "It was like war," one said. "The guys with me became my buddies." Sidney Fine in *Sit-Down* describes what happened. Committees organized recreation, information, classes, a postal service, sanitation. Courts were set up to deal with those who didn't take their turn washing dishes or who threw rubbish or smoked where it was prohibited or brought in liquor. The "punishment" consisted of extra duties; the ultimate punishment was expulsion from the plant. A restaurant owner across the street prepared three meals a day for two thousand strikers. There were classes in parliamentary procedure, public speaking, history of the labor movement. Graduate students at the University of Michigan gave courses in journalism and creative writing.

There were injunctions, but a procession of five thousand armed workers encircled the plant and there was no attempt to enforce the injunction. Police attacked with tear gas and the workers fought back with firehoses. Thirteen strikers were wounded by gunfire, but the police were driven back. The governor called out the National Guard. By this time the strike had spread to other General Motors plants. Finally there was a settlement, a six-month contract, leaving many questions unsettled but recognizing that from now on, the company would have to deal not with individuals but with a union.

In 1936 there were forty-eight sitdown strikes. In 1937 there were 477: electrical workers in St. Louis; shirt workers in Pulaski, Tennessee; broom workers in Pueblo, Colorado; trash collectors in Bridgeport, Connecticut; gravediggers in New Jersey; seventeen blind workers at the New York Guild for the Jewish Blind; prisoners in an Illinois penitentiary; and even thirty members of a National Guard Company who had served in the Fisher Body sit-down, and now sat down themselves because they had not been paid.

The sit-downs were especially dangerous to the system because they were not controlled by the regular union leadership. An AFL business agent for the Hotel and Restaurant Employees said:

You'd be sitting in the office any March day of 1937, and the phone would ring and the voice at the other end would say: "My name is Mary Jones; I'm a soda clerk at Liggett's; we've thrown the manager out and we've got the keys. What do we do now?" And you'd hurry over to the company to negotiate and over there they'd say, "I think it's the height of irresponsibility to call a strike before you've ever asked for a contract" and all you could answer was, "You're so right."

It was to stabilize the system in the face of labor unrest that the Wagner Act of 1935, setting up a National Labor Relations Board, had been passed. The wave of strikes in 1936, 1937, 1938, made the need even more pressing. In Chicago, on Memorial Day, 1937, a strike at Republic Steel brought the police out, firing at a mass picket line of strikers, killing ten of them. Autopsies showed the bullets had hit the workers in the back as they were running away: this was the Memorial Day Massacre. But Republic Steel was organized, and so was Ford Motor Company, and the other huge plants in steel, auto, rubber, meatpacking, the electrical industry.

The Wagner Act was challenged by a steel corporation in the courts, but the Supreme Court found it constitutional—that the government could regulate interstate commerce, and that strikes hurt interstate commerce. From the trade unions' point of view, the new law was an aid to union organizing. From the government's point of view it was an aid to the stability of commerce.

Unions were not wanted by employers, but they were more controllable—more stabilizing for the system than the wildcat strikes, the factory occupations of the rank and file. In the spring of 1937, a *New York Times* article carried the headline "Unauthorized Sit-Downs Fought by CIO Unions." The story read: "Strict orders have been issued to all organizers and representatives that they will be dismissed if they authorize any stoppages of work without the consent of the international officers. . . ." The *Times* quoted John L. Lewis, dynamic leader of the CIO: "A CIO contract is adequate protection against sit-downs, lie-downs, or any other kind of strike."

The Communist party, some of whose members played critical roles in organizing CIO unions, seemed to take the same position. One Communist leader in Akron was reported to have said at a party strategy meeting after the sit-downs: "Now we must work for regular relations between the union and the employers—and strict observance of union procedure on the part of the workers."

Thus, two sophisticated ways of controlling direct labor action developed in the mid-thirties. First, the National Labor Relations Board would give unions legal status, listen to them, settling certain of their grievances. Thus it could moderate labor rebellion by channeling energy into elections—just as the constitutional system channeled possibly troublesome energy into voting. The NLRB would set limits in economic conflict as voting did in political conflict. And second, the workers' organization itself, the union, even a militant and aggressive union like the CIO, would channel the workers' insurrectionary energy into contracts, negotiations, union meetings, and try to minimize strikes, in order to build large, influential, even respectable organizations.

The history of those years seems to support the argument of Richard Cloward and Frances Piven, in their book *Poor People's Movements,* that labor won most during its spontaneous uprisings, before the unions were recognized or well organized: "Factory workers had their greatest influence, and were able to exact their most substantial concessions from government, during the Great Depression, in the years before they were organized into unions. Their power during the Depression was not rooted in organization, but in disruption."

Piven and Cloward point out that union membership rose enormously in the forties, during the Second World War (the CIO and AFL had over 6 million members each by 1945), but its power was less than before—its gains from the use of strikes kept getting whittled down. The members appointed to the NLRB were less sympathetic to labor, the Supreme Court declared sit-downs to be illegal, and state governments were passing laws to hamper strikes, picketing, boycotts.

The coming of World War II weakened the old labor militancy of the thirties because the war economy created millions of new jobs at higher wages. The New Deal had succeeded only in reducing unemployment from 13 million to 9 million. It was the war that put almost everyone to work, and the war did something else: patriotism, the push for unity of all classes against enemies overseas, made it harder to mobilize anger against the corporations. During the war, the CIO and AFL pledged to call no strikes.

Still, the grievances of workers were such—wartime "controls" meant their wages were being controlled better than prices—that they felt impelled to engage in many wildcat strikes: there were more strikes in 1944 than in any previous year in American history, says Jeremy Brecher.

The thirties and forties showed more clearly than before the dilemma of working people in the United States. The system responded to workers' rebellions by finding new forms of control—internal control by their own organizations as well as outside control by law and force. But along with the new controls came new concessions. These concessions didn't solve basic problems; for many people they solved nothing. But they helped enough people to create an atmosphere of progress and improvement, to restore some faith in the system.

The minimum wage of 1938, which established the forty-hour week and outlawed child labor, left many people out of its provisions and set very low minimum wages (twenty-five cents an hour the first year). But it was enough to dull the edge of resentment. Housing was built for only a small percentage of the people who needed it. "A modest, even parsimonious, beginning," Paul Conkin says *(F.D.R. and the Origins of the Welfare State),* but the sight of federally subsidized housing projects, playgrounds, vermin-free apartments, replacing dilapidated tenements, was refreshing. The TVA suggested exciting possibilities for regional planning to give jobs, improve areas, and provide cheap power, with local instead of national control. The Social Security Act gave retirement benefits and unemployment insurance, and matched state funds for mothers and dependent children—but it excluded farmers, domestic workers, and old people, and offered no health insurance. As Conkin says: "The meager benefits of Social Security were insignificant in comparison to the building of security for large, established businesses."

The New Deal gave federal money to put thousands of writers, artists, actors, and musicians to work—in a Federal Theatre Project, a Federal Writers Project, a Federal Art Project: murals were painted on public buildings; plays were put on for working-class audiences who had never seen a play; hundreds of books and pamphlets were written and published. People heard a symphony for the first time. It was an exciting flowering of arts for the people, such as had never happened before in American history, and which has not been duplicated since. But in 1939, with the country more stable and the New Deal reform impulse weakened, programs to subsidize the arts were eliminated.

When the New Deal was over, capitalism remained intact. The rich still controlled the nation's wealth, as well as its laws, courts, police, newspapers, churches, colleges. Enough help had been given to enough people to make Roosevelt a hero to millions, but the same system that had brought depression and crisis—the system of waste, of inequality, of concern for profit over human need—remained.

For black people, the New Deal was psychologically encouraging (Mrs. Roosevelt was sympathetic; some blacks got posts in the administration), but most blacks were ignored by the New Deal programs. As tenant farmers, as farm laborers, as migrants, as domestic workers, they didn't qualify for unemployment insurance, minimum wages, social security, or farm subsidies. Roosevelt, careful not to offend southern white politicians whose political support he needed, did not push a bill against lynching. Blacks and whites were segregated in the armed forces. And black workers were discriminated against in getting jobs. They were the last hired, the first fired. Only when A. Philip Randolph, head of the Sleeping-Car Porters Union, threatened a massive march on Washington in 1941 would Roosevelt agree to sign an executive order establishing a Fair Employment Practices Committee. But the FEPC had no enforcement powers and changed little.

Black Harlem, with all the New Deal reforms, remained as it was. There 350,000 people lived, 233 persons per acre compared with 133 for the rest of Manhattan. In twenty-five years, its population had multiplied six times. Ten thousand families lived in rat-infested cellars and basements. Tuberculosis was common. Perhaps half of the married women worked as domestics. They traveled to the Bronx and gathered on street corners—"slave markets," they were called—to be hired. Prostitution crept in. Two young black women, Ella Baker and Marvel Cooke, wrote about this in *The Crisis* in 1935:

> Not only is human labor bartered and sold for the slave wage, but human love is also a marketable commodity. Whether it is labor or love, the women arrive as early as eight a.m. and remain as late as one p.m. or until they are hired. In rain or shine, hot or cold, they wait to work for ten, fifteen, and twenty cents per hour.

In Harlem Hospital in 1932, proportionately twice as many people died as in Bellevue Hospital, which was in the white area downtown. Harlem was a place that bred crime—"the bitter blossom of poverty," as Roi Ottley and William Weatherby say in their essay "The Negro in New York."

On March 19, 1935, even as the New Deal reforms were being passed, Harlem exploded. Ten thousand Negroes swept through the streets, destroying the property of white merchants. Seven hundred policemen moved in and brought order. Two blacks were killed.

In the mid-thirties, a young black poet named Langston Hughes wrote a poem, "Let America Be America Again":

> . . . I am the poor white, fooled and pushed apart,
> I am the Negro bearing slavery's scars.
> I am the red man driven from the land,
> I am the immigrant clutching the hope I seek—
> And finding only the same old stupid plan.
> Of dog eat dog, of mighty crush the weak. . . .
>
> O, let America be America again—
> The land that never has been yet—

> And yet must be—the land where every man is free.
> The land that's mine—the poor man's, Indian's, Negro's
> ME—
> Who made America,
> Whose sweat and blood, whose faith and pain,
> Whose hand at the foundry, whose plow in the rain,
> Must bring back our mighty dream again.
>
> Sure, call me any ugly name you choose—
> The steel of freedom does not stain.
> From those who live like leeches on the people's lives,
> We must take back our land again,
> America! . . .

To white Americans of the thirties, however, North and South, blacks were invisible. Only the radicals made an attempt to break the racial barriers: Socialists, Trotskyists, Communists most of all. The CIO, influenced by the Communists, was organizing blacks in the mass production industries. Blacks were still being used as strikebreakers, but now there were also attempts to bring blacks and whites together against their common enemy. A woman named Mollie Lewis, writing in *The Crisis,* in 1938, told of her experience in a steel strike in Gary, Indiana:

> While the municipal government of Gary continues to keep the children apart in a system of separate schools, their parents are getting together in the union and in the auxiliary. . . . The only public eating place in Gary where both races may be freely served is a cooperative restaurant largely patronized by members of the union and auxiliary. . . .
>
> When the black and white workers and members of their families are convinced that their basic economic interests are the same, they may be expected to make common cause for the advancement of these interests. . . .

There was no great feminist movement in the thirties. But many women became involved in the labor organizing of those years. A Minnesota poet, Meridel LeSeuer, was thirty-four when the great teamsters' strike tied up Minneapolis in 1934. She became active in it, and later described her experiences:

> I have never been in a strike before. . . . The truth is I was afraid. . . . "Do you need any help?" I said eagerly. . . . We kept on pouring thousands of cups of coffee, feeding thousands of men. . . . The cars were coming back. The announcer cried, "This is murder." . . . I saw them taking men out of cars and putting them on the hospital cots, on the floor. . . . The

picket cars keep coming in. Some men have walked back from the market, holding their own blood in. . . . Men, women and children are massing outside, a living circle close packed for protection. . . . We have living blood on our skirts. . . .

Tuesday, the day of the funeral, one thousand more militia were massed downtown.

It was over ninety in the shade. I went to the funeral parlors and thousands of men and women were massed there waiting in the terrific sun. One block of women and children were standing two hours waiting. I went over and stood near them. I didn't know whether I could march. I didn't like marching in parades. . . . Three women drew me in. "We want all to march," they said gently. "Come with us." . . .

Sylvia Woods spoke to Alice and Staughton Lynd years later about her experiences in the thirties as a laundry worker and union organizer:

You have to tell people things they can see. Then they'll say, "Oh, I never thought of that" or "I have never seen it like that." . . . Like Tennessee. He hated black people. A poor sharecropper. . . . He danced with a black woman. . . . So I have seen people change. This is the faith you've got to have in people.

Many Americans began to change their thinking in those days of crisis and rebellion. In Europe, Hitler was on the march. Across the Pacific, Japan was invading China. The Western empires were being threatened by new ones. For the United States, war was not far off.

5.
A People's War?

"We, the governments of Great Britain and the United States, in the name of India, Burma, Malaya, Australia, British East Africa, British Guiana, Hongkong, Siam, Singapore, Egypt, Palestine, Canada, New Zealand, Northern Ireland, Scotland, Wales, as well as Puerto Rico, Guam, the Philippines, Hawaii, Alaska, and the Virgin Islands, hereby declare most emphatically, that this is not an imperialist war." Thus went a skit put on in the United States in the year 1939 by the Communist party.

Two years later, Germany invaded Soviet Russia, and the American Communist party, which had repeatedly described the war between the Axis Powers and the Allied Powers as an imperialist war, now called it a "people's war" against Fascism. Indeed almost all Americans were now in agreement—capitalists, Communists, Democrats, Republicans, poor, rich, and middle class—that this was indeed a people's war.

Was it?

By certain evidence, it was the most popular war the United States had ever fought. Never had a greater proportion of the country participated in a war: 18 million served in the armed forces, 10 million overseas; 25 million workers gave of their pay envelope regularly for war bonds. But could this be considered a manufactured support, since all the power of the nation—not only of the government, but the press, the church, and even the chief radical organizations—was behind the calls for all-out war? Was there an undercurrent of reluctance; were there unpublicized signs of resistance?

It was a war against an enemy of unspeakable evil. Hitler's Germany was extending totalitarianism, racism, militarism, and overt aggressive warfare beyond what an already cynical world had experienced. And yet, did the governments conducting this war—England, the United States, the Soviet Union—represent something significantly different, so that their victory would be a blow to imperialism, racism, totalitarianism, militarism, in the world?

Would the behavior of the United States during the war—in mili-

tary action abroad, in treatment of minorities at home—be in keeping
with a "people's war"? Would the country's wartime policies respect
the rights of ordinary people everywhere to life, liberty, and the pursuit
of happiness? And would postwar America, in its policies at home
and overseas, exemplify the values for which the war was supposed
to have been fought?

These questions deserve thought. At the time of World War II,
the atmosphere was too dense with war fervor to permit them to be
aired.

For the United States to step forward as a defender of helpless
countries matched its image in American high school history textbooks,
but not its record in world affairs. It had instigated a war with Mexico
and taken half of that country. It had pretended to help Cuba win
freedom from Spain, and then planted itself in Cuba with a military
base, investments, and rights of intervention. It had seized Hawaii,
Puerto Rico, Guam, and fought a brutal war to subjugate the Filipinos.
It had "opened" Japan to its trade with gunboats and threats. It had
declared an Open Door Policy in China as a means of assuring that
the United States would have opportunities equal to other imperial
powers in exploiting China. It had sent troops to Peking with other
nations, to assert Western supremacy in China, and kept them there
for over thirty years.

While demanding an Open Door in China, it had insisted (with
the Monroe Doctrine and many military interventions) on a Closed
Door in Latin America—that is, closed to everyone but the United
States. It had engineered a revolution against Colombia and created
the "independent" state of Panama in order to build and control the
Canal. It sent five thousand marines to Nicaragua in 1926 to counter
a revolution, and kept a force there for seven years. It intervened in
the Dominican Republic for the fourth time in 1916 and kept troops
there for eight years. It intervened for the second time in Haiti in
1915 and kept troops there for nineteen years. Between 1900 and 1933,
the United States intervened in Cuba four times, in Nicaragua twice,
in Panama six times, in Guatemala once, in Honduras seven times.
By 1924 the finances of half of the twenty Latin American states were
being directed to some extent by the United States. By 1935, over half
of U.S. steel and cotton exports were being sold in Latin America.

Just before World War I ended, in 1918, an American force of
seven thousand landed at Vladivostok as part of an Allied intervention
in Russia, and remained until early 1920. Five thousand more troops

were landed at Archangel, another Russian port, also as part of an Allied expeditionary force, and stayed for almost a year. The State Department told Congress: "All these operations were to offset effects of the Bolshevik revolution in Russia."

In short, if the entrance of the United States into World War II was (as so many Americans believed at the time, observing the Nazi invasions) to defend the principle of nonintervention in the affairs of other countries, the nation's record cast doubt on its ability to uphold that principle.

What seemed clear at the time was that the United States was a democracy with certain liberties, while Germany was a dictatorship persecuting its Jewish minority, imprisoning dissidents, whatever their religion, while proclaiming the supremacy of the Nordic "race." However, blacks, looking at anti-Semitism in Germany, might not see their own situation in the U.S. as much different. And the United States had done little about Hitler's policies of persecution. Indeed, it had joined England and France in appeasing Hitler throughout the thirties. Roosevelt and his Secretary of State, Cordell Hull, were hesitant to criticize publicly Hitler's anti-Semitic policies; when a resolution was introduced in the Senate in January 1934 asking the Senate and the President to express "surprise and pain" at what the Germans were doing to the Jews, and to ask restoration of Jewish rights, the State Department "caused this resolution to be buried in committee," according to Arnold Offner (American Appeasement).

When Mussolini's Italy invaded Ethiopia in 1935, the U.S. declared an embargo on munitions but let American businesses send oil to Italy in huge quantities, which was essential to Italy's carrying on the war. When a Fascist rebellion took place in Spain in 1936 against the elected socialist-liberal government, the Roosevelt administration sponsored a neutrality act that had the effect of shutting off help to the Spanish government while Hitler and Mussolini gave critical aid to Franco. Offner says:

. . . the United States went beyond even the legal requirements of its neutrality legislation. Had aid been forthcoming from the United States and from England and France, considering that Hitler's position on aid to Franco was not firm at least until November 1936, the Spanish Republicans could well have triumphed. Instead, Germany gained every advantage from the Spanish civil war.

Was this simply poor judgment, an unfortunate error? Or was it the logical policy of a government whose main interest was not stopping

Fascism but advancing the imperial interests of the United States? For those interests, in the thirties, an anti-Soviet policy seemed best. Later, when Japan and Germany threatened U.S. world interests, a pro-Soviet, anti-Nazi policy became preferable. Roosevelt was as much concerned to end the oppression of Jews as Lincoln was to end slavery during the Civil War; their priority in policy (whatever their personal compassion for victims of persecution) was not minority rights, but national power.

It was not Hitler's attacks on the Jews that brought the United States into World War II, any more than the enslavement of 4 million blacks brought Civil War in 1861. Italy's attack on Ethiopia, Hitler's invasion of Austria, his takeover of Czechoslovakia, his attack on Poland—none of those events caused the United States to enter the war, although Roosevelt did begin to give important aid to England. What brought the United States fully into the war was the Japanese attack on the American naval base at Pearl Harbor, Hawaii, on December 7, 1941. Surely it was not the humane concern for Japan's bombing of civilians that led to Roosevelt's outraged call for war—Japan's attack on China in 1937, her bombing of civilians at Nanking, had not provoked the United States to war. It was the Japanese attack on a link in the American Pacific Empire that did it.

So long as Japan remained a well-behaved member of that imperial club of Great Powers who—in keeping with the Open Door Policy— were sharing the exploitation of China, the United States did not object. It had exchanged notes with Japan in 1917 saying "the Government of the United States recognizes that Japan has special interests in China." In 1928, according to Akira Iriye *(After Imperialism)*, American consuls in China supported the coming of Japanese troops. It was when Japan threatened potential U.S. markets by its attempted takeover of China, but especially as it moved toward the tin, rubber, and oil of Southeast Asia, that the United States became alarmed and took those measures which led to the Japanese attack: a total embargo on scrap iron, a total embargo on oil in the summer of 1941.

As Bruce Russett says *(No Clear and Present Danger):* "Throughout the 1930s the United States government had done little to resist the Japanese advance on the Asian continent." But: "The Southwest Pacific area was of undeniable economic importance to the United States—at the time most of America's tin and rubber came from there, as did substantial quantities of other raw materials."

Pearl Harbor was presented to the American public as a sudden, shocking, immoral act. Immoral it was, like any bombing—but not really sudden or shocking to the American government. Russett says: "Japan's strike against the American naval base climaxed a long series of mutually antagonistic acts. In initiating economic sanctions against Japan the United States undertook actions that were widely recognized in Washington as carrying grave risks of war."

Putting aside the wild accusations against Roosevelt (that he knew about Pearl Harbor and didn't tell, or that he deliberately provoked the Pearl Harbor raid—these are without evidence), it does seem clear that he did as James Polk had done before him in the Mexican war and Lyndon Johnson after him in the Vietnam war—he lied to the public for what he thought was a right cause. In September and October 1941, he misstated the facts in two incidents involving German submarines and American destroyers. A historian sympathetic to Roosevelt, Thomas A. Bailey, has written:

Franklin Roosevelt repeatedly deceived the American people during the period before Pearl Harbor. . . . He was like the physician who must tell the patient lies for the patient's own good . . . because the masses are notoriously shortsighted and generally cannot see danger until it is at their throats. . . .

One of the judges in the Tokyo War Crimes Trial after World War II, Radhabinod Pal, dissented from the general verdicts against Japanese officials and argued that the United States had clearly provoked the war with Japan and expected Japan to act. Richard Minear (Victors' Justice) sums up Pal's view of the embargoes on scrap iron and oil, that "these measures were a clear and potent threat to Japan's very existence." The records show that a White House conference two weeks before Pearl Harbor anticipated a war and discussed how it should be justified.

A State Department memorandum on Japanese expansion, a year before Pearl Harbor, did not talk of the independence of China or the principle of self-determination. It said:

. . . our general diplomatic and strategic position would be considerably weakened—by our loss of Chinese, Indian and South Seas markets (and by our loss of much of the Japanese market for our goods, as Japan would become more and more self-sufficient) as well as by insurmountable restrictions upon our access to the rubber, tin, jute, and other vital materials of the Asian and Oceanic regions.

Once joined with England and Russia in the war (Germany and Italy declared war on the United States right after Pearl Harbor), did the behavior of the United States show that her war aims were humanitarian, or centered on power and profit? Was she fighting the war to end the control by some nations over others or to make sure the controlling nations were friends of the United States? In August 1941, Roosevelt and Churchill met off the coast of Newfoundland and released to the world the Atlantic Charter, setting forth noble goals for the postwar world, saying their countries "seek no aggrandizement, territorial or other," and that they respected "the right of all peoples to choose the form of government under which they will live." The Charter was celebrated as declaring the right of nations to self-determination.

Two weeks before the Atlantic Charter, however, the U.S. Acting Secretary of State, Sumner Welles, had assured the French government that they could keep their empire intact after the end of the war: "This Government, mindful of its traditional friendship for France, has deeply sympathized with the desire of the French people to maintain their territories and to preserve them intact." The Department of Defense history of Vietnam (The Pentagon Papers) itself pointed to what it called an "ambivalent" policy toward Indochina, noting that "in the Atlantic Charter and other pronouncements, the U.S. proclaimed support for national self-determination and independence" but also "early in the war repeatedly expressed or implied to the French an intention to restore to France its overseas empire after the war."

In late 1942, Roosevelt's personal representative assured French General Henri Giraud: "It is thoroughly understood that French sovereignty will be re-established as soon as possible throughout all the territory, metropolitan or colonial, over which flew the French flag in 1939." (These pages, like the others in the Pentagon Papers, are marked "TOP SECRET—Sensitive.") By 1945 the "ambivalent" attitude was gone. In May, Truman assured the French he did not question her "sovereignty over Indochina." That fall, the United States urged Nationalist China, put temporarily in charge of the northern part of Indochina by the Potsdam Conference, to turn it over to the French, despite the obvious desire of the Vietnamese for independence.

That was a favor for the French government. But what about the United States' own imperial ambitions during the war? What about the "aggrandizement, territorial or other" that Roosevelt had renounced in the Atlantic Charter?

In the headlines were the battles and troop movements: the invasion of North Africa in 1942, Italy in 1943, the massive, dramatic cross-Channel invasion of German-occupied France in 1944, the bitter battles as Germany was pushed back toward and over her frontiers, the increasing bombardment by the British and American air forces. And, at the same time, the Russian victories over the Nazi armies (the Russians, by the time of the cross-Channel invasion, had driven the Germans out of Russia, and were engaging 80 percent of the German troops). In the Pacific, in 1943 and 1944, there was the island-by-island move of American forces toward Japan, finding closer and closer bases for the thunderous bombardment of Japanese cities.

Quietly, behind the headlines in battles and bombings, American diplomats and businessmen worked hard to make sure that when the war ended, American economic power would be second to none in the world. United States business would penetrate areas that up to this time had been dominated by England. The Open Door Policy of equal access would be extended from Asia to Europe, meaning that the United States intended to push England aside and move in.

That is what happened to the Middle East and its oil. In August 1945 a State Department officer said that "a review of the diplomatic history of the past 35 years will show that petroleum has historically played a larger part in the external relations of the United States than any other commodity." Saudi Arabia was the largest oil pool in the Middle East. The ARAMCO oil corporation, through Secretary of the Interior Harold Ickes, got Roosevelt to agree to Lend Lease aid to Saudi Arabia, which would involve the U.S. government there and create a shield for the interests of ARAMCO. In 1944 Britain and the U.S. signed a pact on oil agreeing on "the principle of equal opportunity," and Lloyd Gardner concludes (Economic Aspects of New Deal Diplomacy) that "the Open Door Policy was triumphant throughout the Middle East."

Historian Gabriel Kolko, after a close study of American wartime policy (The Politics of War), concludes that "the American economic war aim was to save capitalism at home and abroad." In April 1944 a State Department official said: "As you know, we've got to plan on enormously increased production in this country after the war, and the American domestic market can't absorb all that production indefinitely. There won't be any question about our needing greatly increased foreign markets."

Anthony Sampson, in his study of the international oil business (The Seven Sisters), says:

By the end of the war the dominant influence in Saudi Arabia was unquestionably the United States. King Ibn Saud was regarded no longer as a wild desert warrior, but as a key piece in the power-game, to be wooed by the West. Roosevelt, on his way back from Yalta in February 1945, entertained the King on the cruiser *Quincy,* together with his entourage of fifty, including two sons, a prime minister, an astrologer and flocks of sheep for slaughter.

Roosevelt then wrote to Ibn Saud, promising the United States would not change its Palestine policy without consulting the Arabs. In later years, the concern for oil would constantly compete with political concern for the Jewish state in the Middle East, but at this point, oil seemed more important.

With British imperial power collapsing during World War II, the United States was ready to move in. Hull said early in the war:

> Leadership toward a new system of international relationships in trade and other economic affairs will devolve very largely upon the United States because of our great economic strength. We should assume this leadership, and the responsibility that goes with it, primarily for reasons of pure national self-interest.

Before the war was over, the administration was planning the outlines of the new international economic order, based on partnership between government and big business. Lloyd Gardner says of Roosevelt's chief adviser, Harry Hopkins, who had organized the relief programs of the New Deal: "No conservative outdid Hopkins in championing foreign investment, and its protection."

The poet Archibald MacLeish, then an Assistant Secretary of State, spoke critically of what he saw in the postwar world: "As things are now going, the peace we will make, the peace we seem to be making, will be a peace of oil, a peace of gold, a peace of shipping, a peace, in brief . . . without moral purpose or human interest. . . ."

During the war, England and the United States set up the International Monetary Fund to regulate international exchanges of currency; voting would be proportional to capital contributed, so American dominance would be assured. The International Bank for Reconstruction and Development was set up, supposedly to help reconstruct war-destroyed areas, but one of its first objectives was, in its own words, "to promote foreign investment."

The economic aid countries would need after the war was already seen in political terms: Averell Harriman, ambassador to Russia, said in early 1944: "Economic assistance is one of the most effective weapons at our disposal to influence European political events in the direction we desire. . . ."

The creation of the United Nations during the war was presented to the world as international cooperation to prevent future wars. But the U.N. was dominated by the Western imperial countries—the United States, England, and France—and a new imperial power, with military bases and powerful influence in Eastern Europe—the Soviet Union. An important conservative Republican Senator, Arthur Vandenburg, wrote in his diary about the United Nations Charter:

> The striking thing about it is that it is so conservative from a nationalist standpoint. It is based virtually on a four-power alliance. . . . This is anything but a wild-eyed internationalist dream of a world State. . . . I am deeply impressed (and surprised) to find Hull so carefully guarding our American veto in his scheme of things.

The plight of Jews in German-occupied Europe, which many people thought was at the heart of the war against the Axis, was not a chief concern of Roosevelt. Henry Feingold's research *(The Politics of Rescue)* shows that, while the Jews were being put in camps and the process of annihilation was beginning that would end in the horrifying extermination of 6 million Jews and millions of non-Jews, Roosevelt failed to take steps that might have saved thousands of lives. He did not see it as a high priority; he left it to the State Department, and in the State Department anti-Semitism and a cold bureaucracy became obstacles to action.

Was the war being fought to establish that Hitler was wrong in his ideas of white Nordic supremacy over "inferior" races? The United States' armed forces were segregated by race. When troops were jammed onto the *Queen Mary* in early 1945 to go to combat duty in the European theater, the blacks were stowed down in the depths of the ship near the engine room, as far as possible from the fresh air of the deck, in a bizarre reminder of the slave voyages of old.

The Red Cross, with government approval, separated the blood donations of black and white. It was, ironically, a black physician named Charles Drew who developed the blood bank system. He was put in charge of the wartime donations, and then fired when he tried to end blood segregation. Despite the urgent need for wartime labor, blacks were still being discriminated against for jobs. A spokesman for a West Coast aviation plant said: "The Negro will be considered only as janitors and in other similar capacities. . . . Regardless of their training as aircraft workers, we will not employ them." Roosevelt never did anything to enforce the orders of the Fair Employment Practices Commission he had set up.

The Fascist nations were notorious in their insistence that the woman's place was in the home. Yet, the war against Fascism, although it utilized women in defense industries where they were desperately needed, took no special steps to change the subordinate role of women. The War Manpower Commission, despite the large numbers of women in war work, kept women off its policymaking bodies. A report of the Women's Bureau of the Department of Labor, by its director, Mary Anderson, said the War Manpower Commission had "doubts and uneasiness" about "what was then regarded as a developing attitude of militancy or a crusading spirit on the part of women leaders. . . ."

In one of its policies, the United States came close to direct duplication of Fascism. This was in its treatment of the Japanese-Americans living on the West Coast. After the Pearl Harbor attack, anti-Japanese hysteria spread in the government. One Congressman said: "I'm for catching every Japanese in America, Alaska and Hawaii now and putting them in concentration camps. . . . Damn them! Let's get rid of them!"

Franklin D. Roosevelt did not share this frenzy, but he calmly signed Executive Order 9066, in February 1942, giving the army the power, without warrants or indictments or hearings, to arrest every Japanese-American on the West Coast—110,000 men, women, and children—to take them from their homes, transport them to camps far into the interior, and keep them there under prison conditions. Three-fourths of these were Nisei—children born in the United States of Japanese parents and therefore American citizens. The other fourth—the Issei, born in Japan—were barred by law from becoming citizens. In 1944 the Supreme Court upheld the forced evacuation on the grounds of military necessity. The Japanese remained in those camps for over three years.

Michi Weglyn was a young girl when her family experienced evacuation and detention. She tells *(Years of Infamy)* of bungling in the evacuation, of misery, confusion, anger, but also of Japanese-American dignity and fighting back. There were strikes, petitions, mass meetings, refusal to sign loyalty oaths, riots against the camp authorities. The Japanese resisted to the end.

Not until after the war did the story of the Japanese-Americans begin to be known to the general public. The month the war ended in Asia, September 1945, an article appeared in *Harper's Magazine* by Yale Law Professor Eugene V. Rostow, calling the Japanese evacuation "our worst wartime mistake." Was it a "mistake"—or was it an action to be expected from a nation with a long history of racism and which was fighting a war, not to end racism, but to retain the fundamental elements of the American system?

It was a war waged by a government whose chief beneficiary—despite volumes of reforms—was a wealthy elite. The alliance between big business and the government went back to the very first proposals of Alexander Hamilton to Congress after the Revolutionary War. By World War II that partnership had developed and intensified. During the Depression, Roosevelt had once denounced the "economic royalists," but he always had the support of certain important business leaders. During the war, as Bruce Catton saw it from his post in the War Production Board: "The economic royalists, denounced and derided . . . had a part to play now. . . ."

Catton (*The War Lords of Washington*) described the process of industrial mobilization to carry on the war, and how in this process wealth became more and more concentrated in fewer and fewer large corporations. In 1940 the United States had begun sending large amounts of war supplies to England and France. By 1941 three-fourths of the value of military contracts were handled by fifty-six large corporations. A Senate report, "Economic Concentration and World War II," noted that the government contracted for scientific research in industry during the war, and although two thousand corporations were involved, of $1 billion spent, $400 million went to ten large corporations.

Management remained firmly in charge of decisionmaking during the war, and although 12 million workers were organized in the CIO and AFL, labor was in a subordinate position. Labor-management committees were set up in five thousand factories, as a gesture toward industrial democracy, but they acted mostly as disciplinary groups for absentee workers, and devices for increasing production. Catton writes: "The big operators who made the working decisions had decided that nothing very substantial was going to be changed."

Despite the overwhelming atmosphere of patriotism and total dedication to winning the war, despite the no-strike pledges of the AFL and CIO, many of the nation's workers, frustrated by the freezing of wages while business profits rocketed skyward, went on strike. During the war, there were fourteen thousand strikes, involving 6,770,000 workers, more than in any comparable period in American history. In 1944 alone, a million workers were on strike, in the mines, in the steel mills, in the auto and transportation equipment industries.

When the war ended, the strikes continued in record numbers—3 million on strike in the first half of 1946. According to Jeremy Brecher *(Strike!)*, if not for the disciplinary hand of the unions there might have been "a general confrontation between the workers of a great many industries, and the government, supporting the employers."

In Lowell, Massachusetts, for example, according to an unpublished manuscript by Marc Miller ("The Irony of Victory: Lowell During World War II"), there were as many strikes in 1943 and 1944 as in 1937. It may have been a "people's war," but here was dissatisfaction at the fact that the textile mill profits grew 600 percent from 1940 to 1946, while wage increases in cotton goods industries went up 36 percent. How little the war changed the difficult condition of women workers is shown by the fact that in Lowell, among women war workers with children, only 5 percent could have their children taken care of by nursery schools; the others had to make their own arrangements.

Beneath the noise of enthusiastic patriotism, there were many people who thought war was wrong, even in the circumstances of Fascist aggression. Out of 10 million drafted for the armed forces during World War II, only 43,000 refused to fight. But this was three times the proportion of C.O.'s (conscientious objectors) in World War I. Of these 43,000, about 6,000 went to prison, which was, proportionately, four times the number of C.O.'s who went to prison during World War I. Of every six men in federal prison, one was there as a C.O.

Many more than 43,000 refusers did not show up for the draft at all. The government lists about 350,000 cases of draft evasion, including technical violations as well as actual desertion, so it is hard to tell the true number, but it may be that the number of men who either did not show up or claimed C.O. status was in the hundreds of thousands—not a small number. And this in the face of an American community almost unanimously for the war.

Among those soldiers who were not conscientious objectors, who seemed willing fighters, it is hard to know how much resentment there was against authority, against having to fight in a war whose aims were unclear, inside a military machine whose lack of democracy was very clear. No one recorded the bitterness of enlisted men against the special privileges of officers in the army of a country known as a democracy. To give just one instance: combat crews in the air force in the European theater, going to the base movies between bombing missions, found two lines—an officers' line (short), and an enlisted men's line (very long). There were two mess halls, even as they prepared to go into combat: the enlisted men's food was different—worse—than the officers'.

The literature that followed World War II, James Jones's *From Here to Eternity*, Joseph Heller's *Catch-22*, and Norman Mailer's *The Naked and the Dead*, captured this GI anger against the army "brass." In *The Naked and the Dead*, the soldiers talk in battle, and one of them says: "The only thing wrong with this Army is it never lost a war."

Toglio was shocked. "You think we ought to lose this one?"
Red found himself carried away. "What have I against the goddam Japs? You think I care if they keep this fuggin jungle? What's it to me if Cummings gets another star?"
"General Cummings, he's a good man," Martinez said.
"There ain't a good officer in the world," Red stated.

There seemed to be widespread indifference, even hostility, on the part of the Negro community to the war despite the attempts of Negro newspapers and Negro leaders to mobilize black sentiment. Lawrence Wittner *(Rebels Against War)* quotes a black journalist: "The Negro . . . is angry, resentful, and utterly apathetic about the war. 'Fight for what?' he is asking. 'This war doesn't mean a thing to me. If we win I lose, so what?' " A black army officer, home on furlough, told friends in Harlem he had been in hundreds of bull sessions with Negro soldiers and found no interest in the war.

A student at a Negro college told his teacher: "The Army jim-crows us. The Navy lets us serve only as messmen. The Red Cross refuses our blood. Employers and labor unions shut us out. Lynchings continue. We are disenfranchised, jim-crowed, spat upon. What more could Hitler do than that?" NAACP leader Walter White repeated this to a black audience of several thousand people in the Midwest, thinking they would disapprove, but instead, as he recalled: "To my surprise and dismay the audience burst into such applause that it took me some thirty or forty seconds to quiet it."

In January 1943, there appeared in a Negro newspaper this "Draftee's Prayer":

Dear Lord, today
I go to war:
To fight, to die,
Tell me what for?

Dear Lord, I'll fight,
I do not fear,
Germans or Japs;
My fears are here.
America!

But there was no organized Negro opposition to the war. In fact, there was little organized opposition from any source. The Communist party was enthusiastically in support. The Socialist party was divided, unable to make a clear statement one way or the other.

A few small anarchist and pacifist groups refused to back the war. The Women's International League for Peace and Freedom said: ". . . war between nations or classes or races cannot permanently settle conflicts or heal the wounds that brought them into being." The *Catholic Worker* wrote: "We are still pacifists. . . ."

The difficulty of merely calling for "peace" in a world of capitalism, Fascism, Communism—dynamic ideologies, aggressive actions—troubled some pacifists. They began to speak of "revolutionary nonviolence." A. J. Muste of the Fellowship of Reconciliation said in later years: "I was not impressed with the sentimental, easygoing pacifism of the earlier part of the century. People then felt that if they sat and talked pleasantly of peace and love, they would solve the problems of the world." The world was in the midst of a revolution, Muste realized, and those against violence must take revolutionary action, but without violence. A movement of revolutionary pacifism would have to "make effective contacts with oppressed and minority groups such as Negroes, share-croppers, industrial workers."

Only one organized socialist group opposed the war unequivocally. This was the Socialist Workers Party. The Espionage Act of 1917, still on the books, applied to wartime statements. But in 1940, with the United States not yet at war, Congress passed the Smith Act. This took Espionage Act prohibitions against talk or writing that would lead to refusal of duty in the armed forces and applied them to peacetime. The Smith Act also made it a crime to advocate the overthrow of the government by force and violence, or to join any group that advocated this, or to publish anything with such ideas. In Minneapolis in 1943, eighteen members of the Socialist Workers party were convicted for belonging to a party whose ideas, expressed in its Declaration of Principles, and in the *Communist Manifesto,* were said to violate the Smith Act. They were sentenced to prison terms, and the Supreme Court refused to review their case.

A few voices continued to insist that the real war was inside each nation: Dwight Macdonald's wartime magazine *Politics* presented, in early 1945, an article by the French worker-philosopher Simone Weil:

> Whether the mask is labelled Fascism, Democracy, or Dictatorship of the Proletariat, our great adversary remains the Apparatus—the bureaucracy, the police, the military. Not the one facing us across the frontier or the battle-lines, which is not so much our enemy as our brothers' enemy, but the one that calls itself our protector and makes us its slaves. No matter what the circumstances, the worst betrayal will always be to subordinate ourselves to this Apparatus, and to trample underfoot, in its service, all human values in ourselves and in others.

Still, the vast bulk of the American population was mobilized, in the army, and in civilian life, to fight the war, and the atmosphere of war enveloped more and more Americans. Public opinion polls show large majorities of soldiers favoring the draft for the postwar period. Hatred against the enemy, against the Japanese particularly, became widespread. Racism was clearly at work. *Time* magazine, reporting the battle of Iwo Jima, said: "The ordinary unreasoning Jap is ignorant. Perhaps he is human. Nothing . . . indicates it."

So, there was a mass base of support for what became the heaviest bombardment of civilians ever undertaken in any war: the aerial attacks on German and Japanese cities. One might argue that this popular support made it a "people's war." But if "people's war" means a war of people against attack, a defensive war—if it means a war fought for humane reasons instead of for the privileges of an elite, a war against the few, not the many—then the tactics of all-out aerial assault against the populations of Germany and Japan destroy that notion.

Italy had bombed cities in the Ethiopian war; Italy and Germany had bombed civilians in the Spanish Civil War; at the start of World War II German planes dropped bombs on Rotterdam in Holland, Coventry in England, and elsewhere. Roosevelt had described these as "inhuman barbarism that has profoundly shocked the conscience of humanity."

These German bombings were very small compared with the British and American bombings of German cities. In January 1943 the Allies met at Casablanca and agreed on large-scale air attacks to achieve "the destruction and dislocation of the German military, industrial and economic system and the undermining of the morale of the German people to the point where their capacity for armed resistance is fatally weakened." And so, the saturation bombing of German cities began—with thousand-plane raids on Cologne, Essen, Frankfurt, Hamburg. The English flew at night with no pretense of aiming at "military" targets; the Americans flew in the daytime and pretended precision, but bombing from high altitudes made that impossible. The climax of this terror bombing was the bombing of Dresden in early 1945, in which the tremendous heat generated by the bombs created a vacuum into which fire leaped swiftly in a great firestorm through the city. More than 100,000 died in Dresden. (Winston Churchill, in his wartime memoirs, confined himself to this account of the incident: "We made a heavy raid in the latter month on Dresden, then a centre of communication of Germany's Eastern Front.")

The bombing of Japanese cities continued the strategy of saturation bombing to destroy civilian morale; one nighttime fire-bombing of Tokyo took 80,000 lives. And then, on August 6, 1945, came the lone American plane in the sky over Hiroshima, dropping the first atomic bomb, leaving perhaps 100,000 Japanese dead, and tens of thousands more slowly dying from radiation poisoning. Twelve U.S. navy fliers in the Hiroshima city jail were killed in the bombing, a fact that the U.S. government has never officially acknowledged, according to historian Martin Sherwin (A World Destroyed). Three days later, a second atomic bomb was dropped on the city of Nagasaki, with perhaps 50,000 killed.

The justification for these atrocities was that this would end the war quickly, making unnecessary an invasion of Japan. Such an invasion would cost a huge number of lives, the government said—a million, according to Secretary of State Byrnes; half a million, Truman claimed was the figure given him by General George Marshall. (When the papers of the Manhattan Project—the project to build the atom bomb—were released years later, they showed that Marshall urged a warning to the Japanese about the bomb, so people could be removed and only military targets hit.) These estimates of invasion losses were not realistic, and seem to have been pulled out of the air to justify bombings which, as their effects became known, horrified more and more people. Japan, by August 1945, was in desperate shape and ready to surrender. New York Times military analyst Hanson Baldwin wrote, shortly after the war:

The enemy, in a military sense, was in a hopeless strategic position by the time the Potsdam demand for unconditional surrender was made on July 26.

Such then, was the situation when we wiped out Hiroshima and Nagasaki.

Need we have done it? No one can, of course, be positive, but the answer is almost certainly negative.

The United States Strategic Bombing Survey, set up by the War Department in 1944 to study the results of aerial attacks in the war, interviewed hundreds of Japanese civilian and military leaders after Japan surrendered, and reported just after the war:

Based on a detailed investigation of all the facts and supported by the testimony of the surviving Japanese leaders involved, it is the Survey's opinion that certainly prior to 31 December 1945, and in all probability prior to 1 November 1945, Japan would have surrendered even if the atomic bombs had not been dropped, even if Russia had not entered the war, and even if no invasion had been planned or contemplated.

But could American leaders have known this in August 1945? The answer is, clearly, yes. The Japanese code had been broken, and Japan's messages were being intercepted. It was known the Japanese had instructed their ambassador in Moscow to work on peace negotiations with the Allies. Japanese leaders had begun talking of surrender a year before this, and the Emperor himself had begun to suggest, in June 1945, that alternatives to fighting to the end be considered. On July 13, Foreign Minister Shigenori Togo wired his ambassador in Moscow: "Unconditional surrender is the only obstacle to peace. . . ." Martin Sherwin, after an exhaustive study of the relevant historical documents, concludes: "Having broken the Japanese code before the war, American Intelligence was able to—and did—relay this message to the President, but it had no effect whatever on efforts to bring the war to a conclusion."

If only the Americans had not insisted on unconditional surrender—that is, if they were willing to accept one condition to the surrender, that the Emperor, a holy figure to the Japanese, remain in place—the Japanese would have agreed to stop the war.

Why did the United States not take that small step to save both American and Japanese lives? Was it because too much money and effort had been invested in the atomic bomb not to drop it? General Leslie Groves, head of the Manhattan Project, described Truman as a man on a toboggan, the momentum too great to stop it. Or was it, as British scientist P. M. S. Blackett suggested (Fear, War, and the Bomb), that the United States was anxious to drop the bomb before the Russians entered the war against Japan?

The Russians had secretly agreed (they were officially not at war with Japan) they would come into the war ninety days after the end of the European war. That turned out to be May 8, and so, on August 8, the Russians were due to declare war on Japan. But by then the big bomb had been dropped, and the next day a second one would be dropped on Nagasaki; the Japanese would surrender to the United States, not the Russians, and the United States would be the occupier of postwar Japan. In other words, Blackett says, the dropping of the bomb was "the first major operation of the cold diplomatic war with Russia. . . ." Blackett is supported by American historian Gar Alperovitz *(Atomic Diplomacy),* who notes a diary entry for July 28, 1945, by Secretary of the Navy James Forrestal, describing Secretary of State James F. Byrnes as "most anxious to get the Japanese affair over with before the Russians got in."

Truman had said, "The world will note that the first atomic bomb was dropped on Hiroshima, a military base. That was because we wished in this first attack to avoid, insofar as possible, the killing of civilians." It was a preposterous statement. Those 100,000 killed in Hiroshima were almost all civilians. The U.S. Strategic Bombing Survey said in its official report: "Hiroshima and Nagasaki were chosen as targets because of their concentration of activities and population."

The dropping of the second bomb on Nagasaki seems to have been scheduled in advance, and no one has ever been able to explain why it was dropped. Was it because this was a plutonium bomb whereas the Hiroshima bomb was a uranium bomb? Were the dead and irradiated of Nagasaki victims of a scientific experiment? Martin Sherwin says that among the Nagasaki dead were probably American prisoners of war. He notes a message of July 31 from Headquarters, U.S. Army Strategic Air Forces, Guam, to the War Department:

Reports prisoner of war sources, not verified by photos, give location of Allied prisoner of war camp one mile north of center of city of Nagasaki. Does this influence the choice of this target for initial Centerboard operation? Request immediate reply.

The reply: "Targets previously assigned for Centerboard remain unchanged."

True, the war then ended quickly. Italy had been defeated a year earlier. Germany had recently surrendered, crushed primarily by the armies of the Soviet Union on the Eastern Front, aided by the Allied armies on the West. Now Japan surrendered. The Fascist powers were destroyed.

But what about fascism—as idea, as reality? Were its essential elements—militarism, racism, imperialism—now gone? Or were they absorbed into the already poisoned bones of the victors? A. J. Muste, the revolutionary pacifist, had predicted in 1941: "The problem after a war is with the victor. He thinks he has just proved that war and violence pay. Who will now teach him a lesson?"

The victors were the Soviet Union and the United States (also England, France and Nationalist China, but they were weak). Both these countries now went to work—without swastikas, goose-stepping, or officially declared racism, but under the cover of "socialism" on one side, and "democracy" on the other, to carve out their own empires of influence. They proceeded to share and contest with one another the domination of the world, to build military machines far greater than the Fascist countries had built, to control the destinies of more countries than Hitler, Mussolini, and Japan had been able to do. They also acted to control their own populations, each country with its own techniques—crude in the Soviet Union, sophisticated in the United States—to make their rule secure.

The war not only put the United States in a position to dominate much of the world; it created conditions for effective control at home. The unemployment, the economic distress, and the consequent turmoil that had marked the thirties, only partly relieved by New Deal measures, had been pacified, overcome by the greater turmoil of the war. The war brought higher prices for farmers, higher wages, enough prosperity for enough of the population to assure against the rebellions that so threatened the thirties. As Lawrence Wittner writes, "The war rejuvenated American capitalism." The biggest gains were in corporate profits, which rose from $6.4 billion in 1940 to $10.8 billion in 1944. But enough went to workers and farmers to make them feel the system was doing well for them.

It was an old lesson learned by governments: that war solves problems of control. Charles E. Wilson, the president of General Electric Corporation, was so happy about the wartime situation that he suggested a continuing alliance between business and the military for "a permanent war economy."

That is what happened. When, right after the war, the American public, war-weary, seemed to favor demobilization and disarmament, the Truman administration (Roosevelt had died in April 1945) worked to create an atmosphere of crisis and cold war. True, the rivalry with the Soviet Union was real—that country had come out of the war with its economy wrecked and 20 million people dead, but was making an astounding comeback, rebuilding its industry, regaining military strength. The Truman administration, however, presented the Soviet Union as not just a rival but an immediate threat.

In a series of moves abroad and at home, it established a climate of fear—a hysteria about Communism—which would steeply escalate the military budget and stimulate the economy with war-related orders. This combination of policies would permit more aggressive actions abroad, more repressive actions at home.

Revolutionary movements in Europe and Asia were described to the American public as examples of Soviet expansionism—thus recalling the indignation against Hitler's aggressions.

In Greece, which had been a right-wing monarchy and dictatorship before the war, a popular left-wing National Liberation Front (the EAM) was put down by a British army of intervention immediately after the war. A right-wing dictatorship was restored. When opponents of the regime were jailed, and trade union leaders removed, a left-wing guerrilla movement began to grow against the regime, soon consisting of 17,000 fighters, 50,000 active supporters, and perhaps 250,000 sympathizers, in a country of 7 million. Great Britain said it could not handle the rebellion, and asked the United States to come in. As a State Department officer said later: "Great Britain had within the hour handed the job of world leadership . . . to the United States."

The United States responded with the Truman Doctrine, the name given to a speech Truman gave to Congress in the spring of 1947, in which he asked for $400 million in military and economic aid to Greece and Turkey. Truman said the U.S. must help "free peoples who are resisting attempted subjugation by armed minorities or by outside pressures."

In fact, the biggest outside pressure was the United States. The Greek rebels were getting some aid from Yugoslavia, but no aid from the Soviet Union, which during the war had promised Churchill a free hand in Greece if he would give the Soviet Union its way in Rumania, Poland, Bulgaria. The Soviet Union, like the United States, did not seem to be willing to help revolutions it could not control.

Truman said the world "must choose between alternative ways of life." One was based on "the will of the majority . . . distinguished by free institutions"; the other was based on "the will of a minority . . . terror and oppression . . . the suppression of personal freedoms." Truman's adviser Clark Clifford had suggested that in his message Truman connect the intervention in Greece to something less rhetorical, more practical—"the great natural resources of the Middle East" (Clifford meant oil), but Truman didn't mention that.

The United States moved into the Greek civil war, not with soldiers, but with weapons and military advisers. In the last five months of 1947, 74,000 tons of military equipment were sent by the United States to the right-wing government in Athens, including artillery, dive bombers, and stocks of napalm. Two hundred and fifty army officers, headed by General James Van Fleet, advised the Greek army in the field. Van Fleet started a policy—standard in dealing with popular insurrections—of forcibly removing thousands of Greeks from their homes in the countryside, to try to isolate the guerrillas, to remove the source of their support.

With that aid, the rebellion was defeated by 1949. United States economic and military aid continued to the Greek government. Investment capital from Esso, Dow Chemical, Chrysler, and other U.S. corporations flowed into Greece. But illiteracy, poverty, and starvation remained widespread there, with the country in the hands of what Richard Barnet (Intervention and Revolution) called "a particularly brutal and backward military dictatorship."

In China, a revolution was already under way when World War II ended, led by a Communist movement with enormous mass support. A Red Army, which had fought against the Japanese, now fought to oust the corrupt dictatorship of Chiang Kai-shek, which was supported by the United States. The United States by 1949, had given $2 billion in aid to Chiang Kai-shek's forces, but, according to the State Department's own White Paper on China, Chiang Kai-shek's government had lost the confidence of its own troops and its own people. In January 1949, Chinese Communist forces moved into Peking, the civil war was over, and China was in the hands of a revolutionary movement, the closest thing, in the long history of that ancient country, to a people's government, independent of outside control.

The United States was trying, in the postwar decade, to create a national consensus—excluding the radicals, who could not support a foreign policy aimed at suppressing revolution—of conservatives and liberals, Republicans and Democrats, around the policies of cold war and anti-Communism. Such a coalition could best be created by a liberal Democratic President, whose aggressive policy abroad would be supported by conservatives, and whose welfare programs at home (Truman's "Fair Deal") would be attractive to liberals. If, in addition, liberals and traditional Democrats could—the memory of the war was still fresh—support a foreign policy against "aggression," the radical-liberal bloc created by World War II would be broken up. And perhaps, if the anti-Communist mood became strong enough, liberals could support repressive moves at home which in ordinary times would be seen as violating the liberal tradition of tolerance. In 1950, there came an event that speeded the formation of the liberal-conservative consensus—Truman's undeclared war in Korea.

Korea, occupied by Japan for thirty-five years, was liberated from Japan after World War II and divided into North Korea, a socialist dictatorship, part of the Soviet sphere of influence, and South Korea, a right-wing dictatorship, in the American sphere. There had been threats back and forth between the two Koreas, and when on June 25, 1950, North Korean armies moved southward across the 38th parallel in an invasion of South Korea, the United Nations, dominated by the United States, asked its members to help "repel the armed attack." Truman ordered the American armed forces to help South Korea, and the American army became the U.N. army. Truman said: "A return to the rule of force in international affairs would have far-reaching effects. The United States will continue to uphold the rule of law."

The United States' response to "the rule of force" was to reduce Korea, North and South, to a shambles, in three years of bombing and shelling. Napalm was dropped, and a BBC journalist described the result:

In front of us a curious figure was standing, a little crouched, legs straddled, arms held out from his sides. He had no eyes, and the whole of his body, nearly all of which was visible through tatters of burnt rags, was covered with a hard black crust speckled with yellow pus. . . . He had to stand because he was no longer covered with a skin, but with a crust-like crackling which broke easily. . . . I thought of the hundreds of villages reduced to ash which I personally had seen and realized the sort of casualty list which must be mounting up along the Korean front.

Perhaps 2 million Koreans, North and South, were killed in the Korean war, all in the name of opposing "the rule of force."

As for the rule of law Truman spoke about, the American military moves seemed to go beyond that. The U.N. resolution had called for action "to repel the armed attack and to restore peace and security in the area." But the American armies, after pushing the North Koreans back across the 38th parallel, advanced all the way up through North

Korea to the Yalu River, on the border of China—which provoked the Chinese into entering the war. The Chinese then swept southward and the war was stalemated at the 38th parallel until peace negotiations restored, in 1953, the old boundary between North and South.

The Korean war mobilized liberal opinion behind the war and the President. It created the kind of coalition that was needed to sustain a policy of intervention abroad, militarization of the economy at home. This meant trouble for those who stayed outside the coalition as radical critics. Alonzo Hamby noted (Beyond the New Deal) that the Korean war was supported by The New Republic, by The Nation, and by Henry Wallace (who in 1948 had run against Truman on a left coalition Progressive party ticket). The liberals didn't like Senator Joseph McCarthy (who hunted for Communists everywhere, even among liberals), but the Korean war, as Hamby says, "had given McCarthyism a new lease on life."

The left had become very influential in the hard times of the thirties, and during the war against Fascism. The actual membership of the Communist party was not large—fewer than 100,000 probably—but it was a potent force in trade unions numbering millions of members, in the arts, and among countless Americans who may have been led by the failure of the capitalist system in the thirties to look favorably on Communism and Socialism. Thus, if the Establishment, after World War II, was to make capitalism more secure in the country, and to build a consensus of support for the American Empire, it had to weaken and isolate the left.

Two weeks after presenting to the country the Truman Doctrine for Greece and Turkey, Truman issued, on March 22, 1947, Executive Order 9835, initiating a program to search out any "infiltration of disloyal persons" in the U.S. government. In their book The Fifties, Douglas Miller and Marion Nowack comment:

> Though Truman would later complain of the "great wave of hysteria" sweeping the nation, his commitment to victory over communism, to completely safeguarding the United States from external and internal threats, was in large measure responsible for creating that very hysteria. Between the launching of his security program in March 1947 and December 1952, some 6.6 million persons were investigated. Not a single case of espionage was uncovered, though about 500 persons were dismissed in dubious cases of "questionable loyalty." All of this was conducted with secret evidence, secret and often paid informers, and neither judge nor jury. Despite the failure to find subversion, the broad scope of the official Red hunt gave popular credence to the notion that the

government was riddled with spies. A conservative and fearful reaction coursed the country. Americans became convinced of the need for absolute security and the preservation of the established order.

World events right after the war made it easier to build up public support for the anti-Communist crusade at home. In 1948, the Communist party in Czechoslovakia ousted non-Communists from the government and established their own rule. The Soviet Union that year blockaded Berlin, which was a jointly occupied city isolated inside the Soviet sphere of East Germany, forcing the United States to airlift supplies into Berlin. In 1949, there was the Communist victory in China, and in that year also, the Soviet Union exploded its first atomic bomb. In 1950 the Korean war began. These were all portrayed to the public as signs of a world Communist conspiracy.

Not as publicized as the Communist victories, but just as disturbing to the American government, was the upsurge all over the world of colonial peoples demanding independence. Revolutionary movements were growing—in Indochina against the French; in Indonesia against the Dutch; in the Philippines, armed rebellion against the United States.

In Africa there were rumblings of discontent in the form of strikes. Basil Davidson (*Let Freedom Come*) tells of the longest recorded strike (160 days) in African history, of 19,000 railwaymen in French West Africa in 1947, whose message to the governor general showed the new mood of militancy: "Open your prisons, make ready your machine guns and cannon. Nevertheless, at midnight on 10 October, if our demands are not met, we declare the general strike." The year before in South Africa, 100,000 gold mine workers stopped work, demanding ten shillings (about $2.50) a day in wages, the greatest strike in the history of South Africa, and it took a military attack to get them back to work. In 1950, in Kenya, there was a general strike against starvation wages.

So it was not just Soviet expansion that was threatening to the United States government and to American business interests. In fact, China, Korea, Indochina, the Philippines, represented local Communist movements, not Russian fomentation. It was a general wave of anti-imperialist insurrection in the world, which would require gigantic American effort to defeat: national unity for militarization of the budget, for the suppression of domestic opposition to such a foreign policy. Truman and the liberals in Congress proceeded to try to create a new national unity for the postwar years—with the executive order on loyalty oaths, Justice Department prosecutions, and anti-Communist legislation.

In this atmosphere, Senator Joseph McCarthy of Wisconsin could go even further than Truman. Speaking to a Women's Republican Club in Wheeling, West Virginia, in early 1950, he held up some papers and shouted: "I have here in my hand a list of 205—a list of names that were made known to the Secretary of State as being members of the Communist Party and who nevertheless are still working and shaping policy in the State Department." The next day, speaking in Salt Lake City, McCarthy claimed he had a list of fifty-seven (the number kept changing) such Communists in the State Department. Shortly afterward, he appeared on the floor of the Senate with photostatic copies of about a hundred dossiers from State Department loyalty files. The dossiers were three years old, and most of the people were no longer with the State Department, but McCarthy read from them anyway, inventing, adding, and changing as he read. In one case, he changed the dossier's description of "liberal" to "communistically inclined," in another form "active fellow traveler" to "active Communist," and so on.

McCarthy kept on like this for the next few years. As chairman of the Permanent Investigations Sub-Committee of a Senate Committee on Government Operations, he investigated the State Department's information program, its Voice of America, and its overseas libraries, which included books by people McCarthy considered Communists. The State Department reacted in panic, issuing a stream of directives to its library centers across the world. Forty books were removed, including *The Selected Works of Thomas Jefferson,* edited by Philip Foner, and *The Children's Hour* by Lillian Hellman. Some books were burned.

McCarthy became bolder. In the spring of 1954 he began hearings to investigate supposed subversives in the military. When he began attacking generals for not being hard enough on suspected Communists, he antagonized Republicans as well as Democrats, and in December 1954, the Senate voted overwhelmingly to censure him for "conduct . . . unbecoming a Member of the United States Senate." The censure resolution avoided criticizing McCarthy's anti-Communist lies and exaggerations; it concentrated on minor matters—on his refusal to appear before a Senate Subcommittee on Privileges and Elections, and his abuse of an army general at his hearings.

At the very time the Senate was censuring McCarthy, Congress was putting through a whole series of anti-Communist bills. Liberal Hubert Humphrey introduced an amendment to one of them to make

the Communist party illegal, saying: "I do not intend to be a half
patriot. . . . Either Senators are for recognizing the Communist Party
for what it is, or they will continue to trip over the niceties of legal
technicalities and details."

The liberals in the government were themselves acting to exclude,
persecute, fire, and even imprison Communists. It was just that McCarthy had gone too far, attacking not only Communists but liberals, endangering that broad liberal-conservative coalition which was considered
essential. For instance, Lyndon Johnson, as Senate minority leader,
worked not only to pass the censure resolution on McCarthy but also
to keep it within the narrow bounds of "conduct . . . unbecoming a
Member of the United States Senate" rather than questioning McCarthy's anti-Communism.

John F. Kennedy was cautious on the issue, didn't speak out against
McCarthy (he was absent when the censure vote was taken and never
said how he would have voted). McCarthy's insistence that Communism
had won in China because of softness on Communism in the American
government was close to Kennedy's own view, expressed in the House
of Representatives, January 1949, when the Chinese Communists took
over Peking. Kennedy said:

Mr. Speaker, over this weekend we have learned the extent of the disaster
that has befallen China and the United States. The responsibility for the failure
of our foreign policy in the Far East rests squarely with the White House
and the Department of State.

The continued insistence that aid would not be forthcoming unless a
coalition government with the Communists was formed, was a crippling blow
to the National Government.

So concerned were our diplomats and their advisers, the Lattimores and
the Fairbanks [both scholars in the field of Chinese history, Owen Lattimore
a favorite target of McCarthy, John Fairbank, a Harvard professor], with
the imperfection of the democratic system in China after 20 years of war
and the tales of corruption in high places that they lost sight of our tremendous
stake in a non-Communist China. . . .

This House must now assume the responsibility of preventing the onrush-
ing tide of Communism from engulfing all of Asia.

When, in 1950, Republicans sponsored an Internal Security Act
for the registration of organizations found to be "Communist-action"
or "Communist-front," liberal Senators did not fight that head-on. Instead, some of them, including Hubert Humphrey and Herbert Lehman,
proposed a substitute measure, the setting up of detention centers (really,

concentration camps) for suspected subversives, who, when the President declared an "internal security emergency," would be held without trial. The detention-camp bill became not a substitute for, but an addition to, the Internal Security Act, and the proposed camps were set up, ready for use. (In 1968, a time of general disillusionment with anti-Communism, this law was repealed.)

Truman's executive order on loyalty in 1947 required the Department of Justice to draw up a list of organizations it decided were "totalitarian, fascist, communist or subversive . . . or as seeking to alter the form of government of the United States by unconstitutional means." Not only membership in, but also "sympathetic association" with, any organization on the Attorney General's list would be considered in determining disloyalty. By 1954, there were hundreds of groups on this list, including, besides the Communist party and the Ku Klux Klan, the Chopin Cultural Center, the Cervantes Fraternal Society, the Committee for the Negro in the Arts, the Committee for the Protection of the Bill of Rights, the League of American Writers, the Nature Friends of America, People's Drama, the Washington Bookshop Association, and the Yugoslav Seaman's Club.

It was not McCarthy and the Republicans, but the liberal Democratic Truman administration, whose Justice Department initiated a series of prosecutions that intensified the nation's anti-Communist mood. The most important of these was the prosecution of Julius and Ethel Rosenberg in the summer of 1950.

The Rosenbergs were charged with espionage. The major evidence was supplied by a few people who had already confessed to being spies, and were either in prison or under indictment. David Greenglass, the brother of Ethel Rosenberg, was the key witness. He had been a machinist at the Manhattan Project laboratory at Los Alamos, New Mexico, in 1944–1945 when the atomic bomb was being made there and testified that Julius Rosenberg had asked him to get information for the Russians. Greenglass said he had made sketches from memory for his brother-in-law of experiments with lenses to be used to detonate atomic bombs. He said Rosenberg had given him half of the cardboard top to a box of Jell-o, and told him a man would show up in New Mexico with the other half, and that, in June 1945, Harry Gold appeared with the other half of the box top, and Greenglass gave him information he had memorized.

Gold, already serving a thirty-year sentence in another espionage case, came out of jail to corroborate Greenglass's testimony. He had never met the Rosenbergs, but said a Soviet embassy official gave him half of a Jello box top and told him to contact Greenglass, saying, "I come from Julius." Gold said he took the sketches Greenglass had drawn from memory and gave them to the Russian official.

There were troubling aspects to all this. Did Gold cooperate in return for early release from prison? After serving fifteen years of his thirty-year sentence, he was paroled. Did Greenglass—under indictment at the time he testified—also know that his life depended on his cooperation? He was given fifteen years, served half of it, and was released. How reliable a memorizer of atomic information was David Greenglass, an ordinary-level machinist, not a scientist, who had taken six courses at Brooklyn Polytechnical Institute and flunked five of them? Gold's and Greenglass's stories had first not been in accord. But they were both placed on the same floor of the Tombs prison in New York before the trial, giving them a chance to coordinate their testimony.

How reliable was Gold's testimony? It turned out that he had been prepared for the Rosenberg case by four hundred hours of interviews with the FBI. It also turned out that Gold was a frequent and highly imaginative liar. He was a witness in a later trial where defense counsel asked Gold about his invention of a fictional wife and fictional children. The attorney asked: ". . . you lied for a period of six years?" Gold responded: "I lied for a period of sixteen years, not alone six years." Gold was the only witness at the trial to connect Julius Rosenberg and David Greenglass to the Russians. The FBI agent who had questioned Gold was interviewed twenty years after the case by a journalist. He was asked about the password Gold was supposed to have used—"Julius sent me." The FBI man said:

Gold couldn't remember the name he had given. He thought he had said: I come from ——— or something like that. I suggested, "Might it have been Julius?"

That refreshed his memory.

When the Rosenbergs were found guilty, and Judge Irving Kaufman pronounced sentence, he said:

I believe your conduct in putting into the hands of the Russians the A-bomb years before our best scientists predicted Russia would perfect the bomb has already caused the Communist aggression in Korea with the resultant casualties exceeding 50,000 Americans and who knows but that millions more of innocent people may pay the price of your treason. . . .

He sentenced them both to die in the electric chair.

Morton Sobell was also on trial as a co-conspirator with the Rosenbergs. The chief witness against him was an old friend, the best man at his wedding, a man who was facing possible perjury charges by the federal government for lying about his political past. This was Max Elitcher, who testified that he had once driven Sobell to a Manhattan housing project where the Rosenbergs lived, and that Sobell got out of the car, took from the glove compartment what appeared to be a film can, went off, and then returned without the can. There was no evidence about what was in the film can. The case against Sobell seemed so weak that Sobell's lawyer decided there was no need to present a defense. But the jury found Sobell guilty, and Kaufman sentenced him to thirty years in prison. He was sent to Alcatraz, parole was repeatedly denied, and he spent nineteen years in various prisons before he was released.

FBI documents subpoenaed in the 1970s showed that Judge Kauf- man had conferred with the prosecutors secretly about the sentences he would give in the case. Another document shows that after three years of appeal a meeting took place between Attorney General Herbert Brownell and Chief Justice Fred Vinson of the Supreme Court, and the chief justice assured the Attorney General that if any Supreme Court justice gave a stay of execution, he would immediately call a full court session and override it.

There had been a worldwide campaign of protest. Albert Einstein, whose letter to Roosevelt early in the war had initiated work on the atomic bomb, appealed for the Rosenbergs, as did Jean-Paul Sartre, Pablo Picasso, and the sister of Bartolomeo Vanzetti. There was an appeal to President Truman, just before he left office in the spring of 1953. It was turned down. Then, another appeal to the new President, Dwight Eisenhower, was also turned down.

At the last moment, Justice William O. Douglas granted a stay of execution. Chief Justice Vinson sent out special jets to bring the vacationing justices back to Washington from various parts of the country. They canceled Douglas's stay in time for the Rosenbergs to be executed June 19, 1953. It was a demonstration to the people of the country, though very few could identify with the Rosenbergs, of what lay at the end of the line for those the government decided were traitors.

In that same period of the early fifties, the House Un-American Activities Committee was at its heyday, interrogating Americans about their Communist connections, holding them in contempt if they refused to answer, distributing millions of pamphlets to the American public: "One Hundred Things You Should Know About Communism"

("Where can Communists be found? Everywhere"). Liberals often criticized the Committee, but in Congress, liberals and conservatives alike voted to fund it year after year. By 1958, only one member of the House of Representatives (James Roosevelt) voted against giving it money. Although Truman criticized the Committee, his own Attorney General had expressed, in 1950, the same idea that motivated its investigations: "There are today many Communists in America. They are everywhere—in factories, offices, butcher shops, on street corners, in private business—and each carries in himself the germs of death for society."

Liberal intellectuals rode the anti-Communist bandwagon. *Commentary* magazine denounced the Rosenbergs and their supporters. One of *Commentary*'s writers, Irving Kristol, asked in March 1952: "Do we defend our rights by protecting Communists?" His answer: "No."

It was Truman's Justice Department that prosecuted the leaders of the Communist party under the Smith Act, charging them with conspiring to teach and advocate the overthrow of the government by force and violence. The evidence consisted mostly of the fact that the Communists were distributing Marxist-Leninist literature, which the prosecution contended called for violent revolution. There was certainly not evidence of any immediate danger of violent revolution by the Communist party. The Supreme Court decision was given by Truman's appointee, Chief Justice Vinson. He stretched the old doctrine of the "clear and present danger" by saying there was a clear and present conspiracy to make a revolution at some convenient time. And so, the top leadership of the Communist party was put in prison, and soon after, most of its organizers went underground.

Undoubtedly, there was success in the attempt to make the general public fearful of Communists and ready to take drastic actions against them—imprisonment at home, military action abroad. The whole culture was permeated with anti-Communism. The large-circulation magazines had articles like "How Communists Get That Way" and "Communists Are After Your Child." The *New York Times* in 1956 ran an editorial: "We would not knowingly employ a Communist party member in the news or editorial departments . . . because we would not trust his ability to report the news objectively or to comment on it honestly. . . ." An FBI informer's story about his exploits as a Communist who became an FBI agent—"I Led Three Lives"—was serialized in five hundred newspapers and put on television. Hollywood movies had titles like *I Married a Communist* and *I Was a Communist for the FBI*.

Between 1948 and 1954, more than forty anti-Communist films came out of Hollywood.

Even the American Civil Liberties Union, set up specifically to defend the liberties of Communists and all other political groups, began to wilt in the cold war atmosphere. It had already started in this direction back in 1940 when it expelled one of its charter members, Elizabeth Gurley Flynn, because she was a member of the Communist party. In the fifties, the ACLU was hesitant to defend Corliss Lamont, its own board member, and Owen Lattimore, when both were under attack. It was reluctant to defend publicly the Communist leaders during the first Smith Act trial, and kept completely out of the Rosenberg case, saying no civil liberties issues were involved.

Young and old were taught that anti-Communism was heroic. Three million copies were sold of the book by Mickey Spillane published in 1951, *One Lonely Night,* in which the hero, Mike Hammer says: "I killed more people tonight than I have fingers on my hands. I shot them in cold blood and enjoyed every minute of it. . . . They were Commies . . . red sons-of-bitches who should have died long ago. . . ." A comic strip hero, Captain America, said: "Beware, commies, spies, traitors, and foreign agents! Captain America, with all loyal, free men behind him, is looking for you. . . ." And in the fifties, schoolchildren all over the country participated in air raid drills in which a Soviet attack on America was signaled by sirens: the children had to crouch under their desks until it was "all clear."

It was an atmosphere in which the government could get mass support for a policy of rearmament. The system, so shaken in the thirties, had learned that war production could bring stability and high profits. Truman's anti-Communism was attractive. The business publication *Steel* had said in November 1946—even before the Truman Doctrine—that Truman's policies gave "the firm assurance that maintaining and building our preparations for war will be big business in the United States for at least a considerable period ahead."

That prediction turned out to be accurate. At the start of 1950, the total U.S. budget was about $40 billion, and the military part of it was about $12 billion. But by 1955, the military part alone was $40 billion out of a total of $62 billion.

In 1960, the military budget was $45.8 billion—49.7 percent of the budget. That year John F. Kennedy was elected President, and he immediately moved to increase military spending. In fourteen months, the Kennedy administration added $9 billion to defense funds, according to Edgar Bottome *(The Balance of Terror).*

By 1962, based on a series of invented scares about Soviet military build-ups, a false "bomber gap" and a false "missile gap," the United States had overwhelming nuclear superiority. It had the equivalent, in nuclear weapons, of 1,500 Hiroshima-size atomic bombs, far more than enough to destroy every major city in the world—the equivalent, in fact, of 10 tons of TNT for every man, woman, and child on earth. To deliver these bombs, the United States had more than 50 intercontinental ballistic missiles, 80 missiles on nuclear submarines, 90 missiles on stations overseas, 1,700 bombers capable of reaching the Soviet Union, 300 fighter-bombers on aircraft carriers, able to carry atomic weapons, and 1,000 land-based supersonic fighters able to carry atomic bombs.

The Soviet Union was obviously behind—it had between fifty and a hundred intercontinental ballistic missiles and fewer than two hundred long-range bombers. But the U.S. budget kept mounting, the hysteria kept growing, the profits of corporations getting defense contracts multiplied, and employment and wages moved ahead just enough to keep a substantial number of Americans dependent on war industries for their living.

By 1970, the U.S. military budget was $80 billion and the corporations involved in military production were making fortunes. Two-thirds of the 40 billion spent on weapons systems was going to twelve or fifteen giant industrial corporations, whose main reason for existence was to fulfill government military contracts. Senator Paul Douglass, an economist and chairman of the Joint Economic Committee of the Senate, noted that "six-sevenths of these contracts are not competitive. . . . In the alleged interest of secrecy, the government picks a company and draws up a contract in more or less secret negotiations."

C. Wright Mills, in his book of the fifties, *The Power Elite,* counted the military as part of the top elite, along with politicians and corporations. These elements were more and more intertwined. A Senate report showed that the one hundred largest defense contractors, who held 67.4 percent of the military contracts, employed more than two thousand former high-ranking officers of the military.

Meanwhile, the United States, giving economic aid to certain countries, was creating a network of American corporate control over the globe, and building its political influence over the countries it aided. The Marshall Plan of 1948, which gave $16 billion in economic aid to Western European countries in four years, had an economic aim:

to build up markets for American exports. George Marshall (a general, then Secretary of State) was quoted in an early 1948 State Department bulletin: "It is idle to think that a Europe left to its own efforts . . . would remain open to American business in the same way that we have known it in the past."

The Marshall Plan also had a political motive. The Communist parties of Italy and France were strong, and the United States decided to use pressure and money to keep Communists out of the cabinets of those countries. When the Plan was beginning, Truman's Secretary of State Dean Acheson said: "These measures of relief and reconstruction have been only in part suggested by humanitarianism. Your Congress has authorized and your Government is carrying out, a policy of relief and reconstruction today chiefly as a matter of national self-interest."

From 1952 on, foreign aid was more and more obviously designed to build up military power in non-Communist countries. In the next ten years, of the $50 billion in aid granted by the United States to ninety countries, only $5 billion was for nonmilitary economic development.

When John F. Kennedy took office, he launched the Alliance for Progress, a program of help for Latin America, emphasizing social reform to better the lives of people. But it turned out to be mostly military aid to keep in power right-wing dictatorships and enable them to stave off revolutions.

From military aid, it was a short step to military intervention. What Truman had said at the start of the Korean war about "the rule of force" and the "rule of law" was again and again, under Truman and his successors, contradicted by American action. In Iran, in 1953, the Central Intelligence Agency succeeded in overthrowing a government which nationalized the oil industry. In Guatemala, in 1954, a legally elected government was overthrown by an invasion force of mercenaries trained by the CIA at military bases in Honduras and Nicaragua and supported by four American fighter planes flown by American pilots. The invasion put into power Colonel Carlos Castillo Armas, who had at one time received military training at Fort Leavenworth, Kansas.

The government that the United States overthrew was the most democratic Guatemala had ever had. The President, Jacobo Arbenz, was a left-of-center Socialist; four of the fifty-six seats in the Congress were held by Communists. What was most unsettling to American business interests was that Arbenz had expropriated 234,000 acres of land owned by United Fruit, offering compensation that United Fruit called "unacceptable." Armas, in power, gave the land back to United Fruit, abolished the tax on interest and dividends to foreign investors, eliminated the secret ballot, and jailed thousands of political critics.

In 1958, the Eisenhower government sent thousands of marines to Lebanon to make sure the pro-American government there was not toppled by a revolution, and to keep an armed presence in that oil-rich area.

The Democrat-Republican, liberal-conservative agreement to prevent or overthrow revolutionary governments whenever possible— whether Communist, Socialist, or anti–United Fruit—became most evident in 1961 in Cuba. That little island 90 miles from Florida had gone through a revolution in 1959 by a rebel force led by Fidel Castro, in which the American-backed dictator, Fulgencio Batista, was overthrown. The revolution was a direct threat to American business interests. Franklin D. Roosevelt's Good Neighbor Policy had repealed the Platt Amendment (which permitted American intervention in Cuba), but the United States still kept a naval base in Cuba at Guantanamo, and U.S. business interests still dominated the Cuban economy. American companies controlled 80 to 100 percent of Cuba's utilities, mines, cattle ranches, and oil refineries, 40 percent of the sugar industry, and 50 percent of the public railways.

Fidel Castro had spent time in prison after he led an unsuccessful attack in 1953 on an army barracks in Santiago. Out of prison, he went to Mexico, met Argentine revolutionary Che Guevara, and returned in 1956 to Cuba. His tiny force fought guerrilla warfare from the jungles and mountains against Batista's army, drawing more and more popular support, then came out of the mountains and marched across the country to Havana. The Batista government fell apart on New Year's Day 1959.

In power, Castro moved to set up a nationwide system of education, of housing, of land distribution to landless peasants. The government confiscated over a million acres of land from three American companies, including United Fruit.

Cuba needed money to finance its programs, and the United States was not eager to lend it. The International Monetary Fund, dominated by the United States, would not loan money to Cuba because Cuba would not accept its "stabilization" conditions, which seemed to undermine the revolutionary program that had begun. When Cuba now signed a trade agreement with the Soviet Union, American-owned oil companies in Cuba refused to refine crude oil that came from the Soviet Union. Castro seized these companies. The United States cut down on its sugar buying from Cuba, on which Cuba's economy depended, and the Soviet Union immediately agreed to buy all the 700,000 tons of sugar that the United States would not buy.

Cuba had changed. The Good Neighbor Policy did not apply. In the spring of 1960, President Eisenhower secretly authorized the Central Intelligence Agency to arm and train anti-Castro Cuban exiles in Guatemala for a future invasion of Cuba. When Kennedy took office in the spring of 1961 the CIA had 1,400 exiles, armed and trained. He moved ahead with the plans, and on April 17, 1961, the CIA-trained force, with some Americans participating, landed at the Bay of Pigs on the south shore of Cuba, 90 miles from Havana. They expected to stimulate a general rising against Castro. But it was a popular regime. There was no rising. In three days, the CIA forces were crushed by Castro's army.

The whole Bay of Pigs affair was accompanied by hypocrisy and lying. The invasion was a violation—recalling Truman's "rule of law"—of a treaty the U.S. had signed, the Charter of the Organization of American States, which reads: "No state or group of states has the right to intervene, directly or indirectly, for any reason whatever, in the internal or external affairs of any other state."

Four days before the invasion—because there had been press reports of secret bases and CIA training for invaders—President Kennedy told a press conference: ". . . there will not be, under any conditions, any intervention in Cuba by United States armed forces." True, the landing force was Cuban, but it was all organized by the United States, and American war planes, including American pilots, were involved; Kennedy had approved the use of unmarked navy jets in the invasion. Four American pilots of those planes were killed, and their families were not told the truth about how those men died.

The success of the liberal-conservative coalition in creating a national anti-Communist consensus was shown by how certain important news publications cooperated with the Kennedy administration in deceiving the American public on the Cuban invasion. *The New Republic* was about to print an article on the CIA training of Cuban exiles, a few weeks before the invasion. Historian Arthur Schlesinger was given copies of the article in advance. He showed them to Kennedy, who asked that the article not be printed, and *The New Republic* went along.

James Reston and Turner Catledge of the *New York Times,* on the government's request, did not run a story about the imminent invasion. Arthur Schlesinger said of the *New York Times* action: "This was another patriotic act, but in retrospect I have wondered whether, if the press had behaved irresponsibly, it would not have spared the country a disaster." What seemed to bother him, and other liberals in the cold war consensus, was not that the United States was interfering in revolutionary movements in other countries, but that it was doing so unsuccessfully.

Around 1960, the fifteen-year effort since the end of World War II to break up the Communist-radical upsurge of the New Deal and wartime years seemed successful. The Communist party was in disarray—its leaders in jail, its membership shrunken, its influence in the trade union movement very small. The trade union movement itself had become more controlled, more conservative. The military budget was taking half of the national budget, but the public was accepting this.

The radiation from the testing of nuclear weapons had dangerous possibilities for human health, but the public was not aware of that. The Atomic Energy Commission insisted that the deadly effects of atomic tests were exaggerated, and an article in 1955 in the *Reader's Digest* (the largest-circulation magazine in the United States) said: "The scare stories about this country's atomic tests are simply not justified."

In the mid-fifties, there was a flurry of enthusiasm for air-raid shelters; the public was being told these would keep them safe from atomic blasts. A government consultant and scientist, Herman Kahn, wrote a book, *On Thermonuclear War,* in which he explained that it was possible to have a nuclear war without total destruction of the world, that people should not be so frightened of it. A political scientist named Henry Kissinger wrote a book published in 1957 in which he said: "With proper tactics, nuclear war need not be as destructive as it appears. . . ."

The country was on a permanent war economy which had big pockets of poverty, but there were enough people at work, making enough money, to keep things quiet. The distribution of wealth was still unequal. From 1944 to 1961, it had not changed much: the lowest fifth of the families received 5 percent of all the income; the highest fifth received 45 percent of all the income. In 1953, 1.6 percent of the adult population owned more than 80 percent of the corporate stock and nearly 90 percent of the corporate bonds. About 200 giant corporations out of 200,000 corporations—one-tenth of 1 percent of all corporations—controlled about 60 percent of the manufacturing wealth of the nation.

When John F. Kennedy presented his budget to the nation after his first year in office, it was clear that, liberal Democrat or not, there would be no major change in the distribution of income or wealth or tax advantages. *New York Times* columnist James Reston summed up Kennedy's budget messages as avoiding any "sudden transformation of the home front" as well as "a more ambitious frontal attack on the unemployment problem." Reston said:

He agreed to a tax break for business investment in plant expansion and modernization. He is not spoiling for a fight with the Southern conservatives over civil rights. He has been urging the unions to keep wage demands down so that prices can be competitive in the world markets and jobs increased. And he has been trying to reassure the business community that he does not want any cold war with them on the home front.

. . . this week in his news conference he refused to carry out his promise to bar discrimination in Government-insured housing, but talked instead of postponing this until there was a "national consensus" in its favor. . . .

During these twelve months the President has moved over into the decisive middle ground of American politics. . . .

On this middle ground, all seemed secure. Nothing had to be done for blacks. Nothing had to be done to change the economic structure. An aggressive foreign policy could continue. The country seemed under control. And then, in the 1960s, came a series of explosive rebellions in every area of American life, which showed that all the system's estimates of security and success were wrong.

6.
"Or Does It Explode?"

The black revolt of the 1950s and 1960s—North and South—came as a surprise. But perhaps it should not have. The memory of oppressed people is one thing that cannot be taken away, and for such people, with such memories, revolt is always an inch below the surface. For blacks in the United States, there was the memory of slavery, and after that of segregation, lynching, humiliation. And it was not just a memory but a living presence—part of the daily lives of blacks in generation after generation.

In the 1930s, Langston Hughes wrote a poem, "Lenox Avenue Mural":

> What happens to a dream deferred?
>> Does it dry up
>> like a raisin in the sun?
>> Or fester like a sore—
>> And then run?
> Does it stink like rotten meat?
> Or crust and sugar over—
> like a syrupy sweet?
>
> Maybe it just sags like a heavy load.
>
> Or does it explode?

In a society of complex controls, both crude and refined, secret thoughts can often be found in the arts, and so it was in black society. Perhaps the blues, however pathetic, concealed anger; and the jazz, however joyful, portended rebellion. And then the poetry, the thoughts no longer so secret. In the 1920s, Claude McKay, one of the figures of what came to be called the "Harlem Renaissance," wrote a poem that Henry Cabot Lodge put in the *Congressional Record* as an example of dangerous currents among young blacks:

> If we must die, let it not be like hogs
> Hunted and penned in an inglorious spot. . . .
> Like men we'll face the murderous cowardly pack,
> Pressed to the wall, dying, but fighting back!

Countee Cullen's poem "Incident" evoked memories—all different, all the same—out of every black American's childhood:

> Once riding in old Baltimore,
> Heart-filled, head-filled with glee,
> I saw a Baltimorean
> Keep looking straight at me.
>
> Now I was eight and very small,
> And he was no whit bigger,
> And so I smiled, but he poked out
> His tongue, and called me, "Nigger."
>
> I saw the whole of Baltimore
> From May until December;
> Of all the things that happened there
> That's all that I remember.

At the time of the Scottsboro Boys incident, Cullen wrote a bitter poem noting that white poets had used their pens to protest in other cases of injustice, but now that blacks were involved, most were silent. His last stanza was:

> Surely, I said,
>   Now will the poets sing.
> But they have raised no cry.
>   I wonder why.

Even outward subservience—Uncle Tom behavior in real situations, the comic or fawning Negro on the stage, the self-ridicule, the caution—concealed resentment, anger, energy. The black poet Paul Laurence Dunbar, in the era of the black minstrel, around the turn of the century, wrote "We Wear the Mask":

> We wear the mask that grins and lies,
> It hides our cheeks and shades our eyes,—
>
> . . . We sing, but oh, the clay is vile
> Beneath our feet, and long the mile;
> But let the world dream otherwise,
> We wear the mask.

Two black performers of that time played the minstrel and satirized it at the same time. When Bert Williams and George Walker billed themselves as "Two Real Coons," they were, Nathan Huggins says, "intending to give style and comic dignity to a fiction that white men had created. . . ."

By the 1930s the mask was off for many black poets. Langston Hughes wrote "I, Too."

> I, too, sing America
>
> I am the darker brother.
> They send me to eat in the kitchen
> When company comes,
> But I laugh,
> And eat well,
> And grow strong.
>
> Tomorrow,
> I'll be at the table
> When company comes. . . .

Gwendolyn Bennett wrote:

> I want to see lithe Negro girls,
> Etched dark against the sky
> While sunset lingers. . . .
>
> I want to hear the chanting
> Around a heathen fire
> Of a strange black race. . . .
>
> I want to feel the surging
> Of my sad people's soul
> Hidden by a minstrel-smile.

There was Margaret Walker's prose-poem "For My People":

. . . Let a new earth rise. Let another world be born. Let a bloody peace be written in the sky. Let a second generation full of courage issue forth, let a people loving freedom come to growth, let a beauty full of healing and a strength of final clenching be the pulsing in our spirits and our blood. Let the martial songs be written, let the dirges disappear. Let a race of men now rise and take control!

By the 1940s there was Richard Wright, a gifted novelist, a black man. His autobiography of 1937, *Black Boy,* gave endless insights: for instance, how blacks were set against one another, when he told how he was prodded to fight another black boy for the amusement of white men. *Black Boy* expressed unashamedly every humiliation and then:

The white South said that it knew "niggers," and I was what the white South called a "nigger." Well, the white South had never known me—never known what I thought, what I felt. The white South said that I had a "place" in life. Well, I had never felt my "place"; or, rather, my deepest instincts had always made me reject the "place" to which the white South had assigned me. It had never occurred to me that I was in any way an inferior being. And no word that I had ever heard fall from the lips of southern white men had ever made me really doubt the worth of my own humanity.

It was all there in the poetry, the prose, the music, sometimes masked, sometimes unmistakably clear—the signs of a people unbeaten, waiting, hot, coiled.

In *Black Boy*, Wright told about the training of black children in America to keep them silent. But also:

How do Negroes feel about the way they have to live? How do they discuss it when alone among themselves? I think this question can be answered in a single sentence. A friend of mine who ran an elevator once told me: "Lawd, man! Ef it wuzn't fer them polices 'n' them ol' lynch mobs, there wouldn't be nothin' but uproar down here!"

Richard Wright, for a time, joined the Communist party (he tells of this period of his life, and his disillusionment with the party, in *The God That Failed*). The Communist party was known to pay special attention to the problem of race equality. When the Scottsboro case unfolded in the 1930s in Alabama, it was the Communist party that had become associated with the defense of these young black men imprisoned, in the early years of the Depression, by southern injustice.

The party was accused by liberals and the NAACP of exploiting the issue for its own purposes, and there was a half-truth in it, but black people were realistic about the difficulty of having white allies who were pure in motive. The other half of the truth was that black Communists in the South had earned the admiration of blacks by their organizing work against enormous obstacles. There was Hosea Hudson, the black organizer of the unemployed in Birmingham, for instance. And in Georgia, in 1932, a nineteen-year-old black youth named Angelo Herndon, whose father died of miner's pneumonia, who had worked in mines as a boy in Kentucky, joined an Unemployment Council in Birmingham organized by the Communist party, and then joined the party. He wrote later:

All my life I'd been sweated and stepped-on and Jim-Crowed. I lay on my belly in the mines for a few dollars a week, and saw my pay stolen and slashed, and my buddies killed. I lived in the worst section of town, and rode behind the "Colored" signs on streetcars, as though there was something disgusting about me. I heard myself called "nigger" and "darky" and I had to say "Yes, sir" to every white man, whether he had my respect or not.

I had always detested it, but I had never known that anything could be done about it. And here, all of a sudden, I had found organizations in which Negroes and whites sat together, and worked together, and knew no difference of race or color. . . .

Herndon became a Communist party organizer in Atlanta. He and his fellow Communists organized block committees of Unemployment Councils in 1932 which got rent relief for needy people. They organized a demonstration to which a thousand people came, six hundred of them white, and the next day the city voted $6,000 in relief to the jobless. But soon after that Herndon was arrested, held incommunicado, and charged with violating a Georgia statute against insurrection. He recalled his trial:

The state of Georgia displayed the literature that had been taken from my room, and read passages of it to the jury. They questioned me in great detail. Did I believe that the bosses and government ought to pay insurance to unemployed workers? That Negroes should have complete equality with white people? Did I believe in the demand for the self-determination of the Black Belt—that the Negro people should be allowed to rule the Black Belt territory, kicking out the white landlords and government officials? Did I feel that the working-class could run the mills and mines and government? That it wasn't necessary to have bosses at all?

I told them I believed all of that—and more. . . .

Herndon was convicted and spent five years in prison until in 1937 the Supreme Court ruled unconstitutional the Georgia statute under which he was found guilty. It was men like him who represented to the Establishment a dangerous militancy among blacks, made more dangerous when linked with the Communist party.

There were others who made that same connection, magnifying the danger: Benjamin Davis, the black lawyer who defended Herndon at his trial; nationally renowned men like singer and actor Paul Robeson, and writer and scholar W. E. B. Du Bois, who did not hide their support and sympathy for the Communist party. The Negro was not as anti-Communist as the white population. He could not afford to be, his friends were so few—so that Herndon, Davis, Robeson, Du Bois, however their political views might be maligned by the country as a whole, found admiration for their fighting spirit in the black community.

The black militant mood, flashing here and there in the thirties, was reduced to a subsurface simmering during World War II, when the nation on the one hand denounced racism, and on the other hand maintained segregation in the armed forces and kept blacks in low-paying jobs. When the war ended, a new element entered the racial balance in the United States—the enormous, unprecedented upsurge of black and yellow people in Africa and Asia.

President Harry Truman had to reckon with this, especially as the cold war rivalry with the Soviet Union began, and the dark-skinned revolt of former colonies all over the world threatened to take Marxist form. Action on the race question was needed, not just to calm a black population at home emboldened by war promises, frustrated by the basic sameness of their condition. It was needed to present to the world a United States that could counter the continuous Communist thrust at the most flagrant failure of American society—the race question. What Du Bois had said long ago, unnoticed, now loomed large in 1945: "The problem of the 20th century is the problem of the color line."

President Harry Truman, in late 1946, appointed a Committee on Civil Rights, which recommended that the civil rights section of the Department of Justice be expanded, that there be a permanent Commission on Civil Rights, that Congress pass laws against lynching and to stop voting discrimination, and suggested new laws to end racial discrimination in jobs.

Truman's Committee was blunt about its motivation in making these recommendations. Yes, it said, there was "moral reason:" a matter of conscience. But there was also an "economic reason"—discrimination was costly to the country, wasteful of its talent. And, perhaps most important, there was an international reason:

Our position in the post-war world is so vital to the future that our smallest actions have far-reaching effects. . . . We cannot escape the fact that our civil rights record has been an issue in world politics. The world's press and radio are full of it. . . . Those with competing philosophies have stressed— and are shamelessly distorting—our shortcomings. . . . They have tried to prove our democracy an empty fraud, and our nation a consistent oppressor of underprivileged people. This may seem ludicrous to Americans, but it is sufficiently important to worry our friends. The United States is not so strong, the final triumph of the democratic ideal is not so inevitable that we can ignore what the world thinks of us or our record.

The United States was out in the world now in a way it had never been. The stakes were large—world supremacy. And, as Truman's Committee said: ". . . our smallest actions have far-reaching effects."

And so the United States went ahead to take small actions, hoping they would have large effects. Congress did not move to enact the legislation asked for by the Committee on Civil Rights. But Truman—four months before the presidential election of 1948, and challenged from the left in that election by Progressive party candidate Henry Wallace—issued an executive order asking that the armed forces, segregated in World War II, institute policies of racial equality "as rapidly as possible." The order may have been prompted not only by the election but by the need to maintain black morale in the armed forces, as the possibility of war grew. It took over a decade to complete the desegregation in the military.

Truman could have issued executive orders in other areas, but did not. The Fourteenth and Fifteenth Amendments, plus the set of laws passed in the late 1860s and early 1870s, gave the President enough authority to wipe out racial discrimination. The Constitution demanded that the President execute the laws, but no President had used that power. Neither did Truman. For instance, he asked Congress for legislation "prohibiting discrimination in interstate transportation facilities"; but specific legislation in 1887 already barred discrimination in interstate transportation and had never been enforced by executive action.

Meanwhile, the Supreme Court was taking steps—ninety years after the Constitution had been amended to establish racial equality—to move toward that end. During the war it ruled that the "white primary" used to exclude blacks from voting in the Democratic party primaries—which in the South were really the elections—was unconstitutional.

In 1954, the Court finally struck down the "separate but equal" doctrine that it had defended since the 1890s. The NAACP brought a series of cases before the Court to challenge segregation in the public schools, and now in *Brown* v. *Board of Education* the Court said the separation of schoolchildren "generates a feeling of inferiority . . . that may affect their hearts and minds in a way unlikely ever to be undone." In the field of public education, it said, "the doctrine of 'separate but equal' has no place." The Court did not insist on immediate change: a year later it said that segregated facilities should be integrated "with all deliberate speed." By 1965, ten years after the "all deliberate speed" guideline, more than 75 percent of the school districts in the South remained segregated.

Still, it was a dramatic decision—and the message went around the world in 1954 that the American government had outlawed segregation. In the United States too, for those not thinking about the customary gap between word and fact, it was an exhilarating sign of change.

What to others seemed rapid progress to blacks was apparently not enough. In the early 1960s black people rose in rebellion all over the South. And in the late 1960s they were engaging in wild insurrection in a hundred northern cities. It was all a surprise to those without that deep memory of slavery, that everyday presence of humiliation, registered in the poetry, the music, the occasional outbursts of anger, the more frequent sullen silences. Part of that memory was of words uttered, laws passed, decisions made, which turned out to be meaningless.

For such a people, with such a memory, and such daily recapitulation of history, revolt was always minutes away, in a timing mechanism which no one had set, but which might go off with some unpredictable set of events. Those events came, at the end of 1955, in the capital city of Alabama—Montgomery.

Three months after her arrest, Mrs. Rosa Parks, a forty-three-year-old seamstress, explained why she refused to obey the Montgomery law providing for segregation on city buses, why she decided to sit down in the "white" section of the bus:

> Well, in the first place, I had been working all day on the job. I was quite tired after spending a full day working. I handle and work on clothing that white people wear. That didn't come in my mind but this is what I wanted to know: when and how would we ever determine our rights as human beings? . . . It just happened that the driver made a demand and I just didn't feel like obeying his demand. He called a policeman and I was arrested and placed in jail. . . .

Montgomery blacks called a mass meeting. They voted to boycott all city buses. Car pools were organized to take Negroes to work; most people walked. The city retaliated by indicting one hundred leaders of the boycott, and sent many to jail. White segregationists turned to violence. Bombs exploded in four Negro churches. A shotgun blast was fired through the front door of the home of Dr. Martin Luther King, Jr., the twenty-seven-year-old Altanta-born minister who was one of the leaders of the boycott. King's home was bombed. But the black people of Montgomery persisted, and in November 1956, the Supreme Court outlawed segregation on local bus lines.

Montgomery was the beginning. It forecast the style and mood of the vast protest movement that would sweep the South in the next

ten years: emotional church meetings, Christian hymns adapted to current battles, references to lost American ideals, the commitment to
nonviolence, the willingness to struggle and sacrifice. A *New York Times*
reporter described a mass meeting in Montgomery during the boycott:

> One after the other, indicted Negro leaders took the rostrum in a crowded
> Baptist church tonight to urge their followers to shun the city's buses and
> "walk with God."
>
> More than two thousand Negroes filled the church from basement to
> balcony and overflowed into the street. They chanted and sang; they shouted
> and prayed; they collapsed in the aisles and they sweltered in an eighty-five
> degree heat. They pledged themselves again and again to "passive resistance."
> Under this banner they have carried on for eighty days a stubborn boycott
> of the city's buses.

Martin Luther King at that meeting gave a preview of the oratory
that would soon inspire millions of people to demand racial justice.
He said the protest was not merely over buses but over things that
"go deep down into the archives of history." He said:

> We have known humiliation, we have known abusive language, we have
> been plunged into the abyss of oppression. And we decided to raise up only
> with the weapon of protest. It is one of the greatest glories of America that
> we have the right of protest.
>
> If we are arrested every day, if we are exploited every day, if we are
> trampled over every day, don't ever let anyone pull you so low as to hate
> them. We must use the weapon of love. We must have compassion and under-
> standing for those who hate us. We must realize so many people are taught
> to hate us that they are not totally responsible for their hate. But we stand
> in life at midnight, we are always on the threshold of a new dawn.

King's stress on love and nonviolence was powerfully effective in
building a sympathetic following throughout the nation, among whites
as well as blacks. But there were blacks who thought the message naïve,
that while there were misguided people who might be won over by
love, there were others who would have to be bitterly fought, and not
always with nonviolence. Two years after the Montgomery boycott,
in Monroe, North Carolina, an ex-marine named Robert Williams, the
president of the local NAACP, became known for his view that blacks
should defend themselves against violence, with guns if necessary. When
local Klansmen attacked the home of one of the leaders of the Monroe
NAACP, Williams and other blacks, armed with rifles, fired back. The
Klan left. (The Klan was being challenged now with its own tactic of

violence; a Klan raid on an Indian community in North Carolina was repelled by Indians firing rifles.)

Still, in the years that followed, southern blacks stressed nonviolence. On February 1, 1960, four freshmen at a Negro college in Greensboro, North Carolina, decided to sit down at the Woolworth's lunch counter downtown, where only whites ate. They were refused service, and when they would not leave, the lunch counter was closed for the day. The next day they returned, and then, day after day, other Negroes came to sit silently.

In the next two weeks, sit-ins spread to fifteen cities in five southern states. A seventeen-year-old sophomore at Spelman College in Atlanta, Ruby Doris Smith, heard about Greensboro:

> When the student committee was formed . . . I told my older sister . . . to put me on the list. And when two hundred students were selected for the first demonstration I was among them. I went through the food line in the restaurant at the State Capitol with six other students, but when we got to the cashier she wouldn't take our money. . . . The Lieutenant-Governor came down and told us to leave. We didn't and went to the county jail.

In his Harlem apartment in New York, a young Negro teacher of mathematics named Bob Moses saw a photo in the newspapers of the Greensboro sit-inners. "The students in that picture had a certain look on their faces, sort of sullen, angry, determined. Before, the Negro in the South had always looked on the defensive, cringing. This time they were taking the initiative. They were kids my age, and I knew this had something to do with my own life."

There was violence against the sit-inners. But the idea of taking the initiative against segregation took hold. In the next twelve months, more than fifty thousand people, mostly black, some white, participated in demonstrations of one kind or another in a hundred cities, and over 3,600 people were put in jail. But by the end of 1960, lunch counters were open to blacks in Greensboro and many other places.

A year after the Greensboro incident, a northern-based group dedicated to racial equality—CORE (Congress of Racial Equality)—organized "Freedom Rides" in which blacks and whites traveled together on buses going through the South, to try to break the segregation pattern in interstate travel. Such segregation had long been illegal, but the federal government never enforced the law in the South; the President now was John F. Kennedy, but he too seemed cautious about the race question, concerned about the support of southern white leaders of the Democratic party.

The two buses that left Washington, D.C., on May 4, 1961, headed for New Orleans, never got there. In South Carolina, riders were beaten. In Alabama, a bus was set afire. Freedom Riders were attacked with fists and iron bars. The southern police did not interfere with any of this violence, nor did the federal government. FBI agents watched, took notes, did nothing.

At this point, veterans of the sit-ins, who had recently formed the Student Nonviolent Coordinating Committee (SNCC), dedicated to nonviolent but militant action for equal rights, organized another Freedom Ride, from Nashville to Birmingham. Before they started out, they called the Department of Justice in Washington, D.C., to ask for protection. As Ruby Doris Smith reported: ". . . the Justice Department said no, they couldn't protect anyone, but if something happened, they would investigate. You know how they do. . . ."

The racially mixed SNCC Freedom Riders were arrested in Birmingham, Alabama, spent a night in jail, were taken to the Tennessee border by police, made their way back to Birmingham, took a bus to Montgomery, and there were attacked by whites with fists and clubs, in a bloody scene. They resumed their trip, to Jackson, Mississippi.

By this time the Freedom Riders were in the news all over the world, and the government was anxious to prevent further violence. Attorney General Robert Kennedy, instead of insisting on their right to travel without being arrested, agreed to the Freedom Riders' being arrested in Jackson, in return for Mississippi police protection against possible mob violence. As Victor Navasky comments in *Kennedy Justice,* about Robert Kennedy: "He didn't hesitate to trade the freedom riders' constitutional right to interstate travel for Senator Eastland's guarantee of their right to live."

The Freedom Riders did not become subdued in jail. They resisted, protested, sang, demanded their rights. Stokely Carmichael recalled later how he and his fellow inmates were singing in the Parchman jail in Mississippi and the sheriff threatened to take away their mattresses:

I hung on to the mattress and said, "I think we have a right to them and I think you're unjust." And he said, "I don't want to hear all that shit, nigger," and started to put on the wristbreakers. I wouldn't move and started to sing "I'm Gonna Tell God How You Treat Me" and everybody started to sing it, and by this time Tyson was really to pieces. He called to the trusties, "Get him in there!" and he went out the door and slammed it, and left everybody else with their mattresses.

In Albany, Georgia, a small deep-South town where the atmosphere of slavery still lingered, mass demonstrations took place in the winter of 1961 and again in 1962. Of 22,000 black people in Albany, over a thousand went to jail for marching, assembling, to protest segregation and discrimination. Here, as in all the demonstrations that would sweep over the South, little black children participated—a new generation was learning to act. The Albany police chief, after one of the mass arrests, was taking the names of prisoners lined up before his desk. He looked up and saw a Negro boy about nine years old. "What's your name?" The boy looked straight at him and said: "Freedom, Freedom."

There is no way of measuring the effect of that southern movement on the sensibilities of a whole generation of young black people, or of tracing the process by which some of them became activists and leaders. In Lee County, Georgia, after the events of 1961–1962, a black teenager named James Crawford joined SNCC and began taking black people to the county courthouse to vote. One day, bringing a woman there, he was approached by the deputy registrar. Another SNCC worker took notes on the conversation:

REGISTRAR: What do you want?
CRAWFORD: I brought this lady down to register.
REGISTRAR: (after giving the woman a card to fill out and sending her outside in the hall) Why did you bring this lady down here?
CRAWFORD: Because she wants to be a first class citizen like y'all.
REGISTRAR: Who are you to bring people down to register?
CRAWFORD: It's my job.
REGISTRAR: Suppose you get two bullets in your head right now?
CRAWFORD: I got to die anyhow.
REGISTRAR: If I don't do it, I can get somebody else to do it. (No reply)
REGISTRAR: Are you scared?
CRAWFORD: No.
REGISTRAR: Suppose somebody came in that door and shoot you in the back of the head right now. What would you do?
CRAWFORD: I couldn't do nothing. If they shoot me in the back of the head there are people coming from all over the world.
REGISTRAR: What people?
CRAWFORD: The people I work for.

In Birmingham in 1963, thousands of blacks went into the streets, facing police clubs, tear gas, dogs, high-powered water hoses. And meanwhile, all over the deep South, the young people of SNCC, mostly black, a few white, were moving into communities in Georgia, Alabama, Mississippi, Arkansas. Joined by local black people, they were organizing, to register people to vote, to protest against racism, to build up courage against violence. The Department of Justice recorded 1412 demonstrations in three months of 1963. Imprisonment became commonplace, beatings became frequent. Many local people were afraid. Others came forward. A nineteen-year-old black student from Illinois named Carver Neblett, working for SNCC in Terrell County, Georgia, reported:

I talked with a blind man who is extremely interested in the civil rights movement. He has been keeping up with the movement from the beginning. Even though this man is blind he wants to learn all the questions on the literacy test. Imagine, while many are afraid that white men will burn our houses, shoot into them, or put us off their property, a blind man, seventy years old, wants to come to our meetings.

As the summer of 1964 approached, SNCC and other civil rights groups working together in Mississippi, and facing increasing violence, decided to call upon young people from other parts of the country for help. They hoped that would bring attention to the situation in Mississippi. Again and again in Mississippi and elsewhere, the FBI had stood by, lawyers for the Justice Department had stood by, while civil rights workers were beaten and jailed, while federal laws were violated.

On the eve of the Mississippi Summer, in early June 1964, the civil rights movement rented a theater near the White House, and a busload of black Mississippians traveled to Washington to testify publicly about the daily violence, the dangers facing the volunteers coming into Mississippi. Constitutional lawyers testified that the national government had the legal power to give protection against such violence. The transcript of this testimony was given to President Johnson and Attorney General Kennedy, accompanied by a request for a protective federal presence during the Mississippi Summer. There was no response.

Twelve days after the public hearing, three civil rights workers, James Chaney, a young black Mississippian, and two white volunteers, Andrew Goodman and Michael Schwerner, were arrested in Philadelphia, Mississippi, released from jail late at night, then seized, beaten with chains, and shot to death. Ultimately, an informer's testimony led to jail sentences for the sheriff and deputy sheriff and others. That came too late. The Mississippi murders had taken place after the repeated refusal of the national government, under Kennedy or Johnson, or any other President, to defend blacks against violence.

Dissatisfaction with the national government intensified. Later that summer, during the Democratic National Convention in Washington, Mississippi, blacks asked to be seated as part of the state delegation to represent the 40 percent of the state's population who were black. They were turned down by the liberal Democratic leadership, including vice-presidential candidate Hubert Humphrey.

Congress began reacting to the black revolt, the turmoil, the world publicity. Civil rights laws were passed in 1957, 1960, and 1964. They promised much, on voting equality, on employment equality, but were enforced poorly or ignored. In 1965, President Johnson sponsored and Congress passed an even stronger Voting Rights Law, this time ensuring on-the-spot federal protection of the right to register and vote. The effect on Negro voting in the South was dramatic. In 1952, a million southern blacks (20 percent of those eligible) registered to vote. In 1964 the number was 2 million—40 percent. By 1968, it was 3 million, 60 percent—the same percentage as white voters.

The federal government was trying—without making fundamental changes—to control an explosive situation, to channel anger into the traditional cooling mechanism of the ballot box, the polite petition, the officially endorsed quiet gathering. When black civil rights leaders planned a huge march on Washington in the summer of 1963 to protest the failure of the nation to solve the race problem, it was quickly embraced by President Kennedy and other national leaders, and turned into a friendly assemblage.

Martin Luther King's speech there thrilled 200,000 black and white Americans—"I have a dream. . . ." It was magnificent oratory, but without the anger that many blacks felt. When John Lewis, a young Alabama-born SNCC leader, much arrested, much beaten, tried to introduce a stronger note of outrage at the meeting, he was censored by the leaders of the march, who insisted he omit certain sentences critical of the national government and urging militant action.

Eighteen days after the Washington gathering, almost as if in deliberate contempt for its moderation, a bomb exploded in the basement of a black church in Birmingham and four girls attending a Sunday school class were killed. President Kennedy had praised the "deep fervor and quiet dignity" of the march, but the black militant Malcolm X was probably closer to the mood of the black community. Speaking in Detroit two months after the march on Washington and the Birmingham bombing, Malcolm X said, in his powerful, icy-clear, rhythmic style:

> The Negroes were out there in the streets. They were talking about how they were going to march on Washington. . . . That they were going to march on Washington, march on the Senate, march on the White House, march on the Congress, and tie it up, bring it to a halt, not let the government proceed. They even said they were going out to the airport and lay down on the runway and not let any airplanes land. I'm telling you what they said. That was revolution. That was revolution. That was the black revolution.
>
> It was the grass roots out there in the street. It scared the white man to death, scared the white power structure in Washington, D.C. to death; I was there. When they found out that this black steamroller was going to come down on the capital, they called in . . . these national Negro leaders that you respect and told them, "Call it off," Kennedy said. "Look you all are letting this thing go too far." And Old Tom said, "Boss, I can't stop it because I didn't start it." I'm telling you what they said. They said, "I'm not even in it, much less at the head of it." They said, "These Negroes are doing things on their own. They're running ahead of us." And that old shrewd fox, he said, "If you all aren't in it, I'll put you in it. I'll put you at the head of it. I'll endorse it. I'll welcome it. I'll help it. I'll join it."
>
> This is what they did with the march on Washington. They joined it . . . became part of it, took it over. And as they took it over, it lost its militancy. It ceased to be angry, it ceased to be hot, it ceased to be uncompromising. Why, it even ceased to be a march. It became a picnic, a circus. Nothing but a circus, with clowns and all. . . .
>
> No, it was a sellout. It was a takeover. . . . They controlled it so tight, they told those Negroes what time to hit town, where to stop, what signs to carry, what song to sing, what speech they could make, and what speech they couldn't make, and then told them to get out of town by sundown. . . .

The accuracy of Malcolm X's caustic description of the march on Washington is corroborated in the description from the other side— from the Establishment, by White House adviser Arthur Schlesinger, in his book *A Thousand Days.* He tells how Kennedy met with the civil rights leaders and said the march would "create an atmosphere of intimidation" just when Congress was considering civil rights bills. A. Philip Randolph replied: "The Negroes are already in the streets. It is very likely impossible to get them off. . . ." Schlesinger says:

"The conference with the President did persuade the civil rights leaders that they should not lay siege to Capitol Hill." Schlesinger describes the Washington march admiringly and then concludes: "So in 1963 Kennedy moved to incorporate the Negro revolution into the democratic coalition. . . ."

But it did not work. The black could not be easily brought into "the democratic coalition" when bombs kept exploding in churches, when new "civil rights" laws did not change the root condition of black people. In the spring of 1963, the rate of unemployment for whites was 4.8 percent. For nonwhites it was 12.1 percent. According to government estimates, one-fifth of the white population was below the poverty line, and one-half of the black population was below that line. The civil rights bills emphasized voting, but voting was not a fundamental solution to racism or poverty. In Harlem, blacks who had voted for years still lived in rat-infested slums.

In precisely those years when civil rights legislation coming out of Congress reached its peak, 1964 and 1965, there were black outbreaks in every part of the country: in Florida, set off by the killing of a Negro woman and a bomb threat against a Negro high school; in Cleveland, set off by the killing of a white minister who sat in the path of a bulldozer to protest discrimination against blacks in construction work; in New York, set off by the fatal shooting of a fifteen-year-old Negro boy during a fight with an off-duty policeman. There were riots also in Rochester, Jersey City, Chicago, Philadelphia.

In August 1965, just as Lyndon Johnson was signing into law the strong Voting Rights Act, providing for federal registration of black voters to ensure their protection, the black ghetto in Watts, Los Angeles, erupted in the most violent urban outbreak since World War II. It was provoked by the forcible arrest of a young Negro driver, the clubbing of a bystander by police, the seizure of a young black woman falsely accused of spitting on the police. There was rioting in the streets, looting and firebombing of stores. Police and National Guardsmen were called in; they used their guns. Thirty-four people were killed, most of them black, hundreds injured, four thousand arrested. Robert Conot, a West Coast journalist, wrote of the riot *(Rivers of Blood, Years of Darkness):* "In Los Angeles the Negro was going on record that he would no longer turn the other cheek. That, frustrated and goaded, he would strike back, whether the response of violence was an appropriate one or no."

In the summer of 1966, there were more outbreaks, with rock

throwing, looting, and fire bombing by Chicago blacks and wild shootings by the National Guard; three blacks were killed, one a thirteen-year-old boy, another a fourteen-year-old pregnant girl. In Cleveland, the National Guard was summoned to stop a commotion in the black community; four Negroes were shot to death, two by troopers, two by white civilians.

It seemed clear by now that the nonviolence of the southern movement, perhaps tactically necessary in the southern atmosphere, and effective because it could be used to appeal to national opinion against the segregationist South, was not enough to deal with the entrenched problems of poverty in the black ghetto. In 1910, 90 percent of Negroes lived in the South. But by 1965, mechanical cotton pickers harvested 81 percent of Mississippi Delta cotton. Between 1940 and 1970, 4 million blacks left the country for the city. By 1965, 80 percent of blacks lived in cities and 50 percent of the black people lived in the North.

There was a new mood in SNCC and among many militant blacks. Their disillusionment was expressed by a young black writer, Julius Lester:

Now it is over. America has had chance after chance to show that it really meant "that all men are endowed with certain inalienable rights." . . . Now it is over. The days of singing freedom songs and the days of combating bullets and billy clubs with love. . . . Love is fragile and gentle and seeks a like response. They used to sing "I Love Everybody" as they ducked bricks and bottles. Now they sing:

> Too much love,
> Too much love,
> Nothing kills a nigger like
> Too much love.

In 1967, in the black ghettos of the country, came the greatest urban riots of American history. According to the report of the National Advisory Committee on Urban Disorders, they "involved Negroes acting against local symbols of white American society," symbols of authority and property in the black neighborhoods—rather than purely against white persons. The Commission reported eight major uprisings, thirty-three "serious but not major" outbreaks, and 123 "minor" disorders. Eighty-three died of gunfire, mostly in Newark and Detroit. "The overwhelming majority of the persons killed or injured in all the disorders were Negro civilians."

The "typical rioter," according to the Commission, was a young, high school dropout but "nevertheless, somewhat better educated than his non-rioting Negro neighbor" and "usually underemployed or employed in a menial job." He was "proud of his race, extremely hostile to both whites and middle-class Negroes and, although informed about politics, highly distrustful of the political system."

The report blamed "white racism" for the disorders, and identified the ingredients of the "explosive mixture which has been accumulating in our cities since the end of World War II":

> Pervasive discrimination and segregation in employment, education, and housing . . . growing concentrations of impoverished Negroes in our major cities, creating a growing crisis of deteriorating facilities and services and unmet human needs. . . .
>
> A new mood has sprung up among Negroes, particularly the young, in which self-esteem and enhanced racial pride are replacing apathy and submission to the "system."

But the Commission Report itself was a standard device of the system when facing rebellion: set up an investigating committee, issue a report; the words of the report, however strong, will have a soothing effect.

That didn't completely work either. "Black Power" was the new slogan—an expression of distrust of any "progress" given or conceded by whites, a rejection of paternalism. Few blacks (or whites) knew the statement of the white writer Aldous Huxley: "Liberties are not given, they are taken." But the idea was there, in Black Power. Also, a pride in race, an insistence on black independence, and often, on black separation to achieve this independence. Malcolm X was the most eloquent spokesman for this. After he was assassinated as he spoke on a public platform in February 1965, in a plan whose origins are still obscure, he became the martyr of this movement. Hundreds of thousands read his *Autobiography*. He was more influential in death than during his lifetime. NO

Martin Luther King, though still respected, was being replaced now by new heroes: Huey Newton of the Black Panthers, for instance. The Panthers had guns; they said blacks should defend themselves.

Malcolm X in late 1964 had spoken to black students from Mississippi visiting Harlem:

> You'll get freedom by letting your enemy know that you'll do anything to get your freedom; then you'll get it. It's the only way you'll get it. When you get that kind of attitude, they'll label you as a "crazy Negro," or they'll call you a "crazy nigger"—they don't say Negro. Or they'll call you an extremist

or a subversive, or seditious, or a red or a radical. But when you stay radical long enough and get enough people to be like you, you'll get your freedom.

Congress responded to the riots of 1967 by passing the Civil Rights Act of 1968. Presumably it would make stronger the laws prohibiting violence against blacks; it increased the penalties against those depriving people of their civil rights. However, it said: "The provisions of this section shall not apply to acts or omissions on the part of law enforcement officers, members of the National Guard . . . or members of the Armed Forces of the United States, who are engaged in suppressing a riot or civil disturbance. . . ."

Furthermore, it added a section—agreed to by liberal members of Congress in order to get the whole bill passed—that provided up to five years in prison for anyone traveling interstate or using interstate facilities (including mail and telephone) "to organize, promote, encourage, participate in, or carry on a riot." It defined a riot as an action by three or more people involving threats of violence. The first person prosecuted under the Civil Rights Act of 1968 was a young black leader of SNCC, H. Rap Brown, who had made a militant, angry speech in Maryland, just before a racial disturbance there. (Later the Act would be used against antiwar demonstrators in Chicago—the Chicago Eight.)

Martin Luther King himself became more and more concerned about problems untouched by civil rights laws—problems coming out of poverty. In the spring of 1968, he began speaking out, against the advice of some Negro leaders who feared losing friends in Washington, against the war in Vietnam. He connected war and poverty:

. . . it's inevitable that we've got to bring out the question of the tragic mix-up in priorities. We are spending all of this money for death and destruction, and not nearly enough money for life and constructive development . . . when the guns of war become a national obsession, social needs inevitably suffer.

King now became a chief target of the FBI, which tapped his private phone conversations, sent him fake letters, threatened him, blackmailed him, and even suggested once in an anonymous letter that he commit suicide. FBI internal memos discussed finding a black leader to replace King. As a Senate report on the FBI said in 1976, the FBI tried "to destroy Dr. Martin Luther King."

King was turning his attention to troublesome questions. He still insisted on nonviolence. Riots were self-defeating, he thought. But they did express a deep feeling that could not be ignored. And so, nonviolence, he said, "must be militant, massive non-violence." He planned a "Poor

People's Encampment" on Washington, this time not with the paternal approval of the President. And he went to Memphis, Tennessee, to support a strike of garbage workers in that city. There, standing on a balcony outside his hotel room, he was shot to death by an unseen marksman. The Poor People's Encampment went on, and then it was broken up by police action, just as the World War I veterans' Bonus Army of 1932 was dispersed.

The killing of King brought new urban outbreaks all over the country, in which thirty-nine people were killed, thirty-five of them black. Evidence was piling up that even with all of the civil rights laws now on the books, the courts would not protect blacks against violence and injustice:

1. In the 1967 riots in Detroit, three black teen-agers were killed in the Algiers Motel. Three Detroit policemen and a black private guard were tried for this triple murder. The defense conceded, a UPI dispatch said, that the four men had shot two of the blacks. A jury exonerated them.

2. In Jackson, Mississippi, in the spring of 1970, on the campus of Jackson State College, a Negro college, police laid down a 28-second barrage of gunfire, using shotguns, rifles, and a submachine gun. Four hundred bullets or pieces of buckshot struck the girls' dormitory and two black students were killed. A local grand jury found the attack "justified" and U.S. District Court Judge Harold Cox (a Kennedy appointee) declared that students who engage in civil disorders "must expect to be injured or killed."

3. In Boston in April 1970, a policeman shot and killed an unarmed black man, a patient in a ward in the Boston City Hospital, firing five shots after the black man snapped a towel at him. The chief judge of the municipal court of Boston exonerated the policeman.

4. In Augusta, Georgia, in May 1970, six Negroes were shot to death during looting and disorder in the city. The *New York Times* reported:

   A confidential police report indicates that at least five of the victims were killed by the police. . . .

   An eyewitness to one of the deaths said he had watched a Negro police-man and his white partner fire nine shots into the back of a man suspected of looting. They did not fire warning shots or ask him to stop running, said Charles A. Reid, a 38-year-old businessman. . . .

5. In April 1970, a federal jury in Boston found a policeman had used "exces-sive force" against two black soldiers from Fort Devens, and one of them required twelve stitches in his scalp; the judge awarded the servicemen $3 in damages.

These were "normal" cases, endlessly repeated in the history of the country, coming randomly but persistently out of a racism deep in the institutions, the mind of the country. But there was something else—a planned pattern of violence against militant black organizers, carried on by the police and the Federal Bureau of Investigation. On December 4, 1969, a little before five in the morning, a squad of Chicago police, armed with a submachine gun and shotguns, raided an apartment where Black Panthers lived. They fired at least eighty-two and perhaps two hundred rounds into the apartment, killing twenty-one-year-old Black Panther leader Fred Hampton as he lay in his bed, and another Black Panther, Mark Clark. Years later, it was discovered in a court proceeding that the FBI had an informer among the Panthers, and that they had given the police a floor plan of the apartment, including a sketch of where Fred Hampton slept.

Was the government turning to murder and terror because the concessions—the legislation, the speeches, the intonation of the civil rights hymn "We Shall Overcome" by President Lyndon Johnson—were not working? It was discovered later that the government in all the years of the civil rights movement, while making concessions through Congress, was acting through the FBI to harass and break up black militant groups. Between 1956 and 1971 the FBI concluded a massive Counterintelligence Program (known as COINTELPRO) that took 295 actions against black groups. Black militancy seemed stubbornly resistant to destruction. A secret FBI report to President Nixon in 1970 said "a recent poll indicates that approximately 25% of the black population has a great respect for the Black Panther Party, including 43% of blacks under 21 years of age." Was there fear that blacks would turn their attention from the controllable field of voting to the more dangerous arena of wealth and poverty—of class conflict? In 1966, seventy poor black people in Greenville, Mississippi, occupied an unused air force barracks, until they were evicted by the military. A local woman, Mrs. Unita Blackwell, said:

I feel that the federal government have proven that it don't care about poor people. Everything that we have asked for through these years had been handed down on paper. It's never been a reality. We the poor people of Mississippi is tired. We're tired of it so we're going to build for ourselves, because we don't have a government that represents us.

Out of the 1967 riots in Detroit came an organization devoted to organizing black workers for revolutionary change. This was the League of Revolutionary Black Workers, which lasted until 1971 and influenced thousands of black workers in Detroit during its period of activity.

The new emphasis was more dangerous than civil rights, because it created the possibility of blacks and whites uniting on the issue of class exploitation. Back in November 1963, A. Philip Randolph had spoken to an AFL-CIO convention about the civil rights movement, and foreseen its direction: "The Negro's protest today is but the first rumbling of the 'under-class.' As the Negro has taken to the streets, so will the unemployed of all races take to the streets."

Attempts began to do with blacks what had been done historically with whites—to lure a small number into the system with economic enticements. There was talk of "black capitalism." Leaders of the NAACP and CORE were invited to the White House. James Farmer of CORE, a former Freedom Rider and militant, was given a job in President Nixon's administration. Floyd McKissick of CORE received a $14 million government loan to build a housing development in North Carolina. Lyndon Johnson had given jobs to some blacks through the Office of Economic Opportunity; Nixon set up an Office of Minority Business Enterprise.

Chase Manhattan Bank and the Rockefeller family (controllers of Chase) took a special interest in developing "black capitalism." The Rockefellers had always been financial patrons of the Urban League, and a strong influence in black education through their support of Negro colleges in the South. David Rockefeller tried to persuade his fellow capitalists that while helping black businessmen with money might not be fruitful in the short run, it was necessary "to shape an environment in which the business can continue earning a profit four or five or ten years from now." With all of this, black business remained infinitesimally small. The largest black corporation (Motown Industries) had sales in 1974 of $45 million, while Exxon Corporation had sales of $42 billion. The total receipts of black-owned firms accounted for 0.3 percent of all business income.

There was a small amount of change and a lot of publicity. There were more black faces in the newspapers and on television, creating an impression of change—and siphoning off into the mainstream a small but significant number of black leaders.

Some new black voices spoke against this. Robert Allen *(Black Awakening in Capitalist America)* wrote:

If the community as a whole is to benefit, then the community as a whole must be organized to manage collectively its internal economy and its business relations with white America. Black business firms must be treated and operated as social property, belonging to the general black community, not as the private property of individual or limited groups of individuals. This necessitates the dismantling of capitalist property relations in the black community and their replacement with a planned communal economy.

A black woman, Patricia Robinson, in a pamphlet distributed in Boston in 1970 *(Poor Black Woman)*, tied male supremacy to capitalism and said the black woman "allies herself with the have-nots in the wider world and their revolutionary struggles." She said the poor black woman did not in the past "question the social and economic system" but now she must, and in fact, "she has begun to question aggressive male domination and the class society which enforces it, capitalism."

Another black woman, Margaret Wright, said she was not fighting for equality with men if it meant equality in the world of killing, the world of competition. "I don't want to compete on no damned exploitative level. I don't want to exploit nobody. . . . I want the right to be black and me. . . ."

The system was working hard, by the late sixties and early seventies, to contain the frightening explosiveness of the black upsurge. Blacks were voting in large numbers in the South, and in the 1968 Democratic Convention three blacks were admitted into the Mississippi delegation. By 1977, more than two thousand blacks held office in eleven southern states (in 1965 the number was seventy-two). There were two Congressmen, eleven state senators, ninety-five state representatives, 267 county commissioners, seventy-six mayors, 824 city council members, eighteen sheriffs or chiefs of police, 508 school board members. It was a dramatic advance. But blacks, with 20 percent of the South's population, still held less than 3 percent of the elective offices. A *New York Times* reporter, analyzing the new situation in 1977, pointed out that even where blacks held important city offices: "Whites almost always retain economic power." After Maynard Jackson, a black, became mayor of Atlanta, "the white business establishment continued to exert its influence."

Those blacks in the South who could afford to go to downtown restaurants and hotels were no longer barred because of their race. More blacks could go to colleges and universities, to law schools and medical schools. Northern cities were busing children back and forth in an attempt to create racially mixed schools, despite the racial segregation in housing. None of this, however, was halting what Frances Piven and Richard Cloward *(Poor People's Movements)* called "the destruction of the black lower class"—the unemployment, the deterioration of the ghetto, the rising crime, drug addiction, violence.

In the summer of 1977, the Department of Labor reported that the rate of unemployment among black youths was 34.8 percent. A small new black middle class of blacks had been created, and it raised the overall statistics for black income—but there was a great disparity between the newly risen middle-class black and the poor left behind. Despite the new opportunities for a small number of blacks, the median black family income of 1977 was only about 60 percent that of whites; blacks were twice as likely to die of diabetes; seven times as likely to be victims of homicidal violence rising out of the poverty and despair of the ghetto.

A *New York Times* report in early 1978 said: ". . . the places that experienced urban riots in the 1960's have, with a few exceptions, changed little, and the conditions of poverty have spread in most cities."

Statistics did not tell the whole story. Racism, always a national fact, not just a southern one, emerged in northern cities, as the federal government made concessions to poor blacks in a way that pitted them against poor whites for resources made scarce by the system. Blacks, freed from slavery to take their place under capitalism, had long been forced into conflict with whites for scarce jobs. Now, with desegregation in housing, blacks tried to move into neighborhoods where whites, themselves poor, crowded, troubled, could find in them a target for their anger. In the Boston *Globe,* November 1977:

A Hispanic family of six fled their apartment in the Savin Hill section of Dorchester yesterday after a week of repeated stonings and window-smashings by a group of white youths, in what appears to have been racially motivated attacks, police said.

In Boston, the busing of black children to white schools, and whites to black schools, set off a wave of white neighborhood violence. The use of busing to integrate schools—sponsored by the government and the courts in response to the black movement—was an ingenious concession to protest. It had the effect of pushing poor whites and poor blacks into competition for the miserable inadequate schools which the system provided for all the poor.

Was the black population—hemmed into the ghetto, divided by the growth of a middle class, decimated by poverty, attacked by the government, driven into conflict with whites—under control? Surely, in the mid-seventies, there was no great black movement under way.

Yet, a new black consciousness had been born and was still alive. Also, whites and blacks were crossing racial lines in the South to unite as a class against employers. In 1971, two thousand woodworkers in Mississippi, black and white, joined together to protest a new method of measuring wood that led to lower wages. In the textile mills of J. P. Stevens, where 44,000 workers were employed in eighty-five plants, mostly in the South, blacks and whites were working together in union activity. In Tifton, Georgia, and Milledgeville, Georgia, in 1977, blacks and whites served together on the union committees of their plants.

Would a new black movement go beyond the limits of the civil rights actions of the sixties, beyond the spontaneous urban riots of the seventies, beyond separatism to a coalition of white and black in a historic new alliance? There was no way of knowing this in 1978. In 1978, 6 million black people were unemployed. As Langston Hughes said, what happens to a dream deferred? Does it dry up, or does it explode? If it did explode, as it had in the past, it would come with a certain inevitability—out of the conditions of black life in America— and yet, because no one knew when, it would come as a surprise.

7.
The Impossible Victory: Vietnam

From 1964 to 1972, the wealthiest and most powerful nation in the history of the world made a maximum military effort, with everything short of atomic bombs, to defeat a nationalist revolutionary movement in a tiny, peasant country—and failed. When the United States fought in Vietnam, it was organized modern technology versus organized human beings, and the human beings won.

In the course of that war, there developed in the United States the greatest antiwar movement the nation had ever experienced, a movement that played a critical part in bringing the war to an end.

It was another startling fact of the sixties.

In the fall of 1945 Japan, defeated, was forced to leave Indochina, the former French colony it had occupied at the start of the war. In the meantime, a revolutionary movement had grown there, determined to end colonial control and to achieve a new life for the peasants of Indochina. Led by a Communist named Ho Chi Minh, the revolutionists fought against the Japanese, and when they were gone held a spectacular celebration in Hanoi in late 1945, with a million people in the streets, and issued a Declaration of Independence. It borrowed from the Declaration of the Rights of Man and the Citizen, in the French Revolution, and from the American Declaration of Independence, and began: "All men are created equal. They are endowed by their Creator with certain inalienable rights; among these are Life, Liberty, and the pursuit of Happiness." Just as the Americans in 1776 had listed their grievances against the English King, the Vietnamese listed their complaints against French rule:

They have enforced inhuman laws. . . . They have built more prisons than schools. They have mercilessly slain our patriots, they have drowned uprisings in rivers of blood. They have fettered public opinion. . . . They have robbed us of our rice fields, our mines, our forests, and our raw materials. . . .

They have invented numerous unjustifiable taxes and reduced our people, especially our peasantry, to a state of extreme poverty. . . .

. . . from the end of last year, to the beginning of this year . . . more than two million of our fellow-citizens died of starvation. . . .

The whole Vietnamese people, animated by a common purpose, are determined to fight to the bitter end against any attempt by the French colonialists to reconquer their country.

The U.S. Defense Department study of the Vietnam war, intended to be "top secret" but released to the public by Daniel Ellsberg and Anthony Russo in the famous *Pentagon Papers* case, described Ho Chi Minh's work:

. . . Ho had built the Viet Minh into the only Vietnam-wide political organization capable of effective resistance to either the Japanese or the French. He was the only Vietnamese wartime leader with a national following, and he assured himself wider fealty among the Vietnamese people when in August–September, 1945, he overthrew the Japanese . . . established the Democratic Republic of Vietnam, and staged receptions for in-coming allied occupation forces. . . . For a few weeks in September, 1945, Vietnam was—for the first and only time in its modern history—free of foreign domination, and united from north to south under Ho Chi Minh. . . .

The Western powers were already at work to change this. England occupied the southern part of Indochina and then turned it back to the French. Nationalist China (this was under Chiang Kai-shek, before the Communist revolution) occupied the northern part of Indochina, and the United States persuaded it to turn that back to the French. As Ho Chi Minh told an American journalist: "We apparently stand quite alone. . . . We shall have to depend on ourselves."

Between October 1945 and February 1946, Ho Chi Minh wrote eight letters to President Truman, reminding him of the self-determination promises of the Atlantic Charter. One of the letters was sent both to Truman and to the United Nations:

I wish to invite attention of your Excellency for strictly humanitarian reasons to following matter. Two million Vietnamese died of starvation during winter of 1944 and spring 1945 because of starvation policy of French who seized and stored until it rotted all available rice. . . . Three-fourths of cultivated land was flooded in summer 1945, which was followed by a severe drought; of normal harvest five-sixths was lost. . . . Many people are starving. . . . Unless great world powers and international relief organizations bring us immediate assistance we face imminent catastrophe. . . .

Truman never replied.

In October of 1946, the French bombarded Haiphong, a port in northern Vietnam, and there began the eight-year war between the

Vietminh movement and the French over who would rule Vietnam. After the Communist victory in China in 1949 and the Korean war the following year, the United States began giving large amounts of military aid to the French. By 1954, the United States had given 300,000 small arms and machine guns, enough to equip the entire French army in Indochina, and $1 billion; all together, the U.S. was financing 80 percent of the French war effort.

Why was the United States doing this? To the public, the word was that the United States was helping to stop Communism in Asia, but there was not much public discussion. In the secret memoranda of the National Security Council (which advised the President on foreign policy) there was talk in 1950 of what came to be known as the "domino theory"—that, like a row of dominoes, if one country fell to Communism, the next one would do the same and so on. It was important therefore to keep the first one from falling.

A secret memo of the National Security Council in June 1952 also pointed to the chain of U.S. military bases along the coast of China, the Philippines, Taiwan, Japan, South Korea:

> Communist control of all of Southeast Asia would render the U.S. position in the Pacific offshore island chain precarious and would seriously jeopardize fundamental U.S. security interests in the Far East.

And:

> Southeast Asia, especially Malaya and Indonesia, is the principal world source of natural rubber and tin, and a producer of petroleum and other strategically important commodities. . . .

It was also noted that Japan depended on the rice of Southeast Asia, and Communist victory there would "make it extremely difficult to prevent Japan's eventual accommodation to communism."

In 1953, a congressional study mission reported: "The area of Indochina is immensely wealthy in rice, rubber, coal and iron ore. Its position makes it a strategic key to the rest of Southeast Asia." That year, a State Department memorandum said that the French were losing the war in Indochina, had failed "to win a sufficient native support," feared that a negotiated settlement "would mean the eventual loss to Communism not only of Indo-China but of the whole of Southeast Asia, and concluded: "If the French actually decided to withdraw, the U.S. would have to consider most seriously whether to take over in this area."

In 1954, the French, having been unable to win Vietnamese popular support, which was overwhelmingly behind Ho Chi Minh and the revolutionary movement, had to withdraw.

An international assemblage at Geneva presided over the peace agreement between the French and the Vietminh. It was agreed that the French would temporarily withdraw into the southern part of Vietnam, that the Vietminh would remain in the north, and that an election would take place in two years in a unified Vietnam to enable the Vietnamese to choose their own government.

The United States moved quickly to prevent the unification and to establish South Vietnam as an American sphere. It set up in Saigon as head of the government a former Vietnamese official named Ngo Dinh Diem, who had recently been living in New Jersey, and encouraged him not to hold the scheduled elections for unification. A memo in early 1954 of the Joint Chiefs of Staff said that intelligence estimates showed "a settlement based on free elections would be attended by almost certain loss of the Associated States [Laos, Cambodia, and Vietnam—the three parts of Indochina created by the Geneva Conference] to Communist control." Diem again and again blocked the elections requested by the Vietminh, and with American money and arms his government became more and more firmly established. As the *Pentagon Papers* put it: "South Viet Nam was essentially the creation of the United States."

The Diem regime became increasingly unpopular. Diem was a Catholic, and most Vietnamese were Buddhists; Diem was close to the landlords, and this was a country of peasants. His pretenses at land reform left things basically as they were. He replaced locally selected provincial chiefs with his own men, appointed in Saigon; by 1962, 88 percent of these provincial chiefs were military men. Diem imprisoned more and more Vietnamese who criticized the regime for corruption, for lack of reform.

Opposition grew quickly in the countryside, where Diem's apparatus could not reach well, and around 1958 guerrilla activities began against the regime. The Communist regime in Hanoi gave aid, encouragement, and sent people south—most of them southerners who had gone north after the Geneva accords—to support the guerrilla movement. In 1960, the National Liberation Front was formed in the South. It united the various strands of opposition to the regime; its strength came from South Vietnamese peasants, who saw it as a way of changing their daily lives. A U.S. government analyst named Douglas Pike, in his book *Viet Cong,* based on interviews with rebels and captured documents, tried to give a realistic assessment of what the United States faced:

> In the 2561 villages of South Vietnam, the National Liberation Front created a host of nation-wide socio-political organizations in a country where mass organizations . . . were virtually nonexistent. . . . Aside from the NLF there had never been a truly mass-based political party in South Vietnam.

Pike wrote: "The Communists have brought to the villages of South Vietnam significant social change and have done so largely by means of the communication process." That is, they were organizers much more than they were warriors. "What struck me most forcibly about the NLF was its totality as a social revolution first and as a war second." Pike was impressed with the mass involvement of the peasants in the movement. "The rural Vietnamese was not regarded simply as a pawn in a power struggle but as the active element in the thrust. He was the thrust." Pike wrote:

> The purpose of this vast organizational effort was . . . to restructure the social order of the village and train the villages to control themselves. This was the NLF's one undeviating thrust from the start. Not the killing of ARVN (Saigon) soldiers, not the occupation of real estate, not the preparation for some great pitched battle . . . but organization in depth of the rural population through the instrument of self-control.

Pike estimated that the NLF membership by early 1962 stood at around 300,000. The *Pentagon Papers* said of this period: "Only the Viet Cong had any real support and influence on a broad base in the countryside."

When Kennedy took office in early 1961 he continued the policies of Truman and Eisenhower in Southeast Asia. Almost immediately, he approved a secret plan for various military actions in Vietnam and Laos, including the "dispatch of agents to North Vietnam" to engage in "sabotage and light harassment," according to the *Pentagon Papers*. Back in 1956, he had spoken of "the amazing success of President Diem" and said of Diem's Vietnam: "Her political liberty is an inspiration."

One day in June 1963, a Buddhist monk sat down in the public square in Saigon and set himself afire. More Buddhist monks began committing suicide by fire to dramatize their opposition to the Diem regime. Diem's police raided the Buddhist pagodas and temples, wounded thirty monks, arrested 1,400 people, and closed down the pagodas. There were demonstrations in the city. The police fired, killing nine people. Then, in Hué, the ancient capital, ten thousand demonstrated in protest.

Under the Geneva Accords, the United States was permitted to have 685 military advisers in southern Vietnam. Eisenhower secretly sent several thousand. Under Kennedy, the figure rose to sixteen thousand, and some of them began to take part in combat operations. Diem was losing. Most of the South Vietnam countryside was now controlled by local villagers organized by the NLF.

Diem was becoming an embarrassment, an obstacle to effective control over Vietnam. Some Vietnamese generals began plotting to overthrow his regime, staying in touch with a CIA man named Lucien Conein. Conein met secretly with American Ambassador Henry Cabot Lodge, who was enthusiastically for the coup. Lodge reported to Kennedy's assistant, McGeorge Bundy, on October 25 *(Pentagon Papers):* "I have personally approved each meeting between General TranVan Don and Conein who has carried out my orders in each instance explicitly." Kennedy seemed hesitant, but no move was made to warn Diem. Indeed, just before the coup, and just after he had been in touch through Conein with the plotters, Lodge spent a weekend with Diem at a seaside resort. When, on November 1, 1963, the generals attacked the presidential palace, Diem phoned Ambassador Lodge, and the conversation went as follows:

Diem: Some units have made a rebellion and I want to know what is the attitude of the United States?
Lodge: I do not feel well enough informed to be able to tell you. I have heard the shooting, but am not acquainted with all of the facts. Also it is 4:30 A.M. in Washington and the U.S. Government cannot possibly have a view.
Diem: But you must have some general ideas. . . .

Lodge told Diem to phone him if he could do anything for his physical safety.

That was the last conversation any American had with Diem. He fled the palace, but he and his brother were apprehended by the plotters, taken out in a truck, and executed.

Earlier in 1963, Kennedy's Undersecretary of State, U. Alexis Johnson, was speaking before the Economic Club of Detroit:

What is the attraction that Southeast Asia has exerted for centuries on the great powers flanking it on all sides? Why is it desirable, and why is it important? First, it provides a lush climate, fertile soil, rich natural resources, a relatively sparse population in most areas, and room to expand. The countries of Southeast Asia produce rich exportable surpluses such as rice, rubber, teak, corn, tin, spices, oil, and many others. . . .

This is not the language that was used by President Kennedy in his explanations to the American public. He talked of Communism and freedom. In a news conference February 14, 1962 he said: "Yes, as you know, the U.S. for more than a decade has been assisting the government, the people of Vietnam, to maintain their independence."

Three weeks after the execution of Diem, Kennedy himself was assassinated, and his Vice-President, Lyndon Johnson, took office.

The generals who succeeded Diem could not suppress the National Liberation Front. Again and again, American leaders expressed their bewilderment at the popularity of the NLF, at the high morale of its soldiers. The Pentagon historians wrote that when Eisenhower met with President-elect Kennedy in January 1961, he "wondered aloud why, in interventions of this kind, we always seemed to find that the morale of the Communist forces was better than that of the democratic forces." And General Maxwell Taylor reported in late 1964:

The ability of the Viet-Cong continuously to rebuild their units and to make good their losses is one of the mysteries of the guerrilla war. . . . Not only do the Viet-Cong units have the recuperative powers of the phoenix, but they have an amazing ability to maintain morale. Only in rare cases have we found evidences of bad morale among Viet-Cong prisoners or recorded in captured Viet-Cong documents.

In early August 1964, President Johnson used a murky set of events in the Gulf of Tonkin, off the coast of North Vietnam, to launch full-scale war on Vietnam. Johnson and Secretary of Defense Robert McNamara told the American public there was an attack by North Vietnamese torpedo boats on American destroyers. "While on routine patrol in international waters," McNamara said, "the U.S. destroyer *Maddox* underwent an unprovoked attack." It later turned out that the Gulf of Tonkin episode was a fake, that the highest American officials had lied to the public—just as they had in the invasion of Cuba under Kennedy. In fact, the CIA had engaged in a secret operation attacking North Vietnamese coastal installations—so if there had been an attack it would not have been "unprovoked." It was not a "routine patrol," because the *Maddox* was on a special electronic spying mission. And it was not in international waters but in Vietnamese territorial waters.

It turned out that no torpedoes were fired at the *Maddox,* as McNamara said. Another reported attack on another destroyer, two nights later, which Johnson called "open aggression on the high seas," seems also to have been an invention.

At the time of the incident, Secretary of State Rusk was questioned on NBC television:

REPORTER: What explanation, then, can you come up with for this unpro-
            voked attack?

RUSK: Well, I haven't been able, quite frankly, to come to a fully satisfac-
            tory explanation. There is a great gulf of understanding, between
            that world and our world, ideological in character. They see
            what we think of as the real world in wholly different terms.
            Their very processes of logic are different. So that it's very difficult
            to enter into each other's minds across that great ideological
            gulf.

The Tonkin "attack" brought a congressional resolution, passed unanimously in the House, and with only two dissenting votes in the Senate, giving Johnson the power to take military action as he saw fit in Southeast Asia.

Two months before the Gulf of Tonkin incident, U.S. government leaders met in Honolulu and discussed such a resolution. Rusk said, in this meeting, according to the *Pentagon Papers,* that "public opinion on our Southeast Asia policy was badly divided in the United States at the moment and that, therefore, the President needed an affirmation of support."

The Tonkin Resolution gave the President the power to initiate hostilities without the declaration of war by Congress that the Constitution required. The Supreme Court, supposed to be the watchdog of the Constitution, was asked by a number of petitioners in the course of the Vietnam war to declare the war unconstitutional. Again and again, it refused even to consider the issue.

Immediately after the Tonkin affair, American warplanes began bombarding North Vietnam. During 1965, over 200,000 American soldiers were sent to South Vietnam, and in 1966, 200,000 more. By early 1968, there were more than 500,000 American troops there, and the U.S. Air Force was dropping bombs at a rate unequaled in history. Tiny glimmerings of the massive human suffering under this bombardment came to the outside world. On June 5, 1965, the *New York Times* carried a dispatch from Saigon:

As the Communists withdrew from Quangngai last Monday, United States jet bombers pounded the hills into which they were headed. Many Vietnamese—one estimate is as high as 500—were killed by the strikes. The American contention is that they were Vietcong soldiers. But three out of four patients seeking treatment in a Vietnamese hospital afterward for burns from napalm, or jellied gasoline, were village women.

On September 6, another press dispatch from Saigon:

In Bien Hoa province south of Saigon on August 15 United States aircraft accidentally bombed a Buddhist pagoda and a Catholic church . . . it was the third time their pagoda had been bombed in 1965. A temple of the Cao Dai religious sect in the same area had been bombed twice this year.

In another delta province there is a woman who has both arms burned off by napalm and her eyelids so badly burned that she cannot close them. When it is time for her to sleep her family puts a blanket over her head. The woman had two of her children killed in the air strike that maimed her.

Few Americans appreciate what their nation is doing to South Vietnam with airpower . . . innocent civilians are dying every day in South Vietnam.

Large areas of South Vietnam were declared "free fire zones," which meant that all persons remaining within them—civilians, old people, children—were considered an enemy, and bombs were dropped at will. Villages suspected of harboring Viet Cong were subject to "search and destroy" missions—men of military age in the villages were killed, the homes were burned, the women, children, and old people were sent off to refugee camps. Jonathan Schell, in his book *The Village of Ben Suc,* describes such an operation: a village surrounded, attacked, a man riding on a bicycle shot down, three people picnicking by the river shot to death, the houses destroyed, the women, children, old people herded together, taken away from their ancestral homes.

The CIA in Vietnam, in a program called "Operation Phoenix," secretly, without trial, executed at least twenty thousand civilians in South Vietnam who were suspected of being members of the Communist underground. A pro-administration analyst wrote in the journal *Foreign Affairs* in January 1975: "Although the Phoenix program did undoubtedly kill or incarcerate many innocent civilians, it did also eliminate many members of the Communist infrastructure."

After the war, the release of records of the International Red Cross showed that in South Vietnamese prison camps, where at the height of the war 65,000 to 70,000 people were held and often beaten and tortured, American advisers observed and sometimes participated. The Red Cross observers found continuing, systematic brutality at the two principal Vietnamese POW camps—at Phu Quoc and Qui Nhon, where American advisers were stationed.

By the end of the Vietnam war, 7 million tons of bombs had been dropped on Vietnam, more than twice the total bombs dropped on Europe and Asia in World War II—almost one 500-pound bomb for every human being in Vietnam. It was estimated that there were 20 million bomb craters in the country. In addition, poisonous sprays were dropped by planes to destroy trees and any kind of growth—an area the size of the state of Massachusetts was covered with such poison. Vietnamese mothers reported birth defects in their children. Yale biologists, using the same poison (2,4,5,T) on mice, reported defective mice born and said they had no reason to believe the effect on humans was different.

On March 16, 1968, a company of American soldiers went into the hamlet of My Lai 4, in Quang Ngai province. They rounded up the inhabitants, including old people and women with infants in their arms. These people were ordered into a ditch, where they were methodically shot to death by American soldiers. The testimony of James Dursi, a rifleman, at the later trial of Lieutenant William Calley, was reported in the *New York Times:*

Lieutenant Calley and a weeping rifleman named Paul D. Meadlo—the same soldier who had fed candy to the children before shooting them—pushed the prisoners into the ditch. . . .

"There was an order to shoot by Lieutenant Calley, I can't remember the exact words—it was something like 'Start firing.'

"Meadlo turned to me and said: 'Shoot, why don't you shoot?'

"He was crying.

"I said, 'I can't. I won't.'

"Then Lieutenant Calley and Meadlo pointed their rifles into the ditch and fired.

"People were diving on top of each other; mothers were trying to protect their children. . . ."

Journalist Seymour Hersh, in his book *My Lai 4,* writes:

When Army investigators reached the barren area in November, 1969, in connection with the My Lai probe in the United States, they found mass graves at three sites, as well as a ditch full of bodies. It was estimated that between 450 and 500 people—most of them women, children and old men—had been slain and buried there.

The army tried to cover up what happened. But a letter began circulating from a GI named Ron Ridenhour, who had heard about the massacre. There were photos taken of the killing by an army photographer, Ronald Haeberle. Seymour Hersh, then working for an antiwar news agency in Southeast Asia called Dispatch News Service, wrote about it. The story of the massacre had appeared in May 1968 in two French publications, one called *Sud Vietnam en Lutte,* and another published by the North Vietnamese delegation to the peace talks in Paris—but the American press did not pay any attention.

Several of the officers in the My Lai massacre were put on trial, but only Lieutenant William Calley was found guilty. He was sentenced to life imprisonment, but his sentence was reduced twice; he served three years—Nixon ordered that he be under house arrest rather than a regular prison—and then was paroled. Thousands of Americans came to his defense. Part of it was in patriotic justification of his action as necessary against the "Communists." Part of it seems to have been a feeling that he was unjustly singled out in a war with many similar atrocities. Colonel Oran Henderson, who had been charged with covering up the My Lai killings, told reporters in early 1971: "Every unit of brigade size has its My Lai hidden someplace."

Indeed, My Lai was unique only in its details. Hersh reported a letter sent by a GI to his family, and published in a local newspaper:

Dear Mom and Dad:

Today we went on a mission and I am not very proud of myself, my friends, or my country. We burned every hut in sight!

It was a small rural network of villages and the people were incredibly poor. My unit burned and plundered their meager possessions. Let me try to explain the situation to you.

The huts here are thatched palm leaves. Each one has a dried mud bunker inside. These bunkers are to protect the families. Kind of like air raid shelters.

My unit commanders, however, chose to think that these bunkers are offensive. So every hut we find that has a bunker we are ordered to burn to the ground.

When the ten helicopters landed this morning, in the midst of these huts, and six men jumped out of each "chopper", we were firing the moment we hit the ground. We fired into all the huts we could. . . .

It is then that we burned these huts. . . . Everyone is crying, begging and praying that we don't separate them and take their husbands and fathers, sons and grandfathers. The women wail and moan.

Then they watch in terror as we burn their homes, personal possessions and food. Yes, we burn all rice and shoot all livestock.

The more unpopular became the Saigon government, the more desperate the military effort became to make up for this. A secret congressional report of late 1967 said the Viet Cong were distributing about five times more land to the peasants than the South Vietnamese government, whose land distribution program had come "to a virtual standstill." The report said: "The Viet Cong have eliminated landlord domination and reallocated lands owned by absentee landlords and the G.V.N. [Government of Viet Nam] to the landless and others who cooperate with Viet Cong authorities."

The unpopularity of the Saigon government explains the success of the National Liberation Front in infiltrating Saigon and other government-held towns in early 1968, without the people there warning the government. The NLF thus launched a surprise offensive (it was the time of "Tet," their New Year holiday) that carried them into the heart of Saigon, immobilized Tan San Nhut airfield, even occupied the American Embassy briefly. The offensive was beaten back, but it demonstrated that all the enormous firepower delivered on Vietnam by the United States had not destroyed the NLF, its morale, its popular support, its will to fight. It caused a reassessment in the American government, more doubts among the American people.

The massacre at My Lai by a company of ordinary soldiers was a small event compared with the plans of high-level military and civilian leaders to visit massive destruction on the civilian population of Vietnam. Assistant Secretary of Defense John McNaughton in early 1966, seeing that large-scale bombing of North Vietnam villages was not producing the desired result, suggested a different strategy. The air strikes on villages, he said, would "create a counterproductive wave of revulsion abroad and at home." He suggested instead:

Destruction of locks and dams, however—if handled right—might . . . offer promise. It should be studied. Such destruction doesn't kill or drown people. By shallow-flooding the rice, it leads after a time to widespread starvation (more than a million?) unless food is provided—which we could offer to do "at the conference table." . . .

The heavy bombings were intended to destroy the will of ordinary Vietnamese to resist, as in the bombings of German and Japanese population centers in World War II—despite President Johnson's public insistence that only "military targets" were being bombed. The government was using language like "one more turn of the screw" to describe bombing. The CIA at one point in 1966 recommended a "bombing program of greater intensity," according to the *Pentagon Papers,* directed against, in the CIA's words, "the will of the regime as a target system."

Meanwhile, just across the border of Vietnam, in a neighboring country, Laos, where a right-wing government installed by the CIA faced a rebellion, one of the most beautiful areas in the world, the Plain of Jars, was being destroyed by bombing. This was not reported by the government or the press, but an American who lived in Laos, Fred Branfman, told the story in his book *Voices from the Plain of Jars:*

> Over 25,000 attack sorties were flown against the Plain of Jars from May, 1964, through September, 1969; over 75,000 tons of bombs were dropped on it; on the ground, thousands were killed and wounded, tens of thousands driven underground, and the entire aboveground society leveled.

Branfman, who spoke the Laotian language and lived in a village with a Laotian family, interviewed hundreds of refugees from the bombing who poured into the capital city of Vientiane. He recorded their statements and preserved their drawings. A twenty-six-year-old nurse from Xieng Khouang told of her life in her village:

> I was at one with the earth, the air, the upland fields, the paddy and the seedbeds of my village. Each day and night in the light of the moon I and my friends from the village would wander, calling out and singing, through forest and field, amidst the cries of the birds. During the harvesting and planting season, we would sweat and labor together, under the sun and the rain, contending with poverty and miserable conditions, continuing the farmer's life which has been the profession of our ancestors.
>
> But in 1964 and 1965 I could feel the trembling of the earth and the shock from the sounds of arms exploding around my village. I began to hear the noise of airplanes, circling about in the heavens. One of them would stick its head down and, plunging earthward, loose a loud roar, shocking the heart as light and smoke covered everything so that one could not see anything at all. Each day we would exchange news with the neighboring villagers of the bombings that had occurred: the damaged houses, the injured and the dead. . . .
>
> The holes! The holes! During that time we needed holes to save our lives. We who were young took our sweat and our strength, which should have been spent raising food in the ricefields and forests to sustain our lives, and squandered it digging holes to protect ourselves. . . .

One young woman explained why the revolutionary movement in Laos, the Neo Lao, attracted her and so many of her friends:

As a young girl, I had found that the past had not been very good, for men had mistreated and made fun of women as the weaker sex. But after the Neo Lao party began to administer the region . . . it became very different . . . under the Neo Lao things changed psychologically, such as their teaching that women should be as brave as men. For example: although I had gone to school before, my elders advised me not to. They had said that it would not be useful for me as I could not hope to be a high ranking official after graduation, that only the children of the elite or rich could expect that.

But the Neo Lao said that women should have the same education as men, and they gave us equal privileges and did not allow anyone to make fun of us. . . .

And the old associations were changed into new ones. For example, most of the new teachers and doctors trained were women. And they changed the lives of the very poor. . . . For they shared the land of those who had many rice fields with those who had none.

A seventeen-year-old boy told about the Pathet Lao revolutionary army coming to his village:

Some people were afraid, mostly those with money. They offered cows to the Pathet Lao soldiers to eat, but the soldiers refused to take them. If they did take them, they paid a suitable price. The truth is that they led the people not to be afraid of anything.

Then they organized the election of village and canton chief, and the people were the ones who chose them. . . .

In September 1973, a former government official in Laos, Jerome Doolittle, wrote in the *New York Times*:

The Pentagon's most recent lies about bombing Cambodia bring back a question that often occurred to me when I was press attache at the American Embassy in Vientiane, Laos.

Why did we bother to lie?

When I first arrived in Laos, I was instructed to answer all press questions about our massive and merciless bombing campaign in that tiny country with: "At the request of the Royal Laotian Government, the United States is conducting unarmed reconnaissance flights accompanied by armed escorts who have the right to return if fired upon."

This was a lie. Every reporter to whom I told it knew it was a lie. Hanoi knew it was a lie. The International Control Commission knew it was a lie. Every interested Congressman and newspaper reader knew it was a lie. . . .

After all, the lies did serve to keep something from somebody, and the somebody was us.

By early 1968, the cruelty of the war began touching the conscience of many Americans. For many others, the problem was that the United States was unable to win the war, while 40,000 American soldiers were dead by this time, 250,000 wounded, with no end in sight. (The Vietnam casualties were many times this number.)

Lyndon Johnson had escalated a brutal war and failed to win it. His popularity was at an all-time low; he could not appear publicly without a demonstration against him and the war. The chant "LBJ, LBJ, how many kids did you kill today?" was heard in demonstrations throughout the country. In the spring of 1968 Johnson announced he would not run again for President, and that negotiations for peace would begin with the Vietnamese in Paris.

In the fall of 1968, Richard Nixon, pledging that he would get the United States out of Vietnam, was elected President. He began to withdraw troops; by February 1972, less than 150,000 were left. But the bombing continued. Nixon's policy was "Vietnamization"—the Saigon government, with Vietnamese ground troops, using American money and air power, would carry on the war. Nixon was not ending the war; he was ending the most unpopular aspect of it, the involvement of American soldiers on the soil of a faraway country.

In the spring of 1970, Nixon and Secretary of State Henry Kissinger launched an invasion of Cambodia, after a long bombardment that the government never disclosed to the public. The invasion not only led to an outcry of protest in the United States, it was a military failure, and Congress resolved that Nixon could not use American troops in extending the war without congressional approval. The following year, without American troops, the United States supported a South Vietnamese invasion of Laos. This too failed. In 1971, 800,000 tons of bombs were dropped by the United States on Laos, Cambodia, Vietnam. Meantime, the Saigon military regime, headed by President Nguyen Van Thieu, the last of a long succession of Saigon chiefs of state, was keeping thousands of opponents in jail.

Some of the first signs of opposition in the United States to the Vietnam war came out of the civil rights movement—perhaps because the experience of black people with the government led them to distrust any claim that it was fighting for freedom. On the very day that Lyndon Johnson was telling the nation in early August 1964 about the Gulf of Tonkin incident, and announcing the bombing of North Vietnam, black and white activists were gathering near Philadelphia, Mississippi, at a memorial service for the three civil rights workers killed there that summer. One of the speakers pointed bitterly to Johnson's use of force in Asia, comparing it with the violence used against blacks in Mississippi.

In mid-1965, in McComb, Mississippi, young blacks who had just learned that a classmate of theirs was killed in Vietnam distributed a leaflet:

No Mississippi Negroes should be fighting in Viet Nam for the White man's freedom, until all the Negro People are free in Mississippi.

Negro boys should not honor the draft here in Mississippi. Mothers should encourage their sons not to go. . . .

No one has a right to ask us to risk our lives and kill other Colored People in Santo Domingo and Viet Nam, so that the White American can get richer.

When Secretary of Defense Robert McNamara visited Mississippi and praised Senator John Stennis, a prominent racist, as a "man of very genuine greatness," white and black students marched in protest, with placards saying "In Memory of the Burned Children of Vietnam."

The Student Nonviolent Coordinating Committee declared in early 1966 that "the United States is pursuing an aggressive policy in violation of international law" and called for withdrawal from Vietnam. That summer, six members of SNCC were arrested for an invasion of an induction center in Atlanta. They were convicted and sentenced to several years in prison. Around the same time, Julian Bond, a SNCC activist who had just been elected to the Georgia House of Representatives, spoke out against the war and the draft, and the House voted that he not be seated because his statements violated the Selective Service Act and "tend to bring discredit to the House." The Supreme Court restored Bond to his seat, saying he had the right to free expression under the First Amendment.

One of the great sports figures of the nation, Muhammad Ali, the black boxer and heavyweight champion, refused to serve in what he called a "white man's war"; boxing authorities took away his title as champion. Martin Luther King, Jr., spoke out in 1967 at Riverside Church in New York:

Somehow this madness must cease. We must stop now. I speak as a child of God and brother to the suffering poor of Vietnam. I speak for those whose land is being laid waste, whose homes are being destroyed, whose culture is being subverted. I speak for the poor of America who are paying the double price of smashed hopes at home and death and corruption in Vietnam. I speak as a citizen of the world, for the world as it stands aghast at the path we have taken. I speak as an American to the leaders of my own nation. The great initiative in this war is ours. The initiative to stop it must be ours.

Young men began to refuse to register for the draft, refused to be inducted if called. As early as May 1964 the slogan "We Won't Go" was widely publicized. Some who had registered began publicly burning their draft cards to protest the war. One, David O'Brien, burned his draft card in South Boston; he was convicted, and the Supreme Court overruled his argument that this was a protected form of free expression. In October of 1967 there were organized draft-card "turn-ins" all over the country; in San Francisco alone, three hundred draft cards were returned to the government. Just before a huge demonstration at the Pentagon that month, a sack of collected draft cards was presented to the Justice Department.

By mid-1965, 380 prosecutions were begun against men refusing to be inducted; by mid-1968 that figure was up to 3,305. At the end of 1969, there were 33,960 delinquents nationwide.

In May 1969 the Oakland induction center, where draftees reported from all of northern California, reported that of 4,400 men ordered to report for induction, 2,400 did not show up. In the first quarter of 1970 the Selective Service system, for the first time, could not meet its quota.

A Boston University graduate student in history, Philip Supina, wrote on May 1, 1968, to his draft board in Tucson, Arizona:

I am enclosing the order for me to report for my pre-induction physical exam for the armed forces. I have absolutely no intention to report for that exam, or for induction, or to aid in any way the American war effort against the people of Vietnam. . . .

He ended his letter by quoting the Spanish philosopher Miguel Unamuno, who during the Spanish Civil War said: "Sometimes to be Silent is to Lie." Supina was convicted and sentenced to four years in prison.

Early in the war, there had been two separate incidents, barely noticed by most Americans. On November 2, 1965, in front of the Pentagon in Washington, as thousands of employees were streaming out of the building in the late afternoon, Norman Morrison, a thirty-two-year-old pacifist, father of three, stood below the third-floor windows of Secretary of Defense Robert McNamara, doused himself with kerosene, and set himself afire, giving up his life in protest against the war. Also that year, in Detroit, an eighty-two-year-old woman named Alice Herz burned herself to death to make a statement against the horror of Indochina.

A remarkable change in sentiment took place. In early 1965, when the bombing of North Vietnam began, a hundred people gathered on the Boston Common to voice their indignation. On October 15, 1969, the number of people assembled on the Boston Common to protest the war was 100,000. Perhaps 2 million people across the nation gathered that day in towns and villages that had never seen an antiwar meeting.

In the summer of 1965, a few hundred people had gathered in Washington to march in protest against the war: the first in line, historian Staughton Lynd, SNCC organizer Bob Moses, and long-time pacifist David Dellinger, were splattered with red paint by hecklers. But by 1970, the Washington peace rallies were drawing hundreds of thousands of people. In 1971, twenty thousand came to Washington to commit civil disobedience, trying to tie up Washington traffic to express their revulsion against the killing still going on in Vietnam. Fourteen thousand of them were arrested, the largest mass arrest in American history.

Hundreds of volunteers in the Peace Corps spoke out against the war. In Chile, ninety-two volunteers defied the Peace Corps director and issued a circular denouncing the war. Eight hundred former members of the Corps issued a statement of protest against what was happening in Vietnam.

The poet Robert Lowell, invited to a White House function, refused to come. Arthur Miller, also invited, sent a telegram to the White House: "When the guns boom, the arts die." Singer Eartha Kitt was invited to a luncheon on the White House lawn and shocked all those present by speaking out, in the presence of the President's wife, against the war. A teenager, called to the White House to accept a prize, came and criticized the war. In Hollywood, local artists erected a 60-foot Tower of Protest on Sunset Boulevard. At the National Book Award ceremonies in New York, fifty authors and publishers walked out on a speech by Vice-President Humphrey in a display of anger at his role in the war.

In London, two young Americans gate-crashed the American ambassador's elegant Fourth of July reception and called out a toast: "To all the dead and dying in Vietnam." They were carried out by guards. In the Pacific Ocean, two young American seamen hijacked an American munitions ship to divert its load of bombs from airbases in Thailand.

For four days they took command of the ship and its crew, taking amphetamine pills to stay awake until the ship reached Cambodian waters. The Associated Press reported in late 1972, from York, Pennsylvania: "Five antiwar activists were arrested by the state police today for allegedly sabotaging railroad equipment near a factory that makes bomb casings used in the Vietnam war."

Middle-class and professional people unaccustomed to activism began to speak up. In May 1970, the *New York Times* reported from Washington: "1000 'ESTABLISHMENT' LAWYERS JOIN WAR PROTEST." Corporations began to wonder whether the war was going to hurt their long-range business interests; the *Wall Street Journal* began criticizing the continuation of the war.

As the war became more and more unpopular, people in or close to the government began to break out of the circle of assent. The most dramatic instance was the case of Daniel Ellsberg.

Ellsberg was a Harvard-trained economist, a former marine officer, employed by the RAND Corporation, which did special, often secret research for the U.S. government. Ellsberg helped write the Department of Defense history of the war in Vietnam, and then decided to make the top-secret document public, with the aid of his friend, Anthony Russo, a former RAND Corporation man. The two had met in Saigon, where both had been affected, in different experiences, by direct sight of the war, and had become powerfully indignant at what the United States was doing to the people of Vietnam.

Ellsberg and Russo spent night after night, after hours, at a friend's advertising agency, duplicating the 7,000-page document. Then Ellsberg gave copies to various Congressmen and to the *New York Times*. In June 1971 the *Times* began printing selections from what came to be known as the *Pentagon Papers*. It created a national sensation.

The Nixon administration tried to get the Supreme Court to stop further publication, but the Court said this was "prior restraint" of the freedom of the press and thus unconstitutional. The government then indicted Ellsberg and Russo for violating the Espionage Act by releasing classified documents to unauthorized people; they faced long terms in prison if convicted. The judge, however, called off the trial during the jury deliberations, because the Watergate events unfolding at the time, revealed unfair practices by the prosecution.

Ellsberg, by his bold act, had broken with the usual tactic of dissidents inside the government who bided their time and kept their opinions to themselves, hoping for small changes in policy. A colleague urged him not to leave the government because there he had "access," saying, "Don't cut yourself off. Don't cut your throat." Ellsberg replied: "Life exists outside the Executive Branch."

The antiwar movement, early in its growth, found a strange, new constituency: priests and nuns of the Catholic Church. Some of them had been aroused by the civil rights movement, others by their experiences in Latin America, where they saw poverty and injustice under governments supported by the United States. In the fall of 1967, Father Philip Berrigan (a Josephite priest who was a veteran of World War II), joined by artist Tom Lewis and friends David Eberhardt and James Mengel, went to the office of a draft board in Baltimore, Maryland, drenched the draft records with blood, and waited to be arrested. They were put on trial and sentenced to prison terms of two to six years.

The following May, Philip Berrigan—out on bail in the Baltimore case—was joined in a second action by his brother Daniel, a Jesuit priest who had visited North Vietnam and seen the effects of U.S. bombing. They and seven other people went into a draft board office in Catonsville, Maryland, removed records, and set them afire outside in the presence of reporters and onlookers. They were convicted and sentenced to prison, and became famous as the "Catonsville Nine." Dan Berrigan wrote a "Meditation" at the time of the Catonsville incident:

Our apologies, good friends, for the fracture of good order, the burning of paper instead of children, the angering of the orderlies in the front parlor of the charnel house. We could not, so help us God, do otherwise. . . . We say: killing is disorder, life and gentleness and community and unselfishness is the only order we recognize. For the sake of that order, we risk our liberty, our good name. The time is past when good men can remain silent, when obedience can segregate men from public risk, when the poor can die without defense.

When his appeals had been exhausted, and he was supposed to go to prison, Daniel Berrigan disappeared. While the FBI searched for him, he showed up at an Easter festival at Cornell University, where he had been teaching. With dozens of FBI men looking for him in the crowd, he suddenly appeared on stage. Then the lights went out, he hid inside a giant figure of the Bread and Puppet Theatre which was on stage, was carried out to a truck, and escaped to a nearby farmhouse. He stayed underground for four months, writing poems, issuing statements, giving secret interviews, appearing suddenly in a

Philadelphia church to give a sermon and then disappearing again, baffling the FBI, until an informer's interception of a letter disclosed his whereabouts and he was captured and imprisoned.

The one woman among the Catonsville Nine, Mary Moylan, a former nun, also refused to surrender to the FBI. She was never found. Writing from underground, she reflected on her experience and how she came to it:

. . . We had all known we were going to jail, so we all had our toothbrushes. I was just exhausted. I took my little box of clothes and stuck it under the cot and climbed into bed. Now all the women in the Baltimore County jail were black—I think there was only one white. The women were waking me up and saying, "Aren't you going to cry?" I said, "What about?" They said, "You're in jail." And I said, "Yeah, I knew I'd be here.". . .

I was sleeping between two of these women, and every morning I'd wake up and they'd be leaning on their elbows watching me. They'd say, "You slept all night." And they couldn't believe it. They were good. We had good times. . . .

I suppose the political turning point in my life came while I was in Uganda. I was there when American planes were bombing the Congo, and we were very close to the Congo border. The planes came over and bombed two villages in Uganda. . . . Where the hell did the American planes come in?

Later I was in Dar Es Salaam and Chou En-lai came to town. The American Embassy sent out letters saying that no Americans were to be on the street, because this was a dirty Communist leader; but I decided this was a man who was making history and I wanted to see him. . . .

When I came home from Africa I moved to Washington, and had to deal with the scene there and the insanity and brutality of the cops and the type of life that was led by most of the citizens of that city—70 percent black. . . .

And then Vietnam, and the napalm and the defoliants, and the bombings. . . .

I got involved with the women's movement about a year ago. . . .

At the time of Catonsville, going to jail made sense to me, partially because of the black scene—so many blacks forever filling the jails. . . . I don't think it's a valid tactic anymore. . . . I don't want to see people marching off to jail with smiles on their faces. I just don't want them going. The Seventies are going to be very difficult, and I don't want to waste the sisters and brothers we have by marching them off to jail and having mystical experiences or whatever they're going to have. . . .

The effect of the war and of the bold action of some priests and nuns was to crack the traditional conservatism of the Catholic community. On Moratorium Day 1969, at the Newton College of the Sacred Heart near Boston, a sanctuary of bucolic quiet and political silence, the great front door of the college displayed a huge painted red fist. At Boston College, a Catholic institution, six thousand people gathered that evening in the gymnasium to denounce the war.

Students were heavily involved in the early protests against the war. A survey by the Urban Research Corporation, for the first six months of 1969 only, and for only 232 of the nation's two thousand institutions of higher education, showed that at least 215,000 students had participated in campus protests, that 3,652 had been arrested, that 956 had been suspended or expelled. Even in the high schools, in the late sixties, there were five hundred underground newspapers. At the Brown University commencement in 1969, two-thirds of the graduating class turned their backs when Henry Kissinger stood up to address them.

The climax of protest came in the spring of 1970 when President Nixon ordered the invasion of Cambodia. At Kent State University in Ohio, on May 4, when students gathered to demonstrate against the war, National Guardsmen fired into the crowd. Four students were killed. One was paralyzed for life. Students at four hundred colleges and universities went on strike in protest. It was the first general student strike in the history of the United States. During that school year of 1969–1970, the FBI listed 1,785 student demonstrations, including the occupation of 313 buildings.

The commencement day ceremonies after the Kent State killings were unlike any the nation had ever seen. From Amherst, Massachusetts, came this newspaper report:

> The 100th Commencement of the University of Massachusetts yesterday was a protest, a call for peace.
> The roll of the funeral drum set the beat for 2600 young men and women marching "in fear, in despair and in frustration."
> Red fists of protest, white peace symbols, and blue doves were stenciled on black academic gowns, and nearly every other senior wore an armband representing a plea for peace.

Student protests against the ROTC (Reserve Officers Training Program) resulted in the canceling of those programs in over forty colleges and universities. In 1966, 191,749 college students enrolled in ROTC. By 1973, the number was 72,459. The ROTC was depended on to supply half the officers in Vietnam. In September 1973, for the sixth straight month, the ROTC could not fulfill its quota. One army official said: "I just hope we don't get into another war, because if we do, I doubt we could fight it."

The publicity given to the student protests created the impression that the opposition to the war came mostly from middle-class intellectuals. When some construction workers in New York attacked student demonstrators, the news was played up in the national media. However, a number of elections in American cities, including those where mostly blue-collar workers lived, showed that antiwar sentiment was strong in the working classes. For instance, in Dearborn, Michigan, an automobile manufacturing town, a poll as early as 1967 showed 41 percent of the population favored withdrawal from the Vietnam war. In 1970, in two counties in California where petitioners placed the issue on the ballot—San Francisco County and Marin County—referenda asking withdrawal of the U.S. forces from Vietnam received a majority vote.

In late 1970, when a Gallup poll presented the statement: "The United States should withdraw all troops from Vietnam by the end of next year," 65 percent of those questioned said, "Yes." In Madison, Wisconsin, in the spring of 1971, a resolution calling for an immediate withdrawal of U.S. forces from Southeast Asia won by 31,000 to 16,000 (in 1968 such a resolution had lost).

But the most surprising data were in a survey made by the University of Michigan. This showed that, throughout the Vietnam war, Americans with only a grade school education were much stronger for withdrawal from the war than Americans with a college education. In June 1966, of people with a college education, 27 percent were for immediate withdrawal from Vietnam; of people with only a grade school education, 41 percent were for immediate withdrawal. By September 1970, both groups were more antiwar: 47 percent of the college-educated were for withdrawal, and 61 percent of grade school graduates.

There is more evidence of the same kind. In an article in the *American Sociological Review* (June 1968), Richard F. Hamilton found in his survey of public opinion: "Preferences for 'tough' policy alternatives are most frequent among the following groups, the highly educated, high status occupations, those with high incomes, younger persons, and those paying much attention to newspapers and magazines." And a political scientist, Harlan Hahn, doing a study of various city referenda on Vietnam, found support for withdrawal from Vietnam highest in groups of lower socioeconomic status. He also found that the regular polls, based on samplings, underestimated the opposition to the war among lower-class people.

All this was part of a general change in the entire population of the country. In August of 1965, 61 percent of the population thought the American involvement in Vietnam was not wrong. By May 1971 it was exactly reversed; 61 percent thought our involvement *was* wrong. Bruce Andrews, a Harvard student of public opinion, found that the people most opposed to the war were people over fifty, blacks, and women. He also noted that a study in the spring of 1964, when Vietnam was a minor issue in the newspapers, showed that 53 percent of college-educated people were willing to send troops to Vietnam, but only 33 percent of grade school–educated people were so willing.

It seems that the media, themselves controlled by higher-education, higher-income people who were more aggressive in foreign policy, tended to give the erroneous impression that working-class people were superpatriots for the war. Lewis Lipsitz, in a mid-1968 survey of poor blacks and whites in the South, paraphrased an attitude he found typical: "The only way to help the poor man is to get out of that war in Vietnam. . . . These taxes—high taxes—it's going over yonder to kill people with and I don't see no cause in it."

The capacity for independent judgement among ordinary Americans is probably best shown by the swift development of antiwar feeling among American GIs—volunteers and draftees who came mostly from lower-income groups. There had been, earlier in American history, instances of soldiers' disaffection from the war: isolated mutinies in the Revolutionary War, refusal of reenlistment in the midst of hostilities in the Mexican war, desertion and conscientious objection in World War I and World War II. But Vietnam produced opposition by soldiers and veterans on a scale, and with a fervor, never seen before.

It began with isolated protests. As early as June 1965, Richard Steinke, a West Point graduate in Vietnam, refused to board an aircraft taking him to a remote Vietnamese village. "The Vietnamese war," he said, "is not worth a single American life." Steinke was court-martialed and dismissed from the service. The following year, three army privates, one black, one Puerto Rican, one Lithuanian-Italian—all poor—refused to embark for Vietnam, denouncing the war as "immoral, illegal, and unjust." They were court-martialed and imprisoned.

In early 1967, Captain Howard Levy, an army doctor at Fort Jackson, South Carolina, refused to teach Green Berets, a Special Forces elite in the military. He said they were "murderers of women and children" and "killers of peasants." He was court-martialed on the ground that he was trying to promote disaffection among enlisted men by his statements. The colonel who presided at the trial said: "The truth of the statements is not an issue in this case." Levy was convicted and sentenced to prison.

The individual acts multiplied: A black private in Oakland refused to board a troop plane to Vietnam, although he faced eleven years at hard labor. A navy nurse, Lieutenant Susan Schnall, was court-martialed for marching in a peace demonstration while in uniform, and for dropping antiwar leaflets from a plane on navy installations. In Norfolk, Virginia, a sailor refused to train fighter pilots because he said the war was immoral. An army lieutenant was arrested in Washington, D.C., in early 1968 for picketing the White House with a sign that said: "120,000 American Casualties—Why?" Two black marines, George Daniels and William Harvey, were given long prison sentences (Daniels, six years, Harvey, ten years, both later reduced) for talking to other black marines against the war.

As the war went on, desertions from the armed forces mounted. Thousands went to Western Europe—France, Sweden, Holland. Most deserters crossed into Canada; some estimates were 50,000, others 100,000. Some stayed in the United States. A few openly defied the military authorities by taking "sanctuary" in churches, where, surrounded by antiwar friends and sympathizers, they waited for capture and court-martial. At Boston University, a thousand students kept vigil for five days and nights in the chapel, supporting an eighteen-year-old deserter, Ray Kroll.

Kroll's story was a common one. He had been inveigled into joining the army; he came from a poor family, was brought into court, charged with drunkenness, and given the choice of prison or enlistment. He enlisted. And then he began to think about the nature of the war.

On a Sunday morning, federal agents showed up at the Boston University chapel, stomped their way through aisles clogged with students, smashed down doors, and took Kroll away. From the stockade, he wrote back to friends: "I ain't gonna kill; it's against my will. . . ." A friend he had made at the chapel brought him books, and he noted a saying he had found in one of them: "What we have done will not be lost to all Eternity. Everything ripens at its time and becomes fruit at its hour."

The GI antiwar movement became more organized. Near Fort Jackson, South Carolina, the first "GI coffeehouse" was set up, a place where soldiers could get coffee and doughnuts, find antiwar literature, and talk freely with others. It was called the UFO, and lasted for several years before it was declared a "public nuisance" and closed by court action. But other GI coffeehouses sprang up in half a dozen other places across the country. An antiwar "bookstore" was opened near Fort Devens, Massachusetts, and another one at the Newport, Rhode Island, naval base.

Underground newspapers sprang up at military bases across the country; by 1970 more than fifty were circulating. Among them: *About Face* in Los Angeles; *Fed Up!* in Tacoma, Washington; *Short Times* at Fort Jackson; *Vietnam GI* in Chicago; *Graffiti* in Heidelberg, Germany; *Bragg Briefs* in North Carolina; *Last Harass* at Fort Gordon, Georgia; *Helping Hand* at Mountain Home Air Base, Idaho. These newspapers printed antiwar articles, gave news about the harassment of GIs and practical advice on the legal rights of servicemen, told how to resist military domination.

Mixed with feeling against the war was resentment at the cruelty, the dehumanization, of military life. In the army prisons, the stockades, this was especially true. In 1968, at the Presidio stockade in California, a guard shot to death an emotionally disturbed prisoner for walking away from a work detail. Twenty-seven prisoners then sat down and refused to work, singing "We Shall Overcome." They were court-martialed, found guilty of mutiny, and sentenced to terms of up to fourteen years, later reduced after much public attention and protest.

The dissidence spread to the war front itself. When the great Moratorium Day demonstrations were taking place in October 1969 in the United States, some GIs in Vietnam wore black armbands to show their support. A news photographer reported that in a platoon on patrol near Da Nang, about half of the men were wearing black armbands. One soldier stationed at Cu Chi wrote to a friend on October 26, 1970, that separate companies had been set up for men refusing to go into the field to fight. "It's no big thing here anymore to refuse to go." The French newspaper *Le Monde* reported that in four months, 109 soldiers of the first air cavalry division were charged with refusal to fight. "A common sight," the correspondent for *Le Monde* wrote, "is the black soldier, with his left fist clenched in defiance of a war he has never considered his own."

Wallace Terry, a black American reporter for *Time* magazine, taped conversations with hundreds of black soldiers; he found bitterness against army racism, disgust with the war, generally low morale. More and more cases of "fragging" were reported in Vietnam—incidents where servicemen rolled fragmentation bombs under the tents of officers who were ordering them into combat, or against whom they had other grievances. The Pentagon reported 209 fraggings in Vietnam in 1970 alone.

Veterans back from Vietnam formed a group called Vietnam Veterans Against the War. In December 1970, hundreds of them went to Detroit to what was called the "Winter Soldier" investigations, to testify publicly about atrocities they had participated in or seen in Vietnam, committed by Americans against Vietnamese. In April 1971 more than a thousand of them went to Washington, D.C., to demonstrate against the war. One by one, they went up to a wire fence around the Capitol, threw over the fence the medals they had won in Vietnam, and made brief statements about the war, sometimes emotionally, sometimes in icy, bitter calm.

In the summer of 1970, twenty-eight commissioned officers of the military, including some veterans of Vietnam, saying they represented about 250 other officers, announced formation of the Concerned Officers Movement against the war. During the fierce bombings of Hanoi and Haiphong, around Christmas 1972, came the first defiance of B-52 pilots who refused to fly those missions.

On June 3, 1973, the *New York Times* reported dropouts among West Point cadets. Officials there, the reporter wrote, "linked the rate to an affluent, less disciplined, skeptical, and questioning generation and to the anti-military mood that a small radical minority and the Vietnam war had created."

But most of the antiwar action came from ordinary GIs, and most of these came from lower-income groups—white, black, Native American, Chinese.

A twenty-year-old New York City Chinese-American named Sam Choy enlisted at seventeen in the army, was sent to Vietnam, was made a cook, and found himself the target of abuse by fellow GIs, who called him "Chink" and "gook" (the term for the Vietnamese) and said he looked like the enemy. One day he took a rifle and fired warning shots at his tormenters. "By this time I was near the perimeter of the base and was thinking of joining the Viet Cong; at least they would trust me."

Choy was taken by military police, beaten, court-martialed, sentenced to eighteen months of hard labor at Fort Leavenworth. "They beat me up every day, like a time clock." He ended his interview with a New York Chinatown newspaper saying: "One thing: I want to tell all the Chinese kids that the army made me sick. They made me so sick that I can't stand it."

A dispatch from Phu Bai in April 1972 said that fifty GIs out of 142 men in the company refused to go on patrol, crying: "This isn't our war!" The *New York Times* on July 14, 1973, reported that American prisoners of war in Vietnam, ordered by officers in the POW camp to stop cooperating with the enemy, shouted back: "Who's the enemy?" They formed a peace committee in the camp, and a sergeant on the committee later recalled his march from capture to the POW camp:

> Until we got to the first camp, we didn't see a village intact; they were all destroyed. I sat down and put myself in the middle and asked myself: Is this right or wrong? Is it right to destroy villages? Is it right to kill people en masse? After a while it just got to me.

Pentagon officials in Washington and navy spokesmen in San Diego announced, after the United States withdrew its troops from Vietnam in 1973, that the navy was going to purge itself of "undesirables"—and that these included as many as six thousand men in the Pacific fleet, "a substantial proportion of them black." All together, about 700,000 GIs had received less than honorable discharges. In the year 1973, one of every five discharges was "less than honorable," indicating something less than dutiful obedience to the military. By 1971, 177 of every 1,000 American soldiers were listed as "absent without leave," some of them three or four times. Deserters doubled from 47,000 in 1967 to 89,000 in 1971.

One of those who stayed, fought, but then turned against the war was Ron Kovic. His father worked in a supermarket on Long Island. In 1963, at the age of seventeen, he enlisted in the marines. Two years later, in Vietnam, at the age of nineteen, his spine was shattered by shellfire. Paralyzed from the waist down, he was put in a wheelchair. Back in the States, he observed the brutal treatment of wounded veterans in the veterans' hospitals, thought more and more about the war, and joined the Vietnam Veterans Against the War. He went to demonstrations to speak against the war. One evening he heard actor Donald Sutherland read from the post–World War I novel by Dalton Trumbo, *Johnny Got His Gun*, about a soldier whose limbs and face were shot away by gunfire, a thinking torso who invented a way of communicating with the outside world and then beat out a message so powerful it could not be heard without trembling.

> Sutherland began to read the passage and something I will never forget swept over me. It was as if someone was speaking for everything I ever went

through in the hospital. . . . I began to shake and I remember there were tears in my eyes.

Kovic demonstrated against the war, and was arrested. He tells his story in *Born on the Fourth of July:*

> They help me back into the chair and take me to another part of the prison building to be booked.
> "What's your name?" the officer behind the desk says.
> "Ron Kovic," I say. "Occupation, Vietnam veteran against the war."
> "What?" he says sarcastically, looking down at me.
> "I'm a Vietnam veteran against the war," I almost shout back.
> "You should have died over there," he says. He turns to his assistant. "I'd like to take this guy and throw him off the roof."
> They fingerprint me and take my picture and put me in a cell. I have begun to wet my pants like a little baby. The tube has slipped out during my examination by the doctor. I try to fall asleep but even though I am exhausted, the anger is alive in me like a huge hot stone in my chest. I lean my head up against the wall and listen to the toilets flush again and again.

Kovic and the other veterans drove to Miami to the Republican National Convention in 1972, went into the Convention Hall, wheeled themselves down the aisles, and as Nixon began his acceptance speech shouted, "Stop the bombing! Stop the war!" Delegates cursed them: "Traitor!" and Secret Service men hustled them out of the hall.

In the fall of 1973, with no victory in sight and North Vietnamese troops entrenched in various parts of the South, the United States agreed to accept a settlement that would withdraw American troops and leave the revolutionary troops where they were, until a new elected government would be set up including Communist and non-Communist elements. But the Saigon government refused to agree, and the United States decided to make one final attempt to bludgeon the North Vietnamese into submission. It sent waves of B-52s over Hanoi and Haiphong, destroying homes and hospitals, killing unknown numbers of civilians. The attack did not work. Many of the B-52s were shot down, there was angry protest all over the world—and Kissinger went back to Paris and signed very much the same peace agreement that had been agreed on before.

The United States withdrew its forces, continuing to give aid to the Saigon government, but when the North Vietnamese launched attacks in early 1975 against the major cities in South Vietnam, the government collapsed. In late April 1975, North Vietnamese troops entered Saigon. The American embassy staff fled, along with many Vietnamese who feared Communist rule, and the long war in Vietnam was over. Saigon was renamed Ho Chi Minh City, and both parts of Vietnam were unified as the Democratic Republic of Vietnam.

Traditional history portrays the end of wars as coming from the initiatives of leaders—negotiations in Paris or Brussels or Geneva or Versailles—just as it often finds the coming of war a response to the demand of "the people." The Vietnam war gave clear evidence that at least for that war (making one wonder about the others) the political leaders were the last to take steps to end the war—"the people" were far ahead. The President was always far behind. The Supreme Court silently turned away from cases challenging the Constitutionality of the war. Congress was years behind public opinion.

In the spring of 1971, syndicated columnists Rowland Evans and Robert Novak, two firm supporters of the war, wrote regretfully of a "sudden outbreak of anti-war emotionalism" in the House of Representatives, and said: "The anti-war animosities now suddenly so pervasive among House Democrats are viewed by Administration backers as less anti-Nixon than as a response to constituent pressures."

It was only after the intervention in Cambodia ended, and only after the nationwide campus uproar over that invasion, that Congress passed a resolution declaring that American troops should not be sent into Cambodia without its approval. And it was not until late 1973, when American troops had finally been removed from Vietnam, that Congress passed a bill limiting the power of the President to make war without congressional consent; even there, in that "War Powers Resolution," the President could make war for sixty days on his own without a congressional declaration.

The administration tried to persuade the American people that the war was ending because of its decision to negotiate a peace—not because it was losing the war, not because of the powerful antiwar movement in the United States. But the government's own secret memoranda all through the war testify to its sensitivity at each stage about "public opinion" in the United States and abroad. The data is in the *Pentagon Papers.*

In June of 1964, top American military and State Department officials, including Ambassador Henry Cabot Lodge, met in Honolulu. "Rusk stated that public opinion on our SEA policy was badly divided and that, therefore, the President needed an affirmation of support." Diem had been replaced by a general named Khanh. The Pentagon historians write: "Upon his return to Saigon on June 5 Ambassador Lodge went straight from the airport to call on General Khanh . . . the main thrust of his talk with Khanh was to hint that the United States Government would in the immediate future be preparing U.S. public opinion for actions against North Vietnam." Two months later came the Gulf of Tonkin affair.

On April 2, 1965, a memo from CIA director John McCone suggested that the bombing of North Vietnam be increased because it was "not sufficiently severe" to change North Vietnam's policy. "On the other hand . . . we can expect increasing pressure to stop the bombing . . . from various elements of the American public, from the press, the United Nations and world opinion." The U.S. should try for a fast knockout before this opinion could build up, McCone said.

Assistant Secretary of Defense John McNaughton's memo of early 1966 suggested destruction of locks and dams to create mass starvation, because "strikes at population targets" would "create a counterproductive wave of revulsion abroad and at home." In May 1967, the Pentagon historians write: "McNaughton was also very deeply concerned about the breadth and intensity of public unrest and dissatisfaction with the war . . . especially with young people, the underprivileged, the intelligentsia and the women." McNaughton worried: "Will the move to call up 20,000 Reserves . . . polarize opinion to the extent that the 'doves' in the United States will get out of hand—massive refusals to serve, or to fight, or to cooperate, or worse?" He warned:

There may be a limit beyond which many Americans and much of the world will not permit the United States to go. The picture of the world's greatest superpower killing or seriously injuring 1000 non-combatants a week, while trying to pound a tiny backward nation into submission, on an issue whose merits are hotly disputed, is not a pretty one. It could conceivably produce a costly distortion in the American national consciousness.

That "costly distortion" seems to have taken place by the spring of 1968, when, with the sudden and scary Tet offensive of the National Liberation Front, Westmoreland asked President Johnson to send him 200,000 more troops on top of the 525,000 already there. Johnson asked a small group of "action officers" in the Pentagon to advise him on this. They studied the situation and concluded that 200,000 troops would totally Americanize the war and would not strengthen the Saigon government because: "The Saigon leadership shows no signs of a willingness—let alone an ability—to attract the necessary loyalty or support of the people." Furthermore, the report said, sending troops would mean mobilizing reserves, increasing the military budget. There would be more U.S. casualties, more taxes. And:

This growing disaffection accompanied as it certainly will be, by increased defiance of the draft and growing unrest in the cities because of the belief that we are neglecting domestic problems, runs great risks of provoking a domestic crisis of unprecedented proportions.

The "growing unrest in the cities" must have been a reference to the black uprisings that had taken place in 1967—and showed the link, whether blacks deliberately made it or not—between the war abroad and poverty at home.

The evidence from the *Pentagon Papers* is clear—that Johnson's decision in the spring of 1968 to turn down Westmoreland's request, to slow down for the first time the escalation of the war, to diminish the bombing, to go to the conference table, was influenced to a great extent by the actions Americans had taken in demonstrating their opposition to the war.

When Nixon took office, he too tried to persuade the public that protest would not affect him. But he almost went berserk when one lone pacifist picketed the White House. The frenzy of Nixon's actions against dissidents—plans for burglaries, wiretapping, mail openings—suggests the importance of the antiwar movement in the minds of national leaders.

One sign that the ideas of the antiwar movement had taken hold in the American public was that juries became more reluctant to convict antiwar protesters, and local judges too were treating them differently. In Washington, by 1971, judges were dismissing charges against demonstrators in cases where two years before they almost certainly would have been sent to jail. The antiwar groups who had raided draft boards—the Baltimore Four, the Catonsville Nine, the Milwaukee Fourteen, the Boston Five, and more—were receiving lighter sentences for the same crimes.

The last group of draft board raiders, the "Camden 28," were priests, nuns, and laypeople who raided a draft board in Camden, New Jersey, in August 1971. It was essentially what the Baltimore Four had done four years earlier, when all were convicted and Phil Berrigan got six years in prison. But in this instance, the Camden defendants were acquitted by the jury on all counts. When the verdict was in, one of the jurors, a fifty-three-year-old black taxi driver from Atlantic

City named Samuel Braithwaite, who had spent eleven years in the army, left a letter for the defendants:

> To you, the clerical physicians with your God-given talents, I say, well done. Well done for trying to heal the sick irresponsible men, men who were chosen by the people to govern and lead them. These men, who failed the people, by raining death and destruction on a hapless country. . . . You went out to do your part while your brothers remained in their ivory towers watching . . . and hopefully some day in the near future, peace and harmony may reign to people of all nations.

That was in May of 1973. The American troops were leaving Vietnam. C. L. Sulzberger, the *New York Times* correspondent (a man close to the government), wrote: "The U.S. emerges as the big loser and history books must admit this. . . . We lost the war in the Mississippi valley, not the Mekong valley. Successive American governments were never able to muster the necessary mass support at home."

In fact, the United States had lost the war in both the Mekong Valley and the Mississippi Valley. It was the first clear defeat to the global American empire formed after World War II. It was administered by revolutionary peasants abroad, and by an astonishing movement of protest at home.

Back on September 26, 1969, President Richard Nixon, noting the growing antiwar activity all over the country, announced that "under no circumstance will I be affected whatever by it." But nine years later, in his *Memoirs,* he admitted that the antiwar movement caused him to drop plans for an intensification of the war: "Although publicly I continued to ignore the raging antiwar controversy. . . . I knew, however, that after all the protests and the Moratorium, American public opinion would be seriously divided by any military escalation of the war." It was a rare presidential admission of the power of public protest.

From a long-range viewpoint, something perhaps even more important had happened. The rebellion at home was spreading beyond the issue of war in Vietnam.

8.
Surprises

Helen Keller had said in 1911: "We vote? What does that mean?"
And Emma Goldman around the same time: "Our modern fetish is
universal suffrage." After 1920, women were voting, as men did, and
their subordinate condition had hardly changed.

Right after women got the vote, the measure of their social progress
can be seen in an advice column written by Dorothy Dix that appeared
in newspapers all over the country. The woman should not merely be
a domestic drudge, she said:

> . . . a man's wife is the show window where he exhibits the measure of his
> achievement. . . . The biggest deals are put across over luncheon tables; . . .
> we meet at dinner the people who can push our fortunes. . . . The woman
> who cultivates a circle of worthwhile people, who belongs to clubs, who makes
> herself interesting and agreeable . . . is a help to her husband.

Robert and Helen Lynd, studying Muncie, Indiana *(Middletown),* in
the late twenties, noted the importance of good looks and dress in
the assessment of women. Also, they found that when men spoke frankly
among themselves they were "likely to speak of women as creatures
purer and morally better than men but as relatively impractical, emotional, unstable, given to prejudice, easily hurt, and largely incapable
of facing facts or doing hard thinking."

A writer in early 1930, boosting the beauty business, started off
a magazine article with the sentence: "The average American woman
has sixteen square feet of skin." He went on to say that there were
forty thousand beauty shops in the country, and that $2 billion was
spent each year on cosmetics for women—but this was insufficient:
"American women are not yet spending even one-fifth of the amount
necessary to improve their appearance." He then gave an itemized list
of the "annual beauty needs of every woman": twelve hot-oil treatments,
fifty-two facials, twenty-six eyebrow plucks, etc.

It seems that women have best been able to make their first escape
from the prison of wifeliness, motherhood, femininity, housework, beau-
tification, isolation, when their services have been desperately needed—

whether in industry, or in war, or in social movements. Each time practicality pulled the woman out of her prison—in a kind of work-parole program—the attempt was made to push her back once the need was over, and this led to women's struggle for change.

World War II had brought more women than ever before out of the home into work. By 1960, 36 percent of all women sixteen and older—23 million women—worked for paid wages. But although 43 percent of women with school-age children worked, there were nursery schools for only 2 percent—the rest had to work things out themselves. Women were 50 percent of the voters—but (even by 1967) they held 4 percent of the state legislative seats, and 2 percent of the judgeships. The median income of the working woman was about one-third that of the man. And attitudes toward women did not seem to have changed much since the twenties.

"There is no overt anti-feminism in our society in 1964," wrote feminist and sociologist Alice Rossi, "not because sex equality has been achieved, but because there is practically no feminist spark left among American women."

In the civil rights movement of the sixties, the signs of a collective stirring began to appear. Women took the place they customarily took in social movements, in the front lines—as privates, not generals. In the office of the Student Nonviolent Coordinating Committee in Atlanta, a Spelman College student named Ruby Doris Smith, who had been jailed during the sit-ins, expressed her anger at the way women were relegated to the routine office work, and she was joined in her protest by two white women in SNCC, Sandra Hayden and Mary King. The men in SNCC listened to them respectfully, read the position paper they had put together asserting their rights, but did not do very much. Ella Baker, a veteran fighter from Harlem, now organizing in the South, knew the pattern: "I knew from the beginning that as a woman, an older woman in a group of ministers who are accustomed to having women largely as supporters, there was no place for me to have come into a leadership role."

Nevertheless, women played a crucial role in those early dangerous years of organizing in the South, and were looked on with admiration. Many of these were older women like Ella Baker, and Amelia Boynton in Selma, Alabama, and "Mama Dolly" in Albany, Georgia. Younger women—Gloria Richardson in Maryland, Annelle Ponder in Missis-sippi—were not only active, but leaders. Women of all ages demon-strated, went to jail. Mrs. Fannie Lou Hamer, a sharecropper in Ruleville, Mississippi, became legendary as organizer and speaker. She sang hymns; she walked picket lines with her familiar limp (as a child she contracted polio). She roused people to excitement at mass meetings: "I'm sick an' tired o' bein' sick an' tired!"

Around the same time, white, middle-class, professional women were beginning to speak up. A pioneering, early book, strong and influential, was Betty Friedan's *The Feminine Mystique*.

> Just what was the problem that has no name? What were the words women used when they tried to express it? Sometimes a woman would say "I feel empty somehow . . . incomplete." Or she would say, "I feel as if I don't exist." Sometimes. . . . "A tired feeling . . . I get so angry with the children it scares me. . . . I feel like crying without any reason."

Friedan wrote out of her experience as a middle-class housewife, but what she spoke about touched something inside all women:

> The problem lay buried, unspoken for many years in the minds of American women. It was a strange stirring, a sense of dissatisfaction, a yearning that women suffered in the middle of the twentieth century in the United States. Each suburban wife struggled with it alone. As she made the beds, shopped for groceries, matched slip-cover material, ate peanut butter sandwiches with her children, chauffeured Cub Scouts and Brownies, lay beside her husband at night—she was afraid to ask even of herself the silent question—"Is this all?" . . .
>
> But on an April morning in 1959, I heard a mother of four, having coffee with four other mothers in a suburban development fifteen miles from New York, say in a tone of quiet desperation, "the problem." And the others knew, without words, that she was not talking about a problem with her husband, or her children, or her home. Suddenly they realized they all shared the same problem, the problem that has no name. They began, hesitantly, to talk about it. Later, after they had picked up their children at nursery school and taken them home to nap, two of the women cried, in sheer relief, just to know they were not alone.

The "mystique" that Friedan spoke of was the image of the woman as mother, as wife, living through her husband, through her children, giving up her own dreams for that. She concluded: "The only way for a woman, as for a man, to find herself, to know herself as a person, is by creative work of her own."

In the summer of 1964, in McComb, Mississippi, at a Freedom House (a civil rights headquarters where people worked and lived together) the women went on strike against the men who wanted them to cook and make beds while the men went around in cars organizing.

The stirring that Friedan spoke of was true of women everywhere, it seemed:

By 1969, women were 40 percent of the entire labor force of the United States, but a substantial number of these were secretaries, cleaning women, elementary school teachers, saleswomen, waitresses, and nurses. One out of every three working women had a husband earning less than $5,000 a year.

What of the women who didn't have jobs? They worked very hard, at home, but this wasn't looked on as work, because in a capitalist society (or perhaps in any modern society where things and people are bought and sold for money), if work is not paid for, not given a money value, it is considered valueless. Women began to think more about this fact in the 1960s, and Margaret Benston wrote about it ("The Political Economy of Women's Liberation"). Women doing housework were people outside the modern economic system, therefore they were like serfs or peasants, she said.

The women who worked in the typical "woman's job"—secretary, receptionist, typist, salesperson, cleaning woman, nurse—were treated to the full range of humiliations that men in subordinate positions faced at work, plus another set of humiliations stemming from being a woman: gibes at their mental processes, sexual jokes and aggression, invisibility except as sexual objects, cold demands for more efficiency. A commercial "Guide to Clerical Times Standards" printed a question-and-answer column:

Q. I'm a businessman, and my secretary seems to move entirely too slowly. How many times a minute should she be able to open and close a file drawer?

A. Exactly 25 times. Times for other "open and close operations" . . . are .04 minutes for opening or closing a folder, and .026 minutes for opening a standard center desk drawer. If you're worried about her "chair activity," clock her against these standards: "Got up from chair," .033 minutes; "turn in swivel chair," .009 minutes.

A woman factory worker in New Bedford, Massachusetts, in the early seventies, in a medium-sized corporation whose president's dividends from the corporation in 1970 amounted to $325,000, wrote in an organizing newspaper that 9 percent of the workers in her department were women, but all the supervisors were men.

A few years ago I was suspended for three days from work because my children were still young and I had to take time off when they were sick.

. . . They want people who keep quiet, squeal on one another, and are very good little robots. The fact that many have to take nerve pills before starting their day, and a week doesn't go by that there aren't two or three people who break down and cry, doesn't mean a thing to them.

She added: "But times are changing, and from now on, more people will speak out and demand from their so-called bosses that they be treated the way the bosses themselves would like to be treated."

Times indeed were changing. Around 1967, women in the various movements—civil rights, Students for a Democratic Society, antiwar groups—began meeting as women, and in early 1968, at a women's antiwar meeting in Washington, hundreds of women carrying torches paraded to the Arlington National Cemetery and staged "The Burial of Traditional Womanhood." At this point, and later too, there was some disagreement among women, and even more among men, on whether women should battle on specifically women's issues, or just take part in general movements against racism, war, capitalism. But the idea of a feminist focus grew.

In the fall of 1968, a group called Radical Women attracted national attention when they protested the selection of Miss America, which they called "an image that oppresses women." They all threw bras, girdles, curlers, false eyelashes, wigs, and other things they called "women's garbage" into a Freedom Trash Can. A sheep was crowned Miss America. More important, people were beginning to speak of "Women's Liberation."

Some of the New York Radical Women shortly afterward formed WITCH (Women's International Terrorist Conspiracy from Hell), and its members, dressed as witches, appeared suddenly on the floor of the New York Stock Exchange. A leaflet put out by WITCH in New York said:

WITCH lives and laughs in every woman. She is the free part of each of us, beneath the shy smiles, the acquiescence to absurd male domination, the make-up or flesh-suffocating clothes our sick society demands. There is no "joining" WITCH. If you are a woman and dare to look within yourself, you are a WITCH. You make your own rules.

WITCH in Washington, D.C., protested at the United Fruit Company for the corporation's activities in the Third World and its treatment of its women office workers. In Chicago it protested the firing of a radical feminist teacher named Marlene Dixon.

Poor women, black women, expressed the universal problem of women in their own way. In 1964 Robert Coles *(Children of Crisis)* interviewed a black woman from the South recently moved to Boston, who spoke of the desperation of her life, the difficulty of finding happiness: "To me, having a baby inside me is the only time I'm really alive."

Without talking specifically about their problems as women, many women, among the poor, did as they had always done, quietly organized neighborhood people to right injustices, to get needed services. In the mid-1960s, ten thousand black people in a community in Atlanta called Vine City joined together to help one another: they set up a thrift shop, a nursery, a medical clinic, monthly family suppers, a newspaper, a family counseling service. One of the organizers, Helen Howard, told Gerda Lerner *(Black Women in White America)* about it:

> I organized this neighborhood organization, two men and six ladies started it. That was a hard pull. A lot of people joined in later. For about five months we had meetings pretty near every night. We learned how to work with other people. . . . A lot of people were afraid to really do anything. You were afraid to go to the city hall or ask for anything. You didn't even ask the landlord for anything, you were afraid of him. Then we had meetings and then we weren't afraid so much anymore. . . .
>
> The way we got this playground: we blocked off the street, wouldn't let anything come through. We wouldn't let the trolley bus come through. The whole neighborhood was in it. Took record players and danced; it went on for a week. We didn't get arrested, they was too many of us. So then the city put up this playground for the kids. . . .

A woman named Patricia Robinson wrote a pamphlet called *Poor Black Woman,* in which she connected the problems of women with the need for basic social change:

> Rebellion by poor black women, the bottom of a class hierarchy heretofore not discussed, places the question of what kind of society will the poor black woman demand and struggle for. Already she demands the right to have birth control, like middle class black and white women. She is aware that it takes two to oppress and that she and other poor people no longer are submitting to oppression, in this case genocide. She allies herself with the have-nots in the wider world and their revolutionary struggles. She had been forced by historical conditions to withdraw the children from male dominance and to educate and support them herself. In this very process, male authority and exploitation are seriously weakened. Further, she realizes that the children will be used as all poor children have been used through history—as poorly

paid mercenaries fighting to keep or put an elite group in power. Through these steps . . . she has begun to question aggressive male domination and the class society which enforces it, capitalism.

In 1970, Dorothy Bolden, a laundry worker in Atlanta and mother of six, told why in 1968 she began organizing women doing housework, into the National Domestic Workers Union. She said: "I think women should have a voice in making decisions in their community for betterment. Because this woman in the slum is scuffling hard, and she's got a very good intelligent mind to do things, and she's been overlooked for so many years. I think she should have a voice."

Women tennis players organized. A woman fought to be a jockey, won her case, became the first woman jockey. Women artists picketed the Whitney Museum, charging sex discrimination in a sculptors' show. Women journalists picketed the Gridiron Club in Washington, which excluded women. By the start of 1974, women's studies programs existed at seventy-eight institutions, and about two thousand courses on women were being offered at about five hundred campuses.

Women's magazines and newspapers began appearing, locally and nationally, and books on women's history and the movement came out in such numbers that some bookstores had special sections for them. The very jokes on television, some sympathetic, some caustic, showed how national was the effect of the movement. Certain television commercials, which women felt humiliated them, were eliminated after protest.

In 1967, after lobbying by women's groups, President Johnson signed an executive order banning sex discrimination in federally connected employment, and in the years that followed, women's groups demanded that this be enforced. Over a thousand suits were initiated by NOW (National Organization for Women, formed in 1966) against U.S. corporations charging sex discrimination.

The right to abortion became a major issue. Before 1970, about a million abortions were done every year, of which only about ten thousand were legal. Perhaps a third of the women having illegal abortions—mostly poor people—had to be hospitalized for complications. How many thousands died as a result of these illegal abortions no one really knows. But the illegalization of abortion clearly worked against the poor, for the rich could manage either to have their baby or to have their abortion under safe conditions.

Court actions to do away with the laws against abortions were begun in over twenty states between 1968 and 1970, and public opinion grew stronger for the right of women to decide for themselves without government interference. In the book *Sisterhood Is Powerful,* an important collection of women's writing around 1970, an article by Lucinda Cisler, "Unfinished Business: Birth Control," said that "abortion is a woman's right . . . no one can veto her decision and compel her to bear a child against her will. . . ." In the spring of 1969 a Harris poll showed that 64 percent of those polled thought the decision on abortion was a private matter.

Finally, in early 1973, the Supreme Court decided (*Roe* v. *Wade, Doe* v. *Bolton*) that the state could prohibit abortions only in the last three months of pregnancy, that it could regulate abortion for health purposes during the second three months of pregnancy, and during the first three months, a woman and her doctor had the right to decide.

There was a push for child care centers, and although women did not succeed in getting much help from government, thousands of cooperative child care centers were set up.

Women also began to speak openly, for the first time, about the problem of rape. Each year, fifty thousand rapes were reported and many more were unreported. Women began taking self-defense courses. There were protests against the way police treated women, interrogated them, insulted them, when women filed rape charges. A book by Susan Brownmiller, *Against Our Will,* was widely read—it is a powerful, indignant history and analysis of rape, suggesting self-defense, individual or collective:

Fighting back. On a multiplicity of levels, that is the activity we must engage in, together, if we—women—are to redress the imbalance and rid ourselves and men of the ideology of rape. Rape can be eradicated, not merely controlled or avoided on an individual basis, but the approach must be long-range and cooperative, and must have the understanding and good will of many men as well as women. . . .

Many women were active in trying to get a Constitutional amendment, ERA (Equal Rights Amendment), passed by enough states. But it seemed clear that even if it became law, it would not be enough, that what women had accomplished had come through organization, action, protest. Even where the law was helpful it was helpful only if backed by action. Shirley Chisholm, a black Congresswoman, said:

The law cannot do it for us. We must do it for ourselves. Women in this country must become revolutionaries. We must refuse to accept the old, the traditional roles and stereotypes. . . . We must replace the old, negative thoughts about our femininity with positive thoughts and positive action. . . .

Perhaps the most profound effect of the women's movement of the sixties—beyond the actual victories on abortion, in job equality— was called "consciousness raising," often done in "women's groups," which met in homes all across the country. This meant the rethinking of roles, the rejection of inferiority, the confidence in self, a bond of sisterhood, a new solidarity of mother and daughter. The Atlanta poet Esta Seaton wrote "Her Life":

> This is the picture that keeps forming in my mind:
> my young mother, barely seventeen,
> cooking their Kosher dinner on the coal stove,
> that first winter in Vermont,
> and my father, mute in his feelings
> except when he shouted,
> eating to show his love.
>
> Fifty years later her blue eyes would grow cold
> with the shock of that grey house
> and the babies one after another
> and the doctor who said
> "If you don't want any more children
> move out of the house."

For the first time, the sheer biological uniqueness of women was openly discussed. Some theorists (Shulamith Firestone, in *The Dialectics of Sex*, for instance) thought this was more fundamental to their oppression than any particular economic system. It was liberating to talk frankly about what had for so long been secret, hidden, cause for shame and embarrassment: menstruation, masturbation, menopause, abortion, lesbianism.

One of the most influential books to appear in the early seventies was a book assembled by eleven women in the Boston Women's Health Book Collective called *Our Bodies, Ourselves*. It contained an enormous amount of practical information, on women's anatomy, on sexuality and sexual relationships, on lesbianism, on nutrition and health, on rape, self-defense, venereal disease, birth control, abortion, pregnancy, childbirth, and menopause. More important even than the information, the charts, the photos, the candid exploration of the previously unmentioned, was the mood of exuberance throughout the book, the enjoyment of the body, the happiness with the new-found understanding, the new sisterhood with young women, middle-aged women, older women. They quoted the English suffragette Christabel Pankhurst:

> Remember the dignity
> of your womanhood.
> Do not appeal,
> do not beg,
> do not grovel.
> Take courage
> join hands,
> stand beside us.
> Fight with us. . . .

The fight began, many women were saying, with the body, which seemed to be the beginning of the exploitation of women—as sex plaything (weak and incompetent), as pregnant woman (helpless), as middle-aged woman (no longer considered beautiful), as older woman (to be ignored, set aside). A biological prison had been created by men and society. As Adrienne Rich said *(Of Woman Born):* "Women are controlled by lashing us to our bodies." She wrote:

> I have a very clear, keen memory of myself the day after I was married: I was sweeping a floor. Probably the floor did not really need to be swept; probably I simply did not know what else to do with myself. But as I swept that floor I thought: "Now I am a woman. This is an age-old action, this is what women have always done." I felt I was bending to some ancient form, too ancient to question. *This is what women have always done.*
>
> As soon as I was visibly and clearly pregnant, I felt, for the first time in my adolescent and adult life, not-guilty. The atmosphere of approval in which I was bathed—even by strangers on the street, it seemed—was like an aura I carried with me, in which doubts, fears, misgivings met with absolute denial. *This is what women have always done.* . . .

Rich said women could use the body "as a resource, rather than a destiny." Patriarchal systems, she said, whether under capitalism or "socialism," limited women's bodies to their own needs. She discussed the training of passivity in women. Generations of schoolgirls were raised on *Little Women,* where Jo is told by her mother: "I am angry nearly every day of my life, Jo; but I have learned not to show it; and I still hope to learn not to feel it, though it may take me another forty years to do so."

Male doctors used instruments to bring out children, replacing the sensitive hands of midwives, in the era of "anesthetized, technologized childbirth." Rich disagreed with her fellow feminist Firestone, who wanted to change the biological inevitability of childbirth, because it is painful and a source of subordination; she wants, under different social conditions, to make childbirth a source of physical and emotional joy.

One could not talk of Freud's ignorance of women, Rich said, as his one "blind spot," which implied that in other matters his vision was clear; such ignorance distorts all. There is a dilemma of the body:

I know no woman—virgin, mother, lesbian, married, celibate—whether she earns her keep as a housewife, a cocktail waitress, or a scanner of brain waves—for whom her body is not a fundamental problem: its clouded meaning, its fertility, its desire, its so-called frigidity, its bloody speech, its silences, its changes and mutilations, its rapes and ripenings.

Her reply to this: the "repossession of our bodies . . . a world in which every woman is the presiding genius of her own body" as a basis for bringing forth not just children but new visions, new meanings, a new world.

For most women who were not intellectuals, the question was even more immediate: how to eliminate hunger, suffering, subordination, humiliation, in the here and now. A woman named Johnnie Tillmon wrote in 1972:

I'm a woman. I'm a black woman. I'm a poor woman. I'm a fat woman. I'm a middle-aged woman. And I'm on welfare. . . . I have raised six children. . . . I grew up in Arkansas . . . worked there for fifteen years in a laundry . . . moved to California. . . . In 1963 I got too sick to work anymore. Friends helped me to go on welfare. . . .

Welfare's like a traffic accident. It can happen to anybody, but especially it happens to women.

And that is why welfare is a women's issue. For a lot of middle-class women in this country, Women's Liberation is a matter of concern. For women on welfare it's a matter of survival.

Welfare, she said, was like "a supersexist marriage. You trade in *a* man for *the* man. . . . *The* man runs everything . . . controls your money. . . ." She and other welfare mothers organized a National Welfare Rights Organization. They urged that women be paid for their work—housekeeping, child rearing. ". . . No woman can be liberated, until all women get off their knees."

In the problem of women was the germ of a solution, not only for their oppression, but for everybody's. The control of women in society was ingeniously effective. It was not done directly by the state. Instead, the family was used—men to control women, women to control children, all to be preoccupied with one another, to turn to one another for help, to blame one another for trouble, to do violence to one another when things weren't going right. Why could this not be turned around? Could women liberating themselves, children freeing themselves, men and women beginning to understand one another, find the source of their common oppression outside rather than in one another? Perhaps then they could create nuggets of strength in their own relationships, millions of pockets of insurrection. They could revolutionize thought and behavior in exactly that seclusion of family privacy which the system had counted on to do its work of control and indoctrination. And together, instead of at odds—male, female, parents, children—they could undertake the changing of society itself.

It was a time of uprisings. If there could be rebellion inside that most subtle and complex of prisons—the family—it was reasonable that there be rebellions in the most brutal and obvious of prisons: the penitentiary system itself. In the sixties and early seventies, those rebellions multiplied. They also took on an unprecedented political character and the ferocity of class war, coming to a climax at Attica, New York, in September of 1971.

The prison had arisen in the United States as an attempt at Quaker reform, to replace mutilation, hanging, exile—the traditional punishments during colonial times. The prison was intended, through isolation, to produce repentence and salvation, but prisoners went insane and died in that isolation. By mid-nineteenth century, the prison was based on hard labor, along with various punishments: sweat boxes, iron yokes, solitary. The approach was summed up by the warden at the Ossining, New York, penitentiary: "In order to reform a criminal you must first break his spirit." That approach persisted.

Prison officials would convene annually to congratulate themselves on the progress being made. The president of the American Correctional Association, delivering the annual address in 1966, described the new edition of the *Manual of Correctional Standards:* "It permits us to linger, if we will, at the gates of correctional Valhalla—with an abiding pride in the sense of a job superbly done! We may be proud, we may be satisfied, we may be content." He said this just after, in the midst of, and just before the most intense series of prison uprisings the country had ever seen.

There had always been prison riots. A wave of them in the 1920s ended with a riot at Clinton, New York, a prison of 1,600 inmates, which was suppressed with three prisoners killed. Between 1950 and 1953 more than fifty major riots occurred in American prisons. In the early 1960s, prisoners on a work gang in Georgia smashing rocks used the same sledgehammers to break their legs, to call attention to their situation of daily brutality.

At San Quentin prison in California, which housed four thousand prisoners, there was a series of revolts in the late sixties: a race riot in 1967, a united black-white general strike in early 1968 that shut down almost all the prison industries, and then a second strike that summer.

At the Queens House of Detention on Long Island in New York in the fall of 1970, prisoners took over the jail, took hostages, issued demands. The prisoners' negotiating committee included four blacks, one Puerto Rican, one white; they demanded immediate bail hearings on forty-seven cases that they said were examples of racism in the granting of bail. Judges came inside the prison, granted some paroles and reductions, and the hostages were released. But when the prisoners continued to hold out, police stormed the jail with tear gas and clubs· and the revolt was over.

Around the same time, in November 1970, in Folsom prison in California, a work stoppage began which became the longest prison strike in the history of the United States. Most of the 2,400 prisoners held out in their cells for nineteen days, without food, in the face of threats and intimidation. The strike was broken with a combination of force and deception, and four of the prisoners were sent on a fourteen-hour ride to another prison, shackled and naked on the floor of a van. One of the rebels wrote: ". . . the spirit of awareness has grown. . . . The seed has been planted. . . ."

The prisons in the United States had long been an extreme reflection of the American system itself: the stark life differences between rich and poor, the racism, the use of victims against one another, the lack of resources of the underclass to speak out, the endless "reforms" that changed little. Dostoevski once said: "The degree of civilization in a society can be judged by entering its prisons."

It had long been true, and prisoners knew this better than anyone, that the poorer you were the more likely you were to end up in jail. This was not just because the poor committed more crimes. In fact, they did. The rich did not have to commit crimes to get what they wanted; the laws were on their side. But when the rich did commit crimes, they often were not prosecuted, and if they were they could get out on bail, hire clever lawyers, get better treatment from judges. Somehow, the jails ended up full of poor black people.

In 1969, there were 502 convictions for tax fraud. Such cases, called "white-collar crimes," usually involve people with a good deal of money. Of those convicted, 20 percent ended up in jail. The fraud averaged $190,000 per case; their sentences averaged seven months. That same year, for burglary and auto theft (crimes of the poor) 60 percent ended up in prison. The auto thefts averaged $992; the sentences averaged eighteen months. The burglaries averaged $321; the sentences averaged thirty-three months.

Willard Gaylin, a psychiatrist, relates *(Partial Justice)* a case which, with changes in details, could be multiplied thousands of times. He had just interviewed seventeen Jehovah's Witnesses who refused to register for the draft during the Vietnam war, and all had received two-year sentences. He came to a young black man who had notified his draft board he could not in conscience cooperate with the draft because he was repelled by the violence of the Vietnam war. He received a five-year sentence. Gaylin writes: "Hank's was the first five-year sentence I had encountered. He was also the first black man." There were additional factors:

"How was your hair then?" I asked.
"Afro."
"And what were you wearing?"
"A dashiki."
"Don't you think that might have affected your sentence?"
"Of course."
"Was it worth a year or two of your life?" I asked.
"That's all of my life," he said, looking at me with a combination of dismay and confusion. "Man, don't you know! That's what it's all about! Am I free to have my style, am I free to have my hair, am I free to have my skin?"
"Of course," I said. "You're right."

Gaylin found enormous discretion given to judges in the handing out of sentences. In Oregon, of thirty-three men convicted of violating the draft law, eighteen were put on probation. In southern Texas, of sixteen men violating the same law, none was put on probation, and in southern Mississippi, every defendant was convicted and given the maximum of five years. In one part of the country (New England), the average sentence for all crimes was eleven months; in another part (the South), it was seventy-eight months. But it wasn't simply a matter of North and South. In New York City, one judge handling 673 persons brought before him for public drunkenness (all poor; the rich get drunk behind closed doors) discharged 531 of them. Another judge, handling 566 persons on the same charge, discharged one person.

With such power in the hands of the courts, the poor, the black, the odd, the homosexual, the hippie, the radical are not likely to get equal treatment before judges who are almost uniformly white, upper middle class, orthodox.

While in any one year (1972, for instance) perhaps 375,000 people will be in jail (county or city) or in prisons (state or federal), and 54,000 in juvenile detention, there will also be 900,000 under probation and 300,000 on parole—a total of 1,600,000 people affected by the criminal justice system. Considering turnover, in any one year, several million people will come in and go out of this system. It is a population largely invisible to middle-class America, but if 20 million blacks could be invisible for so long, why not four or five million "criminals"? A study by the Children's Defense Fund (Thomas Cottle, *Children in Jail*) in the mid-seventies revealed that more than 900,000 young people under eighteen are jailed in the course of a year.

Anyone trying to describe the reality of prison falters. A man in Walpole prison in Massachusetts wrote:

> Every program that we get is used as a weapon against us. The right to go to school, to go to church, to have visitors, to write, to go to the movies. They all end up being weapons of punishment. None of the programs are *ours*. Everything is treated as a privilege that can be taken away from us. The result is insecurity—a frustration that keeps eating away at you.

Another Walpole prisoner:

> I haven't eaten in the mess hall for four years. I just couldn't take it any more. You'd go into the serving line in the morning and 100 or 200 cockroaches would go running away from the trays. The trays were grimy and the food was raw or had dirt or maggots in it.
>
> Many a night I'd go hungry, living on peanut butter and sandwiches, getting a loaf of bread here or a hunk of bologna there. Other guys couldn't do that because they didn't have my connections or they didn't have money for the canteen.

Communication with the outside world was difficult. Guards would tear up letters. Others would be intercepted and read. Jerry Sousa, a prisoner at Walpole in 1970, sent two letters—one to a judge, the other to the parole board—to tell about a beating by guards. They went unanswered. Eight years later, at a court hearing, he discovered the prison authorities had intercepted them, never sent them out.

The families suffered with the prisoner: "During the last lock-up my four-year-old son sneaked off into the yard and picked me a flower. A guard in the tower called the warden's office and a deputy came in with the State Police at his side. He announced that if any child went into the yard and picked another flower, all visits would be terminated."

The prison rebellions of the late sixties and early seventies had a distinctly different character than the earlier ones. The prisoners in the Queens House of Detention referred to themselves as "revolutionaries." All over the country, prisoners were obviously affected by the turmoil in the country, the black revolt, the youth upsurge, the antiwar movement.

The events of those years underlined what prisoners already sensed—that whatever crimes they had committed, the greatest crimes were being committed by the authorities who maintained the prisons, by the government of the United States. The law was being broken daily by the President, sending bombers to kill, sending men to be killed, outside the Constitution, outside the "highest law of the land." State and local officials were violating the civil rights of black people, which was against the law, and were not being prosecuted for it.

Literature about the black movement, books on the war, began to seep into the prisons. The example set in the streets by blacks, by antiwar demonstrators, was exhilarating—against a lawless system, defiance was the only answer.

It was a system which sentenced Martin Sostre, a fifty-two-year-old black man running an Afro-Asian bookstore in Buffalo, New York, to twenty-five to thirty years in prison for allegedly selling $15 worth of heroin to an informer who later recanted his testimony. The recantation did not free Sostre—he could find no court, including the Supreme Court of the United States, to revoke the judgment. He spent eight years in prison, was beaten ten times by guards, spent three years in solitary confinement, battling and defying the authorities all the way until his release. Such injustice deserved only rebellion.

There had always been political prisoners—people sent to jail for belonging to radical movements, for opposing war. But now a new kind of political prisoner appeared—the man, or woman, convicted of an ordinary crime, who, in prison, became awakened politically.

Some prisoners began making connections between their personal ordeal and the social system. They then turned not to individual rebellion but to collective action. They became concerned—amid an environment whose brutality demanded concentration on one's own safety, an atmosphere of cruel rivalry—for the rights, the safety of others.

George Jackson was one of these new political prisoners. In Soledad prison, California, on an indeterminate sentence for a $70 robbery, having already served ten years of it, Jackson became a revolutionary. He spoke with a fury that matched his condition:

This monster—the monster they've engendered in me will return to torment its maker, from the grave, the pit, the profoundest pit. Hurl me into the next existence, the descent into hell won't turn me. . . . I'm going to charge them reparations in blood. I'm going to charge them like a maddened, wounded, rogue male elephant, ears flared, trunk raised, trumpet blaring. . . . War without terms.

A prisoner like this would not last. And when his book *Soledad Brother* became one of the most widely read books of black militancy in the United States—by prisoners, by black people, by white people—perhaps this ensured he would not last.

All my life I've done exactly what I wanted to do just when I wanted, no more, perhaps less sometimes, but never any more, which explains why I had to be jailed. . . . I never adjusted. I haven't adjusted even yet, with half of my life already in prison.

He knew what might happen:

Born to a premature death, a menial, subsistence-wage worker, odd-job man, the cleaner, the caught, the man under hatches, without bail—that's me, the colonial victim. Anyone who can pass the civil service examination today can kill me tomorrow . . . with complete immunity.

In August 1971 he was shot in the back by guards at San Quentin prison while he was allegedly trying to escape. The state's story (analyzed by Eric Mann in *Comrade George*) was full of holes. Prisoners in jails and state prisons all over the country knew, even before the final autopsy was in, even before later disclosures suggested a government plot to kill Jackson, that he had been murdered for daring to be a revolutionary in prison. Shortly after Jackson's death, there was a chain of rebellions around the country, in San Jose Civic Center jail, in Dallas county jail, in Suffolk county jail in Boston, in Cumberland county jail in Bridgeton, New Jersey, in Bexar county jail in San Antonio, Texas.

The most direct effect of the George Jackson murder was the rebellion at Attica prison in September 1971—a rebellion that came from long, deep grievances, but that was raised to boiling point by the news about George Jackson. Attica was surrounded by a 30-foot wall, 2 feet thick, with fourteen gun towers. Fifty-four percent of the inmates were black; 100 percent of the guards were white. Prisoners spent fourteen to sixteen hours a day in their cells, their mail was read, their reading material restricted, their visits from families conducted through a mesh screen, their medical care disgraceful, their parole system inequitable, racism everywhere. How perceptive the prison administration was about these conditions can be measured by the comment of the superintendent of Attica, Vincent Mancusi, when the uprising began: "Why are they destroying their home?"

Most of the Attica prisoners were there as a result of plea bargaining. Of 32,000 felony indictments a year in New York State, 4,000 to 5,000 were tried. The rest (about 75 percent) were disposed of by deals made under duress, called "plea bargaining," described as follows in the Report of the Joint Legislative Committee on Crime in New York:

> The final climactic act in the plea bargaining procedure is a charade which in itself has aspects of dishonesty which rival the original crime in many instances. The accused is made to assert publicly his guilt on a specific crime, which in many cases he has not committed; in some cases he pleads guilty to a non-existing crime. He must further indicate that he is entering his plea freely . . . and that he is not doing so because of any promises . . . made to him.
>
> In plea bargaining, the accused pleads guilty, whether he is or not, and saves the state the trouble of a trial in return for the promise of a less severe punishment.

When Attica prisoners were up for parole, the average time of their hearing, including the reading of the file and deliberation among the three members, was 5.9 minutes. Then the decision was handed out, with no explanation.

The official report on the Attica uprising tells how an inmate-instructed sociology class there became a forum for ideas about change. Then there was a series of organized protest efforts, and in July an inmate manifesto setting forth a series of moderate demands, after which "tensions at Attica had continued to mount," culminating in a day of protest over the killing of George Jackson at San Quentin, during which few inmates ate at lunch and dinner and many wore black armbands.

On September 9, 1971, a series of conflicts between prisoners and guards ended with a group of inmates breaking through a gate with a defective weld and taking over one of the four prison yards, with forty guards as hostages. Then followed five days in which the prisoners set up a remarkable community in the yard. A group of citizen-observers, invited by the prisoners, included *New York Times* columnist Tom Wicker, who wrote *(A Time to Die):* "The racial harmony that prevailed among the prisoners—it was absolutely astonishing. . . . That prison yard was the first place I have ever seen where there was no racism." One black prisoner later said: "I never thought whites could really get it on. . . . But I can't tell you what the yard was like, I actually cried it was so close, everyone so together. . . .

After five days, the state lost patience. Governor Nelson Rockefeller approved a military attack on the prison (see Cinda Firestone's stunning film *Attica*). National Guardsmen, prison guards, and local police went in with automatic rifles, carbines, and submachine guns in a full-scale assault on the prisoners, who had no firearms. Thirty-one prisoners were killed. The first stories given the press by prison authorities said that nine guards held hostage had their throats slashed by the prisoners during the attack. The official autopsies almost immediately showed this to be false: the nine guards died in the same hail of bullets that killed the prisoners.

The effects of Attica are hard to measure. Two months after the revolt at Attica, men at Norfolk prison in Massachusetts began to organize. On November 8, 1971, armed guards and state troopers, in a surprise raid, moved into the cells at Norfolk, pulled out sixteen men, and shipped them out. A prisoner described the scene:

Between one and two last night I was awakened (I've been a light sleeper since Vietnam) and I looked out my window. There were troopers. And screws. Lots. Armed with sidearms, and big clubs. They were going into dorms and taking people, all kinds of people. . . .

They took a friend of mine. . . . Being pulled outside in our underwear, at 1:30, in bare feet by two troopers and a housescrew. Looking at those troops, with guns, and masks and clubs, with the moon shining off the helmets and the hate that you could see in their faces. Thinking that this is where these guys live, with the guns and the hate, and the helmets and masks, and you, you're trying to wake up, flashing on Kent State and Jackson, and Chicago. And Attica. Most of all, Attica. . . .

That same week at Concord prison in Massachusetts, another raid. It was as if everywhere, in the weeks and months after Attica, the authorities were taking preventive action to break up organizing efforts among the prisoners. Jerry Sousa, a young leader of the prison reform movement at Concord, was taken away, dumped into Walpole in the middle of the night, and immediately put into Nine Block, the dreaded segregation unit. He had been there only a short time when he managed to get a report out to friends. The content of this report tells much about what was happening before and after Attica to the thinking of prisoners:

> We are writing a somber report regarding the circumstances and events leading up to and surrounding the death of prisoner Joseph Chesnulavich which occurred here an hour ago in Nine Block.
>
> Since Christmas eve, vicious prison guards here in Nine Block have created a reign of terror directed toward us prisoners. Four of us have been beaten, one who was prisoner Donald King.
>
> In an attempt to escape constant harassment and inhuman treatment, prisoner George Hayes ate razor blades and prisoner Fred Ahern swallowed a needle . . . they both were rushed to Mass General Hospital.
>
> This evening at 6 P.M. prison guards Baptist, Sainsbury, and Montiega turned a fire extinguisher containing a chemical foam on Joe then slammed the solid steel door sealing him in his cell and walked away, voicing threats of, "We'll get that punk."
>
> At 9:25 P.M. Joe was found dead. . . . Prison authorities as well as news media will label little Joe's death a suicide, but the men here in Block Nine who witnessed this murder know. But are we next?

What was happening was the organization of prisoners—the caring of prisoners for one another, the attempt to take the hatred and anger of individual rebellion and turn it into collective effort for change. On the outside, something new was also happening, the development of prison support groups all over the country, the building of a body of literature about prisons. There were more studies of crime and punishment, a growing movement for the abolition of prisons on the ground that they did not prevent crime or cure it, but expanded it. Alternatives were discussed: community houses in the short run (except for the incorrigibly violent); guaranteed minimum economic security, in the long run.

The prisoners were thinking about issues beyond prison, victims other than themselves and their friends. In Walpole prison a statement asking for American withdrawal from Vietnam was circulated; it was signed by every single prisoner—an amazing organizing feat by a handful of inmates. One Thanksgiving day there, most of the prisoners, not only in Walpole but in three other prisons, refused to eat the special holiday meal, saying they wanted to bring attention to the hungry all over the United States.

Prisoners worked laboriously on lawsuits, and some victories were won in the courts. The publicity around Attica, the community of support, had its effect. Although the Attica rebels were indicted on heavy charges and faced double and triple life terms, the charges were finally dropped. But in general, the courts declared their unwillingness to enter the closed, controlled world of the prison, and so the prisoners remained as they had been so long, on their own.

Even where an occasional "victory" came in the courts it turned out, on close reading, to leave things not much different. In 1973 (*Procunier* v. *Martinez*) the U.S. Supreme Court declared unconstitutional certain mail censorship regulations of the California Department of Corrections. But when one looked closely, the decision, with all its proud language about "First Amendment liberties," said: ". . . we hold that censorship of prison mail is justified if the following criteria are met. . . ." When the censorship could be said to "further an important or substantial government interest" or where it was in the "substantial governmental interests of security, order, and rehabilitation," censorship would be allowed.

In 1978 the Supreme Court ruled that the news media do not have guaranteed rights of access to jails and prisons. It ruled also that prison authorities could forbid inmates to speak to one another, assemble, or spread literature about the formation of a prisoners' union.

It became clear—and prisoners seemed to know this from the start—that their condition would not be changed by law, but by protest, organization, resistance, the creation of their own culture, their own literature, the building of links with people on the outside. There were more outsiders now who knew about prisons. Tens of thousands of Americans had spent time behind bars in the civil rights and antiwar movements. They had learned about the prison system and could hardly forget their experiences. There was a basis now for breaking through the long isolation of the prisoners from the community and finding support there. In the mid-seventies, this was beginning to happen.

It was a time of upsurge. Women, guarded in their very homes, rebelled. Prisoners, put out of sight and behind bars, rebelled. The greatest surprise was still to come.

It was thought that the Indians, once the only occupants of the continent, then pushed back and annihilated by the white invaders, would not be heard from again. In the last days of the year 1890, shortly after Christmas, the last massacre of Indians took place at Pine Ridge, South Dakota, near Wounded Knee Creek. Sitting Bull, the great Sioux leader, had just been assassinated by Indian police in the pay of the United States, and the remaining Sioux sought refuge at Pine Ridge, 120 men and 230 women and children, surrounded by U.S. cavalry, with two Hotchkiss guns—capable of hurling shells over 2 miles—on a rise overlooking the camp. When the troopers ordered the Indians to turn over their weapons, one of them fired his rifle. The soldiers then let loose with their carbines, and the big guns on the hill shelled the tepees. When it was over between 200 and 300 of the original 350 men, women, and children were dead. The twenty-five soldiers who died were mostly hit by their own shrapnel or bullets, since the Indians had only a few guns.

The Indian tribes, attacked, subdued, starved out, had been divided up by putting them on reservations where they lived in poverty. In 1887, an Allotment Act tried to break up the reservations into small plots of land owned by individual Indians, to turn them into American-type small farmers—but much of this land was taken by white speculators, and the reservations remained.

Then, during the New Deal, with a friend of the Indians, John Collier, in charge of the Bureau of Indian Affairs, there was an attempt to restore tribal life. But in the decades that followed, no fundamental change took place. Many Indians stayed on the impoverished reservations. The younger ones often left. An Indian anthropologist said: "An Indian reservation is the most complete colonial system in the world that I know about."

For a time, the disappearance or amalgamation of the Indians seemed inevitable—only 300,000 were left at the turn of the century, from the original million or more in the area of the United States. But then the population began to grow again, as if a plant left to die refused to do so, began to flourish. By 1960 there were 800,000 Indians, half on reservations, half in towns all over the country.

The autobiographies of Indians show their refusal to be absorbed by the white man's culture. One wrote:

Oh, yes, I went to the white man's schools. I learned to read from school books, newspapers, and the Bible. But in time I found that these were not enough. Civilized people depend too much on man-made printed pages. I turn to the Great Spirit's book which is the whole of his creation. . . .

A Hopi Indian named Sun Chief said:

I had learned many English words and could recite part of the Ten Commandments. I knew how to sleep on a bed, pray to Jesus, comb my hair, eat with a knife and fork, and use a toilet. . . . I had also learned that a person thinks with his head instead of his heart.

Chief Luther Standing Bear, in his 1933 autobiography, *From the Land of the Spotted Eagle,* wrote:

True, the white man brought great change. But the varied fruits of his civilization, though highly colored and inviting, are sickening and deadening. And if it be the part of civilization to maim, rob, and thwart, then what is progress?

I am going to venture that the man who sat on the ground in his tipi meditating on life and its meaning, accepting the kinship of all creatures, and acknowledging unity with the universe of things, was infusing into his being the true essence of civilization. . . .

As the civil rights and antiwar movements developed in the 1960s, Indians were already gathering their energy for resistance, thinking about how to change their situation, beginning to organize. In 1961, five hundred tribal and urban Indian leaders met in Chicago. Out of this came another gathering of university-educated young Indians who formed the National Indian Youth Council. Mel Thom, a Paiute Indian, their first president, wrote:

There is increased activity over on the Indian side. There are disagreements, laughing, singing, outbursts of anger, and occasionally some planning. . . . Indians are gaining confidence and courage that their cause is right.

The struggle goes on. . . . Indians are gathering together to deliberate their destiny. . . .

Around this time, Indians began to approach the United States government on an embarrassing topic: treaties. In his widely read 1969 book *Custer Died for Your Sins,* Vine Deloria, Jr., noted that President Lyndon Johnson talked about America's "commitments," and President Nixon talked about Russia's failure to respect treaties. He said: "Indian people laugh themselves sick when they hear these statements."

The United States government had signed more than four hundred treaties with Indians and violated every single one. For instance, back in George Washington's administration, a treaty was signed with the Iroquois of New York: "The United States acknowledge all the land within the aforementioned boundaries to be the property of the Seneka nation. . . ." But in the early sixties, under President Kennedy, the

United States ignored the treaty and built a dam on this land, flooding most of the Seneca reservation.

Resistance was already taking shape in various parts of the country. In the state of Washington, there was an old treaty taking land from the Indians but leaving them fishing rights. This became unpopular as the white population grew and wanted the fishing areas exclusively for themselves. When state courts closed river areas to Indian fishermen, in 1964, Indians had "fish-ins" on the Nisqually River, in defiance of the court orders, and went to jail, hoping to publicize their protest.

A local judge the following year ruled that the Puyallup tribe did not exist, and its members could not fish on the river named for them, the Puyallup River. Policemen raided Indian fishing groups, destroyed boats, slashed nets, manhandled people, arrested seven Indians. A Supreme Court ruling in 1968 confirmed Indian rights under the treaty but said a state could "regulate all fishing" if it did not discriminate against Indians. The state continued to get injunctions and to arrest Indians fishing. They were doing to the Supreme Court ruling what whites in the South had done with the Fourteenth Amendment for many years—ignoring it. Protests, raids, arrests, continued into the early seventies.

Some of the Indians involved in the fish-ins were veterans of the Vietnam war. One was Sid Mills, who was arrested in a fish-in at Frank's Landing on the Nisqually River in Washington on October 13, 1968. He made a statement:

I am a Yakima and Cherokee Indian, and a man. For two years and four months, I've been a soldier in the United States Army. I served in combat in Vietnam—until critically wounded.... I hereby renounce further obligation in service or duty to the United States Army.

My first obligation now lies with the Indian People fighting for the lawful Treaty to fish in usual and accustomed water of the Nisqually, Columbia and other rivers of the Pacific Northwest, and in serving them in this fight in any way possible....

My decision is influenced by the fact that we have already buried Indian fishermen returned dead from Vietnam, while Indian fishermen live here without protection and under steady attack....

Just three years ago today, on October 13, 1965, 19 women and children were brutalized by more than 45 armed agents of the State of Washington at Frank's Landing on the Nisqually river in a vicious, unwarranted attack....

Interestingly, the oldest human skeletal remains ever found in the Western Hemisphere were recently uncovered on the banks of the Columbia River—

the remains of Indian fishermen. What kind of government or society would spend millions of dollars to pick upon our bones, restore our ancestral life patterns, and protect our ancient remains from damage—while at the same time eating upon the flesh of our living People. . . ?

We will fight for our rights.

Indians fought back not only with physical resistance, but also with the artifacts of white culture—books, words, newspapers. In 1968, members of the Mohawk Nation at Akwesasne, on the St. Lawrence River between the United States and Canada, began a remarkable newspaper, *Akwesasne Notes,* with news, editorials, poetry, all flaming with the spirit of defiance. Mixed in with all that was an irrepressible humor. Vine Deloria, Jr., wrote:

Every now and then I am impressed with the thinking of the non-Indian. I was in Cleveland last year and got to talking with a non-Indian about American history. He said that he was really sorry about what had happened to Indians, but that there was a good reason for it. The continent had to be developed and he felt that Indians had stood in the way, and thus had had to be removed. "After all," he remarked, "what did you do with the land when you had it?" I didn't understand him until later when I discovered that the Cuyahoga River running through Cleveland is inflammable. So many combustible pollutants are dumped into the river that the inhabitants have to take special precautions during the summer to avoid setting it on fire. After reviewing the argument of my non-Indian friend I decided that he was probably correct. Whites had made better use of the land. How many Indians could have thought of creating an inflammable river?

In 1969, November 9, there took place a dramatic event which focused attention on Indian grievances as nothing else had. It burst through the invisibility of previous local Indian protests and declared to the entire world that the Indians still lived and would fight for their rights. On that day, before dawn, seventy-eight Indians landed on Alcatraz Island in San Francisco Bay and occupied the island. Alcatraz was an abandoned federal prison, a hated and terrible place nicknamed "The Rock." In 1964 some young Indians had occupied it to establish an Indian university, but they were driven off and there was no publicity.

This time, it was different. The group was led by Richard Oakes, a Mohawk who directed Indian Studies at San Francisco State College, and Grace Thorpe, a Sac and Fox Indian, daughter of Jim Thorpe, the famous Indian college football star and Olympic runner, jumper, hurdler. More Indians landed, and by the end of November nearly six hundred of them, representing more than fifty tribes, were living on Alcatraz. They called themselves "Indians of All Tribes" and issued a proclamation, "We Hold the Rock." In it they offered to buy Alcatraz in glass beads and red cloth, the price paid Indians for Manhattan Island over three hundred years earlier. They said:

We feel that this so-called Alcatraz Island is more than suitable for an Indian reservation, as determined by the white man's own standards. By this we mean that this place resembles most Indian reservations in that:

1. It is isolated from modern facilities, and without adequate means of transportation.
2. It has no fresh running water.
3. It has inadequate sanitation facilities.
4. There are no oil or mineral rights.
5. There is no industry and so unemployment is very great.
6. There are no health care facilities.
7. The soil is rocky and non-productive; and the land does not support game.
8. There are no educational facilities.
9. The population has always exceeded the land base.
10. The population has always been held as prisoners and dependent upon others.

They announced they would make the island a center for Native American Studies for Ecology: "We will work to de-pollute the air and waters of the Bay Area . . . restore fish and animal life. . . ."

In the months that followed, the government cut off telephones, electricity, and water to Alcatraz Island. Many of the Indians had to leave, but others insisted on staying. A year later they were still there, and they sent out a message to "our brothers and sisters of all races and tongues upon our Earth Mother":

We are still holding the Island of Alcatraz in the true names of Freedom, Justice and Equality, because you, our brothers and sisters of this earth, have lent support to our just cause. We reach out our hands and hearts and send spirit messages to each and every one of you—WE HOLD THE ROCK. . . .

We have learned that violence breeds only more violence and we therefore have carried on our occupation of Alcatraz in a peaceful manner, hoping that the government of these United States will also act accordingly. . . .

We are a proud people! We are Indians! We have observed and rejected much of what so-called civilization offers. We are Indians! We will preserve our traditions and ways of life by educating our own children. We are Indians!

We will join hands in a unity never before put into practice. We are Indians! Our Earth Mother awaits our voices.

We are Indians Of All Tribes! WE HOLD THE ROCK!

Six months later, federal forces invaded the island and physically removed the Indians living there.

It had been thought that the Navajo Indians would not be heard from again. In the mid-1800s, United States troops under "Kit" Carson burned Navajo villages, destroyed their crops and orchards, forced them from their lands. But in the Black Mesa of New Mexico they never surrendered. In the late 1960s, the Peabody Coal Company began strip mining on their land—a ruthless excavation of the topsoil. The company pointed to a "contract" signed with some Navajos. It was reminiscent of the "treaties" signed with some Indians in the past that took away all Indian land.

One hundred and fifty Navajos met in the spring of 1969 to declare that the strip mining would pollute the water and the air, destroy the grazing land for livestock, use up their scarce water resources. A young woman pointed to a public relations pamphlet put out by the Peabody Coal Company, showing fishing lakes, grassland, trees, and said: "We're not going to have anything like those you see in the pictures. . . . What is the future going to be like for our children, our children's children?" An elderly Navajo woman, one of the organizers of the meeting, said, "Peabody's monsters are digging up the heart of our mother earth, our sacred mountain, and we also feel the pains. . . . I have lived here for years and I'm not about to move."

The Hopi Indians were also affected by the Peabody operations. They wrote to President Nixon in protest:

Today the sacred lands where the Hopi live are being desecrated by men who seek coal and water from our soil that they may create more power for the whiteman's cities. . . . The Great Spirit said not to allow this to happen. . . . The Great Spirit said not to take from the Earth—not to destroy living things. . . .

It is said by the Great Spirit that if a gourd of ashes is dropped upon the Earth, that many men will die and that the end of this way of life is near at hand. We interpret this as the dropping of atomic bombs on Hiroshima and Nagasaki. We do not want to see this happen to any place or any nation again, but instead we should turn all this energy for peaceful uses, not for war. . . .

In the fall of 1970, a magazine called *La Raza,* one of the countless local publications coming out of the movements of those years to supply information ignored in the regular media, told about the Pit River Indians of northern California. Sixty Pit Indians occupied land they said belonged to them; they defied the Forest Services when ordered to leave. One of them, Darryl B. Wilson, later recalled; "As the flames danced orange making the trees come to life, and the cold creeped out of the darkness to challenge the speaking fire, and our breath came in small clouds, we spoke." They asked the government by what treaty it claimed the land. It could point to none. They cited a federal statute *(25 USCA 194)* that where there was a land dispute between Indian and white "the burden of proof falls on the white man."

They had built a quonset hut, and the marshals told them it was ugly and ruined the landscape. Wilson wrote later:

The whole world is rotting. The water is poisoned, the air polluted, the politics deformed, the land gutted, the forest pillaged, the shores ruined, the towns burned, the lives of the people destroyed . . . and the federals spent the best part of October trying to tell us the quonset hut was "ugly"!

To us it was beautiful. It was the beginning of our school. The meeting place. Home for our homeless. A sanctuary for those needing rest. Our church. Our headquarters. Our business office. Our symbol of approaching freedom. And it still stands.

It was also the center for the reviving of our stricken, diluted and separated culture. Our beginning. It was our sun rising on a clear spring day when the sky holds no clouds. It was a good and pure thing for the heart to look upon. That small place on earth. Our place.

But 150 marshals came, with machine guns, shotguns, rifles, pistols, riot sticks, Mace, dogs, chains, manacles. "The old people were frightened. The young questioned bravery. The small children were like a deer that has been shot by the thunder stick. Hearts beat fast as though a race was just run in the heat of summer." The marshals began swinging their riot sticks, and blood started flowing. Wilson grabbed one marshal's club, was thrown down, manacled, and while lying face down on the ground was struck behind the head several times. A sixty-six-year-old man was beaten to unconsciousness. A white reporter was arrested, his wife beaten. They were all thrown into trucks and taken away, charged with assaulting state and federal officers and cutting trees— but not with trespassing, which might have brought into question the ownership of the land. When the episode was all over, they were still defiant.

Indians who had been in the Vietnam war made connections. At the "Winter Soldier Investigations" in Detroit, where Vietnam veterans testified about their experiences, an Oklahoma Indian named Evan Haney told about his:

The same massacres happened to the Indians 100 years ago. Germ warfare was used then. They put smallpox in the Indians' blankets. . . .

I got to know the Vietnamese people and I learned they were just like us. . . . What we are doing is destroying ourselves and the world.

I have grown up with racism all my life. When I was a child, watching cowboys and Indians on TV, I would root for the cavalry, not the Indians. It was that bad. I was that far toward my own destruction. . . .

Though 50 percent of the children at the country school I attended in Oklahoma were Indians, nothing in school, on television, or on the radio taught anything about Indian culture. There were no books on Indian history, not even in the library. . . .

But I knew something was wrong. I started reading and learning my own culture. . . .

I saw the Indian people at their happiest when they went to Alcatraz or to Washington to defend their fishing rights. They at last felt like human beings.

Indians began to do something about their "own destruction"—the annihilation of their culture. In 1969, at the First Convocation of American Indian Scholars, Indians spoke indignantly of either the ignoring or the insulting of Indians in textbooks given to little children all over the United States. That year the Indian Historian Press was founded. It evaluated four hundred textbooks in elementary and secondary schools and found that not one of them gave an accurate depiction of the Indian.

A counterattack began in the schools. In early 1971, forty-five Indian students at Copper Valley School, in Glennalen, Alaska, wrote a letter to their Congressman opposing the Alaska oil pipeline as ruinous to the ecology, a threat to the "peace, quiet and security of our Alaska."

Other Americans were beginning to pay attention, to rethink their own learning. The first motion pictures attempting to redress the history of the Indian appeared: one was *Little Big Man,* based on a novel by Thomas Berger. More and more books appeared on Indian history, until a whole new literature came into existence. Teachers became sensitive to the old stereotypes, threw away the old textbooks, started using new material. In the spring of 1977 a teacher named Jane Califf, in the New York City elementary schools, told of her experiences with fourth and fifth grade students. She brought into class the traditional textbooks and asked the students to locate the stereotypes in them. She read aloud from Native American writers and articles from *Akwesasne Notes,* and put protest posters around the room. The children then wrote letters to the editors of the books they had read:

Dear Editor,

   I don't like your book called The Cruise of Christopher Columbus. I didn't like it because you said some things about Indians that weren't true. . . . Another thing I didn't like was on page 69, it says that Christopher Columbus invited the Indians to Spain, but what really happened was that he stole them!

censearly,
Raymond Miranda

   On Thanksgiving Day 1970, at the annual celebration of the landing of the Pilgrims, the authorities decided to do something different: invite an Indian to make the celebratory speech. They found a Wampanoag Indian named Frank James and asked him to speak. But when they saw the speech he was about to deliver, they decided they did not want it. His speech, not heard at Plymouth, Massachusetts, on that occasion, said, in part (the whole speech is in *Chronicles of American Indian Protest*):

   I speak to you as a Man—a Wampanoag Man. . . . It is with mixed emotions that I stand here to share my thoughts. . . . The Pilgrims had hardly explored the shores of Cape Cod four days before they had robbed the graves of my ancestors, and stolen their corn, wheat, and beans. . . .

   Our spirit refuses to die. Yesterday we walked the woodland paths and sandy trails. Today we must walk the macadam highways and roads. We are uniting. We're standing not in our wigwams but in your concrete tent. We stand tall and proud and before too many moons pass we'll right the wrongs we have allowed to happen to us. . . .

   For Indians there has never been a clear line between prose and poetry. When an Indian studying in New Mexico was praised for his poetry he said, "In my tribe we have no poets. Everyone talks in poetry." There are, however, "poems," collected in William Brandon's *The Last Americans* and in *The Way* by Shirley Hill Witt and Stan Steiner.

   An Ashinabe "spring poem" translated by Gerald Vizenor:

> as my eyes
> look across the prairie
> i feel the summer
> in the spring

"Snow the Last" by Joseph Concha:

> Snow comes last
> for it quiets down everything

This from a fifth-year group in a Special Navajo Program in the year 1940, called "It is Not!"

> The Navajo Reservation a lonesome place?
> It is Not!
> The skies are sunny,
> Clear blue,
> Or grey with rain.
> Each day is gay—
> in Nature's way.
> It is not a lonesome place at all.
> A Navajo house shabby and small?
> It is Not!
> Inside there's love,
> Good laughter,
> And Big Talk.
> But best—
> it's home
> With an open door
> And room for all
> A Castle could have no more.

In March of 1973 came a powerful affirmation that the Indians of North America were still alive. On the site of the 1890 massacre, on Pine Ridge reservation, several hundred Oglala Sioux and friends returned to the village of Wounded Knee to occupy it as a symbol of the demand for Indian land, Indian rights. The history of that event, in the words of the participants, has been captured in a rare book published by *Akwesasne Notes* (*Voices from Wounded Knee,* 1973).

In the 1970s, 54 percent of the adult males on the Pine Ridge reservation were unemployed, one-third of the families were on welfare or pensions, alcoholism was widespread, and suicide rates were high. The life expectancy of an Oglala Sioux was forty-six years. Just before the Wounded Knee occupation, there was violence at the town of Custer. An Indian named Wesley Bad Heart Bull was killed by a white gas station attendant. The man was let out on $5,000 bond and indicted for manslaughter, facing a possible ten-year term. A gathering of Indians to protest this led to a clash with police. The murder victim's mother, Mrs. Sarah Bad Heart Bull, was arrested, on charges that called for a maximum sentence of thirty years.

On February 27, 1973, about three hundred Oglala Sioux, many of them members of the new militant organization called the American Indian Movement (AIM), entered the village of Wounded Knee and declared it liberated territory. Ellen Moves Camp later said: "We decided that we did need the American Indian Movement in here because our men were scared, they hung to the back. It was mostly the women that went forward and spoke out."

Within hours, more than two hundred FBI agents, federal marshals, and police of the Bureau of Indian Affairs surrounded and blockaded the town. They had armored vehicles, automatic rifles, machine guns, grenade launchers, and gas shells, and soon began firing. Gladys Bissonette said three weeks later: "Since we are here, in Wounded Knee, we've been shot at, over and over, always after dark. But last night we were hit the hardest. I guess the Great Spirit is with us, and no bullets find their way into our bodies. We ran through a hail of bullets one night. . . . We're going to hold our stand until we are completely an independent sovereign nation, Oglala Sioux Nation."

After the siege began, food supplies became short. Indians in Michigan sent food via a plane that landed inside the encampment. The next day FBI agents arrested the pilot and a doctor from Michigan who had hired the plane. In Nevada, eleven Indians were arrested for taking food, clothing, and medical supplies to South Dakota. In mid-April three more planes dropped 1,200 pounds of food, but as people scrambled to gather it up, a government helicopter appeared overhead and fired down on them while groundfire came from all sides. Frank Clearwater, an Indian man lying on a cot inside a church, was hit by a bullet. When his wife accompanied him to a hospital, she was arrested and jailed. Clearwater died.

There were more gun battles, another death. Finally, a negotiated peace was signed, in which both sides agreed to disarm (the Indians had refused to disarm while surrounded by armed men, recalling the 1890 massacre). The United States government promised to investigate Indian affairs, and a presidential commission would reexamine the 1868 treaty. The siege ended and 120 occupiers were arrested. The U.S. government then said that it had reexamined the 1868 treaty, found it valid, but that it was superseded by the U.S. power of "eminent domain"—the government's power to take land.

The Indians had held out for seventy-one days, creating a marvelous community inside the besieged territory. Communal kitchens were set up, a health clinic, and hospital. A Navajo Vietnam veteran:

There's a tremendous amount of coolness considering that we're out-gunned. . . . But people stay because they believe; they have a cause. That's why we lost in Viet Nam, cause there was no cause. We were fighting a rich man's war, for the rich man. . . . In Wounded Knee, we're doing pretty damn good, morale-wise. Because we can still laugh.

Messages of support had come to Wounded Knee from Australia, Finland, Germany, Italy, Japan, England. One message came from some of the Attica brothers, two of whom were Indians: "You fight for our Earth Mother and Her Children. Our spirits fight with you!" Wallace Black Elk replied: "Little Wounded Knee is turned into a giant world."

After Wounded Knee, in spite of the deaths, the trials, the use of the police and courts to try to break the movement, the Native American movement continued.

In the Akwesasne community itself, which put out *Akwesasne Notes,* the Indians had always insisted their territory was separate, not to be invaded by the white man's law. One day New York State police gave three traffic tickets to a Mohawk Indian truck driver, and a council of Indians met with a police lieutenant. At first, he insisted that he had to follow orders and give out tickets, even in Akwesasne territory, although he obviously was trying to be reasonable. He finally agreed that they would not arrest an Indian in the territory or even outside of it without first having a meeting with the Mohawk council. The lieutenant then sat down and lit a cigar. Indian Chief Joahquisoh, a distinguished-looking man with long hair, rose and addressed the lieu-tenant with a serious voice. "There is one more thing before you go," he said looking straight at the lieutenant. "I want to know," he said slowly, "if you've got an extra cigar." The meeting ended in laughter.

Akwesasne Notes continued to publish. On its poetry page, late autumn, 1976, appeared poems reflecting the spirit of the times. Ila Abernathy wrote:

I am grass growing and the shearer of grass,
I am the willow and the splitter of laths,

> weaver and the thing woven, marriage of willow and grass.
> I am frost on the land and the land's life,
> breath and beast and the sharp rock underfoot;
> in me the mountain lives, and the owl strikes,
> and I in them. I am the sun's twin,
> mover of blood and the blood lost,
> I am the deer and the deer's death;
> I am the burr in your conscience:
> acknowledge me.

And Buffy Sainte-Marie:

> You think I have visions
> because I am an Indian.
>
> I have visions because
> there are visions to be seen.

In the sixties and seventies, it was not just a women's movement, a prisoner's movement, an Indian movement. There was general revolt against oppressive, artificial, previously unquestioned ways of living. It touched every aspect of personal life: childbirth, childhood, love, sex, marriage, dress, music, art, sports, language, food, housing, religion, literature, death, schools.

The new temper, the new behavior, shocked many Americans. It created tensions. Sometimes it was seen as a "generation gap"—the younger generation moving far away from the older one in its way of life. But it seemed after a while to be not so much a matter of age— some young people remained "straight" while some middle-aged people were changing their ways and old people were beginning to behave in ways that astounded others.

Sexual behavior went through startling changes. Premarital sex was no longer a matter for silence. Men and women lived together outside of marriage, and struggled for words to describe the other person when introduced: "I want you to meet my . . . friend." Married couples candidly spoke of their affairs, and books appeared discussing "open marriage." Masturbation could be talked about openly, even approvingly. Homosexuality was no longer concealed. "Gay" men and "gay" women—lesbians—organized to combat discrimination against them, to give themselves a sense of community, to overcome shame and isolation.

All this was reflected in the literature and in the mass media. Court decisions overruled the local banning of books that were erotic or even pornographic. A new literature appeared *(The Joy of Sex* and others) to teach men and women how sexual fulfillment could be attained. The movies now did not hesitate to show nudity, although the motion picture industry, wanting to preserve principle as well as profit, set up a classification system (R for Restricted, X for prohibited to children). The language of sex became more common both in literature and in ordinary conversation.

All this was connected with new living arrangements. Especially among young people, communal living arrangements flourished. A few were truly communes—that is, based on the sharing of money and decisions, creating a community of intimacy, affection, trust. Most were practical arrangements for sharing the rent, with varying degrees of friendship and intimate association among the participants. It was no longer unusual for men and women to be "roommates"—in groups of two or three or larger, and without sexual relations—as practical, unself-conscious arrangements.

The most important thing about dress in the cultural change of the sixties was the greater informality. For women it was a continuation of the historic feminist movement's insistence on discarding of "feminine," hampering clothes. Many women stopped wearing bras. The restrictive "girdle"—almost a uniform of the forties and fifties—became rare. Young men and women dressed more nearly alike, in jeans, in discarded army uniforms. Men stopped wearing neckties, women of all ages wore pants more often—unspoken homage to Amelia Bloomer.

There was a new popular music of protest. Pete Seeger had been singing protest songs since the forties, but now he came into his own, his audiences much larger. Bob Dylan and Joan Baez, singing not only protest songs, but songs reflecting the new abandon, the new culture, became popular idols. A middle-aged woman on the West Coast, Malvina Reynolds, wrote and sang songs that fit her socialist thinking and her libertarian spirit, as well as her critique of the modern commercial culture. Everybody now, she sang, lived in "little boxes" and they "all came out just the same."

Bob Dylan was a phenomenon unto himself: powerful songs of protest, personal songs of freedom and self-expression. In an angry song, "Masters of War," he hopes that one day they will die and he will follow their casket "in the pale afternoon." "A Hard Rain's A-Gonna Fall" recounts the terrible stories of the last decades, of starvation and war, and tears, and dead ponies, and poisoned waters, and damp, dirty prisons—"It's a hard rain's a-gonna fall." Dylan sang a bitter antiwar song, "With God on Our Side," and one about the killer of the black activist Medgar Evers, "Only a Pawn in Their Game." He offered a challenge to the old, hope to the new, for "The Times They Are A-Changin'."

The Catholic upsurge against the war was part of a general revolt inside the Catholic Church, which had for so long been a bulwark of conservatism, tied to racism, jingoism, war. Priests and nuns resigned from the church, opened their lives to sex, got married and had children—sometimes without bothering to leave the church officially. True, there was still enormous popularity for the old-time religious revivalists, and Billy Graham commanded the obedience of millions, but now there were small swift currents against the mainstream.

There was a new suspicion of big business, of profiteering as the motive for ruining the environment. There was a reexamination of the "death industry," of moneymaking funerals and profitable tombstones, as in Jessica Mitford's *The American Way of Death*.

With the loss of faith in big powers—business, government, religion—there arose a stronger belief in self, whether individual or collective. The experts in all fields were now looked at skeptically: the belief grew that people could figure out for themselves what to eat, how to live their lives, how to be healthy. There was suspicion of the medical industry and campaigns against chemical preservatives, valueless foods, advertising. By now the scientific evidence of the evils of smoking—cancer, heart disease—was so powerful that the government barred advertising of cigarettes on television and in newspapers.

Traditional education began to be reexamined. The schools had taught whole generations the values of patriotism, of obeying authority, and had perpetuated ignorance, even contempt for people of other nations, races, Native Americans, women. Not just the content of education was challenged, but the style—the formality, the bureaucracy, the insistence on subordination to authority. This made only a small dent in the formidable national system of orthodox education, but it was reflected in a new generation of teachers all over the country, and a new literature to sustain them: Jonathan Kozol, *Death at an Early Age;* George Denison, *The Lives of Children;* Ivan Illich, *De-schooling Society*.

Never in American history had more movements for change been concentrated in so short a span of years. But the system in the course of two centuries had learned a good deal about the control of people. In the mid-seventies, it went to work.

9.
The Seventies: Under Control?

In the early seventies, the system seemed out of control—it could not hold the loyalty of the public. As early as 1970, according to the University of Michigan's Survey Research Center, "trust in government" was low in every section of the population. And there was a significant difference by class. Of professional people, 40 percent had "low" political trust in the government; of unskilled blue-collar workers, 66 percent had "low" trust.

Public opinion surveys in 1971—after seven years of intervention in Vietnam—showed an unwillingness to come to the aid of other countries, assuming they were attacked by Communist-backed forces. Even for countries allied to the United States in the North Atlantic Treaty Organization, or Mexico, right on our southern border, there was no majority opinion for intervening with American troops. As for Thailand, if it were under Communist attack, only 12 percent of whites interrogated would send troops, 4 percent of nonwhites would do so.

In the summer of 1972, antiwar people in the Boston area were picketing Honeywell Corporation. The literature they distributed pointed out that Honeywell was producing antipersonnel weapons used in Vietnam, like the deadly cluster bomb that had riddled thousands of Vietnamese civilians with painful, hard-to-extricate pellets. About six hundred ballots were given to the Honeywell employees, asking if they thought that Honeywell should discontinue making these weapons. Of the 231 persons who returned the ballots, 131 said that Honeywell should stop, 88 said it should not. They were invited to make comments. A typical "no" comment: "Honeywell is not responsible for what the Department of Defense does with the goods it buys. . . ." A typical "yes" comment: "How may we have pride in our work when the entire basis for this work is immoral?"

The Survey Research Center of the University of Michigan had been posing the question: "Is the government run by a few big interests looking out for themselves?" The answer in 1964 had been "yes" from 26 percent of those polled; by 1972 the answer was "yes" from 53 percent of those polled. An article in the *American Political Science*

Review by Arthur H. Miller, reporting on the extensive polling done by the Survey Research Center, said that the polls showed "widespread, basic discontent and political alienation." He added (political scientists often took on the worries of the Establishment): "What is startling and somewhat alarming is the rapid degree of change in this basic attitude over a period of only six years."

More voters than ever before refused to identify themselves as either Democrats or Republicans. Back in 1940, 20 percent of those polled called themselves "independents." In 1974, 34 percent called themselves "independents."

The courts, the juries, and even judges were not behaving as usual. Juries were acquitting radicals: Angela Davis, an acknowledged Communist, was acquitted by an all-white jury on the West Coast. Black Panthers, whom the government had tried in every way to malign and destroy, were freed by juries in several trials. A judge in western Massachusetts threw out a case against a young activist, Sam Lovejoy, who had toppled a 500-foot tower erected by a utility company trying to set up a nuclear plant. In Washington, D.C., in August 1973, a Superior Court judge refused to sentence six men charged with unlawful entry who had stepped from a White House tour line to protest the bombing of Cambodia.

Undoubtedly, much of this national mood of hostility to government and business came out of the Vietnam war, its 55,000 casualties, its moral shame, its exposure of government lies and atrocities. On top of this came the political disgrace of the Nixon administration in the scandals that came to be known by the one-word label "Watergate," and which led to the historic resignation from the presidency—the first in American history—of Richard Nixon in August 1974.

It began during the presidential campaign in June of 1972, when five burglars, carrying wiretapping and photo equipment, were caught in the act of breaking into the offices of the Democratic National Committee, in the Watergate apartment complex of Washington, D.C. One of the five, James McCord, Jr., worked for the Nixon campaign; he was "security" officer for the Committee to Re-elect the President (CREEP). Another of the five had an address book in which was listed the name of E. Howard Hunt, and Hunt's address was listed as the White House. He was assistant to Charles Colson, who was special counsel to President Nixon.

Both McCord and Hunt had worked for many years for the CIA. Hunt had been the CIA man in charge of the invasion of Cuba in

1961, and three of the Watergate burglars were veterans of the invasion. McCord, as CREEP security man, worked for the chief of CREEP, John Mitchell, the Attorney General of the United States.

Thus, due to an unforeseen arrest by police unaware of the high-level connections of the burglars, information was out to the public before anyone could stop it, linking the burglars to important officials in Nixon's campaign committee, to the CIA, and to Nixon's Attorney General. Mitchell denied any connection with the burglary, and Nixon, in a press conference five days after the event, said "the White House has had no involvement whatever in this particular incident."

What followed the next year, after a grand jury in September indicted the Watergate burglars—plus Howard Hunt and G. Gordon Liddy—was that, one after another, lesser officials of the Nixon administration, fearing prosecution, began to talk. They gave information in judicial proceedings, to a Senate investigating committee, to the press. They implicated not only John Mitchell, but Robert Haldeman and John Erlichman, Nixon's highest White House aides, and finally Richard Nixon himself—in not only the Watergate burglaries, but a whole series of illegal actions against political opponents and antiwar activists. Nixon and his aides lied again and again as they tried to cover up their involvement.

These facts came out in the various testimonies:

1. Attorney General John Mitchell controlled a secret fund of $350,000 to $700,000—to be used against the Democratic party—for forging letters, leaking false news items to the press, stealing compaign files.
2. Gulf Oil Corporation, ITT (International Telephone and Telegraph), American Airlines, and other huge American corporations had made illegal contributions, running into millions of dollars, to the Nixon campaign.
3. In September of 1971, shortly after the *New York Times* printed Daniel Ellsberg's copies of the top-secret *Pentagon Papers,* the administration planned and carried out—Howard Hunt and Gordon Liddy themselves doing it—the burglary of the office of Ellsberg's psychiatrist, looking for Ellsberg's records.
4. After the Watergate burglars were caught, Nixon secretly pledged to give them executive clemency if they were imprisoned, and suggested that up to a million dollars be given them to keep them quiet. In fact, $450,000 was given to them, on Erlichman's orders.
5. Nixon's nominee for head of the FBI (J. Edgar Hoover had recently died), L. Patrick Gray, revealed that he had turned over the FBI records on its investigation of the Watergate burglary to Nixon's legal assistant, John Dean, and that Attorney General Richard Kleindienst (Mitchell had just

resigned, saying he wanted to pursue his private life) had ordered him not to discuss Watergate with the Senate Judiciary Committee.

6. Two former members of Nixon's cabinet—John Mitchell and Maurice Stans—were charged with taking $250,000 from a financier named Robert Vesco in return for his help with a Securities and Exchange Commission investigation of Vesco's activities.

7. It turned out that certain material had disappeared from FBI files—material from a series of illegal wiretaps ordered by Henry Kissinger, placed on the telephones of four journalists and thirteen government officials—and was in the White House safe of Nixon's adviser John Erlichman.

8. One of the Watergate burglars, Bernard Barker, told the Senate committee that he had also been involved in a plan to physically attack Daniel Ellsberg while Ellsberg spoke at an antiwar rally in Washington.

9. A deputy director of the CIA testified that Haldeman and Erlichman told him it was Nixon's wish that the CIA tell the FBI not to pursue its investigation beyond the Watergate burglary.

10. Almost by accident, a witness told the Senate committee that President Nixon had tapes of all personal conversations and phone conversations at the White House. Nixon at first refused to turn over the tapes, and when he finally did, they had been tampered with: eighteen and a half minutes of one tape had been erased.

11. In the midst of all this, Nixon's Vice-President, Spiro Agnew, was indicted in Maryland for receiving bribes from Maryland contractors in return for political favors, and resigned from the vice-presidency in October 1973. Nixon appointed Congressman Gerald Ford to take Agnew's place.

12. Over $10 million in government money had been used by Nixon on his private homes in San Clemente and Key Biscayne on grounds of "security," and he had illegally taken—with the aid of a bit of forgery—a $576,000 tax deduction for some of his papers.

13. It was disclosed that for over a year in 1969–1970 the U.S. had engaged in a secret, massive bombing of Cambodia, which it kept from the American public and even from Congress.

It was a swift and sudden fall. In the November 1972 presidential election, Nixon and Agnew had won 60 percent of the popular vote and carried every state except Massachusetts, defeating an antiwar candidate, Senator George McGovern. By June of 1973 a Gallup poll showed 67 percent of those polled thought Nixon was involved in the Watergate break-in or lied to cover up.

By the fall of 1973 eight different resolutions had been introduced in the House of Representatives for the impeachment of President Nixon. The following year a House committee drew up a bill of impeachment to present it to a full House. Nixon's advisers told him it would pass the House by the required majority and then the Senate would vote the necessary two-thirds majority to remove him from office. On August 8, 1974, Nixon resigned.

Six months before Nixon resigned, the business magazine *Dun's Review* reported a poll of three hundred corporation executives. Almost all had voted for Nixon in 1972, but now a majority said he should resign. "Right now, 90% of Wall Street would cheer if Nixon resigns," said a vice-president of Merrill Lynch Government Securities. When he did, there was relief in all sectors of the Establishment.

Gerald Ford, taking Nixon's office, said: "Our long national nightmare is over." Newspapers, whether they had been for or against Nixon, liberal or conservative, celebrated the successful, peaceful culmination of the Watergate crisis. "The system is working," said a long-time strong critic of the Vietnam war, *New York Times* columnist Anthony Lewis. The two journalists who had much to do with investigating and exposing Nixon, Carl Bernstein and Bob Woodward of the Washington *Post,* wrote that with Nixon's departure, there might be "restoration." All of this was in a mood of relief, of gratitude.

No respectable American newspaper said what was said by Claude Julien, editor of *Le Monde Diplomatique* in September 1974. "The elimination of Mr. Richard Nixon leaves intact all the mechanisms and all the false values which permitted the Watergate scandal." Julien noted that Nixon's Secretary of State, Henry Kissinger, would remain at his post—in other words, that Nixon's foreign policy would continue. "That is to say," Julien wrote, "that Washington will continue to support General Pinochet in Chile, General Geisel in Brazil, General Stroessner in Paraguay, etc. . . ."

Months after Julien wrote this, it was disclosed that top Democratic and Republican leaders in the House of Representatives had given secret assurance to Nixon that if he resigned they would not support criminal proceedings against him. One of them, the ranking Republican of the Judiciary Committee, said: "We had all been shuddering about what two weeks of televised floor debates on impeachment would do, how it would tear the country apart and affect foreign policy." The *New York Times*'s articles that reported on Wall Street's hope for Nixon's resignation quoted one Wall Street financier as saying that if Nixon resigned: "What we will have is the same play with different players."

When Gerald Ford, a conservative Republican who had supported all of Nixon's policies, was nominated for President, a liberal Senator from California, Alan Cranston, spoke for him on the floor, saying he had polled many people, Republicans and Democrats, and found "an almost startling consensus of conciliation that is developing around him." When Nixon resigned and Ford became President, the *New York Times* said: "Out of the despair of Watergate has come an inspiring new demonstration of the uniqueness and strength of the American democracy." A few days later the *Times* wrote happily that the "peaceful transfer of power" brought "a cleansing sense of relief to the American people."

In the charges brought by the House Committee on Impeachment against Nixon, it seemed clear that the committee did not want to emphasize those elements in his behavior which were found in other Presidents and which might be repeated in the future. It stayed clear of Nixon's dealings with powerful corporations; it did not mention the bombing of Cambodia. It concentrated on things peculiar to Nixon, not on fundamental policies continuous among American Presidents, at home and abroad.

The word was out: get rid of Nixon, but keep the system. Theodore Sorensen, who had been an adviser to President Kennedy, wrote at the time of Watergate: "The underlying causes of the gross misconduct in our law-enforcement system now being revealed are largely personal, not institutional. Some structural changes are needed. All the rotten apples should be thrown out. But save the barrel."

Indeed, the barrel was saved. Nixon's foreign policy remained. The government's connections to corporate interests remained. Ford's closest friends in Washington were corporate lobbyists. Alexander Haig, who had been one of Nixon's closest advisers, who had helped in "processing" the tapes before turning them over to the public, and who gave the public misinformation about the tapes, was appointed by President Ford to be head of the armed forces of the North Atlantic Treaty Organization. One of Ford's first acts was to pardon Nixon, thus saving him from possible criminal proceedings and allowing him to retire with a huge pension in California.

The Establishment had cleansed itself of members of the club who had broken the rules—but it took some pains not to treat them too harshly. Those few who received jail sentences got short terms, were sent to the most easygoing federal institutions available, and were given special privileges not given to ordinary prisoners. Richard Kleindienst pleaded guilty; he got a $100 fine and one month in jail, which was suspended.

That Nixon would go, but that the power of the President to do anything he wanted in the name of "national security" would stay—this was underscored by a Supreme Court decision in July 1974. The Court said Nixon had to turn over his White House tapes to the special Watergate prosecutor. But at the same time it affirmed "the confidentiality of Presidential communications," which it could not uphold in Nixon's case, but which remained as a general principle when the President made a "claim of need to protect military, diplomatic or sensitive national security secrets."

The televised Senate Committee hearings on Watergate stopped suddenly before the subject of corporate connections was reached. It was typical of the selective coverage of important events by the television industry: bizarre shenanigans like the Watergate burglary were given full treatment, while instances of ongoing practice—the My Lai massacre, the secret bombing of Cambodia, the work of the FBI and CIA—were given the most fleeting attention. Dirty tricks against the Socialist Workers party, the Black Panthers, other radical groups, had to be searched for in a few newspapers. The whole nation heard the details of the quick break-in at the Watergate apartment; there was never a similar television hearing on the long-term break-in in Vietnam.

In the trial of John Mitchell and Maurice Stans for obstruction of justice in impeding a Securities and Exchange Commission investigation of Robert Vesco (a contributor to Nixon), George Bradford Cook, former general counsel of the SEC, testified that on November 13, 1972, he crouched in a Texas rice field while on a goose hunt with Maurice Stans, and told him he wanted to be chairman of the SEC. For this, he would cut out a critical paragraph in the SEC charges against Vesco that referred to Vesco's $200,000 secret contribution to the Nixon campaign.

Corporate influence on the White House is a permanent fact of the American system. Most of it is wise enough to stay within the law; under Nixon they took chances. An executive in the meatpacking industry said during the Watergate events that he had been approached by a Nixon campaign official and told that while a $25,000 contribution would be appreciated, "for $50,000 you get to talk to the President."

Many of these corporations gave money to both sides, so that whichever won they would have friends in the administration. Chrysler Corporation urged its executives to "support the party and candidate of their choice," and then collected the checks from them and delivered the checks to Republican or Democratic campaign committees.

International Telephone and Telegraph was an old hand at giving money on both sides. In 1960 it had made illegal contributions to Bobby Baker, who worked with Democratic Senators, including Lyndon Johnson. A senior vice-president of ITT was quoted by one of his assistants as saying the board of directors "have it set up to 'butter' both sides so we'll be in good position whoever wins." And in 1970, an ITT director, John McCone, who also had been head of the CIA, told Henry Kissinger, Secretary of State, and Richard Helms, CIA director, that ITT was willing to give $1 million to help the U.S. government in its plans to overthrow the Allende government in Chile.

In 1971 ITT planned to take over the $1½ billion Hartford Fire Insurance Company—the largest merger in corporate history. The antitrust division of the Justice Department moved to prosecute ITT for violating the antitrust laws. However, the prosecution did not take place and ITT was allowed to merge with Hartford. It was all settled out of court, in a secret arrangement in which ITT agreed to donate $400,000 to the Republican party. It seemed that Richard Kleindienst, deputy Attorney General, had six meetings with an ITT director named Felix Rohatyn, and then brought in the head of the antitrust division, Richard McLaren, who was persuaded by Rohatyn that to stop the merger would cause a "hardship" for ITT stockholders. McLaren agreed. He was later appointed a federal judge.

One of the items not mentioned in the impeachment charges and never televised in the Senate hearings was the way the government cooperated with the milk industry. In early 1971 the Secretary of Agriculture announced the government would not increase its price supports for milk—the regular subsidy to the big milk producers. Then the Associated Milk Producers began giving money to the Nixon campaign, met in the White House with Nixon and the Secretary of Agriculture, gave more money, and the secretary announced that "new analysis" made it necessary to raise milk price supports from $4.66 to $4.93 a hundredweight. More contributions were made, until the total exceeded $400,000. The price increases added $500 million to the profits of dairy farmers (mostly big corporations) at the expense of consumers.

Whether Nixon or Ford or any Republican or Democrat was President, the system would work pretty much the same way. A Senate subcommittee investigating multinational corporations revealed a document (given passing mention in a few newspapers) in which oil company economists discussed holding back production of oil to keep prices up. ARAMCO—the Arabian-American Oil Corporation, 75 percent of whose stock was held by American oil companies and 25 percent by Saudi Arabia—had made $1 profit on a barrel of oil in 1973. In 1974 it was making $4.50. None of this would be affected by who was President.

Even in the most diligent of investigations in the Watergate affair, that of Archibald Cox, a special prosecutor later fired by Nixon, the corporations got off easy. American Airlines, which admitted making illegal contributions to the Nixon campaign, was fined $5,000; Goodyear was fined $5,000; 3M Corporation was fined $3,000. A Goodyear official was fined $1,000; a 3M official was fined $500. The *New York Times* (October 20, 1973) reported:

> Mr. Cox charged them only with the misdemeanor of making illegal contributions. The misdemeanor, under the law, involved "nonwillful" contributions. The felony count, involving willful contributions, is punishable by a fine of $10,000 and/or a two-year jail term; the misdemeanor by a $1000 fine and/or a one-year jail term.
>
> Asked at the courthouse here how the two executives—who had admitted making the payments—could be charged with making non-willing contributions, Mr. McBride [Cox's staff] replied: "That's a legal question which frankly baffles me as well."

With Gerald Ford in office, the long continuity in American policy was maintained. He continued Nixon's policy of aid to the Saigon regime, apparently still hoping that the Thieu government would remain stable. The head of a congressional committee, John Calkins, visiting South Vietnam just around the time of Nixon's fall from office, reported:

> The South Vietnamese Army shows every sign of being an effective and spirited security force. . . .
>
> Oil exploration will begin very soon. Tourism can be encouraged by continued security of scenic and historic areas and by the erection of a new Hyatt Hotel. . . .
>
> South Vietnam needs foreign investment to finance these and other developments. . . . She has a large labor pool of talented, industrious people whose cost of labor is far less than Hong Kong, Singapore, or even Korea or Taiwan. . . .
>
> I also feel there is much profit to be made there. The combination of serving both God and Mammon had proved attractive to Americans and others in the past. . . . Vietnam can be the next "take off" capitalistic showplace in Asia.

In the spring of 1975, everything that radical critics of American policy in Vietnam had been saying—that without American troops, the Saigon government's lack of popular support would be revealed—came true. An offensive by North Vietnamese troops, left in the South by terms of the 1973 truce, swept through town after town.

Ford continued to be optimistic. He was the last of a long line of government officials and journalists who promised victory. (Secretary of Defense Robert McNamara, February 19, 1963: "Victory is in sight." General William Westmoreland, November 15, 1967: "I have never been more encouraged in my four years in Vietnam." Columnist Joseph Alsop, November 1, 1972: "Hanoi has accepted near-total defeat.") On April 16, 1975, Ford said: "I am absolutely convinced if Congress made available $722 million in military assistance by the time I asked—or sometime shortly thereafter—the South Vietnamese could stabilize the military situation in Vietnam today."

Two weeks later, April 29, 1975, the North Vietnamese moved into Saigon, and the war was over.

Most of the Establishment had already—despite Ford and a few stalwarts—given up on Vietnam. What they worried about was the readiness of the American public now to support other military actions overseas. There were trouble signs in the months before the defeat in Vietnam.

In early 1975 Senator John C. Culver of Iowa was unhappy that Americans would not fight for Korea: "He said that Vietnam had taken a mighty toll on the national will of the American people." Shortly before that, Secretary of Defense James Schlesinger, speaking to the Georgetown Center for Strategic and International Studies, was reported as being "generally gloomy," saying that "the world no longer regarded American military power as awesome."

In March 1975 a Catholic organization, making a survey of American attitudes on abortion, learned other things. To the statement: "The people running this country (government, political, church and civic leaders) don't tell us the truth," more than 83 percent agreed.

New York Times international correspondent C. L. Sulzberger, a consistent supporter of government cold-war foreign policy, wrote in a troubled mood in early 1975 from Ankara, Turkey, that "the glow has worn off from the era of the Truman Doctrine" (when military aid was given to Greece and Turkey). He added: "And one cannot say that the bleak outlook here is balanced by any brilliant United States successes in Greece, where a vast mob recently battered the United States Embassy." He concluded, "There must be something seriously wrong with the way we present ourselves these days." The problem, according to Sulzberger, was not the United States' behavior, but the way this behavior was presented to the world.

It was a few months after these reports, in April of 1975, that Secretary of State Kissinger, invited to be commencement speaker at the University of Michigan, was faced with petitions protesting the invitation, because of Kissinger's role in the Vietnam war. Also a counter-commencement program was planned. He withdrew. It was a low time for the administration. Vietnam was "lost" (the very word supposed it was ours to lose). Kissinger was quoted that April (by Washington *Post* columnist Tom Braden): "The U.S. must carry out some act somewhere in the world which shows its determination to continue to be a world power."

The following month came the *Mayaguez* affair.

The *Mayaguez* was an American cargo ship sailing from South Vietnam to Thailand in mid-May 1975, just three weeks after the victory of the revolutionary forces in Vietnam. When it came close to an island in Cambodia, where a revolutionary regime had just taken power, the ship was stopped by the Cambodians, taken to a port at a nearby island, and the crew removed to the mainland. The crew later described their treatment as courteous: "A man who spoke English greeted us with a handshake and welcomed us to Cambodia." The press reported: "Captain Miller and his men all say they were never abused by their captors. There were even accounts of kind treatment—of Cambodian soldiers feeding them first and eating what the Americans left, of the soldiers giving the seamen the mattresses off their beds." But the Cambodians did ask the crew about spying and the CIA.

President Ford sent a message to the Cambodian government to release the ship and crew, and when thirty-six hours had elapsed and there was no response (the message had been given to the Chinese liaison mission in Washington, but was returned the next day, "ostensibly undelivered," one press account said), he began military operations—U.S. planes bombed Cambodian ships. They strafed the very boat that was taking the American sailors to the mainland.

The men had been detained on a Monday morning. On Wednesday evening the Cambodians released them—putting them on a fishing boat headed for the American fleet. That afternoon, knowing the seamen had been taken off Tang Island, Ford nevertheless ordered a marine assault on Tang Island. That assault began about 7:15 Wednesday evening, but an hour earlier the crewmen were already headed back to the American fleet. About 7:00 P.M. the release had been announced on the radio in Bangkok. Indeed, the boat carrying the returned crewmen was spotted by a U.S. reconnaissance plane that signaled them.

Not mentioned in any press account at the time or in any government statement was a fact that emerged in October 1976 when the General Accounting Office made a report on the *Mayaguez* affair: the U.S. had received a message from a Chinese diplomat saying China was using its influence with Cambodia on the ship "and expected it to be released soon." This message was received fourteen hours before the marine assault began.

No American soldier was hurt by the Cambodians. The marines invading Tang Island, however, met unexpectedly tough resistance, and of two hundred invaders, one-third were soon dead or wounded (this exceeded the casualty rate in the World War II invasion of Iwo Jima). Five of eleven helicopters in the invasion force were blown up or disabled. Also, twenty-three Americans were killed in a helicopter crash over Thailand on their way to participate in the action, a fact the government tried to keep secret. All together, forty-one Americans were killed in the military actions ordered by Ford. There were thirty-nine sailors on the *Mayaguez*. Why the rush to bomb, strafe, attack? Why, even after the ship and crew were recovered, did Ford order American planes to bomb the Cambodian mainland, with untold Cambodian casualties? What could justify such a combination of moral blindness and military bungling?

The answer to this came soon: It was necessary to show the world that giant America, defeated by tiny Vietnam, was still powerful and resolute. The *New York Times* reported on May 16, 1975:

> Administration officials, including Secretary of State Henry Kissinger and Secretary of Defense James Schlesinger were said to have been eager to find some dramatic means of underscoring President Ford's stated intention to "maintain our leadership on a world-wide basis." The occasion came with the capture of the vessel. . . . Administration officials . . . made it clear that they welcomed the opportunity. . . .

Another press dispatch from Washington, in the midst of the *Mayaguez* events, said: "High-ranking sources familiar with military strategy and planning said privately that the seizure of the vessel might provide the test of American determination in Southeast Asia that, they asserted, the U.S. had been seeking since the collapse of allied governments in South Vietnam and Cambodia."

Columnist James Reston wrote: "In fact, the Administration almost seems grateful for the opportunity to demonstrate that the President can act quickly. . . . Officials here have been bridling over a host of silly taunts about the American 'paper tiger' and hope the Marines have answered the charge."

It was not surprising that Secretary of Defense Schlesinger called it a "very successful operation," done "for purposes that were necessary for the well-being of this society." But why would the prestigious *Times* columnist James Reston, a strong critic of Nixon and Watergate, call the *Mayaguez* operation "melodramatic and successful"? And why would the *New York Times*, which had criticized the Vietnam war, talk about the "admirable efficiency" of the operation?

What seemed to be happening was that the Establishment—Republicans, Democrats, newspapers, television—was closing ranks behind Ford and Kissinger, and behind the idea that American authority must be asserted everywhere in the world.

Congress at this time behaved much as it had done in the early years of the Vietnam war, like a flock of sheep. Back in 1973, in a mood of fatigue and disgust with the Vietnam war, Congress had passed a War Powers Act that required the President, before taking military action, to consult with Congress. In the *Mayaguez* affair, Ford had ignored this—he had several aides make phone calls to eighteen Congressmen to inform them that military action was under way. But, as I. F. Stone said (he was the maverick journalist who published the anti-Establishment *I. F. Stone's Weekly*), "Congress raped as easily as it did in the Tonkin Gulf affair." Congressman Robert Drinan of Massachusetts was an exception. Senator McGovern, Nixon's presidential opponent in 1976 and long-time antiwar critic, opposed the action. So did Senator Gaylord Nelson of Wisconsin. Senator Edward Brooke raised questions. Senator Edward Kennedy did not speak out, nor did other Senators who during the Vietnam war had influenced Congress to ban further military action in Indochina but now said their own legislation did not apply.

Secretary of State Kissinger would say: "We are forced into this." When Kissinger was asked why the U.S. was risking the lives of the *Mayaguez* seamen by firing on ships in the area without knowing where they were, he called it a "necessary risk."

Kissinger also said the incident "ought to make clear that there are limits beyond which the United States cannot be pushed, that the United States is prepared to defend those interests, and that it can get public support and congressional support for these actions."

Indeed, Congressmen, Democrats as well as Republicans, who had been critical of the Vietnam war now seemed anxious to pull things together in a unified show of strength to the rest of the world. A week before the *Mayaguez* affair (two weeks before Saigon fell), fifty-six Congressmen had signed a statement saying: "Let no nation read the events in Indochina as the failure of the American will." One of them was a black Congressman from Georgia, Andrew Young.

It was a complex process of consolidation that the system undertook in 1975. It included old-type military actions, like the *Mayaguez* affair, to assert authority in the world and at home. There was also a need to satisfy a disillusioned public that the system was criticizing and correcting itself. The standard way was to conduct publicized investigations that found specific culprits but left the system intact. Watergate had made both the FBI and the CIA look bad—breaking the laws they were sworn to uphold, cooperating with Nixon in his burglary jobs and illegal wiretapping. In 1975, congressional committees in the House and Senate began investigations of the FBI and CIA.

The CIA inquiry disclosed that the CIA had gone beyond its original mission of gathering intelligence and was conducting secret operations of all kinds. For instance, back in the 1950s, it had administered the drug LSD to unsuspecting Americans to test its effects: one American scientist, given such a dose by a CIA agent, leaped from a New York hotel window to his death in the 1950s.

The CIA had also been involved in assassination plots against Castro of Cuba and other heads of state. It had introduced African swine fever virus into Cuba in 1971, bringing disease and then slaughter to 500,000 pigs. A CIA operative told a reporter he delivered the virus from an army base in the Canal Zone to anti-Castro Cubans.

It was also learned from the investigation that the CIA—with the collusion of a secret Committee of Forty headed by Henry Kissinger—had worked to "destabilize" the Chilean government headed by Salvadore Allende, a Marxist who had been elected president in one of the rare free elections in Latin America. ITT, with large interests in Cuba, played a part in this operation. When in 1974 the American ambassador to Chile, David Popper, suggested to the Chilean junta (which, with U.S. aid, had overthrown Allende) that they were violating human rights, he was rebuked by Kissinger, who sent word: "Tell Popper to cut out the political science lectures."

The investigation of the FBI disclosed many years of illegal actions to disrupt and destroy radical groups and left-wing groups of all kinds. The FBI had sent forged letters, engaged in burglaries (it admitted to ninety-two between 1960 and 1966), opened mail illegally, and, in the case of Black Panther leader Fred Hampton, seems to have conspired in murder.

Valuable information came out of the investigations, but it was just enough, and in just the right way—moderate press coverage, little television coverage, thick books of reports with limited readership—to give the impression of an honest society correcting itself.

The investigations themselves revealed the limits of government willingness to probe into such activities. The Church Committee, set up by the Senate, conducted its investigations with the cooperation of the agencies being investigated and, indeed, submitted its findings on the CIA to the CIA to see if there was material that the Agency wanted omitted. Thus, while there was much valuable material in the report, there is no way of knowing how much more there was—the final report was a compromise between committee diligence and CIA caution.

The Pike Committee, set up in the House of Representatives, made no such agreement with the CIA or FBI, and when it issued its final report, the same House that had authorized its investigation voted to keep the report secret. When the report was leaked via a CBS newscaster, Daniel Schorr, to the *Village Voice* in New York, it was never printed by the important newspapers in the country—the *Times,* the Washington *Post,* or others. Schorr was suspended by CBS. It was another instance of cooperation between the mass media and the government in instances of "national security."

The Church Committee, in its report of CIA attempts to assassinate Fidel Castro and other foreign leaders, revealed an interesting point of view. The committee seemed to look on the killing of a head of state as an unpardonable violation of some gentlemen's agreement among statesmen, much more deplorable than military interventions that killed ordinary people. The Committee wrote, in the introduction to its assassination report:

Once methods of coercion and violence are chosen, the probability of loss of life is always present. There is, however, a significant difference between a cold-blooded, targeted, intentional killing of an individual foreign leader and other forms of intervening in the affairs of foreign nations.

The Church Committee uncovered CIA operations to secretly influence the minds of Americans:

The CIA is now using several hundred American academics (administrators, faculty members, graduate students engaged in teaching) who, in addition to providing leads and, on occasion, making introductions for intelligence purposes, write books and other material to be used for propaganda purposes abroad. . . . These academics are located in over 100 American colleges, universities and related institutions. At the majority of institutions, no one other than the individual concerned is aware of the CIA link. At the others, at least one university official is aware of the operational use of academics on his campus. . . . The CIA considers these operational relationships within the U.S. academic community as perhaps its most sensitive domestic area and has strict controls governing these operations. . . .

In 1961 the chief of the CIA's Covert Action Staff wrote that books were "the most important weapon of strategic propaganda." The Church Committee found that more than a thousand books were produced, subsidized, or sponsored by the CIA before the end of 1967.

When Kissinger testified before the Church Committee about the bombing of Laos, orchestrated by the CIA as a secret activity, he said: "I do not believe in retrospect that it was a good national policy to have the CIA conduct the war in Laos. I think we should have found some other way of doing it." There was no indication that anyone on the Committee challenged this idea—that what was done should have been done, but by another method.

Thus, in 1974–1975, the system was acting to purge the country of its rascals and restore it to a healthy, or at least to an acceptable, state. The resignation of Nixon, the succession of Ford, the exposure of bad deeds by the FBI and CIA—all aimed to regain the badly damaged confidence of the American people. However, even with these strenuous efforts, there were still many signs in the American public of suspicion, even hostility, to the leaders of government, military, big business.

Two months after the end of the Vietnam war, only 20 percent of Americans polled thought the collapse of the Saigon government was a threat to United States security.

June 14, 1975, was Flag Day, and President Gerald Ford spoke at Fort Benning, Georgia, where the army staged a march symbolizing its involvement in thirteen wars. Ford commented that he was glad to see so many flags, but a reporter covering the event wrote: "Actually, there were few American flags to be seen near the President's reviewing stand. One, held aloft by demonstrators, bore an inked-in inscription saying, 'No more genocide in our name.' It was torn down by spectators as their neighbors applauded."

That July the Lou Harris poll, looking at the public's confidence in the government from 1966 to 1975, reported that confidence in the military during that period had dropped from 62 percent to 29 percent, in business from 55 percent to 18 percent, in both President and Congress from 42 percent to 13 percent. Shortly after that, another Harris poll reported "65% of Americans oppose military aid abroad because they feel it allows dictatorships to maintain control over their population."

Perhaps much of the general dissatisfaction was due to the economic state of most Americans. Inflation and unemployment had been rising steadily since 1973, which was the year when, according to a Harris poll, the number of Americans feeling "alienated" and "disaffected" with the general state of the country climbed (from 29 percent in 1966) to over 50 percent. After Ford succeeded Nixon, the percentage of "alienated" was 55 percent. The survey showed that people were troubled most of all by inflation.

In the fall of 1975 a *New York Times* survey of 1,559 persons, and interviews with sixty families in twelve cities, showed "a substantial decline in optimism about the future." The *Times* reported:

> Inflation, the apparent inability of the country to solve its economic problems, and a foreboding that the energy crisis will mean a permanent step backward for the nation's standard of living have made inroads into Americans' confidence, expectations, and aspirations. . . .
>
> Pessimism about the future is particularly acute among those who earn less than $7000 annually, but it is also high within families whose annual incomes range from $10,000 to $15,000. . . .
>
> There is also concern that . . . no longer will hard work and a conscientious effort to save money bring them a nice home in the suburbs. . . .

Even higher-income people, the survey found, "are not as optimistic now as they were in past years, indicating that discontent is moving up from the lower middle-income to higher economic levels."

Around the same time, that fall of 1975, public opinion analysts testifying before a congressional committee reported, according to the *New York Times*, "that public confidence in the Government and in the country's economic future is probably lower than it has ever been since they began to measure such things scientifically."

Government statistics suggested the reasons. The Census Bureau reported that from 1974 to 1975 the number of Americans "legally" poor (that is, below an income of $5,500) had risen 10 percent and was now 25.9 million people. Also, the unemployment rate, which had been 5.6 percent in 1974, had risen to 8.3 percent in 1975, and the number of people who exhausted their unemployment benefits increased from 2 million in 1974 to 4.3 million in 1975.

Government figures, however, generally underestimated the amount of poverty, set the "legally" poor level too low, and underestimated the amount of unemployment. For instance, if 16.6 percent of the population averaged six months of unemployment during 1975, or 33.2 percent averaged three months of unemployment, the "average annual figure" given by the government was 8.3 percent, which sounded better.

In the year 1976, with a presidential election approaching, there was worry in the Establishment about the public's faith in the system. William Simon, Secretary of the Treasury under both Nixon and Ford (before then an investment banker earning over $2 million a year), spoke in the fall of 1976 to a Business Council meeting in Hot Springs, Virginia He said that when "so much of the world is lurching towards socialism or totalitarianism" it was urgent to make the American business system understood, because "private enterprise is losing by default—in many of our schools, in much of the communications media, and in a growing portion of the public consciousness." His speech could well be taken to represent the thinking of the American corporate elite:

> Vietnam, Watergate, student unrest, shifting moral codes, the worst recession in a generation, and a number of other jarring cultural shocks have all combined to create a new climate of questions and doubt. . . . It all adds up to a general malaise, a society-wide crisis of institutional confidence. . . .

Too often, Simon said, Americans "have been taught to distrust the very word profit and the profit motive that makes our prosperity possible, to somehow feel this system, that has done more to alleviate human suffering and privation than any other, is somehow cynical, selfish, and amoral." We must, Simon said, "get across the human side of capitalism."

As the United States prepared in 1976 to celebrate the bicentennial of the Declaration of Independence, a group of intellectuals and political leaders from Japan, the United States, and Western Europe, organized into "The Trilateral Commission," issued a report. It was entitled "The Governability of Democracies." Samuel Huntington, a political science professor at Harvard University and long-time consultant to the White House on the war in Vietnam, wrote the part of the report that dealt with the United States. He called it "The Democratic Distemper" and identified the problem he was about to discuss: "The 1960's witnessed a dramatic upsurge of democratic fervor in America." In the sixties, Huntington wrote, there was a huge growth of citizen participation "in the forms of marches, demonstrations, protest movements, and 'cause' organizations." There were also "markedly higher levels of self-consciousness on the part of blacks, Indians, Chicanos, white ethnic groups, students and women, all of whom became mobilized and organized in new ways. . . ." There was a "marked expansion of white-collar unionism," and all this added up to "a reassertion of equality as a goal in social, economic and political life."

Huntington pointed to the signs of decreasing government authority: The great demands in the sixties for equality had transformed the federal budget. In 1960 foreign affairs spending was 53.7 percent of the budget, and social spending was 22.3 percent. By 1974 foreign affairs took 33 percent and social spending 31 percent. This seemed to reflect a change in public mood: In 1960 only 18 percent of the public said the government was spending too much on defense, but in 1969 this jumped to 52 percent.

Huntington was troubled by what he saw:

The essence of the democratic surge of the 1960's was a general challenge to existing systems of authority, public and private. In one form or another, this challenge manifested itself in the family, the university, business, public and private associations, politics, the governmental bureaucracy, and the military services. People no longer felt the same obligation to obey those whom they had previously considered superior to themselves in age, rank, status, expertise, character, or talents.

All this, he said, "produced problems for the governability of democracy in the 1970's. . . ."

Critical in all this was the decline in the authority of the President. And:

To the extent that the United States was governed by anyone during the decades after World War II, it was governed by the President acting with the support and cooperation of key individuals and groups in the executive office, the federal bureaucracy, Congress, and the more important businesses, banks, law firms, foundations, and media, which constitute the private sector's "Establishment."

This was probably the frankest statement ever made by an Establishment adviser.

Huntington further said that the President, to win the election, needed the support of a broad coalition of people. However: "The day after his election, the size of his majority is almost—if not entirely—irrelevant to his ability to govern the country. What counts then is his ability to mobilize support from the leaders of key institutions in a society and government. . . . This coalition must include key people in Congress, the executive branch, and the private-sector 'Establishment.' " He gave examples:

Truman made a point of bringing a substantial number of non-partisan soldiers, Republican bankers, and Wall Street lawyers into his Administration. He went to the existing sources of power in the country to get help he needed in ruling the country. Eisenhower in part inherited this coalition and was in part almost its creation. . . . Kennedy attempted to recreate a somewhat similar structure of alliances.

What worried Huntington was the loss in governmental authority. For instance, the opposition to Vietnam had brought the abolition of the draft. "The question necessarily arises, however, whether if a new threat to security should materialize in the future (as it inevitably will at some point), the government will possess the authority to command the resources, as well as the sacrifices, which are necessary to meet that threat."

Huntington saw the possible end of that quarter century when "the United States was the hegemonic power in a system of world order." His conclusion was that there had developed "an excess of democracy," and he suggested "desirable limits to the extension of political democracy."

Huntington was reporting all this to an organization that was very important to the future of the United States. The Trilateral Commission was organized in early 1973 by David Rockefeller and Zbigniew Brzezinski. Rockefeller was an official of the Chase Manhattan Bank and a powerful financial figure in the United States and the world; Brzezinski, a Columbia University professor, specialized in international relations and was a consultant to the State Department. As reported in the *Far Eastern Economic Review* (March 25, 1977) by Robert Manning:

The initiative for the Commission came entirely from Rockefeller. According to George Franklin, the Commission's executive secretary, Rockefeller "was getting worried about the deteriorating relations between the United States, Europe and Japan." Franklin explained that Rockefeller began to present his ideas to another elite fraternity: ". . . at the Bilderberg Group—a very distinguished Anglo-American group which has been meeting for a long time—Mike Blumenthal said he thought things were in a very serious condition in

the world and couldn't some kind of private group do more about it? . . .
So then David again made his proposal. . . ." Then Brzezinski, a close friend
of Rockefeller's, carried the Rockefeller-funded ball and organized the Commission.

It seems probable that the "very serious condition" mentioned
as the reason for the Trilateral Commission was the need for greater
unity among Japan, Western Europe, and the United States in the face
of a much more complicated threat to tri-continental capitalism than
a monolithic Communism: revolutionary movements in the Third
World. These movements had directions of their own.

The Trilateral Commission wanted also to deal with another situation. Back in 1967, George Ball, who had been Undersecretary of State
for economic affairs in the Kennedy administration and who was director
of Lehman Brothers, a large investment banking firm, told members
of the International Chamber of Commerce:

In these twenty postwar years, we have come to recognize in action,
though not always in words, that the political boundaries of nation-states
are too narrow and constricted to define the scope and activities of modern
business.

To show the growth of international economics for United States corporations, one would only have to note the situation in banking. In 1960
there were eight United States banks with foreign branches; in 1974
there were 129. The assets of these overseas branches amounted to
$3.5 billion in 1960, $155 billion in 1974.

The Trilateral Commission apparently saw itself as helping to create
the necessary international links for the new multinational economy.
Its members came from the highest circles of politics, business, and
the media in Western Europe, Japan, and the United States. They were
from Chase Manhattan, Lehman Brothers, Bank of America, Banque
de Paris, Lloyd's of London, Bank of Tokyo, etc. Oil, steel, auto, aero-
nautic, and electric industries were represented. Other members were
from *Time* magazine, the Washington *Post,* the Columbia Broadcasting
System, *Die Zeit,* the *Japan Times, The Economist* of London, and
more.

1976 was not only a presidential election year—it was the much-
anticipated year of the bicentennial celebration, and it was filled with
much-publicized events all over the country. The great effort that went
into the celebration suggests that it was seen as a way of restoring
American patriotism, invoking the symbols of history to unite people

and government and put aside the protest mood of the recent past.

But there did not seem to be great enthusiasm for it. When the 200th anniversary of the Boston Tea Party was celebrated in Boston, an enormous crowd turned out, not for the official celebration, but for the "People's Bi-Centennial" countercelebration, where packages marked "Gulf Oil" and "Exxon" were dumped into the Boston Harbor, to symbolize opposition to corporate power in America.

A similar intent, to restore legitimacy to the government, was represented in the 1976 elections. Americans were taught, from grade school up, that voting for the President was the supreme act of participation in democracy. Elections gave Americans a feeling that the government was theirs and they were the government. A dramatic change had taken place, however, in attitudes on voting. Surveys showed that the statement: "Voting is the only way that people like me can have any say about how the government runs things," which was once approved by 79 percent of people in their twenties, by 1968 was getting approval from 37 percent.

This diminished faith in voting showed up in the presidential election of 1976. In 1960, 36.6 percent of all Americans eligible to vote did not vote. (There were millions not eligible because they did not meet national residency requirements for citizenship or local residency requirements, or had lost their right to vote by spending time in prison.) In 1976 the percentage of nonvoters rose to 46.7 percent. About 15 million Americans had dropped out of the electoral system and, as in previous elections, those who didn't go to vote were mostly poor, blue-collar workers, with little education, under thirty.

Even those who did vote did not seem to vote with enthusiasm for the political process they were engaging in. Fifty-five percent of the voters in a *CBS News* and *New York Times* survey said that public officials did not care about people like them. A journalist interviewing middle-class residents of Dobbs Ferry, New York, just before the election received these comments: From a restaurant proprietor, "This is the first Presidential election I've seen where people are not interested." From a plumber, "The President of the United States isn't going to solve our problems. The problems are too big." From a teacher, "There's a very strong feeling of disillusionment. You get the old thought that all politicians are corrupt. It's stronger than I've ever seen it before." Those interviewed saw the major problems as high taxes and unemployment.

The Democratic candidate for President in 1976, Jimmy Carter, was a member of the Trilateral Commission. The *Far Eastern Economic Review* article, based apparently on talks with members of the Trilateral Commission and Carter's staff, said:

> There is much evidence to suggest that Carter's ambition [he announced his candidacy in 1972] coincided with similar thought by strategists in and around the Commission, most of whom are liberal Democrats. This is based on the theory that the Watergate-plagued Republican Party was a sure loser for 1976. . . . Peter Bourne, Carter's former deputy campaign chief, has said: "David [Rockefeller] and Zbig [Brzezinski] had both agreed that Carter was the ideal politician to build on."

Carter's job as President, from the point of view of the Establishment, was to halt the rushing disappointment of the American people with the government, with the economic system, with disastrous military ventures abroad. In his campaign, he tried to speak to the disillusioned and angry. His strongest appeal was to blacks, whose rebellion in the late sixties was the most frightening challenge to authority since the labor and unemployed upsurges in the thirties. He was a southern white, former governor of Georgia, whose liberal views on the race question were especially welcome to blacks, and whose promises to include them in government contrasted sharply with Gerald Ford's poor record on racial equality during his long years in Congress.

His appeal was "populist"—that is, he appealed to various elements of American society who saw themselves beleaguered by the powerful and wealthy. Although he himself was a millionaire peanut grower, he presented himself as an ordinary American farmer. Although he had been a supporter of Vietnam until its end, he presented himself as a sympathizer with those who had been against the war, and he appealed to many of the young rebels of the sixties by his promise to cut the military budget. In a much-publicized speech to lawyers, he spoke out against the use of the law to protect the rich. He appointed a black woman, Patricia Harris, as Secretary of Housing and Urban Development, and a black civil rights veteran, Andrew Young, as ambassador to the United Nations. He gave the job of heading the domestic youth service corps to a young former antiwar activist, Sam Brown.

His most crucial appointments, however, followed Huntington's prescription in his Trilateral Report for how a President should behave the day after election. Indeed, the number of Trilateral Commission members appointed to important posts in the Carter administration was startling. Brzezinski became his National Security Adviser. Cyrus

Vance became Secretary of State; he was a member of the board of directors of IBM, Pan American World Airways, and the *New York Times*, a trustee of Yale University and the Rockefeller Foundation, a former Secretary of the Army and Assistant Secretary of Defense during the Vietnam war. His appointment had the enthusiastic approval of his predecessor, Henry Kissinger.

Carter's director of the budget was a wealthy Georgia banker named Bert Lance. Both were presented to the public at the same time, and a reporter commented:

> At Mr. Carter's news conference, Mr. Lance came across as an amiable, self-confident Georgia banker with a gregarious affability of a Southern politician, and Mr. Vance as an experienced lawyer-diplomat with the discreet reserve of a man accustomed to the ways of Yale, Wall Street and the Eastern Establishment.

Vance was a member of the Trilateral Commission. Lance was not.

Walter Mondale, the new Vice-President, was a member of the Trilateral Commission. So were Ambassador to the United Nations Andrew Young, Secretary of the Treasury Michael Blumenthal, and Secretary of Defense Harold Brown. (Brown, according to the *Pentagon Papers*, had, during the Vietnam war, in the spring of 1968, "envisaged the elimination of virtually all the constraints under which the bombing then operated.") Carter's appointments as Assistant Secretary of the Treasury for International Economic Affairs, Undersecretary of State for Economic Affairs, and Assistant for East Asian and Pacific affairs were all members of the Commission. He appointed Admiral Stansfield Turner as head of the CIA, another Trilateral man, and as one of Turner's three deputies a Harvard professor, Robert Bowie, also Trilateral.

All these postelectoral actions were a sharp contrast to the promises and expectations of the campaign, but the consensus of support from both conservatives and liberals suggested the urgent need for the Establishment to try to re-create around Carter the much-damaged national unity. A financial writer wrote not long after Carter's election: "So far, Mr. Carter's actions, commentary, and particularly, his Cabinet appointments have been highly reassuring to the business community." A well-known eastern banker was quoted in the same article as saying: "I don't think Mr. Carter has made a false move since he was elected."

Carter appointed a former Secretary of Defense under Nixon, James Schlesinger, as his Secretary of Energy. Schlesinger was a strong proponent of nuclear energy. His record as Secretary of Defense was described by a member of the Washington press corps:

As Secretary of Defense, Mr. Schlesinger, who looks upon the cold war as a proud chapter in American history, demonstrated an almost missionary drive in seeking to reverse a downward trend in the defense budget. He became spokesman for the concept that a limited nuclear war is possible, with each side attacking the military forces of the other.

Carter's Attorney General, Griffin Bell, was a member of one of the most powerful law firms in Atlanta, King and Spalding, which represented Coca-Cola, and other wealthy corporations. Journalist and veteran Washington correspondent Tom Wicker wrote after Carter had announced his major appointments: "The available evidence is that Mr. Carter so far is opting for Wall Street's confidence."

Carter was attempting to do what previous liberal Democratic administrations had done—for example, Roosevelt and Truman—to please the nation's corporate and military establishment while retaining support from a large section of the people who were the victims of corporate and military policy. The question was whether, in the new condition of the seventies, this could be done successfully.

Carter's election was due in some part to the feeling that the nation must remove itself from the Watergate crowd and the Watergate mentality. Ford had pardoned Nixon. Now, Carter's administration, faced with the fact that a former head of the CIA, Richard Helms, had lied to a Senate committee about CIA operations in Chile, made a deal with Helms which allowed him to plead guilty on two misdemeanor counts and escape prison. The Carter administration seemed reluctant, despite the damaging information on the CIA brought out in congressional hearings, to make any essential changes in the activities of the CIA. The American Civil Liberties Union commented on Carter's first year in office:

In the face of opposition from the intelligence agencies, the President has not fulfilled his campaign promises to curb abuses of civil liberties in the name of national security. Indeed, the Administration has advocated more secrecy.

Carter did initiate more sophisticated policies toward other countries in the world that oppressed their own people. He used Ambassador Andrew Young to build up good will for the United States among the black African nations, urged that South Africa liberalize its policies toward blacks. A peaceful settlement in South Africa was necessary strategically. South Africa was used for radar tracking systems. It had important U.S. corporate investments, and it was a critical source of needed raw materials (diamonds especially). Therefore, what the United States needed was a stable government in South Africa; the continued oppression of blacks might create civil war.

The same approach was used in other countries—combining practical strategic needs with the advancement of civil rights. But because the chief motivation was practicality, not humanity, there was a tendency toward token changes—as in Chile's release of a few prisoners. One of Carter's most publicized stands in foreign policy was his concern for "human rights" all over the world. And during his presidential campaign he proposed that American aid be withheld from "countries that consistently violate human rights." But when Congressman Herman Badillo introduced in Congress a proposal that required the U.S. representatives to the World Bank and other international financial institutions to vote against loans to countries that systematically violated essential rights, by the use of torture or imprisonment without trial, Carter sent a personal letter to every Congressman urging the defeat of this amendment. It won a voice vote in the House, but lost in the Senate.

Carter was continuing the old hypocrisy. The U.S. was supporting, all over the world, regimes that engaged in imprisonment of dissenters, torture, and mass murder: in Chile, in Iran, in Nicaragua, and in Indonesia, where the inhabitants of Timor were being annihilated in a campaign bordering on genocide.

The New Republic magazine, on the liberal side of the Establishment, commented approvingly on the Carter policies: ". . . American foreign policy in the next four years will essentially extend the philosophies developed . . . in the Nixon-Ford years. This is not at all a negative prospect. . . . There should be continuity. It is part of history. . . ."

Carter had presented himself as a friend of the movement against the war, but in fact had advocated aid to the Saigon government right up to the spring of 1975, just before it fell. When Nixon mined Haiphong harbor and resumed bombing of North Vietnam in the spring of 1975, Carter urged that "we give President Nixon our backing and support—whether or not we agree with specific decisions." Once elected, Carter declined to give aid to Vietnam for reconstruction, despite the fact that the land had been devastated by American bombing. Asked about this at a press conference, Carter replied that there was no special obligation on the United States to do this because "the destruction was mutual."

Considering that the United States had crossed half the globe with an enormous fleet of bombers and 2 million soldiers, and after eight years left a tiny nation with over a million dead and its land in ruins, this was an astounding statement. It forecast the direction of the American government's policy in the post-Vietnam period.

One Establishment intention, perhaps, was that future generations see the war not as the Defense Department itself had described it in the *Pentagon Papers*—as a ruthless attack on civilian populations for strategic military and economic interests—but as an unfortunate error. Noam Chomsky, one of the leading antiwar intellectuals during the Vietnam period, looked in mid-1978 at how the history of the Vietnam war was being presented by newspapers and magazines and the "intellectual elite" in the U.S., and wrote that they were "destroying the historical record and supplanting it with a more comfortable story, transferring the moral onus of American aggression to its victims, reducing 'lessons' of the war to the socially neutral categories of error, ignorance, and cost. . . ."

The Carter administration clearly was trying to end the disillusionment of the American people after the Vietnam war by following foreign policies more palatable, less obviously aggressive. Hence, the emphasis on "human rights," the pressure on South Africa and Chile to liberalize their policies. But on close examination, these more liberal policies were designed to leave intact the power and influence of American military and American business in the world.

The renegotiation of the Panama Canal treaty with the tiny Central American republic of Panama was an example. Back in 1903 the United States had engineered a revolution against Colombia, set up the new Panama republic, and dictated a treaty giving the United States military bases, control of the Panama Canal, and sovereignty "in perpetuity." As the *New York Times* commented, when the Carter administration began renegotiating the treaty: "We stole it, and removed the incriminating evidence from our history books."

The canal was a pure example of American imperialism. It saved American companies $1.5 billion a year in delivery costs, and the United States collected $150 million a year in tolls, out of which it paid the Panama government $2.3 million dollars, while maintaining fourteen military bases in the area.

By 1977 the canal had lost military importance. It could not accommodate large tankers or aircraft carriers. And there had been repeated riots in Panama by nationalists demanding that the United States get out. It was the time, therefore, for a new treaty, which, as the *Times* said, could "remove a major irritant in relations with several neighbors, improve the climate for investment throughout the Caribbean, and reduce the risks of sabotage. . . ." The Council of the Americas, an organization representing 220 U.S. corporations with interests in Latin America, favored a new treaty. So the Carter administration negotiated one, which called for a gradual removal of U.S. bases (which could easily be relocated elsewhere in the area) and turned over the canal's legal ownership to Panama after a period. The treaty also contained vague language which could be the basis for American military intervention under certain conditions.

Whatever Carter's sophistication in foreign policy, certain fundamentals operated in the late sixties and the seventies. American corporations were active all over the world on a scale never seen before. There were, by the early seventies, about three hundred U.S. corporations, including the seven largest banks, which earned 40 percent of their net profits outside the United States. They were called "multinationals," but actually, of 1,851 top executives in these companies, it turned out that 98.4 percent were Americans. They were growing at twice and three times the rate of the American economy, and as a group they constituted the third-largest economy in the world, next to the United States and the Soviet Union.

Oil corporations remained powerful in their effect on American foreign policy, and Carter gave no sign of diminishing their power. A government oil economist of many years, John Blair *(The Control of Oil)*, showed in detail how the "Seven Sisters"—Exxon, Mobil, So-Cal, Texaco, Gulf, Royal Dutch Shell, British Petroleum—controlled the supply and marketing of oil in ways that were against the public interest. With the cooperation of national and local governments, the Seven Sisters had followed policies which quickly depleted the American oil supply and forced U.S. dependence on Middle East oil. Much of the blame for increased oil prices after 1973 had been put on the Arab oil countries, but the corporations raised prices far beyond what was necessary, and the consumers, were, as usual, the victims.

It had been U.S. government policy, since 1969, through the establishment of the Overseas Private Investment Corporation, to ensure the multinationals at low rates against the loss of their properties through revolution or war.

The relationship of these global corporations with the poorer countries was an exploiting one, it was clear from U.S. Department of Commerce figures. Whereas U.S. corporations in Europe between 1950 and 1965 invested $8.1 billion and made $5.5 billion in profits, in Latin America they invested $3.8 billion and made $11.3 billion in profits, and in Africa they invested $5.2 billion and made $14.3 billion in profits.

It was the classical imperial situation, where the places with natural wealth became victims of more powerful nations whose power depended on that seized wealth. American corporations depended on the poorer countries for 100 percent of their diamonds, coffee, platinum, mercury, natural rubber, and cobalt. They got 98 percent of their manganese from abroad, 90 percent of their chrome and aluminum. And 20 to 40 percent of certain imports (platinum, mercury, cobalt, chrome, manganese) came from Africa.

The rearrangement of foreign policy after Vietnam, to advance the same interests, but with different tactics, was begun under Ford and continued under Carter. With the Vietnam bases gone, the United States quickly acquired from Britain one of her old colonial possessions in the middle of the Indian Ocean, a little island called Diego Garcia. The island was in an area rich in tin, jute, tea, copper, cobalt, manganese, uranium, and gold, and near the oil fields of the Middle East. The people on that island had been engaged mostly in growing coconuts. This now had to stop as barracks were built, an airfield constructed, a channel dug into the bay big enough for aircraft carriers to come in. The coconut workers were resettled on another island.

Another post-Vietnam necessity was to maintain a huge military presence in other Pacific bases: Japan, Korea, Taiwan, the Philippines— 286 warships, 2,100 planes, and 265,000 sailors and marines, the largest maritime military forces in history. The United States still had over a thousand military bases throughout the world.

Another continuing policy was the training of foreign military officers. The Army had a "School of the Americas" in the Canal Zone, from which 29,000 military leaders in Latin America had graduated since 1949. In 1973, 170 graduates were heads of state, cabinet ministers, commanding generals, or directors of intelligence. Six of those graduates were in the Chilean military junta that overthrew the Allende government. The American commandant of the school told a reporter: "We keep in touch with our graduates and they keep in touch with us."

And yet the United States cultivated a reputation of being generous with its riches. Indeed, it had often given aid to disaster victims. This aid, however, often depended on political loyalty or on meeting cold business demands. In one six-year drought in West Africa, 100,000 Africans died of starvation. A report by the Carnegie Endowment said the Agency for International Development (AID) of the United States had been inefficient and neglectful in giving aid to nomads in the Sahel area of West Africa, an area covering six countries. The response of AID was that those countries had "no close historical, economic, or political ties to the United States." In the summer of 1974, countless died of starvation in Bangladesh (once part of India) because neither U.S. banks nor the U.S. government would give credit to buy grain waiting to be loaded on ships.

In early 1975 the press carried a dispatch from Washington: "Secretary of State Henry A. Kissinger has formally initiated a policy of selecting for cutbacks in American aid those nations that have sided against the U.S. in votes in the United Nations. In some cases, the cutbacks involve food and humanitarian relief."

Most aid was openly military. The Military Assistance Program gave $55 billion to seventy-one countries since World War II. As Senator Alan Cranston told the Foreign Relations Committee after a study: "This aid was intended to help them defend themselves against aggression. But many of the governments have used American money and American-supplied weapons to terrorize and subjugate their own people." What was remarkable was that Americans were beginning to understand this. By 1975, public opinion polls showed that "65 percent of Americans oppose military aid abroad because they feel it allows dictatorships to maintain control over their population."

Congress began to phase out the Military Assistance Program, but it was replaced by the direct sale of arms to the same countries. Whereas in 1969 the United States had exported $1.7 billion in arms, by 1975 the figure was up to $9.5 billion. The Carter administration promised to end the sale of arms to repressive regimes, but when it took office the bulk of the sales continued.

Like his predecessors, Carter was not totally dependent on congressional appropriations of funds for military ventures overseas. There had long been enough statutes on the books to give American Presidents plenty of leeway. Back in 1973, Elliot Richardson, as Secretary of Defense, told the Senate Appropriations Committee that even if it refused to give the $500 million the Pentagon was asking to continue bombing Cambodia, "We can find the money to do it anyway. . . . We could invoke section 3732 authority." This was a statute for the "feed and forage" of troops passed back in 1799 and still alive.

What the Carter administration might change in U.S. foreign policy, it seemed, was not its basic aim of protecting corporate profits, military power, and political influence on the world—but perhaps (with Vietnam a sobering lesson) a smaller emphasis on overt military aggression. A Brookings Institution report of January 1977 showed that after World War II, up to and including the *Mayaguez* incident, the United States had deployed its military forces abroad for political impact on 215 occasions. For instance, when a right-wing coup took place in Brazil in 1964 against a left-wing government, a U.S. naval task force was positioned off the Brazilian coast to support the coup. The study found thirty-three instances in which nuclear forces were deployed for political effect, the latest being during the 1973 war in the Middle East, when American forces were put on a worldwide nuclear alert.

Meanwhile, the education of Americans did not enlighten them much about the sources of U.S. foreign policy. Most college courses on American foreign policy were taught from the standpoint of government policy, looking at strategic problems and alternatives from a government point of view; there was little education on the strategies citizens might use to oppose official policy. Courses on foreign policy generally did not emphasize corporate economic interests. A study in the *Annals of the American Academy of Political and Social Science* in 1972 by Dennis Ray (not widely distributed) concluded:

> The influence of corporations on the foreign policy process . . . remains clouded in mystery. My search through the respectable literature on international relations and U.S. foreign policy shows that less than 5 percent of some 200 books granted even passing attention to the role of corporations in American foreign relations.

Ray found that the most widely used textbooks ignored the fact that "foreign policy decision-makers are heavily recruited from large corporations, investment houses, and law firms."

Indeed, there was a well-financed, well-organized effort to influence teachers on behalf of the government. A series of National Security Programs, by 1976, had reached hundreds of teachers who attended summer seminars and conferences. There they listened to lectures by pro-government academicians and West Point instructors. About a thousand faculty members from four hundred institutions had attended two-day seminars, and this led to eighty-seven colleges and universities giving their own regular courses in "national security."

Was all this rejuvenation of the "national security" slogan a way of building support for large arms budgets? Jimmy Carter, running for election, had told the Democratic Platform Committee: "Without endangering the defense of our nation or commitments to our allies, we can reduce present defense expenditures by about 5 to 7 billion dollars annually." But his first budget in January 1978 proposed not a decrease but an increase of $10 billion in the arms budget. He justified this by saying Ford would have raised it even more. And the administration had just announced that the Department of Agriculture would save $25 million a year by no longer giving free second helpings of milk to 1.4 million needy schoolchildren who got free meals in school.

If Carter's job was to restore faith in the system, here was his greatest failure—solving the economic problems of the people. The price of food and the necessities of life continued to rise faster than wages were rising. Unemployment remained officially at 6 or 8 percent—unofficially, the rates were higher. For certain key groups in the population—young people, and especially young black people—the unemployment rate was 20 percent or 30 percent.

By 1978 it was clear that blacks in the United States, the group most in support of Carter for President, and without whose support he could not have been elected, were bitterly disappointed with his policies. He opposed federal aid to poor people who needed abortions, and when it was pointed out to him that this was unfair, because rich women could get abortions with ease, he replied: "Well, as you know, there are many things in life that are not fair, that wealthy people can afford and poor people cannot."

In early 1978 a survey of public opinion by *CBS News* and the *New York Times* showed that 50 percent of those polled considered themselves worse off economically than a year ago or were in some way dissatisfied with their personal economic situation. "Not surprisingly, the sharpest increases in disapproval of the President's handling of the economy have come among blacks, the elderly, and low-income groups."

Only 43 percent of those polled accepted Carter's view that the energy shortage was serious. More people—almost 50 percent—believed that the people were "just being told" there was a shortage so that oil and gas companies could charge higher prices. Indeed, it was part of Carter's energy plan to end price regulation of natural gas for the consumer. The largest producer of natural gas was Exxon Corporation, and the largest blocks of private stock in Exxon were owned by the Rockefeller family.

Early in Carter's administration congressional investigators charged that Texaco Oil Corporation was withholding from production over 500 billion cubic feet of natural gas in two fields off the coast of Louisiana. That gas could have been used, they said, during the severe gas shortages of the winter, but Texaco did not pump this gas because of a "desire to maximize its profits," according to John Galloway of the House Oversight and Investigations Subcommittee.

In April of 1977 the Federal Energy Administration found that Gulf Oil Corporation had overstated by $79.1 million its costs for crude oil obtained from foreign affiliates. It then passed on these false costs to consumers. In the summer of 1978 the administration announced that a "compromise" had been made with Gulf Oil in which Gulf agreed to pay back $42.2 million. Gulf informed its stockholders that "the payments will not affect earnings since adequate provision was made in prior years."

The lawyer for the Energy Department who worked out the compromise with Gulf said it had been done to avoid a lengthy and costly lawsuit. Would the lawsuit have cost the $36.9 million dropped in the compromise? Would the government have considered letting off a bank robber without a jail term in return for half the loot? The settlement was a perfect example of what Carter had told a meeting of lawyers during his presidential campaign—that the law was on the side of the rich.

The facts on the unequal distribution of wealth in America were clearly not going to be affected by Carter's policies, any more than they had been affected by previous "reform" administrators. According to Andrew Zimbalist, an American economist writing in *Le Monde Diplomatique* in 1977, the top 10 percent of the American population had an income thirty times that of the bottom tenth; the top 1 percent of the nation owned 33 percent of the wealth. The richest 5 percent owned 83 percent of the personally owned corporate stock. The one hundred largest corporations (despite the graduated income tax that misled people into thinking the very rich paid 60 to 70 percent in taxes) paid an average of 26.9 percent in taxes, and the leading oil companies paid 5.8 percent in taxes (these are Internal Revenue Service figures for 1974). Indeed, 244 individuals who earned over $200,000 paid no taxes. (Jimmy Carter paid no income tax for 1976 but gave $6,000 to the Treasury to show his good will.)

Poverty in the cities was much more important than ever before in American history. Fifty years before, 24 percent of Americans lived on farms; now the figure was 4 percent. The cities were bursting with people, many of them black and many of them unemployed. The *U.S. News and World Report* in December 1977 reported that, while the general unemployment rate was 7 percent, for blacks it was 15 percent; for white teenagers it was also 15 percent; and for black teenagers it was 40 percent. Its headline read: YOUNG BLACKS OUT OF WORK—TIME BOMB FOR U.S.

The figures on unemployment and income were matters of life and death. It was found in mid-1977, in a study of death certificates published in the *New England Journal of Medicine*, that the death rate in that area of Boston where most black and Hispanic people lived was 50 percent higher than in the Newton-Wellesley-Weston white suburban neighborhoods.

Not only in the North but also in the South, poverty—after New Deal, Fair Deal, New Frontier, and Great Society—was still deeply entrenched. There were 10 million poor people in the South, the Southern Regional Council reported, two-thirds of those not reached by any form of public welfare assistance.

The President's attempts at post-Vietnam, post-Watergate restoration of faith were not succeeding. True, there was no national movement of protest or rebellion in the mid-seventies comparable with the black protest movement, the antiwar movement, the women's movement. And because there was no visible central movement, the press was full of articles with the theme "The movement is dead." However, if one looked just a bit below the surface, there was massive evidence that the country was not firmly back in the hands of the Establishment, indeed, that people were on the move organizing. And if one looked deeper still, at the economy and its effect on people's lives, there was a huge potential for revolt.

The CIO, which had engaged in the militant strikes of the thirties and the organization of millions of workers in mass production industries, was now comfortably joined with the AFL and served as a control against labor rebellion. But, in the seventies, it faced wildcat strikes all over the country, and rank-and-file insurgencies against established leadership. A long and bitter strike in 1973 of coal miners in Harlan County was part of a rank-and-file movement against the entrenched leaders of the United Mine Workers. In the powerful unions of steel workers and teamsters there were rank-and-file rebellions. No settlement seemed secure. The strikes went on. For instance, in McCreary County, Kentucky, in 1977 a small strike of 160 miners, beset with beatings and arrests, lasted fifteen months. In this, as in Harlan County and many other strikes, women played an important part.

There was a new surge in organizing that 80 percent of the labor force which was unorganized. Women and white-collar workers became the focal point of the new organizing. Teachers and public service workers of all kinds—garbage collectors, fire fighters, police, postal workers—went out on strike. On the campuses, the organization of teachers' unions and secretaries' unions replaced the old issues of the sixties, as bread-and-butter problems became the center of attention instead of war. While striking miners were going to jail in a small town in Kentucky, teachers were going to jail in Franklin, a small town in Massachusetts.

The mass movements of the sixties had disbanded, but they left behind, all over the country, hundreds of thousands of people who were forming into small local groups and battling on a hundred issues, in different ways, for health, safety, peace, equality, and economic justice. Many of them were veterans of the movements of the sixties; many others were young people new to social action. Altogether they constituted a formidable nationwide movement, not unified in structure but sharing a common purpose, to protest against Establishment policies, to work for new ways of living.

In small towns and obscure places that had never seen such things before, there were tenants' organizations, antiutility committees, environmental groups, food cooperatives, work cooperatives, communal housing situations, lawyers' collectives, doctors' collectives, community newspapers. Homosexual men and women were organized into Gay Rights groups, women into women's groups, Chicanos and Puerto Ricans, blacks and Native Americans into their own groups, and sometimes combinations of these into cross-cultural groups.

For instance, in the area of Hampshire County in Western Massachusetts—the scene long ago of Shays' Rebellion—there was a community newspaper called *Outfront,* which in its March 1976 issue reported on an array of activities typical of what was happening in every section of the country in the mid-seventies. Tenants in a government-subsidized housing project were organizing against a rent increase, seventy-five people were protesting sexually discriminatory hiring practices at a local bar-restaurant-inn, eighty students were undertaking an educational campaign to replace the environmentally destructive metal cans with bottles. The Hampshire County Employed-Unemployed Council, an alliance of workers, welfare recipients, and students, was holding a dinner. There was a campaign for rent control in Amherst, a report on a national "Hard Times" conference of two thousand people in Chicago. A women's health care collective was opening. *Outfront* had articles on women's rights, job safety, the Native American movement, repression in Puerto Rico, and other subjects. It printed a list of fifteen work, food, and other cooperatives, fourteen black, Native American, Asian-American, and Third World cultural and political groups, five women's groups, six gay groups, three war veterans' organizations, six tenants' groups, seventeen media groups—radio stations, newspapers, film cooperatives—six day-care groups, three health services, and four labor organizing groups. And there was a full page of "People's Poetry."

This could be duplicated a hundred times around the country. There had not been anything like such extensive local organization in the turbulent sixties. A young graduate of M.I.T. decided, in the early seventies, to gather and publish a directory of anti-Establishment organizations of all kinds, all over the country. His list, published under the title *Alternate America,* had over five thousand groups, and kept growing.

In 1973, in Boston—a city with a very high proportion of women clerical workers, in universities, hospitals, insurance companies—a group of women formed an organization called "9 to 5." It was set up to improve working conditions for women and "to win rights and respect for all women." It organized women workers, negotiated with and put pressure on employers, picketed and demonstrated, brought women together to give them a feeling of support and strength.

As schools opened in the fall of 1978, teachers were on strike in all areas of the country and picket lines were formed outside schools in Cleveland, Philadelphia, New Orleans, Seattle, and other places. The usually cautious television news commentator Walter Cronkite called it "the most stunning action by unaffiliated and uncoordinated labor groups in the nation's recent history." Inflation was hurting; the teachers were demanding wage raises to meet the rise in the cost of living. The president of a teachers' group in Yonkers, New York, said: "It's really something to see all these actions. Our biggest problem used to be that teachers thought they were too good to strike . . . they thought they were artists or professionals. Now, it seems they're ready to join the labor movement."

Not just teachers, but public employees of all sorts—those considered most loyal to government, like firemen and policemen—were defying legislatures, courts, mayors, and demanding improvement in their wages and working conditions. In 1978, firemen and police in Anderson,

Indiana, put their forces together in a strike that left the city prostrate. In San Antonio, Texas, sanitation workers fought against police used to break their strike. But the traditional use of police to break strikes was running into a phenomenon new in American history—the widespread refusal of police to work under conditions dictated by higher authority, the strikes of policemen all over the country, almost all of them for the first time, as in Memphis, Tennessee.

As usual in American history, the millionaire press ignored the local actions going on in a thousand places all over the country, actions that showed people alive, organizing, resisting, trying in small but portentous ways to better their lives by cooperating. For instance, in the mid-seventies, a native of Maine named Russ Christensen, a paratrooper during the Korean war who then went to law school and spent time in Latin America, returned to Maine to give legal help to low-income people, read about Marxism and socialism, and helped form a Maine Woodsmen's Association. The state of Maine is dominated by the paper corporations, and the MWA was the first organization of the men who cut and hauled trees for these companies.

A thousand paper workers joined the Association, they went on strike in 1975, their strike was broken by a court injunction, but the organization was established as a spokesman for the united woodworkers of Maine. Christensen and others were setting up cheap legal service programs and working out ways of cooperatively owning land and housing. He declared himself a socialist, and thought that socialists should run candidates for office as well as doing grass-roots organizing.

When eight women who worked for a bank in the small town of Wilmar, Minnesota, saw a male employee hired who knew less than they did and got twice the pay, they protested, organized, and finally went out on strike in late 1977. They found themselves picketing through the cold Minnesota winter, wearing snowmobile suits, scarves wound around their faces, and heavy boots. It was a small strike, but it was the first bank strike in the history of the state, and a sign of what was beginning to happen across the country in the joining of women's rights to labor struggle.

In the early part of the century, men and women died by the thousands through sickness and accidents resulting from industrial conditions, and mostly without public notice. In the 1970s, working people were beginning to get aroused over the increasing evidence of deadly disease resulting from work situations. It was a condition that could happen under any system of modern technology, but where there was a powerful drive for profit overriding concern for human welfare, as in a capitalist system, the dangers were multiplied, and the remedies more difficult to achieve. In various parts of the United States, both unions and unorganized groups of workers began to campaign to get safer working conditions.

In a small town (Conshohocken) in Pennsylvania in 1978, workers at Lee Tire Company demanded to know exactly what kind of chemicals they were working with, because the labels on the chemical drums had been replaced with code designations which only the employers knew. A similar demand was made by an Oil, Chemical and Atomic Workers Union local at a printing ink company in Minneapolis. In the first instance, the workers' demands were rejected by an arbitrator. In the second, they won in an appeal to the National Labor Relations Board.

Two construction workers at the First National City Bank in Boston, brothers named Leary, discovered in the summer of 1978 that asbestos fibers were coming out of some of the beams in the building. It had recently been discovered that asbestos fibers, inhaled by shipyard workers and other people in construction, caused cancerlike, fatal diseases, often thirty years after inhalation. Hundreds of people worked in that building. When the Leary brothers protested and asked for protective equipment, they were fired. But they publicized what they had found and took their case into the courts. It was another instance of small-scale resistance cropping up in unexpected places.

As the newspapers concentrated on the election campaign of 1976 and the bicentennial events of that year, organizing was going on all over the country, unreported in the press, on the radio or television. Some examples: a farm workers' association in Binghamton, New York; a farm workers' service center in Alamo, Texas; a tenants' union in Madison, Wisconsin, and another in St. Petersburg, Florida (these among hundreds of tenant organizations newly organized in the country). There was a Women's Health Project in Somerville, Massachusetts; a Chicano organizing group in San Juan, Texas; a Legal Defense Committee in Keshena, Wisconsin; a GI organizing project in San Diego, California; a Black Military Resistance League in Norfolk, Virginia; the Fort Bragg GI union in Spring Lake, North Carolina.

Prison support groups were formed in Kansas City, Missouri; Seattle, Washington; St. Louis, Missouri, and dozens of other places. There were alternate newspapers by the hundreds all over the country, and new collectives formed to use audiovisual techniques in organizing people. There were "people's bookstores" in Los Angeles, in Harlem, in Washington, D.C., in small towns in Oregon. Women's groups around the country were increasing too fast to be counted.

Some of the sixties' activists became involved in the seventies in local government—a few were elected mayors of small towns, others to local posts of various kinds. In 1975, they formed a Conference on Alternative State and Local Public Policies, which met annually to exchange experiences and ideas on how to achieve social change within the system. In Eugene, Oregon, a radical became local tax assessor and began to worry the corporations. In California, Tom Hayden, a radical activist of the sixties, ran for U.S. Senator on a program of "Economic Democracy" (he lost, but got over a million votes). When a meeting took place in California in early 1978 to discuss "alternative public policy," more than eight hundred people came.

There was vigorous debate among the new groups on whether radical political energy was best expended inside the political system, through the voting mechanism, or outside it, in protest groups and parallel organizations. But while the debate went on, more and more people were doing both.

With the Vietnam war over, some of the veterans of the antiwar movement took up the battle against the militarization of America and the world arms race. What drove them to action was symbolized in the comments of an air force captain at Whitman Air Force Base in Missouri. He was a launch officer for the Minuteman III, which could wipe out three large cities with its new missile-carrying multiple warheads. The captain told an interviewer: "The fact is, it is possible for 4 officers in a Minuteman Squadron to launch and start World War III without authorization from anyone. . . . Naturally, this would be illegal, but who would be around to punish them?"

In Baltimore, Catholic veterans of jails and demonstrations in the sixties set up a center called Jonah House. From there they went regularly to the Pentagon in Washington, to carry on small but dramatic guerrilla-theater actions against the arms race. They kept being arrested, but, through a small publication, *Year One,* their story got out to people all over the country.

Daniel Berrigan, priest, poet, prisoner of the Vietnam era, was arrested for demonstrating at the Pentagon, and he asked the judge to go into the files of the Department of Defense to see if indeed the protesters were not telling the truth, that "the greatest crime in the history of humanity is being planned there; a conspiracy to hiroshimize every city of the world, to pulverize and vaporize all flesh and bones, to declare the human adventure a cul de sac, all history null and void."

Berrigan asked the judge to look at the evidence in the Pentagon:

And your discovery of evidence, your judicial protest, would sound like the crack of doom. You would be heard, when we are not heard. You would reveal a great crime. You would save lives. You would also restore a degraded judiciary. . . .

You give the nod to murder when the commanders may, again and again, hand us over to you, knowing their enterprise is secure and ours, to say the least, in jeopardy.

You give the nod to murder by honoring the presumption of American authority; the presumption of innocence in high crime, and presumption of guilt in civil disobedience.

You give the nod to murder finally, by sticking to the letter of the law. The letter of this law, quite literally, kills. It will kill you, as it will kill all those who bow to it, countenance it, obey it. It will sweep you into an awesome conspiracy, will add your name to the blueprint of the mad engineers; a blueprint now being drawn up in our judicial district. The blueprint is marked "Last Day."

The antiwar movement was not quite dead, even in the absence of a visible war. An organization called Mobilization for Survival was formed, and branches sprang up around the country to draw attention to the threat of the arms race, of nuclear war, of militarization of the country and neglect of human life. In 1978, twenty thousand people gathered at the United Nations to protest the squandering of human resources and the immense danger of the arms race.

A general worry was developing over the proliferation of nuclear energy plants around the country. The plants were set up, the official word was, to meet the energy shortage. But there were questions about the extent to which the shortage was artificial, created by the corporate energy interests, and how much profit was behind the enthusiasm for nuclear plants. There had been accidents at such plants, so far small, but ominous. And, despite strenuous efforts, no scientific team had been able to come up with a sure solution for the disposal of the wastes from these plants, which were horrifying in their effects. Plutonium, of which microscopic amounts could be deadly to great numbers of people, left poisonous wastes alive for 250,000 years.

Protests multiplied. In 1977, at a nuclear plant in Seabrook, New Hampshire, two thousand well-organized protesters occupied the site. Fourteen hundred were arrested, and the news went around the world.

The following year, sixteen thousand people demonstrated at the same site. Other plants around the country were picketed and became the scenes of protest actions. After a serious and frightening accident at the Three Mile Island nuclear plant in mid-Pennsylvania, there was a wave of fear throughout the country, and an antinuclear rally in Washington drew 100,000 people. Clearly there was more to come in the struggle over nuclear plants.

But what did all this add up to? There was no national movement comparable to those of the thirties and the sixties. It was a time when the Establishment was drawing on all its resources to restore the system, enough to keep the country quiet and obedient. And yet, there were thousands of seeds and shoots of rebellion all around. Was it all an endless cycle of control and rebellion and more control and more rebellion—or was something changing? In the past, aggrieved groups had been set against one another, preventing that unity which was necessary to combat the power of the elite. Was there a new possibility, now, for such unity?

There may have been a clue—when the priest said to the judge, about the arms race: "It will kill you too."

10.
The Coming Revolt of the Guards

The title of this chapter is not a prediction, but a hope, which I will soon explain.

As for the title of this book, it is not quite accurate; a "people's history" promises more than any one person can fulfill, and it is the most difficult kind of history to recapture. I call it that anyway because, with all its limitations, it is a history disrespectful of governments and respectful of people's movements of resistance.

That makes it a biased account, one that leans in a certain direction. I am not troubled by that, because the mountain of history books under which we all stand leans so heavily in the other direction—so tremblingly respectful of states and statesmen and so disrespectful, by inattention, to people's movements—that we need some counterforce to avoid being crushed into submission.

All those histories of this country centered on the Founding Fathers and the Presidents weigh oppressively on the capacity of the ordinary citizen to act. They suggest that in times of crisis we must look to someone to save us: in the Revolutionary crisis, the Founding Fathers; in the slavery crisis, Lincoln; in the Depression, Roosevelt; in the Vietnam-Watergate crisis, Carter. And that between occasional crises everything is all right, and it is sufficient for us to be restored to that normal state. They teach us that the supreme act of citizenship is to choose among saviors, by going into a voting booth every four years to choose between two white and well-off Anglo-Saxon males of inoffensive personality and orthodox opinions.

The idea of saviors has been built into the entire culture, beyond politics. We have learned to look to stars, leaders, experts in every field, thus surrendering our own strength, demeaning our own ability, obliterating our own selves. But from time to time, Americans reject that idea and rebel.

These rebellions, so far, have been contained. The American system is the most ingenious system of control in world history. With a country so rich in natural resources, talent, and labor power the system can afford to distribute just enough wealth to just enough people to limit discontent to a troublesome minority. It is a country so powerful, so big, so pleasing to so many of its citizens that it can afford to give freedom of dissent to the small number who are not pleased.

There is no system of control with more openings, apertures, leeways, flexibilities, rewards for the chosen, winning tickets in lotteries. There is none that disperses its controls more complexly through the voting system, the work situation, the church, the family, the school, the mass media—none more successful in mollifying opposition with reforms, isolating people from one another, creating patriotic loyalty.

One percent of the nation owns a third of the wealth. The rest of the wealth is distributed in such a way as to turn those in the 99 percent against one another: small property owners against the property-less, black against white, native-born against foreign-born, intellectuals and professionals against the uneducated and unskilled. These groups have resented one another and warred against one another with such vehemence and violence as to obscure their common position as sharers of leftovers in a very wealthy country.

Against the reality of that desperate, bitter battle for resources made scarce by elite control, I am taking the liberty of uniting those 99 percent as "the people." I have been writing a history that attempts to represent their submerged, deflected, common interest. To emphasize the commonality of the 99 percent, to declare deep enmity of interest with the 1 percent, is to do exactly what the governments of the United States, and the wealthy elite allied to them—from the Founding Fathers to now—have tried their best to prevent. Madison feared a "majority faction" and hoped the new Constitution would control it. He and his colleagues began the Preamble to the Constitution with the words "We the people . . . ," pretending that the new government stood for everyone, and hoping that this myth, accepted as fact, would ensure "domestic tranquillity."

The pretense continued over the generations, helped by all-embracing symbols, physical or verbal: the flag, patriotism, democracy, national interest, national defense, national security. The slogans were dug into the earth of American culture like a circle of covered wagons on the western plain, from inside of which the white, slightly privileged American could shoot to kill the enemy outside—Indians or blacks or foreigners or other whites too wretched to be allowed inside the circle. The managers of the caravan watched at a safe distance, and when the battle was over and the field strewn with dead on both sides, they would take over the land, and prepare another expedition, for another territory.

The scheme never worked perfectly. The Revolution and the Constitution, trying to bring stability by containing the class angers of the colonial period—while enslaving blacks, annihilating or displacing Indians—did not quite succeed, judging by the tenant uprisings, the slave revolts, the abolitionist agitation, the feminist upsurge, the Indian guerrilla warfare of the pre–Civil War years. After the Civil War, a new coalition of southern and northern elites developed, with southern whites and blacks of the lower classes occupied in racial conflict, native workers and immigrant workers clashing in the North, and the farmers dispersed over a big country, while the system of capitalism consolidated itself in industry and government. But there came rebellion among industrial workers and a great opposition movement among farmers.

At the turn of the century, the violent pacification of blacks and Indians and the use of elections and war to absorb and divert white rebels were not enough, in the conditions of modern industry, to prevent the great upsurge of socialism, the massive labor struggles, before the First World War. Neither that war nor the partial prosperity of the twenties, nor the apparent destruction of the socialist movement, could prevent, in the situation of economic crisis, another radical awakening, another labor upsurge in the thirties.

World War II created a new unity, followed by an apparently successful attempt, in the atmosphere of the cold war, to extinguish the strong radical temper of the war years. But then, surprisingly, came the surge of the sixties, from people thought long subdued or put out of sight—blacks, women, Native Americans, prisoners, soldiers—and a new radicalism, which threatened to spread widely in a population disillusioned by the Vietnam war and the politics of Watergate.

The exile of Nixon, the celebration of the Bicentennial, the presidency of Carter, all aimed at restoration. But though the great tide of the sixties had receded, it left on the beach millions of moving organisms, pockets of energy, in an atmosphere calmed down, but electric with possibility.

In this uncertain situation of the seventies, going into the eighties, it is very important for the Establishment—that uneasy club of business executives, generals, and politicos—to maintain the historic pretension of national unity, in which the government represents all the people, and the common enemy is overseas, not at home, where disasters of economics or war are unfortunate errors or tragic accidents, to be corrected by the members of the same club that brought the disasters. It is important also to make sure this artificial unity of highly privileged and slightly privileged is the only unity—that the 99 percent remain split in countless ways, and turn against one another to vent their angers.

How skillful to tax the middle class to pay for the relief of the poor, building resentment on top of humiliation! How adroit to bus poor black youngsters into poor white neighborhoods, in a violent exchange of impoverished schools, while the schools of the rich remain untouched and the wealth of the nation, doled out carefully where children need free milk, is drained for billion-dollar aircraft carriers. How ingenious to meet the demands of blacks and women for equality by giving them small special benefits, and setting them in competition with everyone else for jobs made scarce by an irrational, wasteful system. How wise to turn the fear and anger of the majority toward a class of criminals bred—by economic inequity—faster than they can be put away, deflecting attention from the huge thefts of national resources carried out within the law by men in executive offices.

But with all the controls of power and punishment, enticements and concessions, diversions and decoys, operating throughout the history of the country, the Establishment has been unable to keep itself secure from revolt. Every time it looked as if it had succeeded, the very people it thought seduced or subdued, stirred and rose. Blacks, cajoled by Supreme Court decisions and congressional statutes, rebelled. Women, wooed and ignored, romanticized and mistreated, rebelled. Indians, thought dead, reappeared, defiant. Young people, despite lures of career and comfort, defected. Working people, thought soothed by reforms, regulated by law, kept within bounds by their own unions, went on strike. Government intellectuals, pledged to secrecy, began giving away secrets. Priests turned from piety to protest. Prisoners, isolated in cages, organized.

To recall this is to remind people of what the Establishment would like them to forget—the enormous capacity of apparently helpless people to resist, of apparently contented people to demand change. To uncover such history is to find a powerful human impulse to assert one's humanity. It is to hold out, even in times of deep pessimism, the possibility of surprise.

True, to overestimate class consciousness, to exaggerate rebellion and its successes, would be misleading. It would not account for the fact that the world—not just the United States, but everywhere else—

is still in the hands of the elites, that people's movements, although they show an infinite capacity for recurrence, have so far been either defeated or absorbed or perverted, that "socialist" revolutionists have betrayed socialism, that nationalist revolutions have led to new dictatorships.

But most histories understate revolt, overemphasize statesmanship, and thus encourage impotency among citizens. When we look closely at resistance movements, or even at isolated forms of rebellion, we discover that class consciousness, or any other awareness of injustice, has multiple levels. It has many ways of expression, many ways of revealing itself—open, subtle, direct, distorted. In a system of intimidation and control, people do not show how much they know, how deeply they feel, until their practical sense informs them they can do so without being destroyed.

History which keeps alive the memory of people's resistance suggests new definitions of power. By traditional definitions, whoever possesses military strength, wealth, command of official ideology, cultural control, has power. Measured by these standards, popular rebellion never looks strong enough to survive.

However, the unexpected victories—even temporary ones—of insurgents show the vulnerability of the supposedly powerful. In a highly developed society, the Establishment cannot survive without the obedience and loyalty of millions of people who are given small rewards to keep the system going: the soldiers and police, teachers and ministers, administrators and social workers, technicians and production workers, doctors, lawyers, nurses, transport and communications workers, garbagemen and firemen. These people—the employed, the somewhat privileged—are drawn into alliance with the elite. They become the guards of the system, buffers between the upper and lower classes. If they stop obeying, the system falls.

That will happen, I think, only when all of us who are slightly privileged and slightly uneasy begin to see that we are like the guards in the prison uprising at Attica—expendable; that the Establishment, whatever rewards it gives us, will also, if necessary to maintain its control, kill us.

Certain new facts may, in our time, emerge so clearly as to lead to general withdrawal of loyalty from the system. The new conditions of technology, economics, and war, in the atomic age, make it less and less possible for the guards of the system—the intellectuals, the home owners, the taxpayers, the skilled workers, the professionals, the servants of government—to remain immune from the violence (physical and psychic) inflicted on the black, the poor, the criminal, the enemy overseas.

All of us have become hostages in the new conditions of doomsday technology, runaway economics, global poisoning, uncontainable war. The atomic weapons, the invisible radiations, the economic anarchy, do not distinguish prisoners from guards, and those in charge will not be scrupulous in making distinctions. There is the unforgettable response of the U.S. high command to the news that American prisoners of war might be near Nagasaki: "Targets previously assigned for Center-board remain unchanged."

There is evidence of growing dissatisfaction among the guards. It had been shown in the early 1960s (Murray Levin, *The Alienated Voter*) that the poor and ignored were the nonvoters, alienated from a political system they felt didn't care about them, and about which they could do little. In the mid-seventies, another study (Donald Warren, *The Radical Center*) found that alienation has spread upward into families above the poverty line. These are white workers, neither rich nor poor, but angry over economic insecurity, unhappy with their work, worried about their neighborhoods, hostile to government—combining elements of racism with elements of class consciousness, contempt for the lower classes along with distrust for the elite, and thus open to solutions from any direction, right or left.

In the twenties, there was a similar estrangement in the middle classes, which could have gone in various directions—the Ku Klux Klan had millions of members at that time—but the work of an organized left wing mobilized a huge amount of this feeling into trade unions, farmers' unions, socialist movements. We may, in the next decade, be in a race for the mobilization of middle-class discontent.

The fact of that discontent is clear. When the surveys of the early seventies showed 70 percent and 80 percent of Americans distrustful of government, business, the military, it meant that this feeling went beyond blacks, the poor, the radicals. It had spread among skilled workers, white-collar workers, professionals; for the first time in the nation's history, perhaps, both the lower classes and the middle classes, the prisoners and the guards, were disillusioned with the system.

There are other signs: the high rate of alcoholism, the high rate of divorce (from one of three marriages ending in divorce, the figure was climbing to one of two), of drug use and abuse, of nervous break-downs and mental illness. Millions of people have been looking desperately for solutions to their sense of impotency, their loneliness, their frustration, their estrangement from other people, from the world, from their work, from themselves. They have been adopting new religions, joining self-help groups of all kinds. It is as if a whole nation were going through a critical point in its middle age, a life crisis of self-doubt, self-examination.

All this, at a time when the middle class is increasingly insecure economically. The system, in its irrationality, has been driven by profit to build steel skyscrapers for insurance companies while the cities decay, to spend billions for weapons of destruction and virtually nothing for children's playgrounds, to give huge incomes to men who make dangerous or useless things, and very little to artists, musicians, writers, actors. Capitalism has always been a failure for the lower classes. It is now beginning to fail for the middle classes.

The threat of unemployment, always inside the homes of the poor, has spread to white-collar workers, professionals. A college education is no longer a guarantee against joblessness, and a system that cannot offer a future to the young coming out of school is in deep trouble. If it happens only to the children of the poor, the problem is manageable; there are the jails. If it happens to the children of the middle class, things may get out of hand.

The poor are accustomed to being squeezed and always short of money, but in recent years the middle classes, too, have begun to feel the press of high prices, high taxes. In the mid-seventies, the property of the average homeowner in Boston was assessed at about 32 percent of its value, while downtown, the National Shawmut Bank of Boston was assessed at 6.9 percent of its value, the First National Bank Building at 8.7 percent. A new group called Fair Share was calling attention to this. A new publication called *Dollars and Sense* was printing the figures. Would taxpayers, whose anger had always been shunted onto welfare recipients, begin to see that their incomes were being dismembered to subsidize welfare payments for the rich?

In the sixties and seventies, there was a dramatic, frightening increase in the number of crimes. It was not hard to understand, when one walked through any big city. There were the contrasts of wealth and poverty, the culture of possession, the frantic advertising. There was the fierce economic competition, in which the legal violence of the state, and the legal robbery of the corporation, led to the illegal crimes of the poor. Most crimes by far involved theft. In the year 1978, 50 percent of prisoners in American jails were black, 31 percent had been unemployed in the month prior to their arrest, 60 percent had earned less than $6,000 in the year prior to their arrest.

The most common and most publicized crimes have been the violent crimes of the young, the poor—a virtual terrorization in the big cities—in which the desperate or drug-addicted attack and rob the middle class, or even their fellow poor. A society so stratified by wealth and education lends itself naturally to envy and class anger.

The critical question in our time is whether the middle classes, so long led to believe that the solution for such crimes is more jails and more jail terms, may begin to see, by the sheer uncontrollability of crime, that the only prospect is an endless cycle of crime and punishment. They might then conclude that physical security for a working person in the city can come only when everyone in the city is working. And that would require a transformation of national priorities, a change in the system.

In the seventies, the fear of criminal assault was joined by an even greater fear. Deaths from cancer began to multiply, and medical researchers seemed helpless to find the cause. It began to be evident that more and more of these deaths were coming from an environment poisoned by military experimentation and industrial greed. The water people drank, the air they breathed, the particles of dust from the buildings in which they worked, had been quietly contaminated over the years by a system so frantic for growth and profit that the safety and health of human beings had been ignored.

A woman in the town of Globe, Arizona, stepped outside her bedroom door one morning in the summer of 1969 and was covered with spray mist from a Forest Service helicopter spraying pesticides in a nearby national forest. She began to investigate, found plants and fruit trees dying nearby, and organized local people in a mock funeral procession carrying the dead plants to the forest supervisor's office. Later she wrote a book called *Sue the Bastards!* But there were limits to what lawsuits could do, what books could do, to poison sprays. In early 1977 she died of cancer, and doctors found herbicides in her body tissue.

The problem of pesticides in the air, of asbestos in buildings, of lead paint on walls, of plutonium in the earth, of industrial wastes in drinking water, is a problem beyond class, race, sex. It could unite people of all classes and groups in fury against those few in the Establishment who, in their demonic pursuit of more weapons, more profits, keep insisting (like the Nuclear Regulatory Commission, like the tobacco companies, like Hoover in 1932 and Lyndon Johnson in the Vietnam war) that everything is all right.

Technology was running wild, and one of its effects, more subtle than radiation poisoning, was fearsome in its own way: there was a growing dependence on computers to replace human thought. An M.I.T. pioneer in computer building, Joseph Weizenbaum, sounded the alarm against the perversion of his own field, in his book *Computer Power and Human Reason*. People were attributing too much wisdom, he said, to science, whose knowledge is not certain. They were giving frightening power to machines, replacing human judgment. The deification of computers was a rejection of direct experience, a replacement of human sensitivity by mechanical devices. What Weizenbaum described has effects on the whole human race, not just one social group. People of all kinds, seeing this, might join to reassert the importance of the living being.

This scary technology, and more, has been adopted by the military. Modern war now means not only the indiscriminate killing of "the enemy"—civilians as well as soldiers, as in World War II, Korea, Vietnam—but the use of weapons that kill friend and foe alike. A tiny group of military planners can launch attacks that will destroy not only "enemy" populations but their own. The people of the United States, the people of the Soviet Union, indeed the population of the world, are at the mercy of a few leaders of the superpowers, who may decide, for their own reasons of strategy, power, or pride, to start the chain of nuclear detonations—or may start it without even deciding.

Small experiences of the recent past suggest larger horrors for the future. In 1976, a book named *Friendly Fire* (by C. D. B. Bryan) told of a U.S. infantryman in Vietnam who was reported to have died on a "noncombat" mission. His parents, grief-stricken and puzzled, investigated. They found the government uncooperative, cold, anxious to minimize and obscure what had happened. What had happened was that their son was killed by "friendly fire," a misdirected artillery shell. The parents turned from quiet residents of Black Hawk County, Iowa, to angry, active opponents of the Vietnam war. The war that was supposed to kill "the enemy" had killed their son. In another war, we may all be killed by "friendly fire."

During the military operations in Vietnam, 20,000 tons of herbicides were dropped by U.S. planes on 5 million acres of the Vietnamese countryside, destroying trees and crops. Among Vietnamese mothers in those areas, birth defects developed in unusual numbers. In 1978 a woman named Claude de Victor, working for the Veterans Administration hospital in Chicago, began to see a pattern of disease and death among former helicopter pilots. Some told of birth defects in babies born to their wives. When she reported this, she was transferred to another job. But shortly after that, a one-paragraph item from Washington appeared on an inside page of the Boston *Globe:*

The Veterans Administration warned its offices across the country yesterday to watch for after-effects among veterans of the Vietnam defoliant "Agent Orange," which some researchers suspect of possible links with cancer or genetic defects. Thousands of veterans were exposed to Orange, the most effective and heavily used of various defoliation compounds of which more than 100 million pounds were sprayed over one-seventh of South Vietnam's land area between 1962 and 1971.

Perhaps much of the general distrust of government reported in recent years comes from a growing recognition of the truth of what the U.S. Air Force bombardier Yossarian said in the novel *Catch-22* to a friend who had just accused him of giving aid and comfort to the enemy: "The enemy is anybody who's going to get you killed, no matter which side he's on. And don't you forget that, because the longer you remember it the longer you might live." The next line in the novel is: "But Clevinger did forget, and now he was dead."

In the late seventies, the American system seemed out of control— a runaway capitalism, a runaway technology, a runaway militarism, a runaway of government from the people it claimed to represent. Crime was out of control, cancer was out of control. Prices and taxes and unemployment were out of control. Auto accidents, the decay of cities, and the breakup of families were out of control. The nuclear arms race was out of control. And people seemed to sense all this.

Let us imagine the prospect—for the first time in the nation's history—of a population united for fundamental change. Would the elite turn as so often before, to its ultimate weapon—foreign intervention—to unite the people with the Establishment, in war? Here, too, the situation may be different today. The defeat of the colossal U.S. military machine in Vietnam was a turning point; the American Empire may have reached its limits, and must now retreat, recognizing that human beings abroad, if determined enough to rebel against harsh regimes, cannot be defeated even with the most terrible of weapons. Ordinary weapons may be not enough—and nuclear weapons too much— to deal with popular revolutions. And Americans may no longer go along with military intervention.

In the late seventies, there was growing evidence of U.S. impotence in the world arena. It could not stop, in 1979, a popular revolution in Iran, where in the past the CIA had its way. And in the same year in Nicaragua, the very dynasty installed by U.S. Marines before World War II was toppled by a revolutionary army, and the U.S. government seemed unable to prevent this.

With the Establishment's inability either to solve severe economic problems at home or to manufacture abroad a safety valve for domestic discontent, Americans might be ready to demand not just more tinkering, more reform laws, another reshuffling of the same deck, another New Deal, but radical change. Let us be utopian for a moment so that when we get realistic again it is not that "realism" so useful to the Establishment in its discouragement of action, that "realism" anchored to a certain kind of history empty of surprise. Let us imagine what radical change would require of us all.

The society's levers of powers would have to be taken away from those whose drives have led to the present state—the giant corporations, the military, and their politician collaborators. We would need—by a coordinated effort of local groups all over the country—to reconstruct the economy for both efficiency and justice, producing in a cooperative way what people need most. We would start on our neighborhoods, our cities, our workplaces. Work of some kind would be needed by everyone, including people now kept out of the work force—children, old people, "handicapped" people. Society could use the enormous energy now idle; the skills and talents now unused. Everyone could share the routine but necessary jobs for a few hours a day, and leave most of the time free for enjoyment, creativity, labors of love, and yet produce enough for an equal and ample distribution of goods. Certain basic things would be abundant enough to be taken out of the money system and be available—free—to everyone: food, housing, health care, education, transportation.

The great problem would be to work out a way of accomplishing this without a centralized bureaucracy, using not the incentives of prison and punishment, but those incentives of cooperation which spring from natural human desires, which in the past have been used by the state in times of war, but also by social movements that gave hints of how people might behave in different conditions. Decisions would be made by small groups of people in their workplaces, their neighborhoods—a network of cooperatives, in communication with one another, a neighborly socialism avoiding the class hierarchies of capitalism and the harsh dictatorships that have taken the name "socialist."

People with time, in friendly communities, might create a new, diversified, nonviolent culture, in which all forms of personal and group expression would be possible. Men and women, black and white, old and young, could then cherish their differences as positive attributes, not as reasons for domination. New values of cooperation and freedom might then show up in the relations of people, the upbringing of children.

To do all that, in the complex conditions of control in the United States, would require combining the energy of all previous movements in American history—of labor insurgents, black rebels, Native Americans, women, young people—along with the new energy of an angry middle class. People would need to begin to transform their immediate environments—the workplace, the family, the school, the community—by a series of struggles against absentee authority, to give control of these places to the people who live and work there.

These struggles would involve all the tactics used at various times in the past by people's movements: demonstrations, marches, civil disobedience; strikes and boycotts and general strikes; direct action to redistribute wealth, to reconstruct institutions, to revamp relationships; creating—in music, literature, drama, all the arts, and all the areas of work and play in everyday life—a new culture of sharing, of respect, a new joy in the collaboration of people to help themselves and one another.

There would be many defeats. But when such a movement took hold in hundreds of thousands of places all over the country it would be impossible to suppress, because the very guards the system depends on to crush such a movement would be among the rebels. It would be a new kind of revolution, the only kind that could happen, I believe, in a country like the United States. It would take enormous energy, sacrifice, commitment, patience. But because it would be a process over time, starting without delay, there would be the immediate satisfactions that people have always found in the affectionate ties of groups striving together for a common goal.

All this takes us far from American history, into the realm of imagination. But not totally removed from history. There are at least glimpses in the past of such a possibility. In the sixties and seventies, for the first time, the Establishment failed to produce national unity and patriotic fervor in a war. There was a flood of cultural changes such as the country had never seen—in sex, family, personal relations—exactly those situations most difficult to control from the ordinary centers of power. And never before was there such a general withdrawal of confidence from so many elements of the political and economic system. In every period of history, people have found ways to help one another—even in the midst of a culture of competition and violence—if only for brief periods, to find joy in work, struggle, companionship, nature.

The prospect is for times of turmoil, struggle, but also inspiration. There is a chance that such a movement could succeed in doing what the system itself has never done—bring about great change with little violence. This is possible because the more of the 99 percent that begin to see themselves as sharing needs, the more the guards and the prisoners see their common interest, the more the Establishment becomes isolated, ineffectual. The elite's weapons, money, control of information would be useless in the face of a determined population. The servants of the system would refuse to work to continue the old, deadly order, and would begin using their time, their space—the very things given them by the system to keep them quiet—to dismantle that system while creating a new one.

The prisoners of the system will continue to rebel, as before, in ways that cannot be foreseen, at times that cannot be predicted. The new fact of our era is the chance that they may be joined by the guards. We readers and writers of books have been, for the most part, among the guards. If we understand that, and act on it, not only will life be more satisfying, right off, but our grandchildren, or our great grandchildren, might possibly see a different and marvelous world.

11.
The Challenge of 1984

Did the people of the United States elect Ronald Reagan as President in 1980? There is no clear-cut answer to that. He won by the barest of majorities, getting 50.7 percent of the votes, while outgoing President Jimmy Carter received 41 percent of the popular vote and John Anderson (a liberal Republican running on a third-party ticket) received 8.2 percent. Only 54 percent of the voting-age population voted, so that, of the total who were eligible to vote, 27 percent voted for Reagan, while a much higher percentage (46 percent) did not vote at all.

Thus, the largest party in the election, by far, was what political scientist and elections specialist Walter Dean Burnham calls "the party of non-voters." It is the poor who have been the non-voters in America, the alienated and hopeless, and in 1980, once again, they could find no party in the election to represent their interests. For instance, three million blacks who voted in the 1976 elections did not vote in 1980.

Even those Americans who voted saw no "important differences" between the candidates and parties, according to a *New York Times* survey. The largest percentage of these (38 percent) told the *Times* that they voted for Reagan because "it is time for a change"; only 11 percent said their main reason was that "he's a real conservative." The Republican victory (which also gave them control of the Senate and many more Republicans in the House of Representatives) represented, according to Burnham's study of the election, not enthusiasm for Reagan but "a more pervasive and intense public discontent than anything seen in modern years."

Carter had entered the White House after the deep public disillusionment with American politics that came out of the Vietnam war and the Watergate affair. Distrust of business and government was high. Yet his presidency clearly failed to restore confidence in the American system, it is evident from an examination of his last years (1978–1980) in office.

Carter inherited the inflation of prices caused by heavy spending for the war in Vietnam. This was part of a general growth in the military budget since 1950, and enormous military expenses are not healthy for any economy because they use up huge labor and capital resources without satisfying any basic human need. Dollars are poured into the economy, but faster than the growth of goods people can buy—so prices go up. And in 1973, the Arab oil countries tripled the price of oil imported by the United States, and because energy costs had become so basic to all production, this led to general high prices.

From 1950 to 1965 the annual rate of inflation averaged 1.8 percent. After 1973, prices rose so fast that by 1979 inflation was at 13 percent. Orthodox economic theory said that if prices rose, the economy would become more productive and employment would grow. But just the opposite happened: prices rose, productivity kept declining, and this combination of inflation and stagnation became known as stagflation.

By 1980, the economy did not seem to be growing at all. The steel industry was functioning at a fraction of its capacity, apparently unable to afford new equipment; it was inefficient compared to Japanese steel-making. Between 1973 and 1978 steel production actually declined. And the auto industry could not compete with foreign cars in quality and efficiency.

Jimmy Carter became desperate in 1979, with the approach of an election year, as unemployment and inflation, along with his unpopularity, rose quickly. He might have tried bold approaches—controlling prices, having the government act to create full employment, cutting military spending and building the economy through civilian projects. But he would not even support a strong Full Employment Bill (to create publicly financed jobs), which was passed finally by Congress in meaningless form. Against his own campaign promises, he held to a rising military budget, thus making it impossible to devote great sums to help the poor.

Carter appointed a conservative, Paul Volcker, to head the Federal Reserve System (the superbank of the country), and Volcker promptly raised the System's interest rates to the highest point in postwar history. Higher interest rates made it difficult for businesses to invest and grow. They laid off workers. In October 1979, unemployment was 6 percent of the labor force. A year later it was 7.7 percent, and going up. Thus, the economy was in trouble, and Carter, running for election, was in trouble.

In 1979, as Carter weakly proposed benefits for the poor, and Congress strongly turned them down, a black woman, Marian Wright Edelman, director of the Children's Defense Fund in Washington, pointed to some facts. One of every seven American children (10 million altogether) had no known regular source of primary health care. One of every three children under seventeen (18 million altogether) had never seen a dentist. In an article on the *New York Times* op-ed page, she wrote:

> The Senate Budget Committee recently . . . knocked off $88 million from a modest $288 million Administration request to improve the program that screens and treats children's health problems. At the same time the Senate found $725 million to bail out Litton Industries and to hand to the Navy at least two destroyers ordered by the Shah of Iran. . . .

In the last months of the Carter administration, a report to the President and Congress by the National Advisory Council on Economic Opportunity found that 25 million Americans were living in poverty (defined as below an annual income of $7,450 for a nonfarm family of four) and "another 40 million are near poor, so that one-third of our citizens are materially deprived." The report also pointed out that while the number of poor people declined in the 1960s as a result of the new social programs under the Johnson administration, it remained quite constant during the 1970s. The shallowness of Carter's concern for the poor was shown when the Democrat-controlled Congress cut off Medicare payments to help poor women pay for abortions and Carter, asked if that was fair, replied (echoing John Kennedy), "Life isn't fair."

Carter made some efforts to hold on to social programs, but this was undermined by his very large military budgets. Further, he approved tax "reforms" which benefited mainly the corporations. Economist Robert Lekachman, writing in *The Nation,* noted the sharp increase in corporate profits (44 percent) in the last quarter of 1978 over the previous year's last quarter. He wrote: "Perhaps the President's most outrageous act occurred last November when he signed into law an $18 billion tax reduction, the bulk of whose benefits accrue to affluent individuals and corporations."

In 1979, while the poor were taking cuts, the salary of the chairman of Exxon Oil was being raised to $830,000 a year, and that of the chairman of Mobil Oil to over a million dollars a year. That year, while Exxon's net income rose 56 percent to over $4 billion, three thousand small independent gasoline stations went out of business. In the summer of 1980, the financial writer of the *New York Times* reported on the legislation for "windfall taxes"—to tax the huge extra profits the oil companies would make after the Carter administration deregulated oil prices:

> Recent rumors that the oil industry had lost a serious measure of its awesome influence in Congress appear, like reports of Mark Twain's death, to be greatly exaggerated. . . . the bill that cleared the House last week contained provisions that recaptured for the oil companies an estimated $12.4 billion. . . .

Thus, as his term was coming to an end, with consumer prices and unemployment both going up quickly, Carter did not seem capable of taking action bold enough to change the basic troubles of the economic system, which went much deeper than the price of oil. He was unwilling to curb corporate power and military dominance of the economy, though he had been elected by large numbers of black and white working-class and middle-class people. And as American world power diminished even further during his presidency—a leftist revolution overthrowing the U.S.-supported Somoza dictatorship in Nicaragua in 1979, a revolution against the U.S.-supported Shah in Iran the same year—he turned more and more to military solutions, which then put even more strain on the economy.

Thus, violating his campaign pledges, Carter increased the military budget. During the 1976 presidential campaign Carter had written the Democratic Platform Committee: "Without endangering the defense of our nation or our commitments to our allies, we can reduce present defense expenditures by $5 billion to $7 billion annually." But he proposed in 1980 that the U.S. spend a thousand billion dollars (a trillion dollars) in the next five years on its military forces. His Department of Defense Budget for 1981 included $16.5 billion for research and development of new weapons, including the MX (Missile X), a bizarre system of 200 missile-launchers, each carrying ten thermonuclear warheads, which were to be moved around continually among 2,400 empty silos to deceive the Russians. The money allocated for the MX was calculated by economist Emma Rothschild of M.I.T. to be more than the combined research and development budgets for the Departments of Labor, Education, and Transportation, the Federal Drug Administration, and the Centers for Disease Control.

The computerizing of nuclear defense systems was creating danger of hair-trigger alerts. In June of 1980, there were two false alarms of a Soviet nuclear attack, and in one case 100 B-52s with nuclear weapons were prepared to fly toward Soviet targets before the failure in the computer system was discovered (a malfunction in a tiny electronic circuit worth 46 cents). In one and a half years, there had been 147 false nuclear attack warnings. The Associated Press quoted a Pentagon official as saying that, in general, the system worked: ". . . the principal exception occurs in crisis situations." By 1980, the Defense Department acknowledged, for the first time, that twenty-seven nuclear accidents (called Broken Arrows) had taken place since 1950; that year, a nine-megaton warhead (its power equivalent to five hundred Hiroshima-type bombs) was accidentally ejected from a Titan II missile site, killing one person and wounding others.

The Soviet invasion of Afghanistan in 1979 created more public support for Carter's increasingly tough and militaristic policies. In fact, the U.S. could not do anything about the invasion of Afghanistan, beyond a feeble call to boycott the Olympic Games in Moscow. But it could use the invasion to justify aid to dictatorial regimes battling left-wing rebels.

A report by the Carter administration to Congress in July 1977 had said that "a number of countries with deplorable records of human rights observance are also countries where we have important security and foreign policy interests." El Salvador, the Philippines, Nicaragua, Iran were among these. Thus, Carter asked Congress in the spring of 1980 for $5.7 million in credits for the military junta fighting off a rebellion in El Salvador. In the Philippines, after the 1978 National Assembly elections, President Marcos imprisoned ten of the twenty-one opposition candidates; many prisoners were tortured, many civilians were killed. Still, Carter urged Congress to give Marcos $300 million in military aid for the next five years.

The U.S. had helped maintain the Somoza dictatorship in Nicaragua for decades. On the eve of the left-wing revolution there, the *New York Times* correspondent wrote that "as the political situation became steadily more polarized last summer, Washington appeared to operate on the assumption that General Somoza was in full control of the country. . . . But Washington apparently misread . . . the pace and shape of events in Nicaragua."

In Iran, toward the end of 1978, the long years of resentment against the Shah's dictatorship culminated in mass demonstrations. On September 8, 1978, hundreds of demonstrators were massacred by the Shah's troops, and on the next day (according to a UPI dispatch from Teheran), Carter affirmed his support for the Shah:

Troops opened fire on demonstrators against the Shah for the third straight day yesterday and President Jimmy Carter telephoned the royal palace to express support for Shah Mohammed Reza Pahlevi, who faced the worst crisis of his 37 year reign.

Nine members of parliament walked out on a speech by Iran's new premier, shouting that his hands were "stained with blood" in the crackdown on conservative Moslems and other protesters.

On December 13, 1978, Nicholas Gage reported for the *New York Times:*

The staff of the United States Embassy here has been bolstered by dozens of specialists flown in to back an effort to help the Shah against a growing challenge to his rule, according to embassy sources. . . .

The new arrivals, according to the embassy sources, include a number of Central Intelligence Agency specialists on Iran, in addition to diplomats and military personnel.

In early 1979, as the crisis in Iran was intensifying, the former chief analyst on Iran for the CIA told *New York Times* reporter Seymour Hersh "that he and his colleagues knew of the tortures of Iranian dissenters by Savak, the Iranian secret police set up during the late 1950's by the Shah with help from the C.I.A. Furthermore, the 38-year old Mr. Leaf said, a senior C.I.A. official was involved in instructing officials in Savak on torture techniques, although Mr. Leaf said that to his knowledge no Americans did any of the torturing. The C.I.A.'s torture seminars, Mr. Leaf said, 'were based on German torture techniques from World War II.' "

Enormous demonstrations in Iran in the summer of 1979 became too much for the Shah's military to handle. The revolutionaries were successful; the Shah fled, and when the United States accepted him into the country, presumably for medical treatment, the anti-American feelings of the revolutionaries in Iran reached a high point. On November 4, 1979, the U.S. embassy was taken over by student militants, with fifty-two embassy employees held hostage, and the demand made that the Shah be returned to Iran for punishment.

For the next fourteen months, with the hostages still held in the embassy compound, that issue took the forefront of foreign news in the United States and aroused powerful nationalist feelings. When Carter responded by ordering the Immigration Service to start deportation proceedings against Iranian students who lacked valid visas, the *New York Times* gave cautious but clear approval. By spring, patriotic tempers were flaring. One Connecticut resident wrote to the *Times* that the President should, in accord with the Alien Enemy Act, "issue a proclamation that all Iranian citizens now residing in the United States should be arrested forthwith" and those "in sympathy with the present policies of the Iranian Government" be put in "alien enemy camps" until the hostages were freed. Bumper stickers began to appear on autos all over the country: "Bomb Iran."

It was a rare journalist bold enough to point out, as Alan Richman of the Boston *Globe* did when the fifty-two were released alive and apparently well, that there was a certain lack of proportion in American reactions to this and other violations of human rights: "There were 52 of them, a number easy to comprehend. It wasn't like 15,000 innocent people permanently disappearing in Argentina. . . . They spoke our language. There were 3000 people summarily shot in Guatemala last year who did not."

In a March 23, 1980, editorial entitled "Poor America," the *New York Times* said that Jimmy Carter and Ronald Reagan, beginning their presidential campaigns, were ignoring an important reality.

The neglected reality is American weakness. . . . Rich as it is, it cannot afford the material and political ambitions, commitments and values that it embraced a generation ago. The Russians are no longer easily contained because they have matched America in military power. Allies are turning into rivals because some have overtaken America in both productive power and energy dependence. The rest of the world is no longer easy to pacify because it can now choose among rival benefactors, and parts of it are very rich indeed.

To Americans concerned with that loss of power and, even more, concerned with inflation and unemployment, Reagan, running for President, offered aggressive statements about American power ("there are limits to our patience") and vague economic solutions ("less government, more freedom").

Reagan's specific policies were not vague. He cut the national budget for health, education, welfare, the arts, children, old people, pregnant women, the unemployed, environmental protection—while giving large benefits to the wealthy. It was disclosed shortly after he took office that twenty-three oil industry executives and investors contributed $270,000 to redecorate the White House living quarters. According to the Associated Press: "The solicitation drive by Mr. Tuttle came four weeks after the President decontrolled oil prices, a decision worth $2 billion to the oil industry. . . . Jack Hodges of Oklahoma City, owner of Core Oil and Gas Company, said: 'The top man of this country ought to live in one of the top places. Mr. Reagan has helped the energy business. . . .' "

With the billions taken from the poor, Reagan proposed to build up the military. He planned $140 billion in cuts in social programs through 1984, and an increase of $181 billion for "defense" in the same period.

He also promised tax cuts of $196 billion, and said he would still balance the budget because the tax cuts would so stimulate the economy as to generate new revenue. Nobel-Prize-winning economist Wassily Leontief remarked dryly: "This is not likely to happen. In fact, I personally guarantee that it will not happen." Indeed, Department of Commerce figures showed that periods of lowered corporate taxes (1973–1975, 1979–1982) did not at all show higher capital investment, but a steep drop. The sharpest rise of capital investment (1975–1979) took place when corporate taxes were slightly higher than they had been for the preceding five years.

Reagan claimed that cuts in social spending for the poor would ultimately not hurt them, because of comparable cuts in income taxes. But a study by the Congressional Budget Office in February 1982 analyzed the effect of the Reagan administration's budget proposals. It found that by 1983, 23 percent of all families, those earning less than $10,000 a year, would gain $120 in tax cuts, but lose $360 in benefits. The richest 1 percent of the nation's families, making over $80,000 a year, would lose an average of $120 in benefits, but gain $15,250 in tax cuts.

The human consequences of Reagan's budget cuts went deep. For instance, Social Security disability benefits were terminated for 350,000 people. A man injured in an oil field accident was forced to go back to work, the federal government overruling both the company doctor and a state supervisor who testified that he was too disabled to work. The man died, and federal officials said: "We have a P.R. problem." A war hero of Vietnam, Roy Benavidez, who had been presented with the Congressional Medal of Honor by Reagan, was told by Social Security officials that the shrapnel pieces in heart, arms, and leg did not prevent him from working. He denounced the Reagan administration before a Congressional committee.

In the spring of 1983, the Congressional Budget Office released a study of the food stamp program, born in the sixties, which provided an average of $120 a month to eight million poor households. It found that the Reagan proposals for reducing the food stamp program (by a billion dollars a year for four years) would cause 62 percent of all food stamp households to lose benefits, and those with elderly or disabled members would experience the greatest average benefit reduction, nearly $21 a month, or 26 percent of their benefit.

The Reagan administration pointed to a decline in inflation (12 percent in 1980, 4 percent in 1982) as proof that its policies were working. But this was accompanied by increasing unemployment: by the fall of 1982, the equivalent of eleven million people for a whole year; in fact, thirty million people were unemployed all or part of the year, for an average of four months each. One result was that over sixteen million Americans lost medical insurance, which was often tied to holding a job. In Michigan, where the unemployment rate was the highest in the country, the infant death rate began to rise in 1981. At Cook County Hospital in Chicago, admissions for tuberculosis jumped from 300 to 600 cases in one year, which hospital officials said was because tubercular patients could not afford to buy antibiotics.

In 1982, over 3 million children and 2,700 schools could no longer be part of the school lunch program under the new requirements. Over a million of those children came from very poor families and depended on school lunches for as much as half of their daily nutrition. By the spring of 1983, 2 million children had entered the ranks of the officially declared "poor" since Reagan took office, and 12 million children—a quarter of the nation's children—were living in poverty. Of those 12 million, 8 million were receiving public assistance, 4 million were not.

A *New York Times* editorial estimated that 9 million women and children nationally were in need of the W.I.C. (women-infants-children) program that provided baby formula, diet supplements, and checkups for poor pregnant and nursing women and their children. The Reagan budget provided money for only a quarter of these. In parts of Detroit, one-third of the children were dying before their first birthday, and the *Times* commented: "Given what's happening to the hungry in America, this Administration has cause only for shame."

By the fall of 1982, on the eve of Congressional elections, even Reagan Republicans in Congress were clearly becoming sensitive to their constituents who were hurt by the budget cuts while more money was given to the military. The *Times* Washington correspondent wrote: "Republican leaders report a shifting mood in Congress on military spending, both because of the weakened economy and sharp cuts in social programs."

However, once the elections were over (the Democrats gained seats in both the House and the Senate), the Reagan budget proposals made in 1983 for 1984 and beyond called for a 10 percent increase in military spending and freezes or cuts in most domestic programs. The President proposed to raise the military budget from $209 billion in 1983 (Carter, as he left office, had himself proposed a rise to $205 billion in arms for 1983) and then even larger growth for the next five years, so that the total for the military would be over $1.5 trillion. For 1983, omitting fixed expenses like Social Security payments and interest on the national debt, arms costs would be 43 percent of federal spending.

All that money was to finance a more aggressive foreign policy. In the 1970s, after twenty-five years of being far behind the United States in the production and deployment of nuclear missiles, the Soviet Union began to catch up. The American decision in 1970 to put multiple warheads on its missile launchers had spurred the Soviet Union to deploy its own series (SS-1 through SS-22) of multiple missiles, which was then pointed to by Reagan to justify an even faster military buildup.

At the same time, officials in the Reagan administration began to speak of nuclear war as if it could be tolerated and even won. Vice-President George Bush told a reporter (Robert Scheer) during the 1980 campaign that in a nuclear exchange between the United States and the Soviet Union, "you can have a winner," in the sense that: "You have survivability of command in control, survival of industrial potential, protection of a percentage of our citizens, and you have a capability that inflicts more damage on the opposition than it can inflict on you." Scheer asked: "Do you mean like 5 percent would survive? 2 percent?" Bush answered: "More than that."

Other officials in the Reagan administration seemed to be trying to persuade Americans that defense measures would enable "survival." One of these (Thomas K. Jones, a deputy undersecretary in the Defense Department) was quoted as saying that in case of a nuclear attack, people should: "Dig a hole, cover it with a couple of doors, and then throw three feet of dirt on top. It's the dirt that does it." And: "Everybody's going to make it if there are enough shovels to go around." One booklet put out by a federal agency on "emergency management" said: "A close look at the facts shows with fair certainty that with reasonable protective measures, the United States could survive nuclear attack and go on to recover within a relatively few years."

Carter's Secretary of Defense, James Schlesinger, had said in 1975: "Under no circumstances could we disavow the first use of nuclear weapons." The Reagan administration proceeded with the same kind of strategy, even more intensely. The Carter proposal for the MX was revived. Critics called it a foolish, expensive, and dangerous scheme, pointing out that it would only lead the Russians to expand their missile production so that they could aim at all 2,400 silos.

During the Carter years, a small but determined movement against nuclear arms began to grow. The pioneers were a tiny group of Christian pacifists who had been active against the Vietnam war (former priest Philip Berrigan and his wife, Elizabeth McAlister, a former nun, were among this core). At the end of the war, they stationed themselves in a communal house in Baltimore and elsewhere around Washington, D.C. Again and again, they would be arrested for engaging in nonviolent acts of dramatic protest against nuclear war at the Pentagon and the White House—occupying forbidden areas, pouring their own blood on symbols of the war machine. This was largely ignored by the press, but the numbers of protesters grew. In 1980, small delegations of peace activists from all over the country maintained a constant series of demonstrations at the Pentagon, in which over a thousand people were arrested for acts of nonviolent civil disobedience.

In September of 1980, Philip Berrigan, his brother Daniel Berrigan (the Jesuit priest and poet), Molly Rush (a mother of six), Anne Montgomery (a nun and counselor to young runaways and prostitutes in Manhattan), with four of their friends, made their way past a guard in the General Electric plant at King of Prussia, Pennsylvania, where nose cones for nuclear missiles were manufactured. They used sledgehammers to smash two of the nose cones, and smeared their own blood over missile parts, blueprints, and furniture. Arrested, tried, sentenced to years in prison, they said they were trying to set an example: to do as the Bible suggested, to beat swords into plowshares.

The "Ploughshares Eight," explaining their action, said: "In confronting G.E., we choose to obey God's law of life, rather than a corporate summons to death. Our beating of swords into plowshares is a way to enflesh this biblical call." They also pointed to the huge allocations of taxpayers' money to corporations producing weaponry, of which GE was the fifth largest: "G.E. drains $3 million a day from the public treasury—an enormous larceny against the poor." Before the trial, Daniel Berrigan had written in the *Catholic Worker:*

I know of no sure way of predicting where things will go from there, whether others will hear and respond, or how quickly or slowly. Or whether the act will fail to vitalize others, will come to a grinding halt then and there, its actors stigmatized or dismissed as fools. One swallows dry and takes a chance.

Whatever the direct effect of the actions of the "Ploughshares Eight" on the American nation, it was clear that the movement against nuclear war was growing, from a small number of men and women willing to go to jail to make others stop and think, to millions of Americans frightened at the thought of nuclear holocaust and beginning to express themselves in various ways.

Even the very middle-American Pennsylvania jurors who convicted the Ploughshares Eight showed remarkable sympathy with their actions. One juror, Michael DeRosa, told reporter Patricia Moore of the Boston *Globe:* "I didn't think they really went to commit a crime. They went to protest." Another, Mary Ann Ingram, said the jury argued about that. DeRosa told the reporter: "We convicted them on three things and we really didn't want to convict them on anything. But we had to because of the way the judge said the only thing you can use is what you get under the law." And Ingram: "These people are not criminals. Here are people who are trying to do some good for the country. But the judge said nuclear power wasn't the issue."

When Carter, responding to the Soviet Union's invasion of Afghanistan, called for the registration of young men for a military draft, over 800,000 (10 percent) failed to register. One mother wrote to the *New York Times:*

To the Editor:

Thirty-six years ago I stood in front of the crematorium. The ugliest force in the world had promised itself that I should be removed from the cycle of life —that I should never know the pleasure of giving life. With great guns and great hatred, this force thought itself the equal of the force of life.

I survived the great guns, and with every smile of my son, they grow smaller. It is not for me, Sir, to offer my son's blood as lubricant for the next generation of guns. I remove myself and my own from the cycle of death.

Isabella Leitner
Bronx, July 3, 1980

Former Nixon aide Alexander Haig warned, in an interview in the French journal *Politique Internationale* in the fall of 1980, that there might reappear in the U.S. the conditions that forced President Nixon to stop the draft. "There is a Jane Fonda on every doorstep," he said.

One of the young men who refused to register, James Peters, wrote an open letter to President Carter:

Dear Mr. President: On July 23, 1980, I, as a male born in September, 1960, am expected to report to my local post office for the purpose of registering with the Selective Service System. I hereby inform you, Mr. President, that I will *not* register on July 23, or at any time thereafter. . . . We have tried militarism, and it has failed the human race in every way imaginable. . . .

At least twenty antidraft groups were working in southern states by early 1981, according to the Southern Student Activist Network in Atlanta, Georgia.

Carter's own preelection statements against Reagan were used to criticize his call for increased military spending. An official of the Center for War/Peace Studies pointed out that, as Carter himself had said, a single American Poseidon submarine carried 160 warheads, each with three times the power of the Hiroshima bomb, enough to destroy every major city in the Soviet Union, and that the United States possessed forty of those submarines. If deterrence was the object, and not an actual nuclear war, why were hundreds of billions more dollars being allocated for more weapons?

In the fall of 1980, local referenda in three districts in western Massachusetts permitted voters to say whether they believed in a mutual Soviet-American halt to testing, production, and deployment of all nuclear weapons, and wanted Congress to devote those funds instead to civilian use. Two peace groups had worked for nine months on the campaign, and all three districts approved the resolution (94,000 to 65,000), even those that voted for Reagan as President. Similar referenda received majority votes between 1978 and 1981 in San Francisco, Berkeley, Oakland, Madison, and Detroit.

Women were in the forefront of the new antinuclear movement. In the spring of 1980, a young specialist in nuclear arms, Randall Forsberg, organized the Council for a Nuclear Weapons Freeze, whose simple program—a mutual Soviet-American freeze on the production of new nuclear weapons—began to catch on throughout the country. On November 16–17, 1980, two thousand women assembled in Washington to discuss militarism and violence, and then marched on the Pentagon, surrounding it in a great circle linking arms or stretching to hold the ends of brightly colored scarves. One hundred forty women were arrested for blocking the Pentagon entrance.

Also in 1980, a small group of doctors began to organize meetings around the country to teach citizens the medical consequences of nuclear war. They were the core of the Physicians for Social Responsibility, and Dr. Helen Caldicott, their president, became one of the most powerful and eloquent national leaders of the movement. At one of their symposia, Howard Hiatt, dean of the Harvard School of Public Health, gave a detailed account of what the explosion of one 20-megaton bomb at ground level would do to downtown Boston. The area of total destruction would be a circle with a diameter of eight miles, and would include most of the medical facilities and personnel in the Boston area; 5,000 of the 6,500 physicians in the area would be immediately killed or fatally injured. Hiatt spoke graphically:

As far as 40 miles away, retinal burns cause blindness. The pressure wave released by the bomb travels faster than the speed of sound. That wave is followed by winds of over 1000 miles per hour fanning the many fires caused by the initial blast and thermal radiation. . . . Within the radius of the firestorm . . . two million fatalities. Many of the survivors are badly burned, blinded, and otherwise seriously wounded. Many are disoriented. These are the short-term effects; the problem of radiation sickness will grow in the days and weeks ahead.

Hiatt pointed out that existing facilities in the United States could take care of 200 severe burn cases, and that a nuclear war could cause 25 million such cases, at a time when three-fourths of the nation's doctors were dead or seriously wounded.

In December of 1981, the annual meeting of the American Medical Association passed a resolution asking doctors to inform the President and the Congress about "the medical consequences of nuclear war." The *New York Times* reported: "The resolution, passed by an overwhelming voice vote at a convention in Las Vegas, marks a departure for the normally conservative organization and lends another voice to the growing movement against nuclear weapons."

That year, town meetings in fourteen Vermont communities passed resolutions asking their representatives to support a nuclear freeze. Hundreds of churches around the nation called community meetings on the issue of nuclear war. In Utah and Idaho, opposition by the Mormon Church caused the United States government to abandon plans to station MX silos in those states.

In Amarillo, Texas, Bishop Leroy Matthieson of the Roman Catholic diocese began a campaign against the neutron bomb (a new type of nuclear weapon, with lower explosive power and higher radiation levels, thus more dangerous to people than to property). He was joined by all twelve Roman Catholic bishops in Texas, who said: "We . . . fully support his appeal to those involved in the manufacture of these weapons in every nation to consider seriously the moral and ethical implications of what they are doing." In a November 1980 national meeting of Catholic bishops, the majority opposed any use of nuclear weapons. The archbishop of San Francisco, John R. Quinn, said: "Something is stirring very deeply in the soul of humanity."

It seemed clear that Reagan's first year in office had provoked fear of nuclear war on a scale never before experienced in the country. That fall of 1981, the City Council of Cambridge, Massachusetts, responding to a state civil defense brochure which outlined plans for an evacuation of the city's population in case of nuclear attack (residents were told to drive out on the major highway leading from the city and take bankbooks and credit cards with them), held hearings on the danger of nuclear war. Then they printed and mailed 30,000 booklets to the city's residents, and instead of passing on the evacuation plans, told them of the devastation a nuclear war would bring, urging them to contact their Congressmen and demand control of the arms race.

In local elections in Boston in November 1981, a resolution calling for increased federal spending on social programs "by reducing the amount of our tax dollars spent on nuclear weapons and programs of foreign military intervention" won a majority in every one of Boston's twenty-two wards, including both white and black working-class districts. Ward 9, all black, passed it by 1,172 to 74. Ward 7, in conservative Irish-Catholic South Boston, passed it by 1,960 to 1,167. That month, there were meetings on 151 college campuses across the country on the dangers of nuclear war, and gatherings in forty-two states, organized by the Union of Concerned Scientists.

Meanwhile, those small groups of religious pacifists were continuing their acts of civil disobedience. At Groton, Connecticut, and on the opposite coast, at Bangor, Washington, demonstrations took place each time a new Trident submarine was commissioned. These were huge ships, each carrying twenty-four missiles with ten warheads on each. Nine people arrested at Groton for defacing one of the submarines became known as the Trident Nine, and one of them, Vincent Kay, explained the action:

> By damaging missile hatches and sonar devices we have done no violence to anyone; likewise, the underground network of resistance working to destroy the ovens of Auschwitz, Belsen, Dachau, Chelmno and Treblinka were trying their hardest at that point to focus on the destruction of private property, not human beings. . . .
>
> Each Trident submarine costs taxpayers some two to three billion dollars. . . . Half a Trident (one billion dollars) equals the cost of 360 health centers, each treating 40,000 people annually.

Another of those arrested in such an action was Peter DeMott, a thirty-three-year-old Vietnam veteran who took a van belonging to the General Dynamics/Electric Boat Corporation, which made the Trident, and rammed it into the rudder of an unfinished Trident. He was sentenced to a year in jail.

Ruth McKay, a sixty-three-year-old Sunday school teacher and grandmother in Hudson, New Hampshire, prepared to go to court in the fall of 1982 for refusing to pay $802 of her income tax because she calculated that this part of her tax would go for military purposes. She was one of about 13,000 people classified in 1980 by the Internal Revenue Service as "illegal tax protesters."

As militarist as the Reagan administration was, it had to proceed cautiously in the face of mounting protests in the United States and abroad. In Europe, hundreds of thousands demonstrated in West Germany, Holland, Italy, and England against the planned deployment of new nuclear missiles in Europe by the United States. In October 1981 alone, over a million people demonstrated in Europe for nuclear disarmament. In Rumania, the most independent of Russia's East European vassals, hundreds of thousands demonstrated for both Soviet and American disarmament.

One American soldier in Germany, James Bergeron of Vermont, decided to join a peace demonstration there, and was arrested, threatened with court-martial, then discharged because, as his commanding colonel put it: "there is a strong possibility that his trial may trigger public demonstrations in the Ludwigsburg/Kornwestheim area, adding to the disruptive influence on morale and discipline that this case is generating." Bergeron explained his action: "I am opposed to war. . . . Our resources are needed for impoverished humanity."

That summer of 1981, the *New York Times* reported that the military could not get sufficient manpower through volunteers, and yet the government hesitated to renew draft registration because, as Secretary of Defense Caspar Weinberger explained: "President Reagan believes that resuming the draft to meet manpower problems would lead to public unrest comparable to that in the 60's and 70's." William Beecher, a former Pentagon reporter, wrote in November 1981 that Reagan was "obviously concerned, even alarmed by the mounting voices of discontent and suspicion over emerging U.S. nuclear strategy both in the streets of Europe and more recently on American campuses."

The Reagan administration began to prosecute draft resisters. One of these, Benjamin Sasway, cited U.S. military intervention in El Salvador as a good reason not to register for the draft. A right-wing columnist and Reagan supporter (William A. Rusher, of the *National Review*) wrote indignantly that one heritage of the sixties was a new generation of antiwar teachers:

Almost certainly there was a teacher, or teachers, who taught Benjamin Sasway to look at American society as a hypocritical, exploitative, materialistic roadblock on the path of human progress. The generation of the Vietnam protesters is now in its early 30's, and the academicians among them are already ensconced in the faculties of the country's high schools and colleges. . . . What a pity our jurisprudence doesn't allow us to reach and penalize the real architects of this sort of destruction!

In the Boston area, a group called Educators for Social Responsibility began working on educational materials for elementary and high schools dealing with questions of nuclear war, as evidence began to grow that children were already thinking about it and worried about it. Interviewed by the Boston *Globe,* a twelve-year-old named Piper said:

I learned about the bomb from the newspapers and radio. I just think it's so stupid that so many innocent people will die. And it's just because some people in the government can't get along with other people in other governments. . . . (her voice trembling) Sometimes I just get so, so scared thinking that tomorrow I might not wake up and that would just be the end.

And a seventeen-year-old named Susan:

What scares me is that President Reagan wants to build up the military. He is trying to say "this way we'll be more secure," but what he's saying is making me more scared.

That summer of 1982, youngsters in New England formed the Children's Campaign for Nuclear Disarmament, soliciting letters to President Reagan to stop the construction of nuclear bombs in the United States. One boy wrote to the President:

I hate nuclear weapons. I hope you understand. I am scared, President Reagan, if someone flies over my house and drops a bomb. My name is Jonas. I am 4½. I live in Cabot, Vermont.

Nationally syndicated columnist Russell Baker commented in late 1982 on the almost hysterical preoccupation with "security":

For five weeks I traveled across beautiful autumnal America. It was like a booby hatch for the criminally insane. . . . At various stops along the route there were campaigning politicians clamoring for use of the electric chair, the gallows or the gas chamber as devices for restoring public civility. Everywhere one was confronted with what seemed like a national obsession for more and more security.

Nowhere was this more chillingly apparent than in Beverly Hills, whose sumptuous houses must contain vast riches. Every other house, it seemed, bore a large placard announcing the identity of its private security guard service, and most of these carried a supplemental placard that said "Armed Response." . . .

Very little of this "security" existed in the country 20 years ago, but now it is a national passion. The irony is that the more "security" we buy, the less secure we are.

On June 12, 1982, there took place in Central Park, New York City, the largest political demonstration in the history of the country, as close to a million people gathered to express their determination to bring an end to the arms race. By then, the number of peace groups in the country had grown with amazing speed. In the Boston area alone, there were forty-one organizations working for nuclear disarmament, including groups like Musicians Against Nuclear Arms and Nurses Alliance for the Prevention of Nuclear War. Even so conservative an organization as the National Taxpayers Union, with more than 100,000 members, turned against Reagan's military budget. The group's newsletter told its members: "Our new age of nuclear hawkery may not only increase your tax burden and lower your standard of living, but it may soon prove hazardous to your health."

The idea of a nuclear freeze, which had worked its way up from conferences and church gatherings to hundreds of town meetings in New England, and referenda in California, soon had won approval in twelve city councils and five state legislatures; Congress, as the fall 1982 elections were coming, could not ignore it. On June 23, 1982, two weeks after the huge New York City rally, the *Times*'s Washington correspondent reported: "The House Foreign Affairs Committee, in a rebuff to President Reagan, approved a resolution today that called for a freeze in American and Soviet nuclear arsenals." An Associated Press poll of March 1982 showed three of four Americans favored a freeze by both countries.

Scientists who had worked on the atomic bomb added their voices to the growing movement. George Kistiakowsky, a Harvard University chemistry professor who had worked on the first atomic bomb, and later was science adviser to President Eisenhower, became a spokesman for the disarmament movement in his seventies, and died at the age of eighty-two after a three-year battle with cancer. His last public remarks were in an editorial for the *Bulletin of Atomic Scientists* in December 1982: "I tell you as my parting words: Forget the channels. There simply is not enough time left before the world explodes. Concentrate instead on organizing, with so many others of like mind, a mass movement for peace such as there has not been before."

That same month, another man devoted to disarmament died, but this was an obscure protester named Norman D. Mayer, sixty-six years old, a maintenance man from Florida and an ex-Navy man. The circumstances were strange. Mayer drove a truck to the Washington Monument, said it was loaded with explosives, and threatened to blow up the monument unless the government agreed to a nationwide media debate on nuclear weapons. When he started to drive the van out of the monument grounds, police fired, and he was hit by four bullets, dying of a bullet in his head. No explosives were found in his truck, and it was never explained why, with police "sharpshooters" firing, Mayer had to be killed in order to stop the truck.

Sam Bass Warner, a historian, was moved to write to the *New York Times*. Norman Mayer, he said, had sought relief from his anxiety about nuclear warfare "by imitating the U.S. Government: in the name of peace he threatened terrible violence." He had only asked for radio and television time. But, Warner wrote:

> To stop the scheduled programming, to have our leaders interrupt their rounds, to give in to such blackmail by one "crazy" man, was a higher price than we were willing to pay for the lives of seven tourists, the many park police and the structural stability of the monument.
>
> Instead, the police responded with a pre-emptive strike, and riddled Mr. Mayer and his van with their gunfire.
>
> We should attend to Mr. Mayer's death, and honor his self-sacrifice. He was telling us something very important about ourselves.
>
> His was, to be sure, an insane form of political theater, but the troubled among us often express what the rest of us dare not. . . . Mr. Mayer gave public expression to deep cleavages within the soul of the nation.

In less than three years, there had come about a remarkable change in public opinion. At the time of Reagan's election, nationalist feeling—drummed up by the recent hostage crisis in Iran and by the Russian invasion of Afghanistan—was strong; the University of Chicago's National Opinion Research Center found that only 12 percent of those it polled thought too much was being spent on arms. But when it took another poll in the spring of 1982, 32 percent thought too much was being spent on the military. And in the spring of 1983, a *New York Times*/CBS News poll found that 48 percent believed too much was being spent on this.

By then, the nuclear freeze had been endorsed by 368 city and county councils across the country, by 444 New England town meetings and 17 state legislatures, and by the House of Representatives. A Harris poll at this time (March 1983) indicated that 79 percent of the population wanted a nuclear freeze agreement with the Soviet Union. Further, among evangelical Christians—a group of 40 million people presumed to be conservative and pro-Reagan—a Gallup poll sampling showed 60 percent favoring a nuclear freeze; 22 percent (high for such a group) said the United States should freeze its nuclear growth even if the Soviet Union refused.

A year after the great Central Park demonstration of nearly a million people, it was estimated by a newspaper devoted to nuclear issues *(Nuclear Times)* that there were over three thousand antiwar groups across the country. A typical local organization was the 400-member Lehigh-Pocono Committee of Concern, in Bethlehem, Pennsylvania, which put up a lemonade stand at the city's annual fair and held a "bike ride for peace" to raise $7,000.

The antinuclear feeling in the country was increasingly reflected in the culture—in books, magazine articles, plays, motion pictures. The *New York Times* Information Bank, repository for data from about 75 journals, reported that in 1978, nuclear war was mentioned in 278 articles; in 1982, there were 1,612 such articles. Jonathan Schell's impassioned book against the arms race, *The Fate of the Earth,* became a national best-seller. A documentary film on the arms race made in Canada was forbidden to enter the country by the Reagan administration, but a federal court ordered it admitted, and it won an Academy Award in 1983. Other documentaries began to circulate widely, even to be shown in neighborhood theaters. In 1983, millions of Americans saw a Hollywood film, *War Games,* which depicted the frightening possibility that computer errors and bureaucratic stupidity might lead to a third world war.

One of the signs of change in public opinion and in the national atmosphere was the occasional refusal of judges and juries to send to jail people of conscience who broke the law to make a statement about human life. In June of 1983, a jury in Minneapolis acquitted of "trespassing" thirty-six people who had invaded and sat in at the Honeywell Corporation to protest the production of parts for nuclear weapons. The forewoman of the jury admired the defendants' "total commitment" and said: "I have to give them a lot of credit for standing by their beliefs."

With the buildup of the disarmament movement, there was also a growing fear that the United States might once again, as in Vietnam, intervene with force against popular revolutions and become embroiled in war. Thus, Reagan's policy of giving military aid to El Salvador brought immediate reactions. The Boston *Globe* reported on one demonstration (March 13, 1981) when Reagan had barely taken office:

It was a scene reminiscent of the 1960's, a rally of students in Harvard Yard shouting anti-war slogans, a candlelight march through the streets of Cambridge.... 2000 persons, mostly students, gathered to protest U.S. involvement in El Salvador. . . . Students from Tufts, MIT, Boston University and Boston College, the University of Massachusetts, Brandeis, Suffolk, Dartmouth, Northeastern, Vassar, Yale, and Simmons were represented.

During commencement exercises that spring at Syracuse University, when Reagan's Secretary of State, Alexander Haig, was given an honorary doctorate in "public service," two hundred students and faculty turned their backs on the presentation. During Haig's address, the press reported, "Nearly every pause in Mr. Haig's 15-minute address was punctuated by chants: 'Human needs, not military greed!' 'Get out of El Salvador!' 'Washington guns killed American nuns!' "

The last slogan was a reference to the execution in the fall of 1980 of four American nuns by Salvadoran soldiers. Thousands of people in El Salvador were being murdered each year by "death squads" connected to a government armed by the United States, and the American public was beginning to pay attention to events in this tiny Central American country. In December 1981, a foreign aid bill passed by Congress included an amendment requiring that before the United States sent military aid to El Salvador, it must certify that the government was making a significant effort to control its armed forces and to control "gross violations of internationally recognized human rights."

Reagan, over the next two years, continued to certify that these conditions were met, even while executions and torture were taking place in El Salvador. An Associated Press dispatch of early 1983 reported that two civil liberties groups called abuses of human rights in El Salvador "worse than ever":

In a 115-page report, Americas Watch and the American Civil Liberties Union charged that government security forces or allied paramilitary groups killed at least 5339 civilians last year.

The Reagan Administration, however, is expected to certify to Congress today that the Salvadoran government has made enough progress in protecting human rights to justify continued military support in its war against leftist guerrillas.

American public opinion clearly was opposed to such support for El Salvador. A *Times*/CBS poll reported (March 21, 1982) that only 16 percent of its sampling favored Reagan's program of sending military and economic aid to El Salvador, while 63 percent said "stay out."

In the spring of 1983, it was disclosed that an American physician was working with the Salvadoran rebels. He had been an Air Force pilot in Southeast Asia, became disillusioned with U.S. policy there, saw at first hand that his government was lying, and refused to fly any more missions. The Air Force response was to commit him to a psychiatric hospital, then to discharge him as psychologically unfit. He went to medical school, and then volunteered to be a doctor with the guerrillas in El Salvador. Serving on the Guazapa front, he carried no weapons, and found that much of his work was to give instructions in nutrition and health care to peasants.

In another Central American country, Nicaragua, the Reagan administration seemed determined to overthrow the leftist government which took power in 1979 after a popular revolution ended decades of dictatorship by the Somoza family, supported by the United States. In December 1982, Congress included an amendment to an appropriations bill which forbade U.S. support for groups trying to overthrow the government of Nicaragua. Despite this, the Reagan administration was openly giving arms to Nicaraguan counterrevolutionaries based in neighboring Honduras.

The government's public explanation for its actions against Nicaragua were summed up by Reagan's first Secretary of State, Alexander Haig, who said that the Sandinista government (Sandino had been a Nicaraguan rebel of the 1920s) "had steadily increased the drift toward totalitarianism." Considering these charges, Warren Hoge, the *New York Times* correspondent in Nicaragua, wrote: "it is indisputable that Nicaraguans today suffer less state repression of fundamental freedoms under their leftist government than do the people of countries in the region like Guatemala and El Salvador whose right-wing governments do not draw the same kind of critical comments from Washington."

There was much talk in the American press in the early eighties about the political cautiousness of a new generation of college students concerned mostly with their own careers. But when, at the Harvard commencement of June 1983, Mexican writer Carlos Fuentes criticized American intervention in Latin America, and said, "Because we are your true friends, we will not permit you to conduct yourselves in Latin American affairs as the Soviet Union conducts itself in Central European and Central Asian affairs," he was interrupted twenty times by applause and received a standing ovation when he finished.

The Reagan presidency, with its clear guns-over-butter budgets, and its revival of the traditional U.S. interventionism in Latin America, seemed to be doing something that no previous administration had done so starkly: uniting the issues of war and economic deprivation. But the foundation for a new movement on economic issues had begun to be created under Carter, with a rapid growth of local groups organizing around domestic issues: rent control, consumers' problems, corporate prices and profits, war veterans' issues, environmental dangers, nuclear radiation, women's rights, discrimination against homosexuals. One gets a sense of this from even a small sampling of the "alternative press"—hundreds of small newspapers published around the country by 1980—as well as from other sources. Some examples:

1. The building of two nuclear reactors at Seabrook, New Hampshire, was postponed by demonstrations, local votes against the facilities, and the

difficulty of getting investors. A couple in their sixties, Louisa and Tony Santasucci, who owned 10 acres of land abutting the Seabrook nuclear plant, offered their land as a sanctuary for the 1,500 nuclear protesters who camped there in 1979 in brightly colored tents, warming themselves in the fall chill by hundreds of campfires. Tony Santasucci talked about the advantages of solar energy, told his wife with awe of how he had seen a solar oven bake bread. "I've learned from the kids," he told a reporter, and explained why he gave them land:

> I don't have to let those people camp here. But I don't like to see them pushed around. I don't want to be a hero or anything, but what's right is right and what's wrong is wrong. At my age, how much longer do I have to go? But the young kids, they got a long time.

2. Protests against nuclear power spread across the country. In the summer of 1979, 500 protesters were arrested at the construction site of Oklahoma's first nuclear power plant at Inola. Other demonstrations took place in Texas, Colorado, Arkansas, and New York. The effectiveness of these protests was acknowledged by the Mobil Oil Company in an advertisement in the *New York Times* published to boost nuclear power, which complained that "a withering storm of 'anti-nuke' protest has contributed to the killing of plans for dozens of facilities, retarded others, and dried up the flow of new orders." Indeed, in 1980, with 66 existing reactors, 90 more were planned, but 15 of the new projects were dropped and 60 postponed. Public hostility to nuclear power was growing, it seemed from a nationwide survey by Associated Press/NBC News in November 1981, which found that 56 percent of those polled opposed the construction of new nuclear plants.

3. In April 1980, a study by the Pennsylvania Health Department found through telephone interviews that nearly 13 percent of the 37,000 people living within a five-mile radius of Three Mile Island (where a frightening nuclear accident had taken place) had become antinuclear activists.

4. A group called POWER (People Outraged With Energy Rates) was only one of twenty similar organizations that sprang up in New York City after the Three Mile Island accident. It aimed at Consolidated Edison's electric bills and campaigned to get households to withhold part of their electric bill payments in protest against the raising of rates.

5. Labor rank-and-file insurgency grew in the last years of the Carter administration. Union members rebelling against the powerful Teamsters Union, as Teamsters for a Democratic Union, won several local elections in Michigan, Wisconsin, Oklahoma, and Florida. Pete Camarata, who had been beaten up at the 1976 national teamster convention for daring to speak up against the union leadership, was one of those elected in Michigan. He said: "Maybe it will take 10 to 15 years but at the next convention it won't be one guy standing up and getting his head beat in."

6. In 1979, the Youth Project, a public foundation set up to help activist

groups all over the country "achieve social justice," listed 77 groups to which it had given seed money and personnel. A sampling suggests the range of community groups active in the nation:

Abortion Rights of Washington
Baltimore Rent Control Campaign
Black Hills Alliance
Brown Lung Association
California Health Action Coalition
Council of Senior West Virginians
Detroit Anti-Hunger & Youth Advocacy Center
Florida Consumers Federation
Iowa Family Farm Coalition
Maricopa County Organizing Project
Minnesota Prisoners Union
Natural Organic Farmers Association (Vermont)
New Mexico People & Energy Project
North Carolina Organizing Project
Oregon Fair Share
Powder River Energy Project (Wyoming)
Rhode Island Jewelry Workers Organizing Committee
Salud & Educación Para el Campesino de Texas
South Carolina Committee Against Hunger
United League of Mississippi
Working Women (Cleveland)
Mohawk Nation Project
Pennsylvania ACORN

For instance, the Maricopa County Organizing Project was formed to improve conditions of Mexicans who, poor and landless, had been driven to seek work on farms in Arizona. Vulnerable to deportation, they lived in camps among the citrus groves without shelter, blankets, safe water, or toilets. The project helped them to organize and by 1979 had doubled and sometimes tripled their wages, provided sanitary drinking water and blankets for the winter months, and brought national attention to their situation. The North Carolina Organizing Project held a regional workshop in mid-1979 to bring together people most affected by the fact that huge military expenditures were leaving no money for community health centers, housing, and public service jobs. The aim was to educate and organize on national budget priorities.

7. Puerto Ricans on New York's Lower East Side invented a utopian name for their area—Losaida, as they put it, was "an entity that dwells in the minds of its creators and lovers." It was an area of 25,000 people—mostly Puerto Rican, some black, some European, Chinese, Indian, white—among whom they set out to create a culture, and a resistance movement. "No heat

—no rent" became the most popular graffiti slogan on walls and sidewalks. They picked one burned-out gutted shell of a building to concentrate on, and made it into a comfortable multifamily cooperative. On East Sixth Street, the Nuyorican Poets' Café was founded, with wine and beer at 50 cents. Music and art groups flourished.

8. In the Mahoning Valley region around Youngstown, Ohio, after 10,000 steelworkers lost their jobs by the closing of three steel mills from 1977 to 1979, rank-and-file steelworkers, struggling against both the ruthlessness of the corporations and the cautiousness of top union officials, fought back. They decided on a novel tactic: to buy the steel mills themselves and have the workers run them cooperatively. When U.S. Steel refused, they took direct action. On January 28, 1980, 100 steelworkers crashed through a glass door of the U.S. Steel offices in Youngstown and occupied the building, demanding to meet with the corporate chairman. This made national television news. At the rally of 600 people that preceded the sit-in, union leader Ed Mann quoted Frederick Douglass: "Power concedes nothing without a demand. It never did, and it never will."

The occupation was ended that day with the hope that U.S. Steel would talk with them about selling the plants. But after a meeting of executives of American steel companies in Washington, the chairman of the board of U.S. Steel said: "We obviously would not be interested in selling the plants to a group of people that can only be successful if they were massively subsidized by the Federal government. We are not, in other words, interested in creating subsidized competition for ourselves."

Staughton Lynd, attorney for the steelworkers, who wrote a history of the battle against the closings, concluded: "The main thing to be learned from the Youngstown experience is that workers *must* seek to take part in decisions about what products to make, where capital should be invested, when a new plant should be built or an old plant shut down."

9. The Palmetto Alliance of Charleston, South Carolina, succeeded in 1979, after several years of education and organizing, in getting the city to set strict regulations on the transport of nuclear materials through the city. New York City had passed such an ordinance in 1976 and then towns in Connecticut, Massachusetts, California, Wisconsin, Virginia, and 39 towns in Vermont had followed.

10. Carter's reintroduction of draft registration brought some arguments that women should be included as a matter of "equality." At a Washington conference on Women and the Draft (March 1, 1980), Janis Kelly spoke on what factors were "common to all armies and distinguish them from other large groups of people, such as symphony orchestras." She said:

First, and most important, an army is an instrument of mass murder. ... To hear most liberals talk, you'd think the army was primarily an equal opportunity program. ... I say to Jimmy Carter, to the Joint Chiefs of Staff, and to the moral idiots who work in the Pentagon, *Don't even think about drafting women.* If you come after our sisters, we will hide them. They will vanish into our communities like drops of water into the ocean.

11. At an "International Survival Gathering" sponsored by the Black Hills Alliance in Rapid City, South Dakota, representatives of 23 Indian nations and people from 36 other countries in the world drew up a 21-point program against corporate, government, and military control of the land, saying: "We believe that the land is not to be owned, but to be shared. . . . We challenge our concerned sisters and brothers throughout the world to unite with us in the struggle to liberate the land and all people from the economic and political domination of the transnational corporations and the governments that serve them."

This scattered local ferment of the late seventies was provoked into something resembling a national movement of class protest by the election of Reagan and the quick juxtaposition by his administration of spending hundreds of billions for war and cutting hundreds of billions in social services. A book on the Reagan policies by social critics Frances Piven and Richard Cloward carried both a description and a prediction in its title: *The New Class War.*

It was not hard to see the physical decay of cities and countryside. In 1981, a report by the Council of State Planning Agencies, produced by the staffs of the nation's governors, and entitled *America in Ruins,* found huge deterioration in vital services all over the country: there were problems with clean water, transportation, bridges, highways, waste disposal. The report said that "the maintenance of public facilities essential to national economic renewal has been deferred."

At the same time, a report on *World Military & Social Expenditures* by Ruth Sivard for the period 1960–1980 showed that among nine leading industrial countries (Japan, Denmark, Canada, Italy, Sweden, West Germany, France, England, and the United States), the country whose military expenditures were largest as a percent of gross national product (7 percent) was the United States, which also had the lowest annual rate of growth (3 percent) in manufacturing productivity. The country with the lowest GNP percentage for military expenditures (1 percent) was Japan, which had the highest (9 percent) rate of growth in manufacturing productivity.

Seymour Melman of Columbia University made the effect of the Reagan priorities graphic with facts and figures: the cost of two B-1 bombers ($400 million) could pay to rebuild Cleveland's water supply system; the cost of the Navy's F-18 fighter program ($34 billion) would modernize the country's machine-tool stock to bring it to the level of

Japan's; the cost of 46 heavy tanks ($120 million) would pay for 500 top-quality city buses; the cost overrun, to 1981, in the Army's heavy tank program ($13 billion) would supply the missing capital needed to maintain water supplies for 150 cities for twenty years.

As federal funds for localities diminished, home owners rebelled against increased property taxes. As cities and states began to cut funds for vital services—police, fire, health, schools—the reactions were angry. In early 1981, after seeing a film depicting the occupation of a closed fire station in Brooklyn, a hundred Bostonians broke into a closed police substation in South Boston to demand its reopening. That spring and summer, East Boston residents took to the streets, and for fifty-five nights blocked major thoroughfares and the Sumner Tunnel during rush hour, to protest cutbacks in funds for fire, police, and teachers. The police superintendent, John Doyle, said: "Maybe these people are starting to take lessons from the protests of the 60's and the 70's." The Boston *Globe* reported: "The demonstrators in East Boston were mostly middle-aged, middle-or working-class people who said they had never protested anything before."

As Reagan's budget took away federal funds for the arts, and suggested that the performing arts get more from private donors, two historic Broadway theaters were razed to make way for a luxury fifty-story hotel, and two hundred theater people picketed and demonstrated. When, after reading plays and singing songs through the afternoon, the picketers were ordered to disperse by the police, several refused and were arrested, including some of the nation's best-known theater personalities: producer Joseph Papp, singer Tammy Grimes, actresses Estelle Parsons and Celeste Holm, actors Richard Gere and Michael Moriarty.

The 1982 budget proposed cutting half of the funds for the National Endowment for the Humanities, which had supported projects in film, theater, and scholarly research. The humanities, said the budget report, were "a matter of low national priority." The United States already was among the stingiest of all industrialized nations in the aid it gave to the arts. The total sum given in 1981 by the NEH was less than the cost of two B-1 bombers. An Associated Press story from Washington reported on testimony to a Congressional committee on the NEH cuts:

Powerful voices in the performing arts—actress Jean Stapleton, actor James Earl Jones and Boston Pops conductor John Williams—sharply criticized yesterday President Ronald Reagan's proposal to slash federal subsidies for the arts and humanities by 50 percent. . . .

"No one argues the priority of a bullet, but we have a hard time pinning down the priority of the arts endeavors," Jones told a House appropriations sub-committee.

A newspaper put out by the North Shore Community Action Program in Massachusetts announced in the fall of 1981 that it was discontinuing publication because Reagan's budget cuts had eliminated the Community Services Administration, which funded the paper. In its farewell letter to its readers, the staff said: "As is now clear, the War on Poverty has become a War Against the Poor." But, it declared:

In spite of all this grim news, we want our friends (as well as our enemies) to know that the struggle will continue. For the past few months, representatives of local tenants unions, North Shore Welfare Rights, as well as other concerned people, have been meeting. . . .

One year after Reagan's election, hundreds of people were gathering in Columbus, Ohio, as part of the Ohio Conference on Responsible Economics, representing dozens of community and trade union groups, to discuss actions to deal with deteriorating economic conditions in Ohio. In the spring and fall of 1982, thousands of people based in the Midwest, in an organization called National People's Action, led by Dale Cincotta, a mother of six sons who had long battled for better schooling on Chicago's West Side, called for a "Reclaim America Week." The idea was for thousands to cross the country eastward to New York City and there demonstrate against corporate America in time to influence the November 1982 elections. The demonstration declared its purposes:

Reclaim America for the jobless and the underemployed. Reclaim America for the right to affordable home heating fuel. Reclaim America for the right to buy or rent a safe, sound, affordable home. Reclaim America for senior citizens. Reclaim America for the small farmers and the small businesses. Reclaim America for the citizens of this country who have built its strength and dignity.

The budget cuts spurred strikes across the country, often by groups unaccustomed to striking. In the fall of 1982, United Press International reported:

Angered by layoffs, salary cuts and uncertainty about job security, more school teachers throughout the country have decided to go on strike.

Teachers' strikes last week in seven states, from Rhode Island to Washington, have idled more than 300,000 students. In Philadelphia, a strike by the 21,000 member Teachers Federation showed no sign that it would end soon. . . .

Elsewhere in Pennsylvania, more than 43,000 elementary, secondary, and college students were out of class because of teachers' disputes.

In Elgin, Illinois, classes for 25,000 students in the state's third largest school district were canceled by a walkout of 1300 teachers in a salary dispute.

In Royal Oak, Michigan, 550 teachers went on strike Friday, canceling classes for more than 9600 students. This made a total of six teacher strikes in Michigan with 2000 teachers and about 41,000 students affected.

In North Providence, Rhode Island, teachers voted Friday to continue their strike. . . . All 18 schools remained closed in the Evergreen School District, on the east side of Vancouver, Washington. The district has 12,000 students and 600 teachers.

Just as the black revolt had brought many blacks into local office in the sixties and seventies, the economic crisis under Carter and Reagan brought some socialists to power as mayors in middle-sized towns across the country. In Burlington, Vermont's largest city, three months after Reagan took office, voters surprised everyone by electing a thirty-nine-year-old Socialist, Bernard Sanders, as mayor. It was not just a college town (the University of Vermont), but a heavily ethnic, blue-collar city. Sanders did not campaign as a Socialist but as a populist spokesman for low-income home owners and tenants, even winning the support of the police union because he favored higher salaries for police. Sanders appealed to Burlington voters' sense of economic justice:

We have a city that is trying to help a developer build $200,000 luxury waterfront condominiums with pools and health clubs and boutiques and all sorts of upper-middle-class junk just five blocks away from an area where people are literally not eating in order to pay their rent and fuel bills.

On the West Coast at this time, environmental and economic issues spurred the birth and growth of the Campaign for Economic Democracy, which had chapters in over twenty California communities by the fall of 1981. In the town of Santa Monica, the CED helped elect a mayor (Ruth Goldway) and a majority of the city council, by appealing to tenants seeking rent control. The following year, CED leader Tom Hayden, who in 1978 had run for the U.S. Senate and won over a million votes (extraordinary, for a person known as a radical), was elected to the California legislature.

Coal miners throughout the country, reacting to Reagan's cuts in federal contributions to a disability program for miners with black lung disease, called a two-day "memorial strike." Five thousand people demonstrated at the White House to protest this.

There was some evidence, in the summer of 1981, that when economic distress grew strong enough, even the nationalistic claims of "defense" were not enough to keep workers at their jobs. In Oak Ridge, Tennessee, 4,400 workers, in a dispute over work assignments, grievance procedures, and salaries, stopped production of components for nuclear weapons.

Bitter feelings were being aroused by the new emphasis, in Washington, and in many local governments, on cutting needy people adrift with the idea that "private enterprise" would give them jobs. One woman wrote to her local newspaper in November 1981:

> I am on Aid to Families with Dependent Children, and both my children are in school. . . . I have graduated from college with distinction, 128th in a class of over 1000, with a B.A. in English and sociology. I have experience in library work, child care, social work and counseling.
>
> I have been to the CETA office. They have nothing for me. . . . I also go every week to the library to scour the newspaper Help Wanted ads. I have kept a copy of every cover letter that I have sent out with my resume; the stack is inches thick. I have applied for jobs paying as little as $8000 a year.
>
> I work part-time in a library for $3.50 an hour; welfare reduces my allotment to compensate. . . .
>
> It appears we have employment offices that can't employ, governments that can't govern and an economic system that can't produce jobs for people ready to work. . . .
>
> Last week I sold my bed to pay for the insurance on my car, which, in the absence of mass transportation, I need to go job hunting. I sleep on a piece of foam rubber somebody gave me.
>
> So this is the great American dream my parents came to this country for: Work hard, get a good education, follow the rules, and you will be rich. I don't want to be rich. I just want to be able to feed my children and live with some semblance of dignity. . . .
>
> Diana D. Violeta
> Mattapoisett

The Reagan budget cuts fell most heavily on women, blacks, and the elderly. Women and their children made up 93 percent of the recipients of Aid to Families with Dependent Children. They made up 100 percent of the recipients of a food supplement program providing infant formula, orange juice, eggs, and cereal for babies and women at risk, from which Reagan wanted to cut $300 million. Thirty-seven feminist groups, studying the budget, denounced the Reagan program: "The net effect of the Reagan proposal is a redistribution of income, widening the income gap between the rich and the lower classes."

The staff of the House Select Committee on Aging found that the administration's budget cuts would have "a devastating impact on the lives of low-income elderly people." There would be sharp reductions in health care for 5 million older people, and 2.5 million would get smaller Social Security checks, while 725,000 would pay higher rents due to decreased subsidies, and 187,000 who received free advice from the Legal Services Corporation would now have to hire private attorneys or do without the help.

Surveying a series of news events in the first week of January 1983, David Nyhan of the Boston *Globe* wrote: "there is something brewing in the land that bodes ill for those in Washington who ignore it. People have moved from the frightened stage to the angry stage and are acting out their frustrations in ways that will test the fabric of civil order." He pointed to these events:

1. When unemployed or bankrupt home owners in the Pittsburgh area could no longer make mortgage payments, and foreclosure sales were scheduled, 60 pickets jammed the courthouse to protest the auction, and Allegheny sheriff Eugene Coon halted the proceedings.
2. In Little Washington, Pennsylvania, when a 50-year-old computer science teacher who led a teachers' strike was sent to jail, 2,000 people demonstrated outside the jailhouse in his support, and the Pittsburgh *Post-Gazette* called it "the largest crowd in Washington County since the 1794 Whiskey Rebellion."
3. The foreclosure of a 320-acre wheat farm in Springfield, Colorado, was interrupted by 200 angry farmers, who had to be dispersed by tear gas and Mace.
4. In Miami, blacks rioted in the ghetto after police shot a young black, a scenario reminiscent of the hundreds of black urban riots of the 1960s; behind all this was a 60 percent unemployment rate for young blacks.

As reporter Nyhan wrote: "when schoolteachers and steelworkers and farmers start acting up at the same time, it's time to take stock of national policy."

When Reagan arrived in Pittsburgh in April 1983 to make a speech, three thousand persons, many of them unemployed steelworkers, demonstrated against him, standing in the rain outside his hotel. One unemployed steelworker said: "A lot of these steelworkers voted for Reagan in 1980, and they realize they made a big mistake now." By June 1983, there were over fifty local committees of laid-off steelworkers around the country, planning a national conference. One man, in McKeesport, Pennsylvania, was about to have his house taken away for failure to meet his mortgage payments, when the Monongahela Valley Unemployed Committee put pressure on the local bank to reduce his payments, and saved his house. Around this same time, demonstrations by the unemployed were taking place in Detroit, Flint, Chicago, Cleveland, Los Angeles, Washington—over twenty cities in all.

Reagan's policies on racial equality created overwhelming hostility to his presidency among American blacks. According to a report of the American Civil Liberties Union in the fall of 1982: "The Reagan Administration has turned its back on civil rights. While the President portrays himself as an unbiased man, sincerely dedicated to equal opportunity for minorities, his Justice Department betrays this image by attempting to slow down, and even reverse, the civil rights gains of the past 20 to 30 years." It gave examples:

1. The Reagan administration reversed a Justice Department stand of the Carter years, and supported a Seattle law opposing student reassignment to achieve integration in the public schools.
2. Reagan's Justice Department reversed the position it had taken under Carter and argued unsuccessfully in the Supreme Court that the Internal Revenue Service could not deny tax exemption to two private schools—Goldsboro Christian Schools and Bob Jones University—which refused to admit blacks.
3. The Reagan administration tried to get Congress to eliminate a crucial section of the Voting Rights Act of 1965, which had been very effective in safeguarding the right of blacks to vote in southern states. (Congress would not comply.)

The U.S. Commission on Civil Rights, an investigative body set up by legislation in the early years of the black movement, declared in early 1983 that the Reagan administration had not cooperated with it, had refused to supply vital information, and was impeding the commission's work. Reagan, shortly afterward, used his power of appointment to remove three people from the commission and to appoint three new members, whose views were closer to his own.

In the summer of 1983, the U.S. Census Bureau issued figures which showed that between 1960 and 1981, the gap between white and black family income had remained virtually the same: median black family income was 55 percent of white family income in 1960, 56 percent in 1981. Over the same period, the unemployment ratio remained the same: twice as many blacks unemployed. More blacks were going to school in the 1980s, but data on occupations gave clues as to their economic situation: while blacks were 12 percent of the population, they were over 50 percent of the private household cleaners and servants and one-third of maids and garbage collectors, but only 3 percent of physicians, lawyers, and engineers.

As 1984 came near, the growing discontent with Reagan's policies around the country became the basis for a plan to register many of the people—mostly poor—who formed that half of the population which did not bother to vote in the presidential elections. The idea, put forward by two writers on welfare politics and social movements, Frances Piven and Richard Cloward, was that there were opportunities in food-stamp lines, welfare offices, unemployment lines, etc., for mass registration of voters by the social service workers there. Such registration activities, they foresaw, would probably lead to conflict with the authorities, who would try to suppress them, and thus generate protest movements. The combination of new, angry voters, and allied protest movements, Piven and Cloward suggested, might bring about a changed Democratic party, more clearly attuned to the interests of the poor and lower middle classes.

In fact, local elections in 1982 brought record numbers of blacks and Hispanics—former members of "the party of non-voters"—to the polls, in many cases electing nonwhites to office, including Harold Washington, a black man, as mayor of Chicago, and Toney Anaya, a Chicano, as governor of New Mexico.

What Reagan had done, as no president before him, was to join the two issues of disarmament and social welfare. It was guns versus children, and this was expressed dramatically by the head of the Children's Defense Fund, Marian Wright Edelman, in a commencement speech to students, faculty, and parents at the Milton Academy in Massachusetts in the summer of 1983. She said:

You are graduating into a nation and world teetering on the brink of moral and economic bankruptcy. Since 1980, our President and Congress have been turning our national plowshares into swords and been bringing good news to the rich at the expense of the poor. . . . Hunger is the enemy faced daily by hundreds of people throughout the world. Children are the major victims. Our misguided national and world choices are literally killing children daily. . . .

A recent study of child deaths by the Maine Department of Human Services says that poor children in America die at a rate three times that of non-poor children, and that poverty is the ultimate cause of death for 11,000 American children each year. . . . Yet governments throughout the world, led by our own, spend over $600 billion a year on arms, while an estimated 1 billion of our world's people live in poverty and 600 million are under- or unemployed.

Where is the human commitment and political will to find the relative pittance of money needed to protect children? What kind of world allows 40,000 children to die needlessly every day? UNICEF estimates that for $6 billion a year we could save 20,000 children a day by 1990. . . . At home, where are the strong political voices speaking out for investing in children rather than bombs; mothers rather than missiles? . . .

Just one hour's worth of President Reagan's proposed defense increase in military spending would pay for free school lunches for 19,000 children for a school year.

She urged that her listeners act: "Pick a piece of the problem that you can help solve while trying to see how your piece fits into the broader social change puzzle."

Her words seemed to represent a growing mood which worried the administration. An aide in Reagan's budget office warned the President that "we are being savaged by the fairness issue" and "our political base has been badly eroded." This political fear led the Reagan administration and Congress to withdraw some of the proposed cutbacks in human services. In his first year, Reagan proposed $11 billion in cuts in preventive health measures for children and support programs for poor families; Congress enacted $9 billion in cuts. In its second year, the administration proposed $9 billion in cuts in these same programs; Congress accepted only $1 billion in cuts. In the third year, Reagan proposed $3.5 billion in cuts in these programs. The Washington correspondent of the *New York Times* reported: "Political concerns about the fairness of Mr. Reagan's programs have forced the Administration to curtail its efforts to make further cutbacks in programs for the poor."

Neither Reagan, nor Carter before him, could cope with something that had been going on for a long time: the deterioration of the American economy. Just after World War II, the United States was the central economic power in the world, producing 40 percent of the world's goods and services; by the late 1970s, this was down to 20 percent. And where in 1953 (according to a report by the Federal Reserve Bank of New York) Western industrial countries imported 30 percent of their manufactured goods from the United States, by 1976 they imported only 13 percent.

Most comments on "the American economy" described it, talking about an "upswing" or a "downswing," through the eyes of businessmen and corporations. Overall statistics, and words like "prosperity" or "decline," or (as I have used it above) "the deterioriation of the American economy," have, through history, concealed what life was like for ordinary people. The prosperity of the 1920s ignored millions in want. In the postwar "boom" of the 1950s, as Michael Harrington showed in his book *The Other America,* millions were living in misery. From 1948 to 1978, during thirty years of what everyone called "rapid economic growth," the relative position of women's earnings declined (as Lester Thurow pointed out in *The Zero-Sum Society*) from 61 percent of what males earned to 57 percent.

General employment figures have always misled. In 1978, total male unemployment was 5.2 percent, but it was 13.5 percent for white males sixteen to nineteen years old, and 34.4 percent for black males sixteen to nineteen years old. The media describe the economy for corporate stockholders; the Dow Jones average may be "up," according to the seven o'clock news, yet this may mean nothing to unemployed steelworkers in Youngstown, black teenagers in Harlem, women secretaries in Boston or Atlanta, old people in Los Angeles or Detroit.

Another statistical deception: if unemployment is "only" 5 percent, that assumes the same 5 percent of the population are unemployed 365 days of that year. But most of the unemployed are unemployed only part of the year, so that a 5 percent rate of whole-year unemployment (which is the rate always used in public announcements) equals a 10 percent rate of six-month unemployment, or a 20 percent rate of three-month unemployment. In 1981, the annual unemployment figure was 8.3 million people, but the Bureau of Labor Statistics said 23.4 million were unemployed for all or part of that year.

Class privilege was embedded in American society long before Reagan drastically cut federal aid to poor people. What class you were born in, much more than your intelligence and ability, determined your success, as one could see from a study done in 1979 for the Carnegie Council on Children by Richard de Lone *(Small Futures: Children, Inequality and the Limits of Liberal Reform).* The de Lone study showed that two youngsters might have the same score on "intelligence" tests, but if the father of one was a lawyer making $45,000 a year and the other's father was a high-school dropout working as a janitor or messenger, the kid from the wealthier background was four times more likely to enter college, twelve times more likely to finish college, twenty-seven times more likely to land a job that would put him or her in the top tenth of American incomes.

Even after the New Deal and the Great Society reforms, according to the de Lone study, the federal government was giving fifteen times more money to the rich, in tax exemptions, than to the poor, as Aid to Families with Dependent Children. The "welfare state" had always been first, and massively, for the welfare of the rich, and only later, and moderately, for the welfare of the poor.

The social programs of the sixties—Medicaid and Medicare (the paying of medical costs for the poor and the elderly), increases in unemployment insurance and Social Security pensions, food stamps, public service employment—did not do much more than maintain the historic American maldistribution of wealth. The Census Bureau showed no significant changes in income distribution from 1947 to 1981 between upper and lower classes: the poorest fifth of the population continued to receive about 5 percent of all income, the highest-paid about 42 percent.

An electorate forced to choose between Carter or Reagan could only despair (or decide not to vote), because neither was capable of dealing with an economic crisis whose roots were deeper than any single presidency. Those roots, according to economists Samuel Bowles, David Gordon, and Thomas Weisskopf *(Beyond the Waste Land)*, lay in the American capitalist system, which began to be in trouble again in the sixties, after the brief "prosperity" of the war and postwar years. It was an incredibly wasteful system, not utilizing the labor of millions of people (unemployed, women, older people) and misusing the labor of millions of others (in the armed forces, or the excessive numbers working on luxury goods or in sales, advertising, or other largely unproductive activities). These economists calculated a thousand billion dollars of waste in the year 1980 alone.

Capitalism did not put people to work unless there was a profit in it—however people needed work, and however much work was needed to produce essential goods. Such a system, driven by corporate profit, could build up the economy, but at the expense of millions of people at home and abroad. When, as in the sixties, the people at home began to rebel and demand more benefits, the system, its profits threatened, turned more and more to overseas ventures. The Defense Department report for fiscal 1980 said: "Our economy has come to depend heavily on imports of energy supplies and raw materials, and nine per cent of our GNP now results from the sale of U.S. goods and services abroad." Indeed, by 1979, one-third of all U.S. corporate profits came from international activity, according to financial writer Richard Lyons in the *New York Times.*

Was it possible that a system which was fueled by profiteering at the expense of poor people abroad and at home had run out of time and space? It could only maintain itself, it seemed, by militarizing the economy, and this aroused people at home to rebellion. It could less and less calm such rebellion by reforms, because it needed the reform money to put down revolutions abroad. And the revolutions abroad were succeeding in spite of this.

At home, support for counterrevolutionary intervention was harder and harder to maintain. Under Carter, despite all the nationalist fervor aroused by the Iranian seizure of American hostages in Teheran, 53 percent of the public, several months after the seizure, opposed even a naval oil blockade of Iran. Under Reagan, despite his efforts to rouse patriotic fervor to support his military budgets, the public was not responding as before; the largest disarmament movement in the history of the country was developing. And public opinion opposed U.S. military involvement in Central America, however much the President pointed to geographical proximity. It seems that the Vietnam war had made foreign adventures on behalf of "national security" much less believable.

Would Reagan (or another President) try to force war and deprivation on an unwilling American population by using the laws, the courts, the police, superpatriotism, and red scares—as in World War I and the 1950s? A National Security Council Memorandum of 1950 (N.S.C. 68) had warned of "an excess of tolerance" in America as an obstacle to an aggressive foreign policy. Could enough dissidents be jailed, enough Americans be intimidated, others be manipulated by secrecy and misinformation, so that the country could be militarized and impoverished without rebellion? Would the Orwellian warning of a totalitarian 1984 be fulfilled for the United States—a new phase of our national history, corresponding to a new desperation of those who want to maintain their power and their privilege?

All this was certainly a possibility. But there was also evidence that the American public, which had come to distrust government deeply, would defend its own interests—that is, defend democracy—even more powerfully than it did during the sixties. In 1982, only 33 percent of the public, according to the Institute for Social Research, University of Michigan, believed the government could be trusted to do what was right most or all of the time. (Back in 1964, 76 percent of the population had such faith.)

Confidence in government had taken a brief upturn when Reagan was first elected, but as his term was coming to an end, it dropped again; the economy was still stagnating, the cities were still decaying, the military was still consuming a huge percentage of the national budget, unemployment—especially among the young—was very high. The traditional political leadership of Republicans and Democrats seemed to have no answers that would give confidence to young people that they were emerging from school into a society that would offer them creative work, a prosperous future, and freedom from the awful threat of nuclear war.

It was not remarkable, in 1983, that the poor at home would either join movements or stay out of politics; or that the poor abroad would rebel, after long suffering, and overthrow governments. What was remarkable was that more and more young Americans, not very poor, going to college to "make good," were showing signs of alienation, even rebelliousness. A few of my students' comments, written in their journals, on the state of the world in the spring of 1983:

A student majoring in biology: "Do you think anything good that has happened in the world had anything to do with government? I work in Roxbury (a black neighborhood). I know the government doesn't work. Not for the people of Roxbury, and not for the people anywhere. It works for people with money."

Another student: "War . . . The idea of not being able to hide, not being able to run, is like a nightmare to me. I have already written so much about war and now I am speechless. I can only think of Thomas Jefferson: 'I tremble for my country when I reflect that God is just.' "

A graduate of a Catholic high school: "America to me is a society, a culture. America is my home; if someone were to rob that culture from me, then perhaps there would be reason to resist. I will not die, however, to defend the honor of the government."

A young woman: "As a white middle class person I've never felt discriminated against at all. But I'll say this: If anyone ever tried to make me sit in a different schoolroom, use a different bathroom, or anything like that, I would knock them right on their ass. . . . The people are the last ones that need their rights stated on paper, for if they're abused or injusticed by government or authority, they can act on the injustice directly, which is direct action. When you look at the issue of statements of rights and laws, it's really government and authority and institutions and corporations that need laws and rights to insulate them from the physicality, the directness of the people."

A freshman studying engineering: "And yet there is the attitude that many hold 'Better Dead than Red.' This is stupid. 'Well, if I can't have it the way I want it, nobody'll have it at all.' Come on now. Have you ever seen a human being squashed against a brick wall? Have you ever seen a person die of radiation poisoning? How about watching the life of a severely deformed child develop? Have you ever thought about what it would be like to feel a light so powerful that you can see the bones in your body? Consider what death is, stupid! Death is final. It's the end of agony and the end of beauty. You have no more choices, no more hope. . . . Better to live under the bleakest conditions than to end that beautiful rush of air into one's lungs. . . . Think, man. Would you take these things from your children? Live so that they may live. Fight to live in peace. Fight for peace. Destroy those things of ultimate destruction."

A few months after these statements were made, by mostly white, middle-class college students, there was a huge gathering in Washington of a quarter of a million people, black and white—domestic workers, unemployed, young, old, laborers and secretaries, teachers and lawyers —a remarkable coalition gathered together to commemorate the twentieth anniversary of the 1963 March on Washington for racial equality. John Herbers, a journalist who had been covering the black movement for twenty years, wrote:

> The diverse outpouring of Americans from across the nation was evidence of a revival of the activist left since Ronald Reagan was elected President in 1980; it was affirmation of the formation of new coalitions of groups—labor, blacks, Hispanic Americans, women, anti-nuclear activists and environmentalists, among others—that have frequently been at odds in recent years.

The passionate statements of young people being prepared by higher education to take their dutiful places in society, and the silent presence of hundreds of thousands of Americans aware of both racial inequality and economic injustice—these were small signs of possible tumultuous change as the United States moved uncertainly toward the twenty-first century.

Bibliography

This book, written in a few years, is based on twenty years of teaching and research in American history, and as many years of involvement in social movements. But it could not have been written without the work of several generations of scholars, and especially the current generation of historians who have done immense work in the history of blacks, Indians, women, and working people of all kinds. It also could not have been written without the work of many people, not professional historians, who were stimulated by the social struggles around them to put together material about the lives and activities of ordinary people trying to make a better world, or just trying to survive.

To indicate every source of information in the text would have meant a book impossibly cluttered with footnotes, and yet I know the curiosity of the reader about where a startling fact or pungent quote comes from. Therefore, as often as I can, I mention in the text authors and titles of books for which the full information is in this bibliography. Where you cannot tell the source of a quotation right from the text, you can probably figure it out by looking at the asterisked books for that chapter. The asterisked books are those I found especially useful and often indispensable.

I have gone through the following standard scholarly periodicals: *American Historical Review, Mississippi Valley Historical Review, Journal of American History, Journal of Southern History, Journal of Negro History, Labor History, William and Mary Quarterly, Phylon, The Crisis, American Political Science Review, Journal of Social History.*

Also, some less orthodox but important periodicals for a work like this: *Monthly Review, Science and Society, Radical America, Akwesasne Notes, Signs: Journal of Women in Culture and Society, The Black Scholar, Bulletin of Concerned Asian Scholars, The Review of Radical Political Economics, Socialist Revolution, Radical History Review.*

1. The Empire and the People

Aptheker, Herbert, ed. *A Documentary History of the Negro People in the United States.* New York: Citadel, 1973.

Beale, Howard K. *Theodore Roosevelt and the Rise of America to World Power.* New York: Macmillan, 1962.

Beisner, Robert. *Twelve Against Empire: The Anti-Imperialists, 1898–1902.* New York: McGraw-Hill, 1968.

*Foner, Philip. *A History of the Labor Movement in the United States.* 4 vols. New York: International Publishers, 1947–1964.

*———. *The Spanish-Cuban-American War and the Birth of American Imperialism.* 2 vols. New York: Monthly Review Press, 1972.

Francisco, Luzviminda. "The First Vietnam: The Philippine-American War, 1899–1902," *Bulletin of Concerned Asian Scholars,* 1973.

*Gatewood, Willard B. *"Smoked Yankees" and the Struggle for Empire: Letters from Negro Soldiers, 1898–1902.* Urbana: University of Illinois Press, 1971.

Lafeber, Walter. *The New Empire: An Interpretation of American Expansion.* Ithaca, N.Y.: Cornell University Press, 1963.

Pratt, Julius. "American Business and the Spanish-American War," *Hispanic-American Historical Review*, 1934.

Schirmer, Daniel Boone. *Republic or Empire: American Resistance to the Philippine War.* Cambridge, Mass.: Schenkman, 1972.

Williams, William Appleman. *The Roots of the Modern American Empire.* New York: Random House, 1969.

————. *The Tragedy of American Diplomacy.* New York: Dell, 1972.

Wolff, Leon. *Little Brown Brother.* Garden City, N.Y.: Doubleday, 1961.

Young, Marilyn. *The Rhetoric of Empire.* Cambridge, Mass.: Harvard University Press, 1968.

2. The Socialist Challenge

*Aptheker, Herbert. *A Documentary History of the Negro People in the United States.* New York: Citadel, 1974.

*Baxandall, Rosalyn, Gordon, Linda, and Reverby, Susan, eds. *America's Working Women.* New York: Random House, 1976.

Braverman, Harry. *Labor and Monopoly Capital: The Degradation of Work in the Twentieth Century.* New York: Monthly Review, 1975.

Brody, David. *Steelworkers in America: The Non-Union Era.* Cambridge, Mass.: Harvard University Press, 1960.

Chafe, William. *Women and Equality: Changing Patterns in American Culture.* New York: Oxford University Press, 1977.

Cochran, Thomas, and Miller, William. *The Age of Enterprise.* New York: Macmillan, 1942.

Dancis, Bruce. "Socialism and Women," *Socialist Revolution*, January–March 1976.

Dubofsky, Melvyn. *We Shall Be All: A History of the Industrial Workers of the World.* New York: Quadrangle, 1974.

Du Bois, W. E. B. *The Souls of Black Folk.* New York: Fawcett, 1961.

Faulkner, Harold. *The Decline of Laissez Faire 1897–1917.* White Plains, N.Y.: M.E. Sharpe, 1977.

*Flexner, Eleanor. *A Century of Struggle.* Cambridge, Mass.: Harvard University Press, 1975.

Flynn, Elizabeth Gurley. *The Rebel Girl.* New York: International Publishers, 1973.

Foner, Philip, ed. *Helen Keller: Her Socialist Years.* New York: International Publishers, 1967.

*————. *A History of the Labor Movement in the United States.* 4 vols. New York: International Publishers, 1947–1964.

Gilman, Charlotte Perkins. *Women and Economics.* New York: Harper & Row, 1966.

*Ginger, Ray. *The Bending Cross: A Biography of Eugene Victor Debs.* New Brunswick: Rutgers University Press, 1969.

Goldman, Emma. *Anarchism and Other Essays.* New York: Dover, 1970.

Green, James. *Grass-Roots Socialism: Radical Movements in the Southwest, 1895–1943.* Baton Rouge: Louisana State University Press, 1978.

Hays, Samuel. "The Politics of Reform in Municipal Government in the Progressive Era," *Pacific Northwest Quarterly*, October 1964. (Reprinted by New England Free Press.)

Haywood, Bill. *The Autobiography of Big Bill Haywood.* New York: International Publishers, 1929.

James, Henry. *The American Scene.* Bloomington: Indiana University Press, 1968.

Hofstadter, Richard. *The American Political Tradition.* New York: Random House, 1954.

Jones, Mary. *The Autobiography of Mother Jones.* Chicago: Charles Kerr, 1925.

Kaplan, Justin. *Mr. Clemens and Mark Twain: A Biography.* New York: Simon & Schuster, 1966.

*Kolko, Gabriel. *The Triumph of Conservatism.* New York: Free Press, 1977.

*Kornbluh, Joyce, ed. *Rebel Voices: An I.W.W. Anthology.* Ann Arbor: University of Michigan Press, 1964.

*Lerner, Gerda, ed. *Black Women in White America.* New York: Random House, 1973.

*————. *The Female Experience: An American Documentary.* Indianapolis: Bobbs-Merrill, 1977.

London, Jack. *The Iron Heel.* New York: Bantam, 1971.

Naden, Corinne J. *The Triangle Shirtwaist Fire, March 25, 1911.* New York: Franklin Watts, 1971.

Sanger, Margaret. *Woman and the New Race.* New York: Brentano's, 1920.

Schoener, Allon, ed. *Portal to America: The Lower East Side, 1870–1925.* New York: Holt, Rinehart and Winston, 1967.

Sinclair, Upton. *The Jungle.* New York: Harper & Row, 1951.

Sochen, June. *Movers and Shakers: American Women Thinkers and Activists, 1900–1970.* New York: Quadrangle, 1974.

Stein, Leon. *The Triangle Fire.* Philadelphia: Lippincott, 1965.

Wasserman, Harvey. *Harvey Wasserman's History of the United States.* New York: Harper & Row, 1972.

*Weinstein, James. *The Corporate Ideal in the Liberal State, 1900–1918.* Boston: Beacon Press, 1968.

*Wertheimer, Barbara. *We Were There: The Story of Working Women in America.* New York: Pantheon, 1977.

Wiebe, Robert H. *The Search for Order, 1877–1920.* New York: Hill & Wang, 1966.

*Yellen, Samuel. *American Labor Struggles.* New York: Pathfinder, 1974.

Zinn, Howard. *The Politics of History.* Boston: Beacon Press, 1970.

3. War Is the Health of the State

Baritz, Loren, ed. *The American Left.* New York: Basic Books, 1971.

*Chafee, Zechariah, Jr. *Free Speech in the United States.* New York: Atheneum, 1969.

Dos Passos, John. *1919.* New York: Signet, 1969.

Du Bois, W. E. B. "The African Roots of War," *Atlantic Monthly,* May 1915.

Fleming, D. F. *The Origins and Legacies of World War I.* Garden City, N.Y.: Doubleday, 1968.

*Fussell, Paul. *The Great War and Modern Memory.* New York: Oxford University Press, 1975.

*Ginger, Ray. *The Bending Cross: A Biography of Eugene Victor Debs.* New Brunswick: Rutgers University Press, 1969.

Goldman, Eric. *Rendezvous with Destiny.* New York: Random House, 1956.

Gruber, Carol S. *Mars and Minerva: World War I and the Uses of Higher Learning in America.* Baton Rouge: Louisiana State University Press, 1975.

Joughin, Louis, and Morgan, Edmund. *The Legacy of Sacco and Vanzetti.* New York: Quadrangle, 1964.

Knightley, Philip. *The First Casualty: The War Correspondent as Hero, Propagandist, and Myth Maker.* New York: Harcourt Brace Jovanovich, 1975.

Kornbluh, Joyce, ed. *Rebel Voices: An I.W.W. Anthology.* Ann Arbor: University of Michigan Press, 1964.

Levin, Murray. *Political Hysteria in America.* New York: Basic Books, 1971.

Mayer, Arno J. *The Politics and Diplomacy of Peace-Making 1918–1919.* New York: Knopf, 1967.

*Peterson, H. C., and Fite, Gilbert C. *Opponents of War, 1917–1918.* Seattle: University of Washington Press, 1968.

Simpson, Colin. *Lusitania.* Boston: Little, Brown, 1973.

Sinclair, Upton. *Boston.* Cambridge, Mass.: Robert Bentley, 1978.

Weinstein, James. *The Corporate Ideal in the United States 1900–1918.* Boston: Beacon Press, 1969.

4. Self-help in Hard Times

Adamic, Louis. *My America, 1928–1938.* New York: Harper & Row, 1938.

*Baxandall, Rosalyn, Gordon, Linda, and Reverby, Susan, eds. *America's Working Women.* New York: Random House, 1976.

Bellush, Bernard. *The Failure of the N.R.A.* New York: W. W. Norton, 1976.

Bernstein, Barton, J., ed. *Towards a New Past: Dissenting Essays in American History.* New York: Pantheon, 1968.

Bernstein, Irving. *The Lean Years: A History of the American Worker, 1920–1933.* Boston: Houghton Mifflin, 1960.

———. *The Turbulent Years: A History of the American Worker, 1933–1941.* Boston: Houghton Mifflin, 1969.

Borden, Morton, ed. *Voices of the American Past: Readings in American History.* Lexington, Mass.: D. C. Heath, 1972.

Boyer, Richard, and Morais, Herbert. *Labor's Untold Story.* United Front, 1955.

*Brecher, Jeremy. *Strike!* Boston, Mass.: South End Press, 1979.

Buhle, Paul. "An Interview with Luigi Nardella," *Radical History Review,* Spring 1978.

*Cloward, Richard A., and Piven, Frances F. *Poor People's Movements.* New York: Pantheon, 1977.

Conkin, Paul. *F.D.R. and the Origins of the Welfare State.* New York: Crowell, 1967.

Curti, Merle. *The Growth of American Thought.* New York: Harper & Row, 1943.

*Fine, Sidney. *Sit-Down: The General Motors Strike of 1936–1937.* Ann Arbor: University of Michigan Press, 1969.

Galbraith, John Kenneth. *The Great Crash: 1929.* Boston: Houghton Mifflin, 1972.

General Strike Committee. *The Seattle General Strike.* Charlestown, Mass.: gum press, 1972.

*Hallgren, Mauritz. *Seeds of Revolt.* New York: Knopf, 1934.

*Lerner, Gerda, ed. *Black Women in White America: A Documentary History.* New York: Random House, 1977.

Lewis, Sinclair. *Babbitt.* New York: Harcourt Brace Jovanovich, 1949.

Lynd, Alice and Staughton, eds. *Rank and File: Personal Histories by Working-Class Organizers.* Boston: Beacon Press, 1974.

Lynd, Robert and Helen. *Middletown.* New York: Harcourt Brace Jovanovich, 1959.

Mangione, Jerre. *The Dream and the Deal: The Federal Writers Project, 1935–1943.* Boston: Little, Brown, 1972.

Mills, Frederick C. *Economic Tendencies in the United States: Aspects of Pre-War and Post-War Changes.* New York: National Bureau of Economic Research, 1932.

Ottley, Roi, and Weatherby, William J. "The Negro in New York: An Informal History," *Justice Denied: The Black Man in White America,* ed. William Chace and Peter Collier. New York: Harcourt Brace Jovanovich, 1970.

Painter, Nell, and Hudson, Hosea. "A Negro Communist in the Deep South," *Radical America,* July–August 1977.

Renshaw, Patrick. *The Wobblies.* New York: Anchor, 1968.

*Rosengarten, Theodore. *All God's Dangers: The Life of Nate Shaw.* New York: Knopf, 1974.

Steinbeck, John. *The Grapes of Wrath.* New York: Viking, 1939.

Swados, Harvey, ed. *The American Writer and the Great Depression.* Indianapolis: Bobbs-Merrill, 1966.

*Terkel, Studs. *Hard Times: An Oral History of the Great Depression in America.* New York: Pantheon, 1970.

Wright, Richard. *Black Boy.* New York: Harper & Row, 1937.

Zinn, Howard. *La Guardia in Congress.* Ithaca, N.Y.: Cornell University Press, 1959.

5. A People's War?

Alperovitz, Gar. *Atomic Diplomacy.* New York: Vintage, 1967.

Aronson, James. *The Press and the Cold War.* Indianapolis: Bobbs-Merrill, 1970.

Barnet, Richard J. *Intervention and Revolution: The U.S. and the Third World.* New York: New American Library, 1969.

Blackett, P. M. S. *Fear, War and the Bomb: Military and Political Consequences of Atomic Energy.* New York: McGraw-Hill, 1948.

Bottome, Edgar. *The Balance of Terror: A Guide to the Arms Race.* Boston: Beacon Press, 1972.

Butow, Robert. *Japan's Decision to Surrender.* Stanford: Stanford University Press, 1954.

Catton, Bruce. *The War Lords of Washington.* New York: Harcourt Brace, 1948.

Chomsky, Noam. *American Power and the New Mandarins.* New York: Pantheon, 1969.

Davidson, Basil. *Let Freedom Come: Africa in Modern History.* Boston: Little, Brown, 1978.

Feingold, Henry L. *The Politics of Rescue: The Roosevelt Administration and the Holocaust.* New Brunswick, N.J.: Rutgers University Press, 1970.

Freeland, Richard M. *The Truman Doctrine and the Origins of McCarthyism.* New York: Knopf, 1971.

Gardner, Lloyd. *Economic Aspects of New Deal Diplomacy.* Madison: University of Wisconsin Press, 1964.

Griffith, Robert W. *The Politics of Fear: Joseph R. McCarthy and the Senate.* Rochelle Park, N.J.: Hayden, 1971.

Hamby, Alonzo L. *Beyond the New Deal: Harry S. Truman and American Liberalism.* New York: Columbia University Press, 1953.

Irving, David. *The Destruction of Dresden.* New York: Ballantine, 1965.

Kahn, Herman. *On Thermonuclear War.* New York: Free Press, 1969.

*Kolko, Gabriel. *The Politics of War: The World and United States Foreign Policy, 1943–1945.* New York: Random House, 1968.

Lemisch, Jesse. *On Active Service in War and Peace: Politics and Ideology in the American Historical Profession.* Toronto: New Hogtown Press, 1975.

Mailer, Norman. *The Naked and the Dead.* New York: Holt, Rinehart and Winston, 1948.

Miller, Douglas, and Nowak, Marion. *The Fifties: The Way We Really Were.* New York: Doubleday, 1977.

Miller, Marc. "The Irony of Victory: Lowell During World War II." Unpublished doctoral dissertation. Boston University, 1977.

Mills, C. Wright. *The Power Elite.* New York: Oxford University Press, 1970.

Minear, Richard H. *Victor's Justice: The Tokyo War Crimes Trial.* Princeton, N.J.: Princeton University Press, 1973.

Offner, Arnold. *American Appeasement: U.S. Foreign Policy and Germany, 1933–1938.* New York: W. W. Norton, 1976.

Rostow, Eugene V. "Our Worst Wartime Mistake," *Harper's,* September 1945.

Russett, Bruce. *No Clear and Present Danger.* New York: Harper & Row, 1972.

Sampson, Anthony. *The Seven Sisters: The Great Oil Companies and the World They Shaped.* New York: Viking, 1975.

Schneir, Walter and Miriam. *Invitation to an Inquest.* New York: Doubleday, 1965.

*Sherwin, Martin. *A World Destroyed: The Atom Bomb and the Grand Alliance.* New York: Knopf, 1975.

Stone, I. F. *The Hidden History of the Korean War.* New York: Monthly Review Press, 1969.

United States Strategic Bombing Survey. *Japan's Struggle to End the War.* Washington: Government Printing Office, 1946.

Weglyn, Michi. *Years of Infamy: The Untold Story of America's Concentration Camps.* New York: William Morrow, 1976.

Wittner, Lawrence S. *Rebels Against War: The American Peace Movement, 1941–1960.* New York: Columbia University Press, 1969.

*Zinn, Howard. *Postwar America: 1945–1971.* Indianapolis: Bobbs-Merrill, 1973.

———. *The Pentagon Papers.* 4 vols. Boston: Beacon Press, 1971.

6. "Or Does It Explode?"

Allen, Robert. *Black Awakening in Capitalist America.* Garden City, N.Y.: Doubleday, 1969.

Bontemps, Arna, ed. *American Negro Poetry.* New York: Hill & Wang, 1974.

Broderick, Francis, and Meier, August. *Black Protest Thought in the Twentieth Century.* Indianapolis: Bobbs-Merrill, 1971.

Cloward, Richard A., and Piven, Frances F. *Poor People's Movements.* New York: Pantheon, 1977.

Conot, Robert. *Rivers of Blood, Years of Darkness.* New York: Morrow, 1968.

Cullen, Countee. *On These I Stand.* New York: Harper & Row, 1947.

Herndon, Angelo. "You Cannot Kill the Working Class," *Black Protest,* ed. Joanne Grant. New York: Fawcett, 1975.

Huggins, Nathan I. *Harlem Renaissance.* New York: Oxford University Press, 1971.

Hughes, Langston. *Selected Poems of Langston Hughes.* New York: Knopf, 1959.

Lerner, Gerda, ed. *Black Women in White America: A Documentary History.* New York: Random House, 1977.

Malcolm X. *Malcolm X Speaks.* New York: Meret, 1965.

Navasky, Victor. *Kennedy Justice.* New York: Atheneum, 1977.

Perkus, Cathy, ed. *Cointelpro: The FBI's Secret War on Political Freedom.* New York: Monad Press, 1976.

Wright, Richard. *Black Boy.* New York: Harper & Row, 1937.

Zinn, Howard. *Postwar America: 1945–1971.* Indianapolis: Bobbs-Merrill, 1973.

———. *SNCC: The New Abolitionists.* Boston: Beacon Press, 1964.

7. The Impossible Victory: Vietnam

*Branfman, Fred. *Voices from the Plain of Jars.* New York: Harper & Row, 1972.

Green, Philip, and Levinson, Sanford. *Power and Community: Dissenting Essays in Political Science.* New York: Pantheon, 1970.

Hersch, Seymour. *My Lai 4: A Report on the Massacre and Its Aftermath.* New York: Random House, 1970.

Kovic, Ron. *Born on the Fourth of July.* New York: McGraw-Hill, 1976.

Lipsitz, Lewis. "On Political Belief: The Grievances of the Poor," *Power and Community: Dissenting Essays in Political Science,* ed. Philip Green and Sanford Levinson. New York: Pantheon, 1970.

Modigliani, Andrew. "Hawks and Doves, Isolationism and Political Distrust: An Analysis of Public Opinion on Military Policy," *American Political Science Review,* September 1972.

Pike, Douglas. *Viet Cong.* Cambridge, Mass.: MIT Press, 1966.

Schell, Jonathan. *The Village of Ben Suc.* New York: Knopf, 1967.

Zinn, Howard. *Vietnam: The Logic of Withdrawal.* Boston: Beacon Press, 1967.

*———. *Pentagon Papers.* 4 vols. Boston: Beacon Press, 1971.

8. Surprises

Akwesasne Notes. *Voices from Wounded Knee, 1973.* Mohawk Nation, Rooseveltown, N.Y.: Akwesasne Notes, 1974.

Baxandall, Rosalyn, Gordon, Linda, and Reverby, Susan, eds. *America's Working Women.* New York: Rándom House, 1976.

Benston, Margaret. "The Political Economy of Women's Liberation," *Monthly Review,* Fall 1969.

Boston Women's Health Book Collective. *Our Bodies, Ourselves.* New York: Simon & Schuster, 1976.

Brandon, William. *The Last Americans.* McGraw-Hill, 1974.

*Brown, Dee. *Bury My Heart at Wounded Knee.* New York: Holt, Rinehart and Winston, 1971.

Brownmiller, Susan. *Against Our Will: Men, Women and Rape.* New York: Simon & Schuster, 1975.

Coles, Robert. *Children of Crisis.* Boston: Little, Brown, 1967.

Cottle, Thomas J. *Children in Jail.* Boston: Beacon Press, 1977.

The Council on Interracial Books for Children, ed. *Chronicles of American Indian Protest.* New York: Fawcett, 1971.

Deloria, Vine, Jr. *Custer Died for Your Sins.* New York: Macmillan, 1969.

———. *We Talk, You Listen.* New York: Macmillan, 1970.

Firestone, Shulamith. *The Dialectics of Sex.* New York: Bantam, 1970.

Friedan, Betty. *The Feminine Mystique*. New York: W. W. Norton, 1963.

Gaylin, Willard. *Partial Justice*. New York: Knopf, 1974.

Jackson, George. *Soledad Brother: The Prison Letters of George Jackson*. New York: Coward McCann, 1970.

Lerner, Gerda, ed. *Black Women in White America: A Documentary History*. New York: Random House, 1977.

Lifton, Robert Jay, ed. *The Woman in America*. Boston: Beacon Press, 1967.

Lynd, Robert and Helen. *Middletown*. New York: Harcourt Brace Jovanovich, 1959.

*McLuhan, T. C. *Touch the Earth: A Self-Portrait of Indian Existence*. New York: Simon & Schuster, 1976.

Mann, Eric. *Comrade George: An Investigation into the Life, Political Thought, and Assassination of George Jackson*. New York: Harper & Row, 1974.

*Mitford, Jessica. *Kind and Usual Punishment: The Prison Business*. New York: Knopf, 1973.

Morgan, Robin, ed. *Sisterhood Is Powerful: An Anthology of Writings from the Women's Liberation Movement*. New York: Random House, 1970.

The Prison Research Project, Urban Planning Aid. *The Price of Punishment: Prisons in Massachusetts*. Cambridge, Mass.: Urban Planning Aid, 1974.

Rich, Adrienne. *Of Woman Born*. New York: Bantam, 1977.

Rothman, David J. and Sheila, eds. *Sources of American Social Tradition*. New York: Basic Books, 1975.

Steiner, Stan. *The New Indians*. New York: Harper & Row, 1968.

*Witt, Shirley Hill, and Steiner, Stan. *The Way: An Anthology of American Indian Literature*. New York: Knopf, 1974.

Wicker, Tom. *A Time to Die*. New York: Quadrangle, 1975.

Zinn, Howard, ed. *Justice in Everyday Life*. New York: Morrow, 1974.

9. The Seventies: Under Control?

Blair, John M. *The Control of Oil*. New York: Pantheon, 1977.

Dommergues, Pierre. "L'Essor Du conservatisme Americain," *Le Monde Diplomatique*, May 1978.

*Evans, Les, and Myers, Allen. *Watergate and the Myth of American Democracy*. New York: Pathfinder Press, 1974.

Frieden, Jess. "The Trilateral Commission," *Monthly Review*, December 1977.

Gardner, Richard. *Alternative America: A Directory of 5000 Alternative Lifestyle Groups and Organizations*. Cambridge, Richard Gardner, 1976.

Glazer, Nathan, and Kristol, Irving. *The American Commonwealth 1976*. New York: Basic Books, 1976.

New York Times. *The Watergate Hearings*. Bantam, 1973.

*U.S., Congress, Senate Committee to Study Governmental Operations with Respect to Intelligence Activities. *Hearings*. 94th Congress. 1976.

10. The Coming Revolt of the Guards

Bryan, C. D. B. *Friendly Fire*. New York: Putnam, 1976.

Levin, Murray B. *The Alienated Voter*. New York: Irvington, 1971.

Warren, Donald I. *The Radical Center: Middle America and the Politics of Alienation.* Notre Dame, Ind.: University of Notre Dame Press, 1976.

Weizenbaum, Joseph. *Computer Power and Human Reason.* San Francisco: Freeman, 1976.

11. The Challenge of 1984

Certain books were important sources for this chapter. On the 1980 election, the essays in Thomas Ferguson and Joel Rogers, *The Hidden Election*, were indispensable, especially those by Walter Dean Burnham, Gerald Epstein, Alan Stone, and Ira Katznelson. On the political economy of the Carter-Reagan policies: Michael Parenti, *Democracy for the Few*, Alan Wolfe, *America's Impasse: The Rise & Fall of the Politics of Growth* (South End Press, 1981), Robert Zevin, *A Greater Good: Potentials for an Intelligent Economy* (Houghton Mifflin, 1983), Lester Thurow, *The Zero-Sum Society* (Basic Books, 1980). An important study on class inequality in America: Richard H. de Lone, *Small Futures: Children, Inequality and the Limits of Liberal Reform* (Harcourt Brace Jovanovich, 1979). A critical analysis of the U.S. economy. Samuel Bowles, David Gordon, and Thomas Weisskopf, *Beyond the Waste Land* (Anchor Press, 1983). Some good data on the Reagan programs: Stephen Rousseas, *The Political Economy of Reagonomics* (M. E. Sharpe, 1982). On legal services for the poor and the Carter-Reagan policies: Loren Siegel and David Landau, "No Justice for the Poor" (Public Policy Report of the American Civil Liberties Union, March 1983). For analysis of the disarmament movement: Dave Dellinger and Michael Albert, *Beyond Survival* (South End Press, 1983). On Reagan's racial policies: "Civil Liberties in Reagan's America" (American Civil Liberties Union, 1982). On the Piven-Cloward registration proposal: *Social Policy*, Winter 1982–1983.

Since most of the chapter deals with very recent events, I relied heavily on the press, especially the *New York Times* and the Boston *Globe*, but also the Washington *Post*. Certain periodicals were especially useful: *New York Review of Books, Catholic Worker, The Nation, In These Times, Bulletin of Atomic Scientists, Radical America, Monthly Review, WIN*. I also used articles from the alternative press, like *Campus Unrest, Resist Newsletter, Sojourners, Peacework*, as well as others reprinted in *Alternative Papers* (Temple University Press, 1982). The Alternative Press Index, at the Alternative Press Center, Baltimore, Maryland, has a long, useful list. Anyone who wants the date of a specific newspaper item should contact me at Boston University.

Index